Democracy, Citizenship and the Global City

Does the city have a future in democracy? With economic, cultural and social globalization, new spaces of democracy have been created with which individuals and groups identify, and which constitute themselves as political and social agents. While the cyberspace of the internet and international organizations such as the IMF, UN, World Bank, the European Union and Greenpeace receive widespread attention, the bedrock of democracy and citizenship, the city, has been neglected in the popular media and in scholarship.

Globalization is now contesting the sovereignty claimed by the nation-state. This state is under increasing pressure from multinational organizations and corporations, as well as sub-national regions, territories and cities. Yet, rather than declaring its death and creating a nostalgic image of the city-state as it existed before the nation-state, the task of political and social theory is to articulate empirically founded but normative ideas about how the city must be rethought as a space of democracy in the global era.

Using an interdisciplinary approach, *Democracy, Citizenship and the Global City* is an innovative and influential collection of essays featuring contributions from prominent social and political theorists: Robert A. Beauregard, Anna Bounds, Janine Brodie, Richard Dagger, Gerard Delanty, Judith A. Garber, Robert J. Holton, Warren Magnusson, Raymond Rocco, Nikolas Rose, Evelyn S. Ruppert, Saskia Sassen, Bryan S. Turner, John Urry, Gerda R. Wekerle and Nira Yuval-Davis.

Engin F. Isin is Associate Professor at York University, Canada.

Innis centenary series: governance and change in the global era
Daniel Drache
Series Editor

Harold Innis, one of Canada's most distinguished economists, described the Canadian experience as no one else ever has. His visionary works in economic geography, political economy and communications theory have endured for over fifty years and have had tremendous influence on scholarship, the media and the business community.

The volumes in the Innis Centenary Series illustrate and expand Innis's legacy. Each volume is written and edited by distinguished members of the fields Innis touched. Each addresses provocative and challenging issues that have profound implications not only for Canada but for the 'new world order', including the impact of globalization on governance, international development and national decision-making; interactions among the state, social movements and the environment; the nature of the 'market' in the future; the effect of new communications technology on economic restructuring; and the role of the individual in effecting positive social change.

The complete series will provide a unique guide to many of the major challenges we face as we enter the twenty-first century.

The Innis Centenary Series is supported by the Robarts Centre for Canadian Studies and York University. Proposals for future volumes in the series are actively encouraged and most welcome. Please address all enquiries to the editor, by email drache@yorku.ca or by fax 1.416.736.5739.

Other titles in the series include:
States Against Markets
Edited by Robert Boyer and Daniel Drache

Political Ecology
Edited by David Bell, Leesa Fawcett, Roger Keil and Peter Penz

Health Reform
Edited by Daniel Drache and Terry Sullivan

Democracy, Citizenship and the Global City

Edited by
Engin F. Isin

London and New York

First published 2000 by Routledge
11 New Fetter Lane, London EC4P 4EE

Simultaneously published in the USA and Canada
by Routledge
29 West 35th Street, New York, NY 10001

Routledge is an imprint of the Taylor & Francis Group

Typeset in Goudy by Taylor & Francis Books Ltd
Printed and bound in Great Britain by Biddles Ltd, Guildford and King's
Lynn

British Library Cataloguing in Publication Data
A catalogue record for this book is available from the British Library

Library of Congress Cataloging in Publication Data
Democracy, citizenship, and the global city / [eidted by] Engin F. Isin.
p.cm. – (Innis centenary series)
Includes bibliographical references and index.
1. Municipal government 2. Cities and towns. 3. Citizenship.
4. Democracy. 5. Globalization.
I. Isin, Engin F. (Engin Fahri), 1959– II. Series
JS67 .D45 2000
321.8–dc21   00–025432

ISBN 0–415–21667–2 (hbk)
ISBN 0–415–21668–0 (pbk)

Contents

Contributors

Robert A. Beauregard, Professor, New School for Social Research, New York, USA.

Anna Bounds, Ph.D. Candidate, New School for Social Research, New York, USA.

Janine Brodie, Professor, Department of Political Science, University of Alberta, Edmonton, Canada.

Richard Dagger, Professor, Department of Political Science, Arizona State University, Tempe, USA.

Gerard Delanty, Professor, Department of Sociology, University of Liverpool, Liverpool, UK.

Judith A. Garber, Associate Professor, Department of Political Science, University of Alberta, Edmonton, Canada.

Robert J. Holton, Professor, Department of Sociology, Flinders University, Adelaide, Australia.

Engin F. Isin, Associate Professor, Division of Social Science and Graduate Programmes in Sociology, Political Science, Social and Political Thought, and Geography, York University, Toronto, Canada.

Warren Magnusson, Professor, Department of Political Science, University of Victoria, Victoria, Canada.

Raymond Rocco, Associate Professor, Department of Political Science, University of California at Los Angeles, Los Angeles, USA.

Nikolas Rose, Professor, Department of Sociology, Goldsmiths College, University of London, London, UK.

Evelyn S. Ruppert, Ph.D. Candidate, Department of Sociology, York University, Toronto, Canada.

Saskia Sassen, Professor, Department of Sociology, University of Chicago, Chicago, USA.

Bryan S. Turner, Professor, Faculty of Social and Political Sciences, University of Cambridge, Cambridge, UK.

John Urry, Professor, Department of Sociology, Lancaster University, Lancaster, UK.

Gerda R. Wekerle, Professor, Faculty of Environmental Studies and Graduate Programme, Women's Studies and Geography, York University, Toronto, Canada.

Nira Yuval-Davis, Professor, Gender and Ethnic Studies, University of Greenwich, London, UK.

Acknowledgements

This volume grew out of a symposium entitled 'Rights to the City: Citizenship, Democracy and Cities in a Global Age' held at York University in Toronto on 26–8 June 1998. While the symposium brought together some three hundred delegates from twenty countries, its substantive focus was liberal democracies in predominantly English-speaking states such as Canada, America, Great Britain, Australia and New Zealand, a focus that this volume maintains.

The symposium was funded by York University, Social Science and Humanities Research Council (SSHRC) and Metropolis Project, Ministry of Citizenship and Immigration Canada. I am grateful to the Division of Social Science and the Urban Studies Programme at York University, which provided funding as well as logistic support. I also thank President Lorna Marsden and Vice Presidents Michael Stevenson and Brock Fenton, as well as George Fallis, the Dean of the Faculty of Arts, York University and Meyer Burstein at Metropolis Project, Citizenship and Immigration Canada, for their support. Urban Studies Programme Assistant Daisy Couto was helpful beyond the call of duty in organizing the symposium. Under her direction, the following graduate students at York University assisted with the organization and operation of the symposium: Kate Anderson, Sarah Bassnett, Peter Fargey, Mary Iannaci, Jennifer Keesmaat, Mark Lede, Emily MacNair, Susan Moore, Andrew Paravantes, Suzanne Peters, Noah Pond, Cheryl Teelucksingh, Graham Todd, Krys Verrall, Deborah Whatley, Jonathon Whatley and Joanne Wolfson. I am grateful for their assistance. My colleagues Pablo Idahosa, Ute Lehrer and Beth Moore Milroy provided excellent direction in chairing sessions. Evelyn S. Ruppert was a magnificent organizer and not only took care of numerous details but also helped shape the symposium from its inception. I am grateful for her diligent, careful, sensitive yet indefatigable approach, without which the symposium would not have been possible.

A special issue of *Citizenship Studies*, vol. 3, no. 2 (1999), published those papers from the symposium with an historical and empirical focus. They are by Zygmunt Bauman, Thomas Bender, Engin F. Isin, Richard Ohmann, Raymond Rocco, Martin Thom and Iris Marion Young. The special issue complements the theoretical chapters in this volume, which includes two additional chapters by Richard Dagger and Robert A. Beauregard and Anna Bounds. I am grateful to two doctoral students in Sociology at York University, Kate Anderson and Mark Lede, who provided superb editorial assistance for the special issue as well as the current volume. I thank Daniel Drache, Innis Centenary Series Editor, for his unflinching support and efficacious and wise editorial guidance in bringing this volume into fruition. He read the entire manuscript twice and made valuable suggestions. Andreja Zivkovic, Robert Langham and Heidi Bagtazo at the Routledge editorial office in London were most helpful in spearheading the manuscript. Four anonymous reviewers of the original draft provided very useful criticisms which made the manuscript so much better than it would have been. My deepest gratitude is to the authors themselves who have taken this project to heart as a project of solidarity right from the beginning and put up with my idiosyncrasies and deficiencies as an editor.

Finally, I would like to express my appreciation to all participants in the symposium who collectively produced a most interesting occasion.

Engin F. Isin
Cambridge, UK
January 2000

Introduction

Democracy, citizenship and the city

Engin F. Isin

> The solution of the problems of democratic government rests in the cities. ...
> The political problem of the modern city is the problem of democracy. ... The
> fanaticism of party, religion, race, professions, nationalism, and militarism must
> somehow be met in the government of the city first and last and after that little
> is left of world problems.
>
> (Innis, 1945, pp. 482, 485, 486)

This volume is concerned with the question of the impact of post-
modernization and globalization on the government of cities and citizens in
western democracies, especially in predominantly English-speaking states such
as Canada, America, Great Britain, Australia and New Zealand. 'Government'
implies not only the institutions and organizations of city government but also
the governmental practices as conduct of conduct, and hence its analysis
involves considering citizenship. If we define post-modernization as both a
process of fragmentation through which various group identities have been
formed, and discourses through which 'difference' has become a dominant
strategy, its effect on citizenship has been twofold. On the one hand, various
groups that have been marginalized and excluded from *modern* citizenship have
been able to seek recognition (Fraser, 1997; Young, 1990). Groups based upon
ethnic, 'racial', ecological and sexual identities have articulated claims for
citizenship to include group-differentiated rights. Women have fought to
expand their citizenship rights to include social rights such as access to
childcare, pay equity and rights to safe cities; ethnic and racialized minorities
have sought recognition and representation; aboriginal peoples have sought
representation and self-government rights; gays and lesbians have struggled to
claim rights that are already extended to heterosexual couples, such as spousal
benefits and common-law arrangements; immigrants have struggled for
naturalization and political rights; and various ability groups have demanded
recognition of their needs to become fully functional citizens of their polities.
These challenged one of the most venerable premises of modernization –
universalization – by exposing its limits. On the other hand, these various
claims have strained the boundaries of citizenship and pitted group against
group in the search for identity and recognition. As a result, while ostensibly

making claims to citizenship, some members of these groups have become trapped or encased within specific identities, unable to move beyond the straitjacket that they have unintentionally created. This called into question another venerable premise of modernization that would have us believe in the disappearance of such allegiances. Either way, post-modernization of politics has, therefore, stretched the capacity of the modern nation-state and citizenship to accommodate and recognize these diverse and conflicting demands, but it has also posed intractable dilemmas about how to conduct ourselves (Rose, 1999, pp. 194–6).

If we define globalization as both a process by which the increasing inter-connectedness of places becomes the defining moment and as a discourse through which 'globalism' becomes a dominant strategy, its effect on citizenship has also been twofold. On the one hand, with the rise of global flows of capital, images, ideas, labour, crime, music and regimes of governance, the sources of authority of citizenship rights and obligations have expanded from the nation-state to other international organizations, corporations and agencies such as the World Bank, the IMF, IBM, the internet, Greenpeace, Amnesty International, Microsoft and Coca-Cola. On the other hand, the dominance of such global agents was accompanied by the decline of the capacity of the nation-states to set sovereign policies. In a very complex relay of events, nation-states have retrenched from certain citizenship rights and instead imposed new obligations on their citizens, which has in turn intensified tensions within states where taken-for-granted citizenship rights began to disappear (e.g. unemployment insurance, welfare or right to legal counsel) and new obligations (e.g. workfare) were implemented. Similarly, increased international migration has raised the question of the rights and responsibilities of aliens, immigrants and refugees (Cohen, 1999).

While some believe that globalization means the rise of the world as one single place, others refute whether globalization has become as widespread as claimed and point to increased post-modernization of culture and politics in which diversity, fragmentation and difference dominate. But few would disagree that post-modernization and globalization are occurring simultaneously and are engendering new patterns of global differentiation in which some states, societies and social groups are becoming increasingly enmeshed with each other, while others are becoming increasingly marginalized. A new configuration of power relations is crystallizing as the old geographical divisions rapidly give way to new spaces which the familiar constructs of core–periphery, North–South, First World and Third World no longer represent. Globalization has recast modern patterns of inclusion and exclusion between nation-states by forging new hierarchies which cut across and penetrate all regions of the world (Held et al., 1999, p. 8). North and South, First World and Third World are no longer 'out there' but nestled together within global cities. It is doubtful whether we can any longer divide the world into discrete, contiguous and contained territorial zones as a representation of reality. Instead, the socio-political geography of the world seems to be crystallizing into overlapping networks of various flows of intensity, extensity and velocity in which global city-regions are the primary nodes. These complex and overlapping networks connect the fate of one global city-region to the fate of another in distant parts of the world and increasingly concentrate and intensify various activities in these nodes. Events that take place in these nodes resonate beyond their immediate spheres precisely because they are nodes within highly complex and overlapping networks rather than self-contained and isolated territories.

As a result many argue that post-modernization and globalization are not simply a continuation of modern capitalism on a global scale but political, economic and cultural transformations of modern capitalism into new regimes of accumulation and modes of regulation (Hoogvelt, 1997). That cities and regions, or, more precisely, global city-regions, are the fundamental spaces of this emerging political economy further erodes the credibility of modernization theories that would have us believe in national trajectories that will follow the disappearance of religion, tradition and particularism. Instead, in global city-regions we are witnessing a general trend towards the proliferation of identities and projects, and an overall incredulity towards grand narratives. Global city-regions give us not only the geographic metaphors with which we think about the social world, but also the concrete sites in which to investigate the complex relays of post-modernization and globalization that engender spaces for new identities and projects which modernization either contained or prohibited, and generate new citizenship rights and obligations. But these processes are not unfolding according to immutable logic or necessary laws. Rather, each node, whether it is Bombay, Istanbul, Shanghai, Mexico City, New York or London, is drawn into these overlapping networks of flows in different ways and articulates very different patterns of inclusion, exclusion, rights, obligations and social struggles depending on its national, regional, social and political trajectories. Moreover, while the metaphors of North and South, centre and periphery may no longer capture these processes, it does not mean that inequalities and differences brought about and institutionalized by such older divisions have suddenly ceased to exist. Rather, we observe strange multiplicities and events: in some global cities as even basic civil or political rights are trampled upon by authorities, new rights, for example sexual or technological rights, are also being claimed. To appreciate how these complex transformations affect citizenship we need to reflect briefly on its modernity.

The modernity of citizenship

Modern citizenship was born of the nation-state in which certain rights and obligations are allocated to individuals under its authority. Modern citizenship rights that draw from the nation-state typically include civil rights (free speech and movement, rule of law), political rights (voting, seeking electoral office) and social rights (welfare, unemployment insurance and health care). The precise combination and depth of such rights vary from one state to another but a modern democratic state is expected to uphold a combination of citizenship rights and obligations. That said, however, three points must be borne in mind to avoid the assumption that citizenship rights and obligations are 'natural'. First, while under some states civil rights such as bodily control rights (medical and sexual control over the body) are guaranteed, other states deny their citizens even basic civil rights such as the rights of access to courts and counsel. Similarly, while some states guarantee political rights and go so far as to franchise prisoners, others deny even the most basic refugee or naturalization rights. Citizenship obligations vary too, ranging from states in which military service is required to those states where jury duty and taxes are the only responsibilities. Second, while many nation-states have elaborate rules and criteria for 'naturalization', the granting of citizenship to those not born in their territories, such rules and criteria are often contested and debated, and vary widely. Third, some of the most fundamental citizenship rights are remarkably recent. We would be well served to remember that the basic political right to franchise was extended to all adult men without property qualifications as recently as, for example, 1920 in Canada, 1918 in Britain and 1901 in Australia. The term 'all' should be interpreted cautiously too, as it did not include aboriginals in settler societies. Similarly, the franchise was only extended to all women as recently as 1918 in Canada, 1928 in Britain and 1902 in Australia. French women have been able to vote since 1944 and American women since 1920.

Thus, what determines the composition of rights and obligations that pertains to a given nation-state depends on its historical trajectory. The typologies developed by Esping-Anderson (1990) and Janoski (1998) to classify citizenship rights according to these trajectories are useful. Esping-Anderson (1990) distinguishes between liberal, corporatist and social democratic states, each of which rests upon a different interpretation of citizenship. While warning that there is no pure example of each, Esping-Anderson argues that in liberal democracies such as America, Switzerland and Australia, the state relies on markets to allocate social rights, and emphasizes civil and political rights. In corporatist states such as Austria, France, Germany and Italy, social rights are accorded a greater role but are not available universally. By contrast, in social democratic states such as Sweden, Norway, Finland, Denmark and the Netherlands, social rights are given the highest priority and the state provides universal benefits such as the right to free vocational or higher education. There are, of course, states that do not neatly fit into these types. Canada, for example, combines a liberal emphasis on individual rights with a social democratic tradition of social rights, especially in the areas of health and education. Britain also combines liberal and social democratic traditions.

Modern political theories about citizenship – liberalism, communitarianism and republicanism – have grown out of these trajectories and roughly correspond to these three types of states. Liberalism puts a strong emphasis on the individual, and most rights involve liberties that adhere to each and every person. Communitarianism puts strong emphasis on the community (or the society or the nation), whose primary concern is with the cohesive and just functioning of society. Republican theories in both their social and radical variants put emphasis on both individual and group rights and underline the role of conflict and contest in the expansion or construction of such rights. While communitarian theories emphasize obligations, democratic theories focus on the importance of rights. Further, not all theories fit into these types. Prominent theorists such as Will Kymlicka (1995) and Charles Taylor (1994), because they reflect Canadian dispositions, combine liberalism and communitarianism, which may appear contradictory to outsiders but sensible to Canadians. At any rate, in many democracies in the postwar era the debate *and* struggles over citizenship rights and obligations have been waged over either *expansion* or *protection* of rights. The *expansion* of the following rights have been most prominent: civil rights, such as medical and sexual control over the body; political rights, such as the rights to naturalization, to aboriginal self-government as well as social movement or protest rights; social rights, such as old age pensions, unemployment insurance, health and education; and participation rights, reflected in job placement programs, affirmative action for minorities, collective bargaining, wage earner and union investment funds. The *protection* of the following rights has occupied governmental agendas: civil rights, such as the right of aliens to immigrate; political rights, such as minority rights to equal and fair treatment; social rights, such as welfare; and participation rights such as job security and workers' compensation. These debates and struggles have been mostly directed via the nation-state as both the source of authority and arbiter of justice.

Citizenship unbound

While useful in the understanding of various theories and practices of citizenship rights and obligations across various postwar democratic states, these typologies can no longer capture the changing nature of citizenship at the dawn of the twenty-first century (Isin and Wood, 1999). In the last two decades of the twentieth century, post-modernization and globalization have challenged the nation-state as the *sole* source of authority of citizenship and democracy. Under the twin pressures of post-modernization and globalization, the blurred boundaries of citizenship rights and obligations and the forms of democracy associated with them brought citizenship on to the political *and* intellectual agendas. This has also broadened the way in which citizenship is understood and debated. Rather than merely focusing on citizenship as legal rights, there is now agreement that citizenship must also be defined as a social process through which individuals and social groups engage in claiming, expanding or losing rights. Being politically engaged means practising substantive citizenship, which in turn implies that members of a polity always struggle to shape its fate. This can be considered as the sociological definition of citizenship in that the emphasis is less on legal rules and more on norms, practices, meanings and identities.

There is no doubt that the debates and struggles over citizenship rights and obligations will intensify not only at the level of the state where, as we have seen, many of these rights are defined, enacted and allocated, but also at other levels. On the global or international level, there is already a lively debate and struggle over cosmopolitan citizenship and democracy (see Hutchings and Dannreuther, 1999; Held, 1995). At sub-national levels, the renewed emphasis on citizenship not only as legal rights and obligations but also as social practices through which citizens make themselves has heightened the role of the city in democracy once again.

The work of cities: modernity of city government

The premise of this volume is that if post-modernization and globalization have brought citizenship on to the political and theoretical agendas, they have also intensified the role of the city in democracy (Garcia, 1996; Holston, 1999; Isin, 1999). Global cities are spaces where the very meaning, content and extent of citizenship are being made and transformed. Being at the interstices of global networks of flows of commodities, services, capital, labour, images and ideas, the global city, both as a milieu and object of struggles for recognition, engenders new political groups that claim either new types of rights or seek to expand modern civil, political and social rights (Sandercock, 1998). In an evocative phrase, Sassen (1996) describes global cities as places where 'the work of globalization gets done'. We can extend her phrasing and describe cities as places where the work of post-modernization also gets done. Many social groups have effectively demonstrated that modern civil, political and social rights do not adequately address their needs and so claim new rights on the basis of such identities as gender, ethnicity, ecology and sexuality. Their struggles for recognition and social justice revolve around new claims to citizenship, inclusion and engagement with the polity to which they seek membership in a qualitatively different way. While these groups seek rights allocated by senior levels of government such as states and provinces, their organizations, symbols and other resources draw upon the city and use it as an organizing principle. Similarly, as Clarke and Gaile (1998, pp. 211–12) illustrate, the work of globalization results in reduced real wages and social benefits, limited job retraining opportunities, lack of affordable housing, discriminatory housing and employment practices, environmental hazards, inaccessible and unaccountable political processes, unhealthy work conditions and restricted educational opportunities, which are all confronted and contested in cities.

How is the role of the city in democracy different under the twin pressures of post-modernization and globalization? 'The solution of the problems of democratic government rests in the cities. … The political problem of the modern city is the problem of democracy' (Innis, 1945, pp. 482, 485). So said Harold Innis in 1945 in an address reflecting on the problems of democracy. A Canadian political economist, Innis is known for his studies on the fur trade, cod fisheries and the lumber industry, which in his later work were linked up with broader processes of imperial and colonial political economy and with even broader civilizational processes of writing, communication and dialogue. It was his ability to explore specific problems within broader processes that perhaps allowed him to see the city as a microcosm in which 'city' became synonymous with 'democracy'. Ambiguously, Innis was both traditional and prescient in his observation. Traditional in the sense that he appears to have been merely expressing a modern liberal faith in city government as a locus of democracy, and prescient in the sense that, now at the beginning of the twenty-first century, we are reconsidering the problems of democracy being entangled with the city. But this is where his prescience becomes particularly poignant and less ambiguous. For Innis the city was not merely a locus of democracy but its vanguard: 'The fanaticism of party, religion, race, professions, nationalism, and militarism must somehow be met in the government of the city first and last and after that little is left of world problems' (Innis, 1945, p. 486). Innis was already thinking differently from the liberal or modern tradition about the city, and seeing it as the concentration of and the solution to the problems of the world arising from difference. Unfortunately, Innis never expanded on his reflections on city government, but he left us the modernity of the work of cities as a question.

To begin to answer that question, we must first outline the rationalities of modern city government. However, one of the thorniest problems besetting thought on city government is its modernity. Beginning with its first advocates such as Alexis de Tocqueville (1835) and John Stuart Mill (1861), historicism has been a prevalent aspect of thinking about city government (Stoker, 1996; Magnusson, 1986). The glorious images of 'ancient institutions' and 'tradition' have always dominated thought on city government. There are understandable genealogical reasons why the dominant groups in the nineteenth century made such historical linkages but we cannot explore them here (Isin, 1995). It is, nevertheless, important to emphasize that the modern democratic conception of the city that emerged in the early nineteenth century expressed a particular conception of local government which became synonymous with democracy. While citizenship originated in the city and played an important role in the history of citizenship in western civilization (Heater, 1990; Riesenberg, 1992), the significance of the city as a milieu cultivating and engendering citizenship does not derive from this history. It is beyond doubt that the relationship between the city and citizenship has a venerable and inextricable history. The western historical imagination is full of images of the birth of democracy and citizenship in ancient Greek cities, its republican transformations in ancient Roman cities, and its revival in medieval European cities. But these images obfuscate and obscure rather than reveal and expose the modernity of city government.

The modernity of local government is a relatively recent concept. In Britain, America and Canada its emergence can be traced from the period after 1835 in which a reformed framework for local government was gradually put in place.

Moreover, it was not until the early decades of the twentieth century that the institution in its modern form could be said to have been established. Although by the end of the nineteenth century the basic structures had crystallized, the capacity of local government was still restricted by a heavy dependence on local rates for finance, and it was not until the 1920s that any scheme for state support for local services was provided on any significant scale (Loughlin, 1996, p. 79). What emerged in the twentieth century was that local government was locked into a network of government that operated at various scales (nation, region, city) and capacities. Neither autonomous nor subordinate, modern city government was a technology defined by a tension between state and local authorities (Isin, 1992). The modern city government that crystallized in the twentieth century therefore had no functional affinity with historical forms of city government either in medieval European or ancient Greek and Roman cities. After the nineteenth-century reforms and the twentieth-century transformations, any appeal to a tradition of local self-government could no longer comfortably rest on ancient tradition and history. The various shifts in the patterns of life and work and the comprehensive nature of the institutional reforms make such claims highly implausible. Nor can such appeals be based on some authoritative constitutional norms in Britain, America, Australia or Canada. If tradition is to be invented it must now be found to rest on modern practices and thus on a set of political understandings which have commanded widespread support throughout the twentieth century.

Moreover, throughout the twentieth century local government has been subjected to almost continuous review and change. Major responsibilities have been removed from local government, new powers and duties have been given, a variety of new checks and control mechanisms have been devised, and reforms have been made to the structure of the institution.

> Given this process of more or less continuous change, it might plausibly be argued that there is no basic institutional identity to local government and that local authorities have simply been shaped in accordance with specific functional requirements of the central State.
>
> (Loughlin, 1996, p. 79)

As Loughlin says, however, this view of modern local government is also misguided in that while it is not autonomous, neither is it a subordinate government; it is an agency that is equipped with a considerable capacity for independent action while being locked into an extensive network of government (Loughlin, 1996, p. 80). Since the early nineteenth century there has always been a *productive* tension between local and central authorities regarding appropriate governmental capacities and practices. It is this tension that produces a continuous incitement to government.

Modern local government embodies complex organizations equipped with a capacity for effective governance and vested with a degree of political legitimacy which justifies its discretionary power. It is because of this tradition that the formal legal status of local government presents a potentially distortive picture. British local government, for example, while constrained in principle by the *ultra vires* doctrine, 'has in fact been vested with considerable autonomy. Although formally subordinate, local government has, as a result of the changes in government during the twentieth century, acquired a relatively important position in an interdependent network government' (Loughlin, 1996, p. 83). This pattern of governmental practice suggests that the modern institution of local government exists not simply because it is the agency which is able most efficiently to deliver particular services. While local government strives to achieve efficiency, its status also serves to reflect certain basic political values. Modern local government is not only an agency for service delivery but also an institution of democratic governance. The inefficiencies that accrue from that function are viewed in balance with its efficient service delivery function. Some degree of inefficiency is accepted for maintaining robust local institutions which are able to mediate between the individual and state and which are responsive to the interests of locality (Loughlin, 1996, p. 83).

The essential features of modern local government are often identified as democracy and efficiency as though they are contradictory functions (Stoker, 1996; Sharpe, 1970; Loughlin, 1996, pp. 80–2). Thus, the emphasis on the authority (ability to perform governmental functions), autonomy (capacity to deliver services according to local needs), taxation (powers to raise revenue) and representation (legitimacy for accountability) functions of modern local government have received widespread attention and, depending on political persuasion, scorn or admiration. However, the exclusive focus on authority, autonomy, taxation and representation resulted in too much emphasis on institutional and organizational arrangements of local government as opposed to its rationalities within the broader network of government. Given these considerations, let me emphasize the following rationalities of modern local government: loyalty, virtue, civics, discipline and subsidiarity. We cannot explore them in detail here but a brief outline will be useful to evaluate whether post-modernization and globalization have issued fundamental changes in them.

Loyalty

The city in modern democracy is simultaneously the milieu and object of *loyalty*. The citizen as a man (later also woman) of property constitutes himself (later also herself) as an agent capable of political judgement while at the same time investing himself in the city, which becomes his work. The citizen identifies with the city and owes allegiance and loyalty to it. But this identification does not contradict with his identification with the nation. Rather, it becomes the foundation of the nation-state. By using our new language we can say that the work of modern nationalism actually got done in the city in the sense that the loyalty to the nation-state was bred and nurtured in the city via the bourgeois public sphere. While considering loyalty a fundamental aspect of the city, the sociological tradition arose out of a concern with the relationship between loyalty and citizenship and the city as an intermediate association between the individual and the state (Durkheim, 1890, 1894; Tönnies, 1887).

Virtue

The city is also where the citizen becomes *virtuous* through his (later also her) engagements in politics, defined as a broad field in which a citizen conducts himself (later also herself) upon the conduct of others. The civic virtue of the citizen consists in the fact that his conduct oriented toward the city is not only his right but also his obligation. The city becomes a space of government in the sense that the citizen constitutes himself as both subject and object of conduct in the public sphere. The exercise of this right *and* obligation can be as passive as simply voting, or as active as taking part in the everyday life of politics. For the political tradition this was a fundamental aspect of the city fostering democracy (Mill, 1861; de Tocqueville, 1835).

Civics

That a subject becomes a citizen by developing loyalty and virtue toward the city means that the city becomes a breeding ground for active citizenship and democracy. Virtue of the modern citizen is *civic* precisely because it is expressed through a loyalty to his (later also her) city as a particular place rather than an idea. The city is where citizens are habituated into democratic imagination by practice, experience and education. But *civics* is not taught in the city as though it is a course but is learned and bred as a disposition, a habitus. The citizen makes himself in the city by learning how to orient himself toward others through everyday experience. The city makes man governable. For the philosophical tradition this was a fundamental aspect of the relationship between city and citizenship (Arkes, 1981; Rousseau, 1762; Strauss, 1964).

Discipline

While the city is constituted as a space of liberty for the citizen, it is also constituted as a space of *discipline* for strangers and outsiders – non-citizens. It is not that liberty does not require discipline. On the contrary, breeding the loyalty, virtue and civics in constituting citizens as capable subjects requires conduct upon conduct and discipline. In fact, liberty and discipline presuppose each other. But those who lack certain attributes of citizens – strangers and outsiders – are subject to further institutions of discipline such as prisons and asylums. The city may be a space where the citizen conducts himself in public as a political agent with rights and liberties, but it is also a space where those who lack or are denied such citizenship rights are subjected to discipline and punishment. The tensions between liberty and order, and between discipline and civility in the modern city constitute citizenship as a space where the 'normalcy' of citizens is articulated against the 'pathologies' of non-citizens. As the legal tradition emphasized, modernity of the city as a corporation consisted precisely in the public rights of self-government vested in it by the modern nation-state to act on the conduct of its subjects (Frug, 1980; Gierke, 1900; 1934; Maitland, 1898).

Subsidiarity

The modern city is also the space where it is most appropriate to deliver public services such as education, welfare, parks, prisons, recreation and the like. The city is the closest level of government to the citizen and is approachable and direct. The *subsidiarity* of the city consists in the fact that there is a shared relationship between the state and the city in delivering public services to the citizen. While there is always a tension in terms of allocating resources to the city to deliver services, and the exact nature, extent and combination of these services, the city is the appropriate level of government to deliver these services because these matters arise and can be decided locally. The economic tradition on the city highlighted this aspect of local government as its essence (Tiebout, 1956; Boyne, 1998).

Post-modernization, globalization and modern city government

While these rationalities of modern local government can be related to its democracy and efficiency roles, and are expressed in its institutions, they are not reducible to them. Neither are they reducible to one another. Loyalty, virtue, civics, discipline and subsidiarity are distinct but related rationalities of modern local government. Moreover, they are neither coherent nor complementary aspects of city government in that there is always a competition among them. Finally, institutional arrangements such as authority, autonomy, taxation and representation derive from these broader rationalities of local government rather than being its constitutive aspects. Thus, considering institutions of modern local government in isolation from its broader rationalities results in a distorted view of the modern city government. Accordingly, we must now answer the question whether post-modernization and globalization have transformed modern city government by exploring these transformations in its rationalities rather than its institutions or organizations.

While certain features of city, government and citizenship changed throughout the twentieth century (women and the poor, for example, won the franchise and subsidiarity changed after the Great Depression), have post-modernization and globalization in the late twentieth century radically altered these formative features? At first glance, despite post-modernization and globalization, it may appear that all five rationalities of the modern city government remain relatively the same. One could argue that, while the city may no longer be the only object of loyalty, the majority of citizens still spend their everyday lives in the city and develop certain affinities with it. The city may no longer be the only place in which citizens practice virtue, yet the institutions of 'civil society' still form and operate within and through the city. The city may no longer be the milieu where citizens learn civics, but the public spaces of the city, from streets to squares, are still where citizens enact their public selves. The city may no longer appear the most appropriate level of government according to the principle of subsidiarity, but essential public services, especially for real property, are still delivered by city governments. The city may no longer be the space of discipline, in the operation of schools, hospitals, prisons and asylums, but it still takes care of imposing law and order on the everyday lives of its unruly and on dangerous strangers and outsiders. So while its modern rationalities may have weakened, the city may still be the place where the problem of government is being posed and articulated.

Nonetheless, it would be a mistake to ignore the significant transformations that post-modernization and globalization have wrought on the rationalities of the modern city as a milieu and object of citizenship and democracy. Let us consider each in turn. There has been a widespread decline in loyalty to and identification of citizens with their city governments in the past twenty years. Three main reasons have been suggested for this decline: (1) there are other sources of identification such as occupation and consumption that are not territorialized and are extensively organized stretching across fixed borders; (2) the city has become fragmented both territorially and governmentally and is more difficult to identify with than its modern counterpart; and (3) the increased spatial mobility of certain segments of the citizen body loosens and stratifies such loyalties to place. Thus, the citizen is able to conduct himself or herself in various domains, such as the professions, the workplace, the shopping mall and the internet, that are more dominant spheres of virtue and loyalty than the city. The citizen learns to create himself or herself in a multiply situated manner rather than in a singular place or mode. Moreover, many services that the city used to deliver according to the subsidiarity principle are either privatized or shifted to other levels and types of government such as quangos (quasi-autonomous non-governmental bodies). This has led some to argue that it is more appropriate to speak about local governance than local government (Andrew and Goldsmith, 1998; Wilson, 1998). In addition, the institutions of the discipline of citizens, strangers and outsiders have either shifted elsewhere or transformed into new modes of control and surveillance (Jones, 1998). As a result, *has the modern city government become an empty shell whose territory marks out the once-meaningful boundaries of the political?* This volume explores this question from a variety of perspectives. Each chapter takes the city as its theoretical object and addresses the question of democratic government and citizenship through the city. But this does not mean that this book is driven by a nostalgic view of the city as a replica of the autonomous Greek polis, the medieval commune or the New England town. Nor is it driven by a belief in the death of the nation-state. On the contrary, each chapter attends seriously to matters relating to post-modernization and globalization, and considers the nation-state not as a disappearing but perhaps as a strengthening institution that allocates citizenship rights and responsibilities. At the same time, however, the chapters recognize the changing nature of state sovereignty and its impact on the city, and begin to articulate the global city as a new space of politics in which new rights-claims are made, and in which new ways of being political/being a citizen are forged, experimented with and enacted.

Making claims on the city: rights to the global city

That the claims for group-differentiated rights actually arise out of the city and are connected with post-modernization and globalization is fairly easy to illustrate. Consider the question of immigrants in North America and Europe and their political status. While the debate rages over the national issues of whether immigrants should be given political and social rights, the majority of immigrants settle in cities and use urban resources to mobilize and articulate their demands for recognition. In Germany it is impossible to understand citizenship rights for Turks without examining their spatial concentrations in major cities such as Berlin or Frankfurt (Barbieri, 1998). Similarly, it is impossible to understand the complexities that arise from Latino citizenship in America without understanding the settlement patterns and forms such groups have engendered (Rocco, 1996). Cities, particularly global cities, have therefore become political spaces where the concentration of different groups and their identities are intertwined with the articulation of various claims to citizenship rights (Sassen, 1996). It is within this domain of groups and identities that the appropriation and use of urban space is articulated, which in turn constitutes urban citizenship as a field of debate and struggle.

This was defined above as the *work* of cities. It is useful at this point to draw upon the work of Henri Lefebvre, who was concerned with establishing an analytical approach to the city within the framework of his theory of social space, in which the city was a political space for claiming rights for social groups. In the late 1960s, he articulated his concept of the right to the city and the city as work, as *oeuvre*, which was the dominant mode of its production in western history. By contrast, modern capitalism constituted the city as a product. While the emphasis was on the city's use value in the former, it was on the city's exchange value in the latter. Lefebvre believed that to claim the rights of ages, sexes, conditions of work, training, education, culture, leisure, health and housing, it was imperative to think through the city (Lefebvre, 1996, p. 157). The recognition of these rights required the pluralization of groups whose everyday lives were bound up with the city. The struggle to define and appropriate the spaces of the city was crucial in claiming these rights (Lefebvre, 1974, pp. 410–11). For Lefebvre, 'the right to the city manifests itself as a superior form of rights: right to freedom, to individualization and socialization, to habitat and to inhabit' (Lefebvre, 1996, p. 173). Accordingly, 'the right to the *oeuvre* [the city as a work of art], to participation and *appropriation* (clearly distinct from the right to property), are implied in the right to the city' (Lefebvre, 1996, p. 174). Neither a natural nor a contractual right, the right to the city 'signifies the rights of citizens and city dwellers, and of groups they (on the basis of social relations) constitute, to appear on all the networks and circuits of communication, information and exchange' (Lefebvre, 1996, pp. 194–5). It follows that,

> To exclude the *urban* from groups, classes, individuals, is also to exclude them from civilization, if from not society itself. The *right* to the city le-gitimates the refusal to allow oneself to be removed from urban reality by a discriminatory and segregative organization.
>
> (Lefebvre, 1996, p. 195)

Thus

> This right of the citizen ... proclaims the inevitable crisis of city centres based upon segregation and establishing it: centres of decision-making, wealth, power, of information and knowledge, which reject towards pe-ripheral spaces all those who do not participate in political privileges. Equally, it stipulates the right to meetings and gathering ...
>
> (Lefebvre, 1996, p. 195)

It is noteworthy that Lefebvre identified the dominant groups in the con-temporary city as the 'new masters' (Lefebvre, 1996, p. 161). He observed that they already claimed the central areas of New York, Paris and other major cities, and he described the new global city as 'New Athens'. What he is referencing here is not the glorious ancient Athens as the birthplace of democracy but the ancient Athens of deep class and group cleavages between citizens and slaves, outsiders and oppressed groups. It is not that the New Athens had slaves in the ancient sense of that term, but that in the global city the new masters created a social space that catered to their exclusive use while surrounding them with masses to provide services. Lefebvre observed that the new masters were made up of a very small minority, as in ancient Athens, and were comprised of 'directors, heads, presidents of this and that, elites, leading writers and artists, well-known entertainers and media people ...' (Lefebvre, 1996, p. 161). Underneath this layer were 'executives, administrators, professionals and scholars'. He was particularly concerned with the rise of this secondary layer of the dominant groups – in the intriguing parlance of Bourdieu (1979), the dominated fraction of the dominant class – because their interests diverged not only from the working classes and the subjugated groups but also from the bourgeoisie. For Lefebvre the right to the city was the right to claim presence in the city, to wrest the use of the city from the privileged new masters and democratize its spaces. Lefebvre saw the rights to the city as an expression of urban citizenship, understood not as membership in a polity – let alone the nation-state – but as a practice of articulating, claiming and renewing group rights in and through the appropriation and creation of spaces in the city.

Lefebvre wrote at a time in which the new politics of the city was just crystallizing (Shields, 1999). Since then, the global flows of ideas, images, sound and capital and labour both emanating from and concentrating in global cities have become the defining moments of our age. Today, the rights of immigrants, ethnic and racialized groups, gays and lesbians, women, the poor and other groups are by and large fought for in global cities. Yet these struggles are not waged on a binary plane against a common adversary, but instead pit groups against groups, and divide, fragment, confuse and shatter identities, rights, sensibilities, loyalties and obligations. The articulation of the right to the city, not as a right to property but as a right to appropriate the city, is a fruitful way of thinking about the rights that arise in the city. But the task of disentangling the interests of various groups and mapping power relations in the global city is intensely difficult. And the conceptual and analytical tools that we inherit from the nineteenth-century sociological, political, philosophical and economic traditions of thought as outlined above are scarcely adequate to the task. The nineteenth-century conception of rights in the city were closely associated with the property rights of the bourgeois man. The city as a corporation institutionalized property rights and incorporated the city into the realm of the state with its rationalities of loyalty, virtue, civics, discipline and subsidiarity. Rethinking rights that arise in the age of the global city requires the articulation of rights *to* the city rather than rights *of* the city as a container of politics. It also requires rethinking citizenship beyond the confines of the city government and 'local' politics. This volume is a contribution to that theoretical and political task.

Overview of this book

This book has four parts. Part I focuses on how globalization affects democracy, citizenship and the city. Dagger focuses on the city as a breeding ground of citizenship and argues that the modern metropolis as it clearly emerged in the second part of the twentieth century is too large, fragmented and its residents too mobile to allow for the creation of collective memory around which citizens can narrate their sense of identity as citizens. Arguing that the modern metropolis cannot serve as a breeding ground for citizenship, Dagger explores the conditions necessary for re-linking the modern metropolis with citizenship. Sassen draws attention to the fact that the so-called 'dual city' hypothesis (the polarization of life chances in the global city) is not an accidental but a rational consequence of globalization: both the centralization of powers and marginalization of groups in the global city represent a joint presence of globalization. But this joint presence is brought into focus by the increasing distance between the two. While Sassen examines globalization as a form of urbanization, Urry is concerned with what happens to the identities and loyalties of groups whose lives are bound up with the global city. After effectively illustrating how the state-centric conception of citizenship runs up against globalization, Urry articulates 'citizenship of flows' as a concept through which rights and responsibilities are defined according to access to flows rather than according to fixed property or location. While he does not draw out the implications of this conception for the global city, following Sassen, citizenship of flows is perhaps most appropriate for thinking about government and the global city. Delanty develops the idea of 'discursive space' to designate the European global city as a space of flows and considers its implications for the European project of citizenship. Emphasizing that discursive space is less a particular place than a network of relationships (a field in Bourdieu's sense), Delanty argues that spaces in which European citizenship is being formed are more like the citizenship of flows described by Urry.

What brings Rose, Brodie, Turner and Isin together in Part II is their concern with government and virtue. Rose and Brodie are concerned about neo-liberal technologies of government that constitute the active citizen as an object of government. Turner is concerned about the changing conceptions of virtue under post-modernization and globalization. Rose situates his reflections on citizenship within the ambiguous tension between the city as a space of and incitement to government. The modern city has been constantly defined as a problem of and incitement to government. While, however, the dream of a rational city (in which all vice, disorder, squalor and crime have been eliminated) dominated most of the twentieth century, it has now been abandoned in favour of the dream of a city that governs itself. But self-government refers here to something fundamentally different from the liberal constitution of the city as municipal government. While the liberal conception of government constituted itself via the unified entity of the municipal corporation, under the advanced liberal dream the unit itself is the individual: the active citizen. Citizenship emerges in the city as a game of practices that make certain actions thinkable, possible and meaningful. Rose is concerned with identifying the various logics of these practices rather than the ostensible meanings ascribed to citizenship. Using 'neo-liberalism' in a more traditional sense, as a governmental regime rather than as technologies of power, Brodie echoes Rose in warning against a possible nostalgia for grounding politics in the local. She urges us to think of glocal citizenship not as a bundle of rights but as a struggle for expanding the public sphere. In turn, by tracing the trajectory of citizenship from the city-state to nation-state and cosmopolitan-state, Turner explores the possible meaning of cosmopolitan virtue as an ironic, post-emotional stance towards loyalty, obligation and responsibility. Such a stance is most compatible with the complexity and differentiation typically found in global cities. Isin tries to make sense of the major reforms enacted recently to govern Toronto. Isin agrees with Rose that under advanced liberal regimes active citizens have been invited to identify themselves with various communities of identity rather than the city as such, which partly explains why the movement in Toronto against those reforms failed rather rapidly. But Isin also brings a sociology of the professions to bear on governing Toronto: he argues that the shift from public-sector professions to private-sector professions, and their interests for a privatized, marketized and managerial city, is capable of imposing a particular order in the city as an effective regime of economic and cultural capital accumulation.

In Part III Yuval-Davis, Holton, Wekerle and Rocco explore how various groups that constitute citizens as active in their own government can be harnessed for the radical and progressive claiming of rights. In other words, taking warnings by Rose, Brodie, Turner and Isin to heart, these chapters illustrate how neo-liberal technologies of government can also be taken in different directions. These chapters are concerned with illustrating how the consequences of post-modernization are being harnessed by various social groups to articulate and claim progressive group rights successfully. Wekerle illustrates with empirical cases how the women's movement has exercised a pluralistic or group-differentiated citizenship. Through a range of global and local practices, women articulated and claimed rights under a variety of identities, as mothers, sisters and workers, and at a variety of spatial levels. They expressed their rights to the city as claims to space and to inclusion in the practices that make those spaces. But how can these practices acquire legitimacy and power? Holton critically examines the challenges posed to liberal conceptions of citizenship based upon individual rights by radical democratic theories arguing for a group-differentiated conception of citizenship. Holton is sympathetic to group-differentiated citizenship, but also draws attention to the dilemma of difference that arises from treating people the same: while such treatment is likely to be insensitive to the particularity, to treat each other as different may equally stigmatize and constrain the other. He is sceptical as to whether such a dilemma can be solved theoretically and wonders if faced with such a dilemma, poetry may play a more active role. Yuval-Davis is confident that group-differentiated citizenship, or what she calls multi-layered citizenship, is not a theoretical luxury but a pragmatic necessity in the face of the complexity that arises in global cities. Once the underlying spatiality of citizenship is recognized, she argues, it becomes obvious that the state or nation cannot deal with the complex ways in which difference is constructed via imaginary and material boundaries and territories. For Rocco, claims to space must be simultaneously associational and spatial. In other words, in order effectively to articulate claims and demand rights, marginal and disfranchised groups must form associations that gain durability, relative permanence and continuity, and making claims to space is a symbolic and material part of this permanence and durability.

Part IV concludes the volume with chapters that critically engage the concepts with which we think about democracy, citizenship and the city. It opens with a proposal for a distinct urban citizenship that bypasses local government institutions. Beauregard and Bounds argue that urban citizenship does not need to be in conflict with other forms of citizenship defined on other scales, such as global or national. They then consider rights and responsibilities that are specific to the urban public realm, which are grouped around the themes of safety, tolerance, political engagement, recognition and freedom. Ruppert illustrates that theoretical articulations about the global city, democracy and citizenship often come up against the messy realities of politics which involve much more than tidy concepts. Ruppert argues that, while the global city literature is becoming increasingly focused on the marginalized and disfranchised and the global city declared as a possible site in which to articulate and claim rights, there is very little concern about specific tactics and strategies that dominant groups use to bypass democratic procedures, institutions and traditions. The governance of global cities has become increasingly managerial, professional, marketized and privatized. Enacting citizenship and making claims in the global city would be difficult if the institutions that allow subjects to become political agents were to disappear. This final part of the volume includes two chapters, which represent a perhaps distinctly Canadian approach to urban studies. Garber and Magnusson question the metaphorical uses of space and urge us to think about the global city politically. Garber makes an important distinction between material and metaphoric space, and wonders what claiming spaces for citizenship would mean in material terms. She takes the post-modern view of the public sphere as metaphorical space to task and argues that a central feature of citizenship as it is enacted in the global city is its intensely concrete character. When individuals and groups articulate and demand rights, they are not simply contesting meanings or representations but also engaging in physical activities of assembling and protesting. These activities generate not a singular, abstract public sphere but plural public spaces, in that they act from, on and in space and make spaces. Without attention to the concrete activities of creating spaces, it becomes very difficult to understand what is political about the use of 'politics of space' as a metaphor. Similarly, Magnusson argues that, despite an overuse of the term 'politics of space', contemporary social and political sciences are intensely apolitical in the sense that they constitute their objects of analysis in chaotic abstractions which naturalize the practices of political agents. Magnusson works his way toward an ontology of space in which the global city no longer refers to a place but to the materialization of specific flows. To that end he recovers 'urbanism as a way of life' and defends it as a stronger conception of the city as specific place.

Conclusion

This volume is at once a challenge and an invitation to think about the city politically, which means to think about democracy and citizenship spatially. The chapters illustrate how our categories and concepts encase our thoughts in particular ways of seeing and hinder our ability to make connections and establish relationships. Refusing, for example, to consider globalization as a monolithic phenomenon, the volume treats it as both a process captured in the term 'time-space compression' *and* a discourse. It also considers globalization as a sufficiently complex phenomenon, involving not only economic but also at least cultural and social forms. Similarly, democracy in this volume does not appear as merely a deliberative institution or as procedural rules but also as a substantive form of government that allows groups to articulate and claim rights and govern themselves. We have already alluded to how citizenship is also understood as embodying social, legal and cultural forms, and not as a unitary construct.

The volume is able to work through such complexities in part because its object, the city, is itself such a complex, diverse and mysterious construct. It is perhaps through this complexity and mysteriousness that the city teaches humility and care to its students. It is perhaps because of its multifarious, confusing and bewildering array of practices that the city is able to teach more about the flows and fleeting images of life than any other object. It is perhaps for these reasons that its students have something unique to contribute to an understanding of politics, democracy and citizenship.

Bibliography

Andrew, C. and Goldsmith, M. (1998) 'From Local Government to Local Governance – and Beyond?', *International Political Science Review*, 19 (2): 101–17.

Arkes, H. (1981) *The Philosopher in the City: The Moral Dimensions of Urban Politics* (Princeton, NJ: Princeton University Press).

Barbieri, W.A. (1998) *Ethics of Citizenship: Immigration and Group Rights in Germany* (Durham, NC: Duke University Press).

Bourdieu, P. (1979 [1984]) *Distinction: A Social Critique of the Judgement of Taste* (Cambridge: Harvard University Press).

Boyne, G.A. (1998) *Public Choice Theory and Local Government: A Comparative Analysis of the UK and the USA* (Basingstoke: Macmillan).

Clarke, S.E. and Gaile, G.L. (1998) *The Work of Cities* (Minneapolis: University of Minnesota Press).

Cohen, J.L. (1999) 'Changing Paradigms of Citizenship and the Exclusiveness of the Demos', *International Sociology*, 14 (3): 245–68.

de Tocqueville, A. (1835 [1945]) *Democracy in America* (New York: Alfred A. Knopf).

Durkheim, E. (1890 [1992]) *Professional Ethics and Civic Morals* (London: Routledge).

—— (1894 [1984]) *The Division of Labor in Society*, ed. L. Coser, trans. W.D. Halls (New York: Free Press).

Esping-Andersen, G. (1990) *The Three Worlds of Welfare Capitalism* (Princeton, NJ: Princeton University Press).

Fraser, N. (1997) *Justice Interruptus: Critical Reflections on the 'Postsocialist' Condition* (New York: Routledge).

Frug, G.E. (1980) 'The City as a Legal Concept', *Harvard Law Review*, 43 (April).

Garcia, S. (1996) 'Cities and Citizenship', *International Journal of Urban and Regional Research*, 20 (1), pp. 7–21.

Gierke, O. (1900) *Political Theories of the Middle Age*, trans. F.W. Maitland (Cambridge: Cambridge University Press).

—— (1934) *Natural Law and the Theory of Society, 1500–1800* (Cambridge: Cambridge University Press).

Heater, D.B. (1990) *Citizenship: The Civic Ideal in World History, Politics, and Education* (London: Longman).

Held, D. (1995) *Democracy and the Global Order: From the Modern State to Cosmopolitan Governance* (Stanford: Stanford University Press).

Held, D. et al. (1999) *Global Transformations: Politics, Economics and Culture* (Cambridge: Polity Press).

Holston, J. (ed.) (1999) *Cities and Citizenship* (Durham, NC: Duke University Press).

Hoogvelt, A. (1997) *Globalisation and the Postcolonial World: The New Political Economy of Development* (Houndmills: Macmillan).

Hutchings, K. and Dannreuther, R. (eds) (1999) *Cosmopolitan Citizenship* (New York: St Martin's Press).

Innis, H.A. (1945 [1995]) 'Democracy and the Free City', in D. Drache (ed.), *Staples, Markets, and Cultural Change: Selected Essays* (Montreal: McGill-Queen's University Press), 482–6.

Isin, E.F. (1992) *Cities Without Citizens: Modernity of the City as a Corporation* (Montreal: Black Rose Books).

—— (1995) 'Rethinking the Origins of Canadian Municipal Government', *Canadian Journal of Urban Research*, 4 (1): 73–92.

—— (1999) 'Cities and Citizenship', *Citizenship Studies*, 3 (2).

Isin, E.F. and Wood, P.K. (1999) *Citizenship and Identity* (London: Sage).

Janoski, T. (1998) *Citizenship and Civil Society: A Framework of Rights and Obligations in Liberal, Traditional, and Social Democratic Regimes* (Cambridge: Cambridge University Press).

Jones, M. (1998) 'Restructuring the Local State: Economic Governance or Social Regulation?', *Political Geography*, 17 (8): 959–88.

Kymlicka, W. (1995) *Multicultural Citizenship* (Oxford: Oxford University Press).

Lefebvre, H. (1974) *The Production of Space*, trans. D. Nicholson-Smith (Oxford: Butterworth).

—— (1996) *Writings on Cities*, trans. E. Kofman and E. Lebas (Oxford: Blackwell).

Loughlin, M. (1996) *Legality and Locality: The Role of Law in Central-Local Government Relations* (Oxford: Clarendon Press).

Magnusson, W. (1986) 'Bourgeois Theories of Local Government', *Political Studies*, 34: 1–18.

Maitland, F.W. (1898) *Township and Borough* (Cambridge: Cambridge University Press).

Mill, J.S. (1861) 'Considerations on Representative Government', in *Collective Works* (London: Routledge), 371–613.

Riesenberg, P. (1992) *Citizenship in the Western Tradition* (Chapel Hill: University of North Carolina Press).

Rocco, R.A. (1996) 'Latino Los Angeles: Reframing Boundaries/Borders', in A.J. Scott and E.W. Soja (eds) *The City: Los Angeles and Urban Theory at the End of the Twentieth Century* (Berkeley, CA: University of California Press).

Rose, N. (1999) *Powers of Freedom: Reframing Political Thought* (Cambridge: Cambridge University Press).

Rousseau, J-J. (1762 [1978]) *On the Social Contract*, ed. R. Masters, trans. J. Masters (New York: St. Martin's Press).

Sandercock, L. (1998) *Towards Cosmopolis: Planning for Multicultural Cities* (Chichester, NY: Wiley).

Sassen, S. (1996) 'Cities and Communities in the Global Economy: Rethinking Our Concepts', *American Behavioral Scientist*, 39: 629–39.

Sharpe, L.J. (1970) 'Theories and Values of Local Government', *Political Studies*, 18: 153–74.

Shields, R. (1999) *Lefebvre, Love, and Struggle: Spatial Dialectics* (London: Routledge).

Stoker, G. (1996) 'Introduction: Normative Theories of Local Government and Democracy', in D.S. King and G. Stoker (eds), *Rethinking Local Democracy* (Basingstoke: Macmillan), 1–27.

Strauss, L. (1964) *The City and Man* (Chicago: University of Chicago Press).

Taylor, C. (1994) 'The Politics of Recognition', in A. Gutmann (ed.), *Multiculturalism: Examining the Politics of Recognition* (Princeton, NJ: Princeton University Press).

Tiebout, C.M. (1956) 'A Pure Theory of Local Expenditures', *Journal of Political Economy*, 64, pp. 416–24.

Tönnies, F. (1887 [1963]) *Community and Association* (New York: Harper and Row).

Wilson, D. (1998) 'From Local Government to Local Governance: Re-casting British Local Democracy', *Democratization*, 5 (1): 90–115.

Young, I.M. (1990) *Justice and the Politics of Difference* (Princeton, NJ: Princeton University Press).

Part I

Citizenship, sovereignty, politics

1 Metropolis, memory and citizenship[1]

Richard Dagger

What is the proper breeding ground for citizenship? Many students of politics, ancients and moderns alike, have thought that it is the city. Other forms of political association, such as province, nation-state and empire, are too large and too remote from the everyday lives of their inhabitants to inspire the kind of interest and effort that citizenship demands. The city, in comparison, is more accessible to its residents, more closely tied to their interests, and more likely to promote the sense of community that is usually associated with citizenship. Yet it is also large enough and diverse enough to offer more scope and substance for political engagement than the village or hamlet. Hence the city is the true home of citizenship.

Cities differ from one another in a remarkable variety of ways, however, and it is unreasonable to think that they all have provided equally hospitable settings for citizenship. In this respect, as in others, what may have been true of Periclean Athens may not be true of modern Los Angeles. I do not mean to deny that cities and citizenship are intimately related, for I believe that, for better or worse, they are. What I want to suggest is that the relationship is nowadays most often for the worse. Far from encouraging citizenship, many cities in one way or another effectively discourage it. The size, the fragmentation, the fluidity of the population of these swollen metropolises all contribute to the loss of civic memory – the memory that, by tying its residents to the past of a city, enables them to play a part in its present and help shape its future. As they contribute to the loss of civic memory, so these factors also contribute to the failure of citizenship.

My purpose here is to demonstrate how and why this happens. But if we are to understand why our cities do not provide an environment conducive to citizenship, we must first understand what citizenship involves. I begin, then, with an explication of that concept.

Citizenship

> We have physicists, geometricians, chemists, astronomers, poets, musicians, and painters in plenty; but we have no longer a citizen among us ...
>
> (Rousseau, 1750, p. 160)

'Citizen' and its cognates derive from the Latin *civis*, and the concept itself can be traced even further to the Greek *politēs*. In both classical Latin and Greek there is a clear connection between the word for citizen and the word we now translate as city-state: between *civis* and *civitas*, *politēs* and *polis*. To be a citizen, then, was to be part of a political community, and a part of it, moreover, in a way that others were not. Others were subjects, as the citizen was, but they were merely subjects. The citizen was a partner in his community, which meant that he enjoyed certain rights – and was subject to certain duties – that were not extended to women, children, resident aliens, slaves and those who could not meet the property qualifications that were sometimes imposed.

In the ancient world the rights and duties of the citizen were always exclusive in nature, designed to distinguish the citizen as somehow superior to others. In the Roman Republic, for example, citizens were legally immune from crucifixion, which was considered a particularly humiliating form of punishment (Sibley, 1970, p. 140). The essential feature of citizenship, however, was that the citizen, and only the citizen, was entitled by law to take a part in the government of his community. As Aristotle saw it, this was at the heart of citizenship: 'as soon as a man becomes entitled to participate in authority, deliberative or judicial, we deem him to be a citizen' (*Politics*, 1275b18–20 [1981, p. 171]).[2]

Legal status was thus the basis of citizenship, but it was hardly the whole of the matter. Not only was the citizen *entitled* to engage in civic affairs, he was *expected* to do so. Because the life of the citizen involved considerably more than casting an occasional vote, this often meant that he would have to devote the better part of his time and energy to public concerns (Fustel de Coulanges, n.d., pp. 334–6). Such devotion was necessary, however, if the individual was to achieve the ideal of citizenship: to be a self-governing member of a self-governed community. Those who preferred a more private existence, even if it proved less arduous than that of the citizen, were regarded, in Pericles' words, 'not as unambitious but as useless' (Thucydides, 1951, p. 105). For the Greeks, such a person was *idios anthropos*: the man who lives for himself (Myres, 1927, p. 341; Jaeger, 1945, p. 111 and p. 444, n. 45).

Here we may have the most telling sign of the distance between the ancient and modern attitudes towards citizenship. For the Greeks, *idiotes* was the opposite of *politēs*. But we have no word to oppose to our 'citizen'; certainly we do not ordinarily contrast citizens with idiots. Nor will 'private' work, for we sometimes describe a person as a 'private citizen'. What this indicates is that citizenship, a prized status in the ancient world, is now largely taken for granted. It has retained its legal basis while losing much of its ethical import. When we nowadays say that someone is a citizen, we normally mean nothing more than that he or she is legally entitled to vote or otherwise participate in public affairs. Whether one puts that title to use (whether one actually does participate) is not usually thought to be a test of one's citizenship. Our view of citizenship tends to be passive and legalistic, and we find nothing remarkable in such statements as, 'A little over a fifth of the citizenry takes almost no part in political life' (Verba and Nie, 1972, p. 79).

This legalistic conception of citizenship is inadequate, in my view, but it is not simply wrong. To be a citizen is, at the least, to be a member of a body politic who enjoys certain rights, and is subject to certain duties, by virtue of one's legal status as a citizen. Holding this status does not require one to exercise the rights of citizenship, such as the right to participate in public affairs. It does make it possible to exercise those rights if one chooses, however, and it provides protection against those who would infringe upon one's rights. Citizenship as legal standing is also something that can be invoked when a person thinks that others are treating him or her as a 'second-class citizen'. In these respects, legal status is surely necessary to an adequate conception of citizenship.

But that is not to say that it is sufficient. If citizenship is nothing more than a matter of legal status, we face the kind of difficulties identified by those who complain of the excessive individualism and civic irresponsibility of too many 'citizens' today (e.g. Etzioni, 1996; Selbourne, 1994). We also neglect the conviction, still widespread (as indicated by Conover et al., 1991), that *real* or *true* citizenship entails a duty to work with others to promote the public good. Some who hold this conviction even argue that mere voting is not enough to satisfy the requirements of citizenship. According to the authors of a recent study of political participation in American cities, for example,

> [r]ebuilding citizenship in America means that reform must move beyond getting more people into private voting booths to getting more people to public forums where they can work with their neighbors to solve the problems of their community. Once America has real citizens, increased voting will be sure to follow. And once we have real citizens, campaigns will be held to higher standards and elections will be more concrete manifestations of the people's will.
>
> (Berry et al., 1993, p. 2)

As this appeal to 'real citizenship' demonstrates, it is still possible to discover traces of the ancient conception of citizenship in contemporary discourse. We may be obliged to attach such adjectives as good, ethical, responsible or real to 'citizen' when we want to distinguish a citizen from those who are citizens only in the legal sense of the word, but the point can be made nonetheless. And when the distinction is drawn today it rests, as it did in Periclean Athens, on the understanding that citizenship is a *public vocation*.

To say that citizenship is a public vocation is to say, first, that the (true) citizen plays a full and active part in the affairs of the community. What counts as a full and active part is difficult to say, for it will vary with the exigencies of the time. As with Oscar Wilde's complaint about socialism, civic life may sometimes seem to take too many evenings. The (good) citizen may share Wilde's abhorrence of too many evenings consumed by meetings, but he or she will not think that any meetings at all are *too* many. Keeping informed about public affairs and making more than an occasional trip to the polls will surely count towards a full and active part in civic life. It would serve no purpose to try to catalogue the activities of the (responsible) citizen here, however. What matters is that these activities set him or her apart from those who regard politics as a nuisance to be avoided or a spectacle to be witnessed – from those who are willing to leave the government of their communities, and their lives, to others.

To say that citizenship is a public vocation is also to say that the mere fact of participation is not enough to establish one as a citizen. The character of one's participation also counts. If citizenship is a public vocation, then it carries with it a responsibility to act with the interests of the community in mind. This point is put nicely by those who remind us that 'every citizen holds office' (Kennedy, 1961; Zwiebach, 1975, p. 87; Van Gunsteren, 1998, p. 25). Every citizen is in a position of public responsibility, and we must judge his or her, and our, actions according to standards similar to those we apply to persons elected or appointed to public office. This means, most significantly, that the citizen is expected to use his or her office not to accomplish his or her own ends but to further those of the public.

Some may regard this as an old-fashioned, outdated conception of citizenship. For those who regard politics as merely another form of economic activity, the citizen is simply a *taxpayer* who wants efficient services or a *consumer* who invests time and energy in politics only when doing so is necessary to protect or promote personal interests. Some even argue that the metropolitan complex consisting of a central city surrounded by a profusion of suburbs is a desirable arrangement because it responds to the preferences of 'citizen-consumers'. According to Charles Tiebout,

> the consumer-voter moves to the community whose local government best satisfies his set of preferences. The greater the number of communities and the greater the variety among them, the closer the community will come to fully realizing his preference position.
>
> (Tiebout, 1956, p. 418)[3]

In residential choice as in other areas of life, on this view, the citizen is simply shopping for the best bargain in the political marketplace.

Someone who rejects the view of the citizen as consumer or taxpayer may also doubt that citizenship is a public vocation. Dennis Thompson (1970, p. 2), for example, holds that 'modern citizenship suggests that citizens are in their political activities to express not only public but also personal interests of individuals and groups'. Whether Thompson is right or wrong here depends on how one distinguishes matters of personal from matters of public interest. In a good many cases the individuals pressing a personal claim are making a public case as well, as happens when a group of parents band together to petition for the installation of a traffic signal. In such cases we commonly acknowledge that the parents are acting as citizens. When someone petitions for a licence to operate a business establishment, however, we are likely to say that the petitioner may be acting *within his or her rights* as a citizen but is not *acting as* a citizen. The parents are required to appeal to the public welfare to make their case, which is to say that their concern is both personal and public. But when it is purely personal, as it seems to be in the second case, it stands outside the bounds of citizenship.[4]

It will not always be easy to separate concerns that are both personal and public from those that are merely personal, for this is often a matter of some controversy. But the fact that it involves us in controversy may be the best indication of the importance we attach to this distinction. Those organizations that seek to distinguish themselves from special interest groups by calling themselves 'citizens' lobbies' testify to its continuing power. Whether these 'citizens' groups' actually do represent the public interest is, of course, open to question. But the important point is that they use 'citizen' as a sign of their professed concern for the public welfare, then contrast this with the 'special' or 'private' nature of other groups. They can do this only because we have not completely lost the notion that citizenship is a public vocation.

If we conceive of citizenship in this way – as ethical citizenship, as a public vocation – then it is easy enough to understand why some political analysts are worried about the failure or eclipse of citizenship. Citizenship demands effort, and it is clear that a large portion of the citizenry (in the legal sense) is not meeting even the minimum demands of citizenship. In the presidential election of 1960 about 63 per cent of the voting age population of America actually voted – the highest turnout in this country since 1912. Since then the percentage of eligible voters who vote in presidential elections has dropped, until in the election of 1996 not even half troubled themselves to vote.

When one looks beyond voting to other forms of political participation, it becomes even more evident that many people regard politics as either beyond or beneath them. As Verba and Nie report in *Participation in America*, fully 22 per cent of the adult population is 'completely inactive politically'. The remaining 78 per cent of the eligible population does participate from time to time, but for most of those in this category political activity is limited to voting now and then. Only about 11 per cent of the adult population may be classified as 'complete activists' for whom public matters are a constant preoccupation and a continual spur to action (1972, pp. 79–80). According to a more recent study (Verba et al., 1995, p. 50–2), voting is the only political activity in which a majority of the American public engages.[5]

But why is this so? In particular, why are rates of political participation so low at the local level, where usually no more than 30 per cent of those eligible to vote even cast a ballot in local elections in America (Bollens and Schmandt, 1982, p. 140)? It is true, of course, that the modern (ethical) citizen must look beyond the affairs of her city to the concerns of the larger associations to which she and the city belong, but it is also true that these larger associations cannot easily accommodate, and are not likely to encourage, widespread and meaningful political activity. That is why anyone who wishes to revive (responsible) citizenship must look to the city. What this now reveals, unfortunately, are not the circumstances in which citizenship flourishes but those in which it is frustrated. That is the prevailing condition in metropolis today, and that is why metropolis must share the blame for the failure of citizenship.

Three enemies of citizenship

Citizenship is connected both etymologically and historically, as previously noted, with the *polis* and the *civitas*. But the city-state was much more than a city; it was an independent, sovereign political unit. For all of the city-state's flaws – especially its reliance on slavery and its exclusion of women from public life – the autonomy the city-state enjoyed was a decided asset when it came to cultivating citizenship. Because of this autonomy, the attention and efforts of the citizens were concentrated on the affairs of the city-state, not divided between several centres of political authority. Autonomy also meant that there was no superior authority to overshadow the city-state and render its politics trivial by comparison. Such is obviously not the case with our cities. Today one of the principal obstacles to the development of (responsible) citizenship appears to be the 'sheer lack of significance at the local level' (Long, 1962, p. 179). Some might argue that this lack of significance is apparent rather than real, but the affairs of a city might not even *appear* to be insignificant were it not for the overwhelming presence of the modern national or multinational state.

Other differences between the city-state and contemporary cities are also pertinent to citizenship (cf. Dahl, 1967, p. 964). Three of these differences – the greater size of our cities, their political fragmentation and the mobility of their citizens – are especially important in this regard, for they all contribute to the loss of civic memory. I shall try to show here how these three factors discourage the inhabitants of our cities from taking the part of the (active) citizen, and in the next section I shall relate them to the loss of civic memory.

Size

Population size has long been regarded as a key to the quality of political life in general and to the character of citizenship in particular.[6] A *polis* must be large enough to be self-sufficient, Aristotle declared, but not so large that its citizens are unable to

> know each other and know what kind of people they are. Where this condition does not exist, both elections and decisions at law are bound to suffer; it is not right in either of these matters to vote at haphazard, which is clearly what takes place when the population is excessive.
>
> (Aristotle, *Politics*, 1326b11–25 [1981, p. 405])

With Aristotle, then, concern with the size of the polity follows largely from his conception of citizenship. Because the self-governing citizen is one who rules and is ruled in turn, he must be able to reach informed judgements about those over whom he rules and who rule over him. Hence the population of the city could not continue to grow indefinitely without diluting the quality of its citizenship.

There is, of course, at least one major difference between Aristotle's time and ours: the advent of mass communication media. Given the benefits of printing press, radio, television and now the internet, we might expect that the size of a city's population would no longer prove an obstacle to (responsible) citizenship. But this does not seem to be the case. Modern means of communication do little to make us familiar with the other residents of metropolis. They may enable us to know something about our cities' leading political figures, but they seldom put us into a position to 'know what kind of people' the other residents of the city are. To make these judgements, we need to observe people in action, preferably in a variety of contexts and over a period of time. Such observation may still be possible for the residents of smaller cities and towns but not for most metropolitans.

Moreover, the sheer size of cities is often overwhelming. When there are so many people about – so many strange people who are almost certain to remain strangers – the individual finds it difficult to feel at home in a city that is familiar, yet foreign. The inhabitants of a metropolis may look to their neighbourhoods for a sense of place or comfort, but when there is no strong neighbourhood tradition, or when that tradition has been eroded, they are likely to feel isolated and alone in an alien city. When people lose touch with the city in this way, they lose interest in its affairs. They may retain an interest in those matters that seem to affect them directly or perceptibly, but these will probably dwindle as the city expands. Thus the inhabitants of the metropolis are likely to believe both that their participation in civic affairs is insignificant, dwarfed as they are by the size of the city, and that these matters are of no real concern to them anyhow.[7] Such an attitude, as well as the environment that fosters it, does not produce (active) citizens.

As the population of a city grows, then, its inhabitants often come to feel more and more remote from its political life. When everyone in the metropolis knows that he or she is only one among hundreds of thousands, or even millions, it is difficult to attach much significance to one's participation in civic affairs. This consideration apparently discourages people from engaging in even the less demanding forms of political action, such as voting. In mathematical terms, as Rousseau pointed out, the chance that one's vote will have any appreciable influence in an election decreases as the size of the body politic increases: the greater the number of voters, the less the weight of anyone's vote (Rousseau, 1762, bk III, chap. 1). This insight has been developed and refined considerably in recent years, and one author has concluded that his chances of casting the vote that determines the winner of a presidential election 'are of about the same order of magnitude as my chances of being killed driving to the polls – hardly a profitable venture' (Meehl, 1977, p. 11). The odds are not so daunting in municipal elections, certainly, but in a metropolis they are great enough to keep at home those people who will only go to the polls when they believe that their vote may well affect the outcome of the election.

The same reasoning applies generally to the cooperation needed to achieve public purposes. If a city suffers from traffic congestion and air pollution, city officials may ask the residents to drive their cars less often. Universal cooperation is seldom necessary in cases of this sort, so any resident of the metropolis may decide that it is in his or her interest not to join a car pool or take the bus but to continue to drive as he or she pleases. As long as the city is large enough to render an individual's cooperation insignificant, and failure to cooperate unnoticeable, the individual will have an incentive to be a free rider. Not everyone takes this point of view; many even appear to be willing to make the sacrifices cooperation requires when they believe that they can trust others to make similar sacrifices. But this basis of trust is often lacking in the metropolis, where the anonymity that comes with size encourages people to pursue private interests rather than a public vocation. The larger the city, the more likely it is that this situation will prevail.[8]

There is, however, a good deal of evidence that shows that those who live in large cities and their suburbs are more likely to vote, at least in national elections, than those living in rural areas, small towns and even relatively small, non-suburban cities. This evidence suggests that the size of a city is positively associated with political participation, if not necessarily with citizenship as a public vocation. But even this conclusion is not warranted. Studies of voting in America indicate that the comparatively high levels of voting among those who live in large metropolitan areas are produced not by the size of those areas but by such social and economic factors as income and education. The residents of metropolis tend to have higher incomes and educational levels than those who live elsewhere, and voting studies have established that both of these variables are positively associated with voting (Rosenstone and Hansen, 1993, pp. 43–5, 134–6). But when the authors of *Participation in America* controlled these factors statistically, so that population could be compared more directly with levels of participation, they found that residents of rural areas and 'isolated villages' have higher voting rates than residents of metropolitan areas. When other forms of political participation are included, moreover, the rate of overall participation is markedly lower in metropolitan areas – in core cities and their suburbs – than in rural areas and 'isolated' communities where the population is generally less than 25,000 (Verba and Nie, 1972, chap. 13).[9] We can add empirical evidence, then, to the logical and psychological reasons for believing that the size of our overgrown cities is a barrier to (responsible) citizenship.

Fragmentation

Another difference between the city-state and the contemporary metropolis that bears on citizenship is the fragmentation of the metropolis – that is, the complications created by the division of authority and the multiplication of boundaries and jurisdictions in urban areas. This fragmentation takes two main forms, the more obvious of which is geographical fragmentation of political authority. Geographical fragmentation occurs especially, if not exclusively, when suburbs spring up around a central city. In America, in particular, there are scores, sometimes hundreds, of suburbs clustered around the central city, each with some government of its own. Added to these municipalities are counties, townships and the various regional coordinating councils that have been established in an attempt to prevent the chaos this geographical fragmentation sometimes seems to threaten.

The second form of fragmentation is functional (Harrigan, 1976, pp. 139–46). Partly as a result of the distrust of urban political machines, many of the functions of city governments have been transferred to special districts or surrendered to the care of supposedly apolitical professionals. This has led to the creation of numerous 'functional fiefdoms' that are virtually independent of city governments (and virtually invisible to the residents of metropolis). Furthermore, new sets of these fiefdoms have compounded the fragmentation of authority in the metropolis as state and federal programmes have been established to deal with problems of economic security, welfare and urban redevelopment.

The consequences of this twofold fragmentation are readily apparent. Superimposed on the layer of municipal governments in the metropolis are a number of other jurisdictions: school districts, police and fire protection districts, sewer districts, cultural districts, transit districts, port authorities, metropolitan councils, and more. In 1977 the 272 Standard Metropolitan Statistical Areas (SMSAs) in America had a total of 25,869 'local governments', or an average of 95.1 each. In the thirty-five SMSAs with populations of a million or more, the average was 293.3, with metropolitan Chicago leading the way with 1,214 local governments (Bollens and Schmandt, 1982, pp. 88–9). By 1992 there were 284 metropolitan areas with a total of 33,004 local governments – an average of 116 apiece (*Census of Governments*, 1992, p. 39, Table 26).

For the inhabitants of the metropolis, the consequences of this fragmentation are often confusion, disorientation and a sense of impotence. It is easy to lose one's bearings, and one's interest, when there is no central political authority to provide a focal point. As jurisdictions proliferate, overlap and cut across each other in an increasingly confusing manner, people may come to believe that charting a course through the maze that confronts them is neither within their capacities nor worth their efforts. Nor will they have much reason to discuss local politics or school board elections with co-workers when they know that those co-workers reside in different municipalities and send their children to school in different districts. Fragmentation thus fosters isolation and apathy, an attitude that is especially prevalent where the effects of the fragmentation of authority are most severe – in the suburbs.

Here again *Participation in America* supplies supporting evidence. The data mentioned in the discussion of community size are helpful with regard to fragmentation also, for the highest rate of overall political participation is to be found in what Verba and Nie call the 'isolated city' – the city that enjoys its own distinct boundaries and identity – rather than in the core city or suburbs. With its relative freedom from fragmentation, the isolated or independent city apparently affords a more hospitable environment for citizenship than the metropolis. Comparisons between the participation rates of those who live in core cities and those who live in their suburbs provide even more telling evidence of the negative effects of metropolitan fragmentation. These comparisons reveal that when the socio-economic characteristics of the population are separated from community characteristics, overall political participation is actually lower in the suburbs – the communities most troubled by the fragmentation of political authority (1972, pp. 233–47). It is hardly surprising, consequently, that Verba and Nie conclude:

> As communities grow in size and, more important, as they lose those characteristics of boundedness that distinguish the independent city from the suburb, participation declines. And it does so most strikingly for communal participation, a kind of participation particularly well attuned to deal with the variety of specific problems faced by groups of citizens. One last obvious point must be made here, for it has important implications. The communities that appear to foster participation – the small and relatively independent communities – are becoming rarer and rarer.
>
> (Verba and Nie, 1972, p. 247)[10]

Mobility

If the size and fragmentation that characterize the metropolis are hostile to (active) citizenship, so too is residential mobility. When the population of any group changes rapidly or frequently, it is difficult for its members to learn who other members are and whether they can be trusted to cooperate. Individuals may also face the question of whether to invest their time and risk their cooperation in an enterprise that they may be part of for only a short time. There is a time-horizon problem in these cases because people are not likely to make the sacrifices required by cooperation in the production of collective goods if they do not take the long-term view (Ostrom, 1990, pp. 34–5, 88, 183–4).

The tendency to move from place to place is not confined to those who live in metropolitan areas, but it does seem to be a feature of predominantly urban societies. Residential mobility certainly plays a significant part in the social and political life of America. 'It is the norm to move', according to one student of mobility (Brown, 1988, p. 6). 'High mobility is at the heart of American culture', according to another, who reports that the average American moves eleven to thirteen times during his or her life (Gober, 1993, pp. 35–6). Since

1950, one-sixth to one-fifth of Americans have changed residence every year; in 1990–1, '17 of every 100 Americans moved to a different home' (Gober, 1993, pp. 2–3). Nor are such rates of mobility confined to America. Residential mobility is typically more than 17 per cent per year in Canada, Australia and New Zealand; the rate ranges from 9 to 15 per cent in France, Sweden, Great Britain, Switzerland, Israel and Japan; and it falls to less than 9 per cent in the Netherlands, Austria, Belgium and Ireland (Gober, 1993, pp. 3–4).

The unsettling effects of such widespread mobility on citizenship should be apparent. In America and other countries without automatic registration, movers must register in their new location in order to vote there. Lack of familiarity with political issues and personalities in the new location will also discourage participation. What may be even more important, however, is the tendency of residential mobility to loosen the ties that bind individuals to a community. Citizenship grows out of attachment to a place and its people that only forms over time. Those who move about frequently are not likely to acquire this attachment. Even those who seem rooted to a place are affected, for they are likely to feel abandoned as the faces about them become less familiar and their neighbourhoods less neighbourly.

High rates of mobility *within* the boundaries of a city can be disruptive, too, largely because whatever sense of community the residents of the metropolis have is often the product of a tie to a particular district or neighbourhood. In large urban areas, these districts and neighbourhoods provide the arenas most accessible to the ordinary citizen and closest to his or her concerns. But these arenas cannot survive when the established patterns of communication and interaction that hold a neighbourhood together are destroyed by the constant shifting of the population. The implications for citizenship, as Jane Jacobs notes, are clear:

> If self-government in the place is to work, underlying any float of popula-
> tion must be a continuity of people who have forged neighbourhood net-
> works. These networks are a city's irreplaceable social capital. Whenever
> the capital is lost … the income from it disappears, never to return until
> and unless new capital is slowly and chancily accumulated.
>
> (Jacobs, 1969, p. 138)

If 'self-government in the place is to work', moreover, there must be a sense of *place* that people share. According to Daniel Kemmis, who wrote these words while mayor of Missoula, Montana,

> people who find themselves together (perhaps against their will) in a
> shared place discover as well that their best possibility for realizing the
> potential of the place is to learn to work together. In this way places breed
> cooperation, and out of this ancient relationship of place to human willing,
> that specific activity which is rightly called 'politics' is born.
>
> (Kemmis, 1990, pp. 122–3)[11]

Professional concerns play an important part, too, for those whose careers encourage or require them to move are less likely to acquire an attachment and devote themselves to civic concerns. Their civic time horizon shortens as they gauge their expected length of residence in a city by the speed with which they can take the next step up the career ladder. Stephen Elkin puts the point well in his study of changes in the politics of Dallas, Texas:

> [A]s Dallas has evolved into a major city with its businessmen and banks conducting business nationally and internationally, the question that increasingly presses on them concerns what incentive they have to remain or take an active interest in city affairs. The businessmen who founded and ran the CCA [Citizen Charter Association] and DCC [Dallas City Council] ... had strong material and civic reasons for devoting themselves to city affairs. They were engaged in making a city that would make them rich and proud and provide a style of living that suited their tastes. The present generation of business executives are as likely as not to have other interests. Their city is already attractive, its government not corrupt. Moreover, they are as likely as not to seek to advance their careers in the national business arena and to seek entertainment outside the city.
>
> (Elkin, 1987, p. 73)

As Elkin indicates, upward mobility that requires geographical mobility complicates the problem of securing civic leadership. Well-educated people typically provide leadership, but they are also the ones most likely to move. In America in the early 1990s, for instance, a college graduate 'was about three times more likely to move to another state than an individual who never completed elementary school' (Gober, 1993, pp. 24–6).

Whether the movement is within, between or simply into cities, the effects are much the same: the sense of community is eroded, and so is the individual's willingness to participate in public affairs and cooperate for public purposes. In the case of cooperation, a fluid population acts, as does a large population, to discourage people from working together to achieve public goods. Under certain conditions, rational-choice theory suggests, rational actors will gradually come to cooperate with one another to produce public goods. These conditions include the requirement that the individuals involved know that (enough of) the others have cooperated in the past. As Taylor points out, this requirement is

> more likely to be met in a small group of players than in a large group – and even more likely in the sort of small community in which people have contact with and can observe the behavior of many of their fellows and which is fairly static, in the sense that there is little mobility in or out.
>
> (Taylor, 1976, p. 93)

When there is a high rate of mobility, the confidence in one another that forms the basis for cooperative action cannot develop. In these circumstances, we can hardly expect people to adopt the public vocation of citizenship.

Several studies support the contention that unstable populations lead to low levels of political participation. In the earliest of these, a study of voting in England shortly after the Second World War, A.H. Birch found a 'clear and positive relation between the stability of population of a town and the proportion of that population that exercises its right to vote' (1950, p. 82). Since then a number of studies have reported that length of residence and other signs of 'community attachment' are positively associated with voting in national elections in America, while residential mobility 'substantially decreases the probability that an individual will vote' (Wolfinger and Rosenstone, 1980, p. 54).[12]

Together with the size and fragmentation of metropolitan areas, then, residential mobility actively discourages (active) citizenship. It does this, as do size and fragmentation, by divorcing citizen from city. When individuals see the city as something distant from their own lives and interests, as something that is not truly *theirs*, they will have little reason to take part in its affairs, to contribute to its well-being, or to make the least sacrifice on its behalf. We simply cannot expect citizens (in the legal sense) to act with the interests of the community in mind when they do not perceive themselves as members of a community. It is equally futile to expect them to perceive themselves in this way when there is no *civic memory* for them to draw upon and to draw them together.

Civic memory

'Civic memory' means simply the recollection of the events, characters and developments that make up the history of one's city or town. Civic memory is therefore something that individuals may possess as individuals, and some no doubt will have better civic memories than others. But it is also a shared recollection of a city's pasts, of its accomplishments and failures, that both reflects and generates a sense of civic identity. When there is no widely shared recollection of this sort – when only a few of a city's inhabitants have more than a nodding acquaintance with its past – then we may say that civic memory has been lost.

Such a loss is devastating to citizenship, for civic memory is related to citizenship as personal memory is to personality. Without memory there is no personality, no sense of self. Indeed, we can think of and act as selves only because we can *recollect* the experiences that constitute ourselves. As Garry Wills says,

> Memory is creative – we come to *be* what we can recognize as the self; and man is not an agent in history until he has acquired this intimate history, the working identity through which other things can be identified.
>
> (Wills, 1979, pp. 223–4; emphasis in original)

What memory is to the self, civic memory is to the city. Civic memory is creative in the sense that it helps to constitute the city by giving it shape and meaning in the minds of its residents. Through the recollection of its people a city comes to be something more than a bewildering agglomeration of streets and buildings and nameless faces. Their memories compose its working identity, and this identity enables them to take the part of the citizen.

Civic memory thus points both backwards and forwards, to the future as well as the past, thereby providing the direction necessary to (ethical) citizenship. Like other forms of memory, it differs in this respect from nostalgia:

> Nostalgia appeals to the feeling that the past offered delights no longer obtainable. ... Memory too may idealize the past, but not in order to condemn the present. ... It sees past, present, and future as continuous. It is less concerned with loss than with our continuing indebtedness to a past the formative influence of which lives on in our patterns of speech, our gestures, our standards of honor, our expectations, our basic disposition toward the world around us.
>
> (Lasch, 1991, p. 83)

In pointing to the past, civic memory is essentially conservative, for it preserves, as it creates, the identity and integrity of a city. When the people and events that formed the city are remembered, the city will be seen not as a curious accident or an incomprehensible jumble, but as something with a story, a past that makes sense of the present. Those residents who know this story, even only some chapters of it, are likely to feel an attachment to the city, to see themselves as part of something enduring and worthwhile. By fostering these attachments, civic memory enables the people of a city to see it as *their* city: an essential perception if they are to regard participation in the government of the city as *self*-government.

That civic memory really works in this way is suggested by the common practice of commemorating the great events and leading figures in a city's history. To *commemorate* someone or something is to *remember together* by committing him, her or it to a common memory. Commemoration takes many forms, from the naming of cities after their founders to public holidays and the erection of statues and stadia in honour of civic leaders and heroes. Regardless of the form, however, these memorial tributes all share a common set of purposes: to recognize those who have contributed to the well-being of the city; to preserve the identity of the city through a common memory; and to celebrate the vitality of the city itself.

In reminding us of a city's past, then, civic memory nourishes the sense of civic identity that is essential to citizenship. It does this by rendering the city familiar and comprehensible, by helping citizens to see that they are part of the city's life just as it is part of theirs. When this memory of the city's past is widely shared, it forges a bond of sympathy, a sense of a common life. These circumstances inspire the individual to act as a (responsible) citizen, a self-governing member of a self-governed community.

Here is where civic memory points to the future. It does this in two ways, each important to the development of citizenship. First, when the spirit of community is alive, the individual finds it difficult to regard his or her city, and the people who compose it, with detachment. The individual sees it, and them, not as something alien, but as something intimately connected to his or her own interests. This attitude is especially likely to arise when he or she can look back to generations of ancestors who have lived in and in some way worked for the city. In this context the individual is likely to regard his or her contributions to the city's life as contributions to his or her own and his or her family's welfare.

Civic memory also points to the future by demonstrating a continuity maintained by those who know and care for the city. The fact that the deeds of others have been remembered is a sign that one's own deeds may be remembered as well. Through the recognition it promises, civic memory supplies both an incentive to civic action and a reward for those who contribute to the city's well-being. This is perhaps obviously true of those whose contributions are heroic or in some way extraordinary, but it is also true of those whose contributions are not. Even those who only do their part may expect to be recognized as (good) citizens by others who know and care for the city.[13]

All of this is to say that civic memory instils in its residents a concern for the health of their city and a willingness to act on that concern. But just as citizenship depends upon civic memory, so civic memory depends upon certain conditions for its preservation – conditions that are far from realized in the conurbations that dominate contemporary life. Certainly the three forces discussed in the previous section – the overwhelming size of the metropolis, the fragmentation of authority it fosters and the mobility of its people – are hostile, each in its own way, to civic memory. They combine to detach us from our surroundings, from place and people, and lead us to think of ourselves as in the city but not of it. It is difficult to regard civic action as an investment in our future, or the future of our children, when it is likely that neither we nor they will long inhabit the city in which we now live. Nor can we expect to be recognized or remembered for our contributions to the city's well-being when the sheer size of metropolis renders the contribution most of us can make all but invisible. When these three conditions prevail, civic memory fails.

Encouraging citizenship

What, then, is the proper breeding ground for citizenship? If it is the city, as I believe, then it is the city as it can be, not as it too often is. Citizenship is a public vocation that we cannot expect more than a few to pursue in the contemporary metropolis. It needs a city large enough to pose problems of some significance, but (ethical) citizenship also requires a city that is more settled and in some ways simpler than the metropolis. If we want to encourage citizenship, then, we must be prepared to reform and redirect our cities.

Some may resist this conclusion. Critics may argue that we should take other measures to promote citizenship – measures that do not require us to reshape our cities and that are to be preferred, for that reason, to those that do. These measures might include, on the one hand, attempts to improve the education and economic well-being of the citizenry and, on the other, attempts to cultivate citizenship in the neighbourhood or workplace.

Although there is something to be said for all these measures, there is this to be said against them: they will not prove adequate to the task. In the case of the first set of measures, we may readily agree that education and economics are closely related to (responsible) citizenship. Citizenship may even presuppose some level of education and material well-being; certainly those who must labour constantly to meet their needs will have neither the time nor the inclination to act as citizens. But there is no reason to believe that educational and economic reforms, desirable as they may be for other reasons, will suffice to bring about widespread (active) citizenship. With regard to political participation, we know that the higher one's educational and economic status, the more likely one is to participate; yet we also know that political participation, at least in the form of voting, has generally declined in recent decades despite rising educational and economic levels for the population as a whole.[14] It seems, moreover, that education and affluence can do little to preserve or restore the civic memory of a rootless people. Schools can devote more time to civic history and problems, and perhaps they should, but residential mobility will render this instruction meaningless for many students. There is room for improvement in these areas, in short, but it is doubtful that such improvement in itself will lead to a revival of (ethical) citizenship.

Nor can we look to the neighbourhood or the workplace to bring about this revival. In the case of the neighbourhood, we can neither develop nor maintain a sense of neighbourhood citizenship in more than a few fortunate places without first solving, or beginning to solve, the problems posed by metropolis and mobility. One of the major obstacles to the creation and preservation of strong neighbourhoods, especially in newer cities, is the centrifugal pull of the metropolis, with its shopping centres, financial districts and industrial parks. Another is residential mobility. And another is the fragmentation of authority in the metropolis – especially the functional fragmentation that makes it difficult for the residents of a neighbourhood or district to exercise control over matters of common concern (Jacobs, 1969, chap. 21). These problems cannot be resolved from within the neighbourhood, so we must conclude that the restoration and (re)creation of neighbourhoods depends in large part upon a redirection of the metropolis.

The attempt to build participation and citizenship through the workplace presents a different problem, for it raises questions about the nature of citizenship. Granting workers the right to participate in the management of their industries and firms may produce worthwhile results; it may increase self-esteem and productivity, reduce alienation and even lead to greater political participation. But will it promote *citizenship*? Citizenship requires a more synoptic perspective than the workplace offers, a perspective that enables the citizen to see the community as a whole and to see himself or herself as part of the community. Democracy of the workplace may take us in this direction, but if it reinforces the worker's tendency to think of himself or herself primarily as a worker, as someone who fills a particular occupation, then it may take us away from it.[15]

Whatever their other merits may be, then, none of these measures is adequate to the task of reviving (ethical) citizenship. Civic memory is necessary to citizenship, and none of these measures deals directly with the forces hostile to civic memory: the size of metropolis, the fragmentation of authority within it, and the high rate of residential mobility. If we are to encourage civic memory, and citizenship with it, we must be prepared to reform and redirect our cities. But how is this to be done?

One possibility is to aim for what Murray Bookchin (1995) calls 'confederal municipalism'. According to Bookchin (p. 235), this will be a 'municipal politics, based on communalist principles' that calls for, among other things, 'the municipalization of the economy – and its management by the community as part of a politics of self-management'. Bookchin thus weds a concern for the recovery of (ethical) citizenship to an anarcho-communist vision of the good society.

A less sweeping, and more conventional, way to attack the problems of metropolis and citizenship is to reduce the size of overgrown metropolises by dispersing population. This strategy would address the problem of fragmentation as well as that of scale, for a redistribution of the population into smaller, more isolated (in Verba and Nie's sense) cities will leave less to fragment. As for residential mobility, there is some reason to believe that redistribution of population will eventually lead to lower rates of residential change. The evidence in this regard is not conclusive, but it does suggest that most Americans, including most of those who reside in large urban areas, would prefer to live in rural, small-town or small urban settings (Hansen, 1975, chap. 3; Sundquist, 1975, pp. 24–30; Fuguitt and Brown, 1990, pp. 592–3). If this remains true, and if educational and employment opportunities are spread about the countryside as part of the policy to encourage dispersal, then people may find it possible to settle and remain settled in the locations they prefer. With the development of the internet and 'telecommuting', in fact, people may be able to take their work with them as they follow their residential preferences.

This approach is attractive because it promises to combat each of the three forces thus identified as enemies of civic memory. Any attempt to put a strategy of this sort into effect will be opposed by those who have investments of one sort or another in the metropolis, however, and in the absence of a natural constituency to support such a policy, the opposition is almost certain to have its way. Even if the opposition can be overcome, it is not clear that we should embark on a programme to redistribute population. No matter how it is planned and executed, the attempt to reduce gigantic cities to a scale more suitable to citizenship is bound to have serious consequences for the organization of the economy, energy use, cultural opportunities, political stability and other aspects of our lives. We may find, upon reflection, that this strategy would promote citizenship at the expense of other things we value.[16]

But that is not to say that the investigation should not be undertaken. Some countries have had modest success with attempts to shift their populations away from congested areas, and we would do well to examine the methods they have used and the results they have achieved (Sundquist, 1975; Harrigan, 1976, chap. 12; De Jong, 1975).

If the attempt to disperse population into more and smaller cities seems too bold, another possibility is to try to redirect the metropolis so that it is more hospitable to citizenship. Attempts to consolidate the municipalities of a metropolitan area, and thus to lessen the geographical fragmentation of authority, are examples of this approach, as are proposals to strengthen city councils and to eliminate non-partisan elections. Other possible reforms might include the establishment of something akin to a federal structure of governments for the metropolis, or perhaps a metropolitan version of democratic centralism.[17]

Measures of this sort are limited, for they are not likely to reduce either the size of metropolis or the rate of residential mobility. They may help to make the government of the metropolis more accessible, more visible and more overtly political, however, and from the standpoint of active citizenship these are worthy accomplishments. If citizenship is to be more than a matter of legal status, the citizens must be able to see themselves as parts of a community whose concerns are their concerns. They must also be able to see that there are important choices to be made in and for the community – choices that shape its character – and that they can play some not insignificant part in making these choices. Insofar as the reforms that this approach suggests lead to a more accessible, more visible and more overtly political government for the metropolis, to that extent they will also be fostering (responsible) citizenship.

Whatever we do, we must begin by confronting the problems of size, fragmentation and mobility. At the least we ought to start to evaluate policies and proposals in terms of their implications for civic memory and citizenship. Had this been done earlier, the programmes that have contributed to the growth of suburbia – such as various mortgage insurance programmes and the Interstate Highway Act in America – might have taken a different form.

In this regard, the most hopeful sign of a proper concern for the relationship between metropolis, memory and citizenship is the emergence among architects and town planners of 'the new urbanism' (Calthorpe, 1993; Katz, 1994; Kunstler, 1996, esp. chap. 5). Because they take civic design seriously as a way of overcoming isolation and promoting community, the proponents of this new urbanism have taken aim at suburban sprawl and the tendency to base town planning on the automobile. In their own designs, they focus on the creation or revival of pedestrian-centred neighbourhoods, houses with front porches, prominent locations for civic buildings, and other devices for encouraging contact among neighbours. Whether the new urbanism becomes more than a hopeful sign of a renewed concern for citizenship and community remains, of course, to be seen.

What we may ultimately have to decide is how much we value the public vocation of citizenship. We may conclude, after all, that (active) citizenship simply costs more than it is worth. But if we value it highly, and if we want to make it possible for all citizens (in the legal sense) to follow this vocation, then we shall have to reform and redirect our cities. However this is done, it will require at least that the sense of community be enhanced and the political character of the community be made more explicit. Citizenship is a political role, and it can only be practised in a *political* community. Which is to say that the reformation and redirection of our cities along the lines sketched here is a necessary condition, if not a sufficient one, for the revival of (ethical) citizenship. Only in this way can we restore civic memory and found cities that can actually be what they potentially are: the breeding grounds of citizenship.

Notes

1 This is a substantially revised version of an essay that appeared, under the same title, in *The American Journal of Political Science*, 25 (1981): 715–37. The revision has aimed at bringing the essay up to date without altering its original focus or spirit.

2 Also 1283b40–1284a3, where Aristotle defines a citizen 'in general' as

> one who has a share both in ruling and in being ruled; this will not be identical in every kind of constitution, but in the best constitution it means one who is able and who chooses to rule and to be ruled with a view to life that is in accordance with goodness.
>
> (Aristotle, 1981, p. 213)

3 For similar views, see Ostrom et al. (1961), Bish (1971) and Teske et al. (1993). For criticism of the idea of the citizen as consumer, see Hollis (1991), Sagoff (1988), esp. p. 8, Kunstler (1996), p. 38 and Dagger (1997), pp. 104–8; for criticism of the citizen as taxpayer, see Bookchin (1995), esp. p. 21.

4 In the case of the person seeking a business licence, it may be instructive to compare his or her role with that of the officials who must rule on the petition. Ordinarily the decision to petition for a business licence is based on personal considerations – the desire to make more money, to be one's own boss – and is justified in those terms. The council's decision to grant or deny the licence is very much a public matter, however, for it is expected to rest on public considerations, such as how this particular establishment will affect traffic, the noise level, the economic condition of the community and so on.

5 And as Verba et al. note (1995, p. 50), these results, as 'is always the case with surveys', indicate that more people said that they voted in the previous year (1988) than really did. They also point out (p. 69) that the USA 'lags far behind other democracies when it comes to voting turnout' – probably because of 'voter registration requirements and the weakness of American political parties as agents of mobilization' – but that 'Americans are as active, or substantially more active, than citizens elsewhere' with regard to 'campaigning, attending political meetings, becoming active in the local community, and contacting officials'.

6 Chap. 1 of Dahl and Tufte (1973) provides a useful survey of political theorists' claims and counterclaims regarding the desirable size of the polity.

7 For social-psychological evidence in support of this observation, see Miller and Godwin (1977), pp. 151–2 and 203. Of the studies cited there, the most pertinent is probably Milgram (1970). Note also Levine (1994–5), who concludes, on the basis of six experiments conducted in thirty-six cities of various sizes in the USA, that 'the citizens of urban environments are clearly less likely to respond to the needs of strangers than are their counterparts in smaller communities' (p. 66).

8 On the relationship between size and cooperation to achieve public goods, see Olson (1971), esp. chap. 2, Taylor (1976), esp. 7.2, and Ullmann-Margalit (1977), pp. 46–7.

9 An 'isolated' community, unlike a suburb, has distinct boundaries and is not caught in the orbit of a larger city. See also the data from France reported in Tarrow (1971).

10 As Downs (1994, p. 11) reports,

Total suburban population [in the USA] rose from 41 million in 1950 to 115 million in 1990, an increase of 181 percent compared with a 65 percent increase in total population. The proportion of Americans living in suburbs rose from 27 percent to 46 percent.

11 Note also Walzer (1990), p. 11: 'Communities are more than just locations, but they are most often successful when they are permanently located'.

12 For evidence on 'community attachment', see Verba et al. (1995, pp. 453–5), Strate et al. (1989), esp. p. 458, Squire et al. (1987), esp. p. 56, and Verba and Nie (1972), pp. 139–46.

13

Some brilliant achievement may win a people's favor at one stroke. But to gain the affection and respect of your immediate neighbours, a long succession of little services rendered and of obscure good deeds, a constant habit of kindness and an established reputation for disinterestedness, are required.

(de Tocqueville, 1969, p. 511)

14 Whether political participation in general has declined in the United States in the last 40 or so years is not clear. Rosenstone and Hansen (1993, chap. 3) report a general decline, but Verba et al. (1995, p. 74), who agree that 'there has been an unambiguous decline in voter turnout', maintain that 'rates of other kinds of political participation have not eroded so sharply. Indeed, over the period [since 1960] some forms of activity – making contributions to electoral campaigns and political organizations and, probably, contacting public officials – have actually increased'. But they go on to say that 'political activity has *not grown at rates that we might have expected on the basis of the substantial increase in levels of educational attainment within the public*' (p. 74; emphasis added).

15 In this regard, note Wolin (1960), p. 434:

the specialized roles assigned the individual, or adopted by him, are not a full substitute for citizenship because citizenship provides what other roles cannot, namely an integrative experience which brings together the multiple role-activities of the contemporary person and demands that the separate roles be surveyed from a more general point of view.

16 We may also find that the merits of large cities, especially the 'economies of scale' they promise, are not as great as they seem. On this point, see Gilbert (1976).

17 See Dagger (1997), pp. 168–71, for elaboration.

Bibliography

Aristotle (1981) *The Politics*, trans. T.A. Sinclair, rev. T.J. Saunders (Baltimore: Penguin Books).

Berry, J.M., Portney, K.E. and Thompson, K. (1993) *The Rebirth of Urban Democracy* (Washington, DC: The Brookings Institution).

Birch, A.H. (1950) 'The Habit of Voting', *Manchester School of Social and Economic Studies*, 28 (January): 75–82.

Bish, R. (1971) *The Public Economy of Metropolitan Areas* (Chicago: Markham).

Bollens, J. and Schmandt, H. (1982) *The Metropolis: Its People, Politics, and Economic Life*, 4th edn (New York: Harper and Row).

Bookchin, M. (1995) *From Urbanization to Cities: Toward a New Politics of Citizenship* (London and New York: Cassell).

Brown, T.A. (1988) *Migration and Politics: The Impact of Population Mobility on American Voting Behavior* (Chapel Hill: University of North Carolina Press).

Calthorpe, P. (1993) *The Next American Metropolis: Ecology, Community, and the American Dream* (New York: Princeton Architectural Press).

Census of Governments (1992), vol. 1, *Government Organization* (Washington, DC: US Government Printing Office).

Conover, P.J., Crewe, I.M. and Searing, D. (1991) 'The Nature of Citizenship in the United States and Great Britain: Empirical Comments on Theoretical Themes', *Journal of Politics*, 53: 800–32.

Dagger, R. (1997) *Civic Virtues: Rights, Citizenship, and Republican Liberalism* (New York: Oxford University Press).

Dahl, R. (1967) 'The City in the Future of Democracy', *The American Political Science Review*, 61 (4): 953–70.

Dahl, R. and Tufte, E. (1973) *Size and Democracy* (Stanford, CA: Stanford University Press).

De Jong, G. (1975) 'Population Redistribution Policies: Alternatives from the Netherlands, Great Britain, and Israel', *Social Science Quarterly*, 56 (September): 262–73.

De Tocqueville, Alexis (1969) *Democracy in America*, trans. G. Lawrence, ed. J.P. Mayer (Garden City, NY: Doubleday).

Downs, A. (1994) *New Visions for Metropolitan America* (Washington, DC: The Brookings Institution).

Elkin, S. (1987) *City and Regime in the American Republic* (Chicago: University of Chicago Press).

Etzioni, A. (1996) *The New Golden Rule: Community and Morality in a Democratic Society* (New York: Basic Books).

Fuguitt, G.V. and Brown, D.L. (1990) 'Residential Preferences and Population Redistribution: 1972–1988', *Demography*, 27: 589–600.

Fustel de Coulanges, N.D. ([1864] [n.d.]) *The Ancient City* (Garden City, NY: Doubleday).

Gilbert, A. (1976) 'The Arguments for Very Large Cities Reconsidered', *Urban Studies*, 13 (February): 27–34.

Gober, P. (1993) 'Americans on the Move', *Population Bulletin*, 48: 1–40.

Hansen, N.M. (1975) *The Challenge of Urban Growth* (Lexington, MA: Lexington Books).

Harrigan, J. (1976) *Political Change in the Metropolis* (Boston, MA: Little, Brown).

Hollis, M. (1991) 'Friends, Romans, and Consumers', *Ethics*, 102: 27–41.

Jacobs, J. (1969) *The Death and Life of Great American Cities* (New York: Modern Library).

Jaeger, W. (1945) *Paideia: The Ideals of Greek Culture*, vol. 1, 2nd edn, trans. G. Highet (New York: Oxford University Press).

Katz, P. (ed.) (1994) *The New Urbanism: Toward an Architecture of Community* (New York: McGraw-Hill).

Kemmis, D. (1990) *Community and the Politics of Place* (Norman: University of Oklahoma Press).

Kennedy, J.F. (1961) 'Every Citizen Holds Office', *NEA Journal*, 50 (October): 18–20.

Kunstler, J.H. (1996) *Home from Nowhere: Remaking Our Everyday World for the Twenty-First Century* (New York: Simon and Schuster).

Lasch, C. (1991) *The True and Only Heaven: Progress and its Critics* (New York: W.W. Norton).

Levine, R. (1994–5) 'Cities with Heart', *The Responsive Community*, 5: 59–67.

Long, N. (1962) 'An Institutional Framework for the Development of Responsible Citizenship', in C. Press (ed.), *The Polity* (Chicago: Rand McNally).

Meehl, P.E. (1977) 'The Selfish Voter Paradox and the Thrown-away Vote Argument', *The American Political Science Review*, 71 (2): 11–30.

Milgram, S. (1970) 'The Experience of Living in Cities', *Science*, 167: 1461–68.

Miller, W.B. and Godwin, R.K. (1977) *Psyche and Demos: Individual Psychology and the Issues of Population* (New York: Oxford University Press).

Myres, J.L. (1927 [1968]) *The Political Ideas of the Greeks* (New York: Greenwood Press).

Olson, M. (1971) *The Logic of Collective Action*, rev. edn (New York: Schocken Books).

Ostrom, E. (1990) *Governing the Commons: The Evolution of Institutions for Collective Action* (Cambridge: Cambridge University Press).

Ostrom, V., Tiebout, C. and Warren, R. (1961) 'The Organization of Government in Metropolitan Areas: A Theoretical Inquiry', *American Political Science Review*, 55: 416–24.

Rosenstone, S. and Hansen, J.M. (1993) *Mobilization, Participation, and Democracy in America* (New York: Macmillan).

Rousseau, J-J. (1750 [1950]) *The Social Contract and Discourses*, trans. G.D.H. Cole (New York: E.P. Dutton).

—— (1762 [1978]) *On the Social Contract*, ed. R. Masters, trans. J. Masters (New York: St Martin's Press).

Sagoff, M. (1988) *The Economy of the Earth: Philosophy, Law, and the Environment* (Cambridge: Cambridge University Press).

Selbourne, D. (1994) *The Principle of Duty: An Essay on the Foundations of the Civic Order* (London: Sinclair-Stevenson).

Sibley, M.Q. (1970) *Political Ideas and Ideologies: A History of Political Thought* (New York: Harper and Row).

Squire, P., Wolfinger, R. and Glass, D. (1987) 'Residential Mobility and Voter Turnout', *American Political Science Review*, 81: 45–65.

Strate, J.M, Parrish, C.J., Elder, C.D. and Ford III, C. (1989) 'Life Span Civic Development and Voting Participation', *American Political Science Review*, 83: 443–64.

Sundquist, J. (1975) *Dispersing Population: What America Can Learn from Europe* (Washington, DC: Brookings Institution).

Tarrow, S. (1971) 'The Urban-Rural Cleavage in Political Involvement: The Case of France', *The American Political Science Review*, 63 (2): 341–57.

Taylor, M. (1976) *Anarchy and Cooperation* (London: John Wiley).

Teske, P., Schneider, M., Mintrom, M. and Best, S. (1993) 'Establishing the Micro Foundations of a Macro Theory: Information, Movers, and the Competitive Local Market for Public Goods', *American Political Science Review*, 87: 702–13.

Thompson, D. (1970) *The Democratic Citizen: Social Science and Democratic Theory in the Twentieth Century* (Cambridge: Cambridge University Press).

Thucydides (1951) *The Peloponnesian War*, trans. J.H. Finley (New York: Modern Library).

Tiebout, C.M. (1956) 'A Pure Theory of Local Expenditures', *Journal of Political Economy*, 64: 416–24.

Ullmann-Margalit, E. (1977) *The Emergence of Norms* (Oxford: Clarendon Press).

Van Gunsteren, H. (1998) *A Theory of Citizenship: Organizing Plurality in Contemporary Democracies* (Boulder, CO and Oxford: Westview Press).

Verba, S. and Nie, N. (1972) *Participation in America: Political Democracy and Social Equality* (New York: Harper and Row).

Verba, S., Schlozman, K.L. and Brady, H.E. (1995) *Voice and Equality: Civic Voluntarism in America* (Cambridge, MA: Harvard University Press).

Walzer, M. (1990) 'The Communitarian Critique of Liberalism', *Political Theory*, 18: 6–23.

Wills, G. (1979) *Confessions of a Conservative* (Garden City, NY: Doubleday).

Wolfinger, R. and Rosenstone, S. (1980) *Who Votes?* (New Haven, CT: Yale University Press).

Wolin, S. (1960) *Politics and Vision: Continuity and Innovation in Western Political Thought* (Boston, MA: Little, Brown).

Zwiebach, B. (1975) *Civility and Disobedience* (New York: Cambridge University Press).

2 The global city

Strategic site/new frontier

Saskia Sassen

One of the impacts of globalization on state sovereignty has been to create operational and conceptual openings for other actors and subjects. Various as yet very minor developments signal that the state is no longer the exclusive subject for international law or the only actor in international relations. Other actors – from NGOs and first-nation peoples to immigrants and refugees who become subjects of adjudication in human rights decisions – are increasingly emerging as subjects of international law and actors in international relations. That is to say, these non-state actors can gain visibility as individuals and as collectivities, and come out of the invisibility of aggregate membership in a nation-state exclusively represented by the sovereign. More generally, the ascendance of a large variety of non-state actors in the international arena signals the expansion of an international civil society.

There is an incipient unbundling of the exclusive authority over territory and people we have long associated with the national state. The most strategic instantiation of this unbundling is probably the global city, which operates as a partly denationalized platform for global capital and, at the same time, is emerging as a key site for the most astounding mix of people from all over the world. The major cities in the world are becoming partly denationalized platforms also for immigrants, refugees and minorities.

There are therefore two strategic dynamics. First, the incipient denationalizing of specific types of national settings, particularly global cities. Second, the formation of conceptual and operational openings for actors other than the national state in cross-border political dynamics, particularly the new global corporate actors and those collectivities whose experience of membership has not been subsumed fully under nationhood in its modern conception, for example minorities, immigrants, first-nation people and many women.[1]

The global city emerges as a strategic site for these new types of operations. It is a nexus where the formation of new claims materializes and assumes concrete forms. The loss of power at the national level produces the possibility for new forms of power and politics at the sub-national level. The national as container of social process and power is cracked (Taylor, 2000; Sachar, 1990). This cracked casing opens up possibilities for a geography of politics that links sub-national spaces. Global cities are foremost in this new geography. One question this engenders is how and whether we are seeing the formation of a new type of transnational politics that localizes in these cities.

Recovering place

Including cities in the analysis of economic globalization is not without its consequences. Economic globalization has mostly been conceptualized in terms of the duality national–global, where the latter gains at the expense of the former. And it has largely been conceptualized in terms of the internationalization of capital and then only the upper circuits of capital. Introducing cities into this analysis allows us to reconceptualize processes of economic globalization as concrete economic complexes situated in specific places. Place is typically seen as neutralized by the capacity for global communications and control. In addition, a focus on cities decomposes the nation-state into a variety of sub-national components, some profoundly articulated with the global economy and others not. It signals the declining significance of the national economy as a unitary category. And even if to a large extent this was a unitary category constructed in political discourse and policy, it has become even less of a fact in the last fifteen years.

Why does it matter to recover place in analyses of the global economy, particularly place as constituted in global cities? Because it allows us to see the multiplicity of economies and work cultures in which the global information economy is embedded. It also allows us to recover the concrete, localized processes through which globalization exists and to argue that a great deal of the multiculturalism in global cities is as much a part of globalization as is international finance. Finally, focusing on cities allows us to specify a geography of strategic places at the global scale, places bound to each other by the dynamics of economic globalization. I refer to this as a new geography of centrality.

Is there a transnational politics embedded in the centrality of place and in the new geography of strategic places, as for instance, in the new worldwide grid of global cities? This is a geography that cuts across national borders and the old North–South divide. But it does so along bounded 'filières'. It is a set of specific and partial rather than all-encompassing dynamics (Sassen, 1998, chap. 10).

Insofar as an economic analysis of the global city recovers the broad array of jobs and work cultures that are part of the global economy though typically not marked as such, it allows us also to examine the possibility of a new politics by traditionally disadvantaged actors operating in this new transnational economic geography. This is a politics that arises out of actual participation as workers in the global economy, but under conditions of disadvantage and lack of recognition – whether factory workers in export processing zones or cleaners on Wall Street.

The centrality of place in a context of global processes makes possible a transnational economic and political opening for the formation of new claims and hence for the constitution of entitlements, notably rights to place. At the limit, this could be an opening for new forms of 'citizenship'. The city has indeed emerged as a site for new claims: not only by global capital, which uses the city as an 'organizational commodity', but also by disadvantaged sectors of the urban population, frequently as internationalized a presence in large cities as capital. The denationalizing of urban space, and the formation of new claims by transnational actors raise the question 'Whose city is it?'

This is a type of political opening that contains unifying capacities across national boundaries and sharpens conflicts within such boundaries. Global capital and the new immigrant workforce are two major instances of transnationalized actors with unifying properties internally and in contestation with each other inside global cities. Global cities are the sites for the over-valorization of corporate capital and the devalorization of disadvantaged workers, subjects upon which the following sections elaborate.

The leading sectors of corporate capital are now global in their organization and operations. And many of the disadvantaged workers in global cities are women, immigrants, people of colour – men and women whose sense of membership is not necessarily adequately captured in terms of the national, and who indeed often evince cross-border solidarities around issues of substance. Both types of actors find the global city a strategic site for their economic and political operations. Immigration, for instance, is one major process through which a new transnational political economy is being constituted, one which is largely embedded in major cities insofar as most immigrants, whether in the USA, Japan or Western Europe, are concentrated in major cities. It is, in my reading, one of the constitutive processes of globalization today, even though not recognized or represented as such in mainstream accounts of the global economy (for a full examination of these issues, see Sassen, 1998, part 1).

The ascendance of international human rights illustrates some of the actual dynamics through which this operational and conceptual opening can be instituted (Jacobson, 1996). International human rights, while rooted in the founding documents of nation-states, are today a force that can undermine the exclusive authority of the state over its nationals and entitle individuals to make claims on grounds that are not derived from the authority of the state (see Soysal, 1994; Franck, 1992).

A new geography of centrality and marginality

Economic globalization can then be seen as materializing in a worldwide grid of strategic places, uppermost among which are major international business and financial centres (Knox and Taylor, 1995; Friedmann, 1995; Stren, 1996). We can think of this global grid as constituting a new economic geography of centrality, one that cuts across national boundaries and across the old North–South divide. It has emerged as a parallel political geography, a transnational space for the formation of new claims by global capital.

This new economic geography of centrality partly reproduces existing inequalities but also is the outcome of a dynamic specific to the current forms of economic growth. It assumes many forms and operates in many terrains, from the distribution of telecommunications facilities to the structure of the economy and of employment. Global cities are sites for immense concentrations of economic power and command centres in a global economy, while cities that were once major manufacturing centres have suffered inordinate declines.

The most powerful of these new geographies of centrality at the inter-urban level bind the major international financial and business centres: New York, London, Tokyo, Paris, Frankfurt, Zurich, Amsterdam, Los Angeles, Sydney, Hong Kong, among others. But this geography now also includes cities such as Sao Paulo, Buenos Aires, Bombay, Bangkok, Taipei and Mexico City. The intensity of transactions among these cities – particularly through the financial markets, transactions in services and investment – has increased sharply, and so have the orders of magnitude involved. At the same time, there has been a sharpening inequality in the concentration of strategic resources and activities between each of these cities and others in the same country.

The growth of global markets for finance and specialized services, the need for transnational servicing networks due to sharp increases in international investment, the reduced role of the government in the regulation of international economic activity and the corresponding ascendance of other institutional arenas, notably global markets and corporate headquarters – all these point to the existence of transnational economic processes with multiple locations in more than one country. We can see here the formation, at least incipient, of a transnational urban system. These cities are not simply in a relationship of competition to each other.

Alongside these new global and regional hierarchies of cities is a vast territory that has become increasingly peripheral, increasingly excluded from the major economic processes that fuel economic growth in the new global economy. A multiplicity of formerly important manufacturing centres and port cities have lost functions and are in decline, not only in the less developed countries but also in the most advanced economies. This is yet another meaning of economic globalization.

But also inside global cities we see a new geography of centrality and marginality (Fainstein et al., 1993; Klosterman, 1996). The downtowns of cities and key nodes in metropolitan areas receive massive investments in real estate and telecommunications while low-income city areas and the older suburbs are starved of resources (see, for example, *The Journal of Urban Technology*, 1995). Highly educated workers see their incomes rise to unusually high levels while low- or medium-skilled workers see their incomes sink. Financial services produce superprofits while industrial services barely survive. These trends are evident, at different levels of intensity, in a growing number of major cities in the developed world, and increasingly in some of the developing countries that have been integrated into the global financial markets (Cohen et al., 1996).

The new urban economy is highly problematic. This is perhaps particularly evident in global cities and their regional counterparts (Sassen, 2000). It sets in motion a whole series of new dynamics of inequality. The new growth sectors – specialized services and finance – contain capabilities for profit-making vastly superior to those of more traditional economic sectors. Many of the latter remain essential to the operation of the urban economy and the daily needs of residents, but their survival is threatened in a situation where finance and specialized services can earn superprofits and bid up prices.[2] Polarization in the profit-making capabilities of different sectors of the economy has always existed. But what we see happening today takes place on another order of magnitude and is engendering massive distortions in the operations of various markets, from housing to labour (Hitz et al., 1995).

What we are seeing is a dynamic of valorization which has sharply increased the distance between the valorized, indeed over-valorized, sectors of the economy and devalorized sectors, even when the latter are part of leading global industries. This devalorization of growing sectors of the economy has been embedded in a massive demographic transition towards a growing presence of women, African-Americans and 'third world' immigrants in the urban workforce (see also Peraldi and Perrin, 1996).

We see here an interesting correspondence between great concentrations of corporate power and large concentrations of 'others'. Global cities in the highly developed world are the terrain where a multiplicity of globalization processes assume concrete, localized forms. A focus on cities allows us to capture, further, not only the upper but also the lower circuits of globalization. These localized forms are, in good part, what globalization is about. We can then also think of cities as one of the sites for the contradictions of the internationalization of capital. If we consider, moreover, that global cities also concentrate a growing share of disadvantaged populations – immigrants in Europe and America, African-Americans and Latinos also in America – then we can see that cities have become a strategic terrain for a whole series of conflicts and contradictions.

The localizations of the global

Economic globalization, then, needs also to be understood in its multiple localizations, rather than purely in terms of the broad, overarching macro-level processes that dominate the mainstream account. Further, we need to see that many of these localizations do not generally get coded as having anything to do with the global economy. The global city can be seen as one strategic instantiation of such multiple localizations.

Many of these localizations are embedded in the demographic transition evident in such cities, where a majority of resident workers are today immigrants and women, often women of colour. These cities are seeing an expansion of low-wage jobs that do not fit the master images about globalization, yet are part of it. Their embeddedness in the demographic transition evident in all these cities, and their consequent invisibility, contribute to the devalorization of these types of workers and work cultures and to the 'legitimacy' of that devalorization.

This can be read as a rupture of the traditional dynamic whereby membership in leading economic sectors contributes conditions towards the formation of a labour aristocracy – a process long evident in western industrialized economies. 'Women and immigrants' come to replace the Fordist/family wage category of 'women and children' (Sassen, 1998, chap. 5).[3] One of the localizations of the dynamics of globalization is the process of economic restructuring in global cities. The associated socio-economic polarization has generated a large growth in the demand for low-wage workers and for jobs that offer few advancement possibilities. This takes place amidst an explosion in the wealth and power concentrated in these cities – that is to say, in conditions where there is also a visible expansion in high-income jobs and high-priced urban space.

'Women and immigrants' emerge as the labour supply that facilitates the imposition of low wages and powerlessness under conditions of high demand for those workers and the location of those jobs in high-growth sectors. It breaks the historic nexus that would have led to empowering workers and legitimates this break culturally.

Another localization which is rarely associated with globalization, informalization, re-introduces the community and the household as an important economic space in global cities. I see informalization in this setting as the low-cost (and often feminized) equivalent of deregulation at the top of the system. As with deregulation (for example, as in financial deregulation), informalization introduces flexibility, reduces the 'burdens' of regulation, and lowers costs, in this case especially the costs of labour. Informalization in major cities of highly developed countries – whether New York, London, Paris or Berlin – can be seen as a downgrading of a variety of activities for which there is an effective demand but also as a devaluing and enormous competition, given low entry costs and few alternative forms of employment. Going informal is one way of producing and distributing goods and services at a lower cost and with greater flexibility. This further devalues these types of activities. Immigrants and women are important actors in the new informal economies of these cities. They absorb the costs of informalizing such activities (see Sassen, 1998, chap. 8).

The reconfiguration of economic spaces associated with globalization in major cities has had differential impacts on women and men, on male-typed and female-typed work cultures, on male- and female-centred forms of power and empowerment. The restructuring of the labour market brings with it a shift of labour market functions to the household or community. Women and households emerge as sites that should be part of the theorization of the particular forms that these elements in labour market dynamics assume today.

These transformations contain possibilities, even if they are limited, for women's autonomy and empowerment. For instance, we might ask whether the growth of informalization in advanced urban economies reconfigures some types of economic relations between men and women? With informalization, the neighbourhood and the household re-emerge as sites for economic activity. This condition has its own dynamic possibilities for women. Economic downgrading through informalization creates 'opportunities' for low-income women entrepreneurs and workers, and thereby reconfigures some of the work and household hierarchies in which women find themselves. This becomes particularly clear in the case of immigrant women who come from countries with rather traditional male-centred cultures.

There is a large literature showing that immigrant women's regular wage work and improved access to other public realms has an impact on their gender relations. Women gain greater personal autonomy and independence while men lose ground. Women gain more control over budgeting and other domestic decisions, and greater leverage in requesting help from men in domestic chores. In addition their access to public services and other public resources gives them a chance to become incorporated in mainstream society – they are often the ones in the household who mediate in this process. It is likely that some women benefit more than others from these circumstances; we need more research to establish the impact of class, education and income on these gendered outcomes. Besides the relatively greater empowerment of women in the household associated with waged employment, there is a second important outcome: their greater participation in the public sphere and their possible emergence as public actors.

There are two arenas where immigrant women are active: institutions for public and private assistance, and the immigrant/ethnic community. The incorporation of women in the migration process strengthens settlement likelihood and contributes to greater immigrant participation in their communities and vis-à-vis the state. For instance, Hondagneu-Sotelo (1994) found that immigrant women come to assume more active public and social roles, which further reinforces their status in the household and the settlement process. Women are more active in community building and community activism and they are positioned differently from men regarding the broader economy and the state. They are the ones who are likely to have to handle the legal vulnerability of their families in the process of seeking public and social services for them.

This greater participation by women suggests the possibility that they may emerge as more forceful and visible actors and make their role in the labour market more visible as well. There is, to some extent, a joining of two different dynamics in the condition of women in global cities described above. On the one hand, they are constituted as an invisible and disempowered class of workers in the service of the strategic sectors constituting the global economy. This invisibility keeps them from emerging as whatever would be the contemporary equivalent of the 'labour aristocracy' of earlier forms of economic organization, when a low-waged worker's position in leading sectors had the effect of empowering that worker, i.e. the possibility of unionizing. On the other hand, the access to (albeit low) wages and salaries, the growing feminization of the job supply, and the growing feminization of business opportunities brought about by informalization, do alter the gender hierarchies in which they find themselves.

Another important localization of the dynamics of globalization is that of the new professional women stratum. Elsewhere I have examined the impact of the growth of top-level professional women on high-income gentrification in these cities – both residential and commercial – as well as in the re-urbanization of middle-class family life (see Sassen, 2000, chap. 9).

What we are seeing is a dynamic of valorization which has sharply increased the distance between the valorized, indeed over-valorized, sectors of the economy and devalorized sectors, even when the latter are part of leading global industries.

A space of power

What makes the localization of the above described processes strategic (even though they involve powerless and often invisible workers), as well as potentially constitutive of a new kind of transnational politics, is that these same cities are also the strategic sites for the valorization of the new forms of global corporate capital.

Global cities are centres for the *servicing* and *financing* of international trade, investment and headquarter operations. That is to say, the multiplicity of specialized activities present in global cities are crucial in the valorization, indeed over-valorization, of leading sectors of capital today. And in this sense they are strategic production sites for today's leading economic sectors. This function is reflected in the ascendance of these activities in their economies. In my analysis what is specific about the shift to services is not merely the growth in service jobs but, most importantly, the growing service intensity in the organization of advanced economies: firms in all industries, from mining to wholesale, buy more accounting, legal, advertising, financial and economic forecasting services today than they did twenty years ago. Whether at the global or regional level, urban regions – core cities, suburbs, edge cities – are adequate and often the best production sites for such specialized services. When it comes to the production of services for the leading globalized sectors, the advantages of location in cities are particularly strong. The rapid growth and dispropor-tionate concentration of such services in cities signals that the latter have re-emerged as significant 'production' sites, having lost this role in the period when mass manufacturing was the dominant sector of the economy. Under mass manufacturing and Fordism, the strategic spaces of the economy were the large-scale integrated factory and the government through their Fordist/Keynesian functions.

Further, the vast new economic topography that is being implemented through electronic space is one moment, one fragment, of an even vaster economic chain that is in good part embedded in non-electronic spaces. There is no fully dematerialized firm or industry. Even the most advanced information industries, such as finance industries, are installed only partly in electronic space. And so are industries that produce digital products, such as software designers. The growing digitization of economic activities has not eliminated the need for major international business and financial centres and all the material resources they concentrate, from state of the art telematics infrastructure to brain talent (Castells, 1989; Graham and Marvin, 1996; Sassen, 1998, chap. 9).[4]

It is precisely because of the territorial dispersal facilitated by telecommunication advances that agglomeration of centralizing activities has expanded immensely. This is not a mere continuation of old patterns of agglomeration but, one could posit, a new logic for agglomeration. Many of the leading sectors in the economy operate globally, in uncertain markets, under conditions of rapid change in other countries (for example, deregulation and privatization), and are subject to enormous speculative pressures. What glues these conditions together into a new logic for spatial agglomeration is the added pressure of speed.

A focus on the *work* behind command functions, on the actual *production process* in the finance and services complex, and on global market*places* has the effect of incorporating the material facilities underlying globalization and the whole infrastructure of jobs typically not marked as belonging to the corporate sector of the economy. An economic configuration very different from that suggested by the concept information economy emerges. We recover the material conditions, production sites and place-boundedness that are also part of globalization and the information economy.

Making claims on the city

These processes signal that there has been a change in the linkages that bind people and places, and in the corresponding formation of claims on the city (Rotzer, 1995). Today the articulation of territory and people is being constituted in a radically different way from past periods at least in one regard, and that is the speed with which that articulation can change. One consequence of this speed is the expansion of the space within which actual and possible linkages can occur (Martinotti, 1993; *Futur Anterieur*, 1995). The shrinking of distance and of time that characterizes the current era finds one of its most extreme forms in electronically based communities of individuals or organizations from all around the globe interacting in real time and simultaneously, as is possible through the internet and kindred electronic networks.

Another radical form assumed today by the linkage of people to territory is the loosening of identities from what have been traditional sources of identity, such as the nation or the village. This unmooring in the process of identity formation engenders new notions of community of membership and of entitlement.

The space constituted by the global grid of global cities, a space with new economic and political potentialities, is perhaps one of the most strategic spaces for the formation of transnational identities and communities. This is a space that is both place-centred, in that it is embedded in particular and strategic sites, and transterritorial, because it connects sites that are not geographically proximate yet are intensely connected to each other. It is the transmigration not only of capital that takes place in this global grid, but also that of people, both rich (i.e. the new transnational professional workforce) and poor (i.e. most migrant workers); and it is a space for the transmigration of cultural forms, for the reterritorialization of 'local' subcultures. An important question is whether it is also a space for a new politics, one going beyond the politics of culture and identity, though at least partly likely to be embedded in these.

Yet another way of thinking about the political implications of this strategic transnational space is the notion of the formation of new claims on that space. Has economic globalization to some degree shaped the formation of claims?[5] There are indeed major new actors making claims on these cities, notably foreign firms who have been increasingly entitled to do business through progressive deregulation of national economies, and the large increase over the last decade in international businesspeople. These are among the new city users. They have profoundly marked the urban landscape. Their claim to the city is not contested, even though the costs and benefits to cities have barely been examined. These claims contribute to the incipient denationalization dynamics discussed in the previous section which, though institutional, tend to have spatial outcomes disproportionately concentrated in global cities.

City users have made an often immense claim on the city and have reconstituted strategic spaces of the city in their image: there is a *de facto* claim to the city, a claim never made problematic. They contribute to changing the social morphology of the city and to constituting what Martinotti (1993) calls the metropolis of second generation, the city of late modernism. The new city of city users is a fragile one, whose survival and successes are centred on an economy of high productivity, advanced technologies and intensified exchanges (Martinotti, 1993).

On the one hand, this raises a question of what the city is for international businesspeople: it is a city whose space consists of airports, top-level business districts, top of the line hotels and restaurants, a sort of urban glamour zone. On the other hand, there is the difficult task of establishing whether a city that functions as an international business centre does in fact recover the costs involved in being such a centre: the costs involved in maintaining a state of the art business district and all it requires, from advanced communications facilities to top-level security (and 'world-class culture').

Perhaps at the other extreme of conventional representations are those who use urban political violence to make their claims on the city, claims that lack the *de facto* legitimacy enjoyed by the new 'city users'. These are claims made by actors struggling for recognition and entitlement, claiming their rights to the city.[6]

There are two aspects in this formation of new claims that have implications for the new transnational politics. One is the sharp and perhaps sharpening differences in the representation of these claims by different sectors, notably international business and the vast population of low income 'others' – African-Americans, immigrants, women (King, 1995). The second aspect is the increasingly transnational element in both types of claims and claimants. It signals a politics of contestation embedded in specific places – global cities – but transnational in character.

At its most extreme, this divergence assumes the form of (1) an over-valorized corporate centre occupying a smaller terrain and one whose edges are sharper than, for example, in the postwar era characterized by a large middle class; and (2) a sharp devalorization of what is outside the centre, which comes to be read as marginal.

A question here is whether the growing presence of immigrants, of African-Americans, of women in the labour force of global cities is what has facilitated the embedding of this sharp increase in inequality (as expressed in earnings and culturally). The new politics of identity and the new cultural politics have brought many of these devalorized or marginal sectors into representation, into the forefront of urban life.

There is something to be captured here – a distinction between powerlessness and a condition of being an actor even though lacking power. I use the term 'presence' to name this condition. In the context of a strategic space such as the global city, the types of disadvantaged people described here are not simply marginal; they acquire presence in a broader political process that escapes the boundaries of the formal polity. This presence signals the possibility of a politics. What this politics will be will depend on the specific projects and practices of various communities. Insofar as the sense of membership of these communities is not subsumed under the national, it may well signal the possibility of a transnational politics centred in concrete localities.

Global capital has made claims on national states and these have responded through the production of new forms of legality (Sassen, 1996, chap. 2). The new geography of global economic processes, the strategic territories for economic globalization, had to be produced, both in terms of the practices of corporate actors and the requisite infrastructure, and in terms of the work of the state in producing or legitimating new legal regimes. These claims very often materialize in claims over the city's land, resources and policies. Disadvantaged sectors which have gained presence are also making claims, but these lack the legitimacy attached to the claims of global capital.

There are two distinct issues here. One is the formation of new legal regimes that negotiate between national sovereignty and the transnational practices of corporate economic actors. The second issue is the particular content of this new regime, one which contributes to strengthen the advantages of certain types of economic actors and to weaken those of others.[7] There is a larger question, at once theoretical and political, that underlies some of these issues – it has to do with which actors gain and which actors lose legitimacy.

Globalization engenders contradictory spaces and it is characterized by contestation, internal differentiation and continuous border crossings. The global city is emblematic of this condition. Global cities concentrate a disproportionate share of global corporate power and are one of the key sites for its over-valorization. But they also concentrate a disproportionate share of the disadvantaged and are one of the key sites for their devalorization. This joint presence happens in a context in which (1) the globalization of the economy has grown sharply and cities have become increasingly strategic for global capital; and (2) marginalized people have found their voice and are making claims on the city as well. This joint presence is further brought into focus by the sharpening of the distance between the two. The centre now concentrates immense power, a power that rests on the capability for global control and the capability to produce superprofits. And marginality, notwithstanding little economic and political power, has become an increasingly strong presence through the new politics of culture and identity, and an emergent transnational politics embedded in the new geography of economic globalization. Both actors, increasingly transnational and in contestation, find in the city the strategic terrain for their operations.

Notes

1 I develop these two arguments at length in Sassen (1996) and in 'Towards a Feminist Analytics of the Global Economy' (Sassen, 1998, chap. 5). I thank the Schoff Fund for its support.
2 Elsewhere I have tried to show how these new inequalities in profit-making capacities of economic sectors, earnings capacities of households, and prices in upscale and downscale markets have contributed to the formation of informal economies in major cities of highly developed countries (see Sassen, 1998). These informal economies negotiate between the new economic trends and regulatory frameworks that were engendered in response to older economic conditions.
3 This newer case brings out, more brutally than did the Fordist contract, the economic significance of these types of actors, a significance veiled or softened in the case of the Fordist contract through the provision of the family wage.
4 Telematics and globalization have emerged as fundamental forces reshaping the organization of economic space. This reshaping ranges from the spatial virtualization of a growing number of economic activities to the reconfiguration of the geography of the built environment for economic activity. Whether in electronic space or in the geography of the built environment, this reshaping involves organizational and structural changes.
5 For a different combination of these elements, see Dunn (1994); *Wissenschaftsforum* (1995).
6 Body-Gendrot (1999) shows how the city remains a terrain for contest, character-ized by the emergence of new actors, who are often younger and younger. It is a terrain where the constraints placed upon, and the institutional limitations of governments to address the demands for equity engender social disorders. She argues that urban political violence should not be interpreted as a coherent ideology but rather as an element of temporary political tactics which permits vulnerable actors to enter into interaction with the holders of power on terms that will be somewhat more favourable to the weak.
7 There are many issues here, from the question of the legitimacy of the right to economic survival to the question of human rights and the question of the represen-tativity of the state. See, for instance, discussions as diverse as Cohen et al. 1996; Franck, 1992; Jacobson, 1996; Reisman, 1990. See also chaps 2 and 3 in Sassen (1996) for a fuller discussion of these issues.

Bibliography

Body-Gendrot, S. (1999) *Controlling Cities* (Oxford: Blackwell).

Castells, M. (1989) *The Informational City* (London: Blackwell).

Cohen, M.A., Ruble, B.A., Tulchin, J.S. and Garland, A.M. (eds) (1996) *Preparing for the Urban Future: Global Pressures and Local Forces* (Washington, DC: Woodrow Wilson Center Press).

Dunn, S. (ed.) (1994) *Managing Divided Cities* (Staffordshire: Keele University Press).

Fainstein, S., Gordon, I. and Harloe, M. (1993) *Divided City: Economic Restructuring and Social Change in London and New York* (New York: Blackwell).

Franck, T.M. (1992) 'The Emerging Right to Democratic Governance', *American Journal of International Law*, 86 (1): 46–91.

Friedmann, J. (1995) 'Where We Stand: A Decade of World City Research', in P.L. Knox and P.J. Taylor (eds), *World Cities in a World-System* (Cambridge: Cambridge University Press).

Futur Anterieur (1995) Special issue: *La Ville-monde aujourd'hui: entre virtualité et ancrage*, T. Pillon and A. Querrien (eds), vols. 30–2 (Paris: L'Harmattan).

Graham, S. and Marvin, S. (1996) *Telecommunications and the City: Electronic Spaces, Urban Places* (London: Routledge).

Hitz, H., Keil, R., Lehrer, U., Ronneberger, K., Schmid, C. and Wolff, R. (eds) (1995) *Capitales Fatales* (Zurich: Rotpunkt Verlag).

Hondagneu-Sotelo, P. (1994) *Gendered Transitions: Mexican Experiences of Immigration* (Berkeley, CA: University of California Press).

Jacobson, D. (1996) *Rights Across Borders: Immigration and the Decline of Citizenship* (Baltimore: Johns Hopkins Press).

The Journal of Urban Technology (1995) Special issue: *Information Technologies and Inner-City Communities*, 3 (1).

King, A.D. (ed.) (1995) *Representing the City. Ethnicity, Capital and Culture in the 21st Century* (London: Macmillan).

Klosterman, R.C. (1996) 'Double Dutch: Polarization Trends in Amsterdam and Rotterdam after 1980', *Regional Studies*, 30 (5).

Knox, P.L. and Taylor, P.J. (eds) (1995) *World Cities in a World-System* (Cambridge: Cambridge University Press).

Martinotti, G. (1993) *La metropoli di seconda generazione* (Bologna: Il Mulino).

Peraldi, M. and Perrin, E. (eds) (1996) *Reseaux productifs et territoires urbains* (Toulouse: Presses Universitaires du Mirail).

Reisman, W.M. (1990) 'Sovereignty and Human Rights in Contemporary International Law', *American Journal of International Law*, 84 (4) (October): 866–76.

Rotzer, F. (1995) *Die Telepolis: Urbanitat im digitalen Zeitalter* (Mannheim: Bollmann).

Sachar, A. (1990) 'The Global Economy and World Cities', in A. Sachar and S. Oberg (eds), *The World Economy and the Spatial Organization of Power* (Aldershot: Avebury).

Sassen, S. (2000) *The Global City: New York, London, Tokyo* (Princeton, NJ: Princeton University Press).

—— (1996) *Losing Control? Sovereignty in an Age of Globalization*, The 1995 Columbia University Leonard Hastings Schoff Memorial Lectures (New York: Columbia University Press).

—— (1998) *Globalization and Its Discontents* (New York: New Press).

Soysal, Y. (1994) *Limits of Citizenship: Migrants and Postnational Membership in Europe* (Chicago: University of Chicago Press).

Stren, R. (1996) 'The Studies of Cities: Popular Perceptions, Academic Disciplines, and Emerging Agendas', in M.A. Cohen, B.A. Ruble, J.S. Tulchin and A.M. Garland (eds), *Preparing for the Urban Future: Global Pressures and Local Forces* (Washington, DC: Woodrow Wilson Center Press).

Taylor, P.J. (2000) 'World Cities and Territorial States: The Rise and Fall of their Mutuality', in P.L. Knox and P.J. Taylor (eds), *World Cities in a World-System* (Cambridge: Cambridge University Press).

3 Global flows and global citizenship[1]

John Urry

Introduction

Across much of the globe over the past decade two of the most powerful issues have been those of 'citizenship' and 'globalization'. As both process and as discourse, 'citizenship' and 'globalization' have swept much else before them, reconstituting social and political life in stunningly powerful ways. In the case of citizenship, movements to demand rights of national citizenship have been enormously powerful in one continent after another. This demand for the rights of the citizen and for the institutions of civil society occurred most strikingly within the former Eastern Europe. In many ways 1989 represents the year of the citizen, being of course two hundred years after the subjects of Paris took to the streets in 1789 demanding citizenship (see Murdock, 1992). Garton Ash argues that during the 1980s and across many diverse societies, people 'wanted to be citizens, individual men and women with dignity and responsibility, with rights but also with duties, freely associating in civil society' (1990, p. 148).

And yet 1989 was also the year when the discourse of 'globalization' really took off, when exponential growth in the analyses of the global began to suggest that there was a putative global reconstitution of economic, political and cultural relationships. One central feature was the sense that people were living in a global village, as the struggles for citizenship were themselves brought instantaneously and 'live' into their homes wherever they were located. The struggles for citizenship, most strikingly in the fall of the Berlin Wall and the crushing of the democracy movement in China, both in 1989, were increasingly globalized, instantaneously transmitted through the global media communication systems. More generally, global money markets, world travel, the internet, globally recognized brands, globally organized corporations, the Rio Earth summit, 'global celebrities' living as global citizens and so on all speak of modes of social experience which transcend each nation-state and its constitution of the national citizen. The lifestyles and citizenship demands of the 'north' and of the 'west' have been globalized, representing a new kind of colonialism.

So just at the moment that almost everyone is seeking to be a citizen of an existing national society or to set up their own national society, globalization appears to be changing what it is to be a citizen. This chapter aims to rethink what we mean by citizenship in the light of economic, political and cultural globalization. Does globalization mean that nationally based forms of citizenship are or will become redundant? How relevant are the classic distinctions between civil, political and social rights in an increasingly globalized world? What are the risks, rights and duties of a global citizen? How is the notion of citizenship increasingly underpinned by a restructuring of contemporary consumerism? Does globalization imply a notion of universal human rights and duties as opposed to those attributed to a national citizen? How might globalization generate new forms of citizenship? How much does globalization involve 'in-human' processes which disrupt the idea of specifically human rights and duties? These questions carry major implications for policy relating to the environment, health, travel, cultural autonomy, the media and oppositional protests. They also relate very directly to whether there is any such thing as 'society' and to the idea of citizenship as the link which binds nation-states and society. Does globalization entail not only the withering away of the nation-state but of society and of its citizens who are uniquely formed within its policed borders? To answer these questions, the Marshallian citizenship trilogy of civil, political and social rights has to be dispensed with, because such distinctions make no sense in relation to 'global ecological rights and duties'.

While there have been very many objections to, and elaborations of, Marshallian arguments (see Mann, 1993; 1996; Hewitt, 1996; Rees, 1996; Runciman, 1996; Walby, 1996), somewhat different arguments that take the analysis of citizenship away from Marshall's particularly national formulation will be developed here. In focusing upon questions of occupation, income and class, Marshall presumes that social citizenship is the ultimate stage of societal achievement. By contrast, we need to consider at the turn of the twenty-first century whether other forms of citizenship are not equally significant and whether social citizenship is the end-point at all. Apart from citizenship within the city, some other important forms of citizenship include: *ecological* citizenship concerned with the rights and responsibilities of the earth citizen (Van Steenbergen, 1994); *cultural* citizenship involving the right to cultural participation (Turner, 1993a); *minority* citizenship involving the rights to enter a society and then to remain within that society (Yuval-Davis, 1997); *cosmopolitan* citizenship concerned with how people may develop an orientation to many other citizens, societies and cultures across the globe (Held, 1995); and *mobility* citizenship concerned with the rights and responsibilities of the visitors to other places and cultures (Urry, 1999).

Each of these citizenships suggests the limitation of the civil–political–social trilogy. That trilogy is organized around the citizenship of *stasis*, of the rights and duties attributed to, and available to, those living and working within a given territory by virtue of their long-term membership of a given society. By contrast, these alternative conceptions could be termed the citizenship of flow, concerned with the causes and consequences of the flows across borders of risks, cultures, migrants and visitors respectively. Such flows involve both threats to, and forms of resistance around, civil, political and social elements. These elements can no longer be distinguished from each other and should not be seen as arriving in different centuries. The citizenship of flow dedifferentiates these various rights and responsibilities (see Urry, 2000).

A major theme in various debates over citizenship concerns the degree to which citizenship is thought to be a property of individuals and how much it is in some ways collective. It has become common to criticize a rights-based approach to citizenship as overly individualistic, and to emphasize the importance of the social practices that can be said to generate or underpin such rights (see Turner, 1993a, p. 2). However, with regard to rights that appear to transcend the boundaries of nation-states, they are constituted through diverse, overlapping and partially contradictory practices which are significantly organized in and through machines, technologies and natures not confined within national borders. This means that contemporary citizenship is loosely 'post-modern' in that there is no single modern rational-legal state which delivers clear and unambiguous rights and duties to all its citizens constituted as a 'nation of strangers' with a common national identity (assuming that we have ever been modern, of course; see Latour, 1993). There are many different social practices, delivering different kinds of rights and duties, over very different geographical reaches, including the city (as shown by Yuval-Davis, 1997). Citizenship is fundamentally contested – but not just between different social groups over access within a nation-state to given rights such as personal property, a job or healthcare. There is contestation over what are the appropriate rights and duties of citizens living within the contemporary world; over what entities should be providing citizenship including those constituted through various technologies, machines and natures; and over what mechanisms there should be to adjudicate between different complexes of rights and duties. All of this is producing a disjunctive, contested and inconsistent citizenship – what Yuval-Davis calls a 'differential multi-tiered citizenship' (1997, p. 12).

The globalization of identity

Some aspects of globalization are reconfiguring the nation and simultaneously displacing 'humans' from the centre of concern (see Appadurai, 1990; Brunn and Leinbach, 1991; Gilroy, 1993; Lash and Urry, 1994; Waters, 1995; Featherstone, et al., 1995; Albrow, 1996; Castells, 1996; Eade, 1997; Urry, 2000). First, there is the development of new *machines and technologies* that dramatically shrink time-space and, in part at least, transcend societal control and regulation. These include fibre-optic cables, jet planes, audiovisual transmissions, digital TV, computer networks including the internet, satellites, credit cards, faxes, electronic point-of-sale terminals, mobile phones, electronic stock exchanges, high-speed trains and virtual reality. There are also large increases in nuclear, chemical and conventional military technologies and weapons, as well as new waste products and health risks, which necessitate inter-societal regulation to ensure personal and national security.

Second, such machines and technologies are organized in terms of various *scapes*. These are the networks of machines, technologies, organizations, texts and actors along which the various flows can be relayed. An example of such a scape is the network of hub airports, which structures the global flows of the 500 million or so international travellers each year. These *flows* consist not just of the flows of people, but also of images, information, money, technologies and waste that are moved within and especially across national borders, and which individual societies are often unable or unwilling to control. Once particular scapes have been established, then individuals and especially corporations within each society will endeavour to become connected to them, by, for example, developing a hub airport, being plugged into the internet, attracting satellite broadcasting, or even reprocessing nuclear waste products. The development of these networked scapes creates new inequalities of access/non-access which do not map onto the jurisdictions of particular societies. Certain scapes have become partially *organized at the global level*. Organizations responsible for facilitating the globalization of scapes and citizenship include the UN, the World Bank, Microsoft, CNN, Greenpeace, the EU, News International, the Oscar ceremony, the World Intellectual Property Organization, UNESCO, the ILO, the Olympic movement, Friends of the Earth, Nobel prizes, Bandaid, the Brundtland Report, the Rio Earth Summit, the European Court of Human Rights, the British Council and the English language and so on. These employ most, if not all, of the machines and technologies listed above.

These scapes generate, for late twentieth century 'humans', new opportunities and *desires*, as well as new *risks*. The former include procuring cheap overseas travel; forming internationalized 'new sociations', especially via the internet; obtaining consumer goods and lifestyles of 'the other'; employing global imagery; participating in global cultural events; listening to 'world music'; and so on. The latter include AIDS, Chernobyl, cultural homogenization, the loss of economic national sovereignty, migration, being exiled and asylum seeking. These 'global' patterns can be described as the hollowing out of existing societies, especially as a plethora of 'sociations' have developed which are concerned with reflecting upon, arguing against, retreating from, providing alternatives to, and campaigning for these various scapes and flows. This generates within any existing 'society' a complex, overlapping, disjunctive order of off-centredness, as these multiple flows are chronically combined and recombined across times and spaces often unrelated to the boundaries of existing societies, often following a kind of hypertextual patterning. Notions of mobility and flow are seen as constitutive of identity, which is less societal and more defined in terms of consuming elements of one or more of the putatively global scapes, so forming or reinforcing new networks (Urry 2000).

These widespread flows across societal borders make it less easy for states to mobilize clearly separate and coherent *nations* in pursuit of societal goals. This can be seen both economically and culturally. Economically, the breaking down of the coherence of 'national economies' has been combined with the increasing political unwillingness of many states to tax and spend, let alone nationalize industries so as to bring them under societal control. States have increasingly shifted to a regulative rather than a direct production/employment function, partly facilitated by new forms of information gathering, storage and retrieval. In many ways, the EU is the quintessential regulatory state (see Ward, 1996, on the European Bathing Waters Directive). Culturally, the hybridization of cultures, the global refugee problem, the importance of travelling cultures, some growth of a sense of global dwelling, diasporas and other notions of the 'unhomely' all problematize the notion of a society which is somehow in and of itself able to mobilize for action. These configurations weaken the power of the societal to draw together its citizens as one, to govern in its unique name, to endow all with national identity and to speak with a single voice. As Rose argues, while

> our political, professional, moral and cultural authorities still speak happily of 'society', the very meaning and ethical salience of this term is under question as 'society' is perceived as dissociated into a variety of ethical and cultural communities with incompatible allegiances and incommensurable obligations.
>
> (Rose, 1996, p. 353)

In some writings, the globalization thesis is an attempted reassertion of a modernist meta-narrative involving the claim that global markets generate economic, political and cultural homogenization. The following argument, however, presumes no necessary homogenization. It is important to distinguish between globalization as outcome and globalization as 'hypothesis', between globalization as 'real' process and globalization as discourse, and between economic/political and cultural/environmental globalizations. Thus, globalization should be seen not as an outcome but as a hypothesis, as both a description of putatively real processes and of certain kinds of discourse, and as something that is as much cultural and environmental as it is economic and political (Urry, 2000).

Global citizenship

Various writers have recently suggested that globalization poses major implications for the concept of national sovereignty and hence of citizenship (see Turner, 1993a; Falk, 1994; Van Steenbergen, 1994; Newby, 1996; Hewitt, 1996). Can citizenship be formulated so that it somehow incorporates the 'global' processes just outlined?

Turner considers citizenship as 'that set of practices (juridical, political, economic and cultural) which define a person as a competent member of society, and which as a consequence shape the flow of resources to persons and social groups' (1993a, p. 2). This definition emphasizes the following features of citizenship: that it is by no means simply juridical; that it is as much cultural as it is social; that it involves the flows of resources, power and inequalities without prioritizing class divisions over others; that it involves social practices and is not only a property of individuals; and that the rights and duties involved are to do with competent societal membership and are not individualized rights. There are, however, three problems with this formulation.

First, given the global flows and processes outlined in the previous section, what does it now mean to say that someone is a competent member of 'society'? Indeed is there any such thing as society any longer? And if not at least in the same sense, where does this leave citizenship focused upon competent societal membership? Elsewhere Turner interestingly outlines a theory of human rights, noting the significance of the UN Charter of Human Rights as a central aspect of 'globalization' (Turner, 1993b; Robertson, 1990). Turner notes that the growth of cultural globalization, the UN, the EU, the European Court of Human Rights, the world refugee problem, aboriginal rights and so on, all suggest that the 'nation-state is not necessarily the most suitable political framework for housing citizenship rights' (1993b, p. 178).

Second, it is unclear just what elements or aspects of social practice are involved in developing citizenship claims as opposed to various other aspects of social life. We can ask where does citizenship begin and where does it end. Are there distinct social practices involved in defining the citizen? What kinds of other rights and duties might be involved and how do they relate to those civil, political and social rights as traditionally conceived within western citizenship literature?

And third, implicit in Turner's definition is a human-centric focus, namely, that only humans should possess rights. Elsewhere he develops a theory of human rights based on the notion of frailty – that humans typically exist under conditions of scarcity, disease and danger, but that in the modern world the institutions which supposedly protect humans are now the cause of new risks to human survival (1993b, pp. 181–2). Citizenship is not protected by societal institutions since they often significantly reinforce human frailty. But what this theory of human precariousness ignores is the literature which maintains that there are 'rights of nature' as well as rights of humans; specifically, that animals as well as humans should possess rights because of their exceptional frailty and their catastrophic dependence upon humans. Nash points out that especially within the USA the notion of natural rights has been exceptionally powerful in facilitating such claims of 'citizenship' (see Nash, 1989, chap. 6, on 'liberating nature'). The failure to honour basic natural rights can generate intense campaigns to establish or to restore the supposedly natural rights of freedom or of liberty. In recent years, domestic, some wild and many laboratory animals have had their rights championed. Petulla wrote in 1980: 'The Marine Mammal Protection Act [and] the Endangered Species Act [embody] the legal idea that a listed non-human resident of the United States is guaranteed, in a special sense, life and liberty' (cited in Nash, 1989, p. 161). More generally Roszak wrote in the 1970s of the rights of inanimate nature: 'We are finally coming to recognize that the natural environment is the exploited proletariat, the downtrodden nigger [sic] of everybody's industrial system ... Nature must also have its natural rights' (cited in Nash, 1989, p. 13).

Little of the existing citizenship literature has engaged with these three points with the exception of two accounts. First, Newby argues that we are all now environmental citizens since each individual's future is tied into what the Brundtland Report called 'our common future'. And yet there are few global institutions in place which are able to articulate such citizenship rights or which are able to ensure even their basic implementation (Newby, 1996). In fact the ensuring of many environmental rights often depends upon individual nation-states acting to protect the rights of the global commons, and hence people's rights of use and access to such commons. Newby asks whether a kind of green Leviathan will be necessary in order to intervene against individual nation-states and to protect global interests. He suggests that in its absence we might all be characterized as 'pre-citizens' with regard to the global environment. While there is considerable organization of the interests of environmental citizens, especially through NGOs, most of the other conditions for ensuring ecological citizenship are tragically missing. We might also note that most of the supposedly global institutions are also problematic for the environment because they are normally organized in terms of nation-states. An example is the General Assembly of the UN with its delegates from each of the 184 countries in the world. This UN structure reinforces the rights of national self-determination, especially of those resources located within the national territory; it leads to the ignoring of issues which do not fit into particular nation-states; it takes no account of regional blocs such as ASEAN or the EU; it neglects powerful internal regions such as Silicon Valley; it fails to represent other organizations which claim to represent global interests such as Greenpeace; and it generally evades consideration of global flows (see Batty and Gray, 1996, pp. 150–1).

Van Steenbergen has further elaborated what might be entailed by ecological citizenship by extending such rights to future generations, to animals and to 'natural' objects (1994; and see Batty and Gray's discussion of human rights to an adequate environment, 1996). Duties and responsibilities for animals and such natural objects have to be undertaken, and this responsibility serves to reconstruct humans as possessors of special powers and responsibilities. Van Steenbergen argues that there is an ecological citizenship consisting of a set of rights (reasonable quality of water and air) and duties (not to consume CFCs) which should be seen as sitting alongside the civil, political and social rights already discussed. As Brundtland states: 'All human beings have the fundamental right to an environment adequate for their health and well-being' (quoted in Batty and Gray, 1996, p. 154). Various American states have affirmed the ecological rights of their citizens, while the South African constitution asserts such an ecological right (Batty and Gray, 1996, p. 153).

However, Van Steenbergen's formulation is too mechanistic. Ecological rights and duties involve the implosion of supposedly separate civil, political and social rights. Indeed, the globalization of risk in many ways highlights the artificiality of Marshall's differentiations and of how contemporary social life involves simultaneous experiences that subsume and fuse Marshall's different dimensions of citizenship. The most interesting aspect of Van Steenbergen's argument is his claim that there are a number of different global citizens whose practices relate to the securing of, or the threatening of, various ecological rights and duties. Extending his analysis somewhat, it is possible to distinguish between seven such social types (see Van Steenbergen, 1994; Ohmae, 1990; Sachs, 1993; Falk, 1994; Rowell, 1996; Castells, 1997): global *capitalists*, who seek to unify the world around global corporate interests which are increasingly 'denationalized'; global *reformers*, who try to use international organizations to moderate and regulate global capitalism; global *environmental managers*, who implement managerial and technical solutions to environmental problems; global *networkers*, who set up and sustain work or leisure networks constituted across national boundaries and having forms of non-national regulation; *earth citizens*, who seek to take responsibility for the globe through a distinct and often highly localized ethics of care; global *cosmopolitans*, who develop a stance and an ideology of openness towards 'other' cultures, peoples and environments; and the global *green backlash*, which in the post-communist era identifies 'environmentalists' as the new global scapegoat to be critiqued and attacked through the media. Each of these types of global citizen involves not just people but networks of machines, technologies, mobilities and social norms. Outcomes in the future will partly depend upon the balance of forces between these different 'global types' and the degree to which any is able to achieve some kind of global hegemony.

The issue of environmental citizenship ought to be seen through the prism of *practices*, *risks*, *rights* and *duties* (see the analogous formulation of citizenship in terms of risk in Therborn, 1995). First, globalization produces a collapse of power of the national society through the development of apparently new global *risks* (Beck, 1992; Macnaghten and Urry, 1998). These include: environmental or health 'bads' resulting from what is now conceptualized as 'global' environmental change; cultural homogenization which destroys local cultures (so-called 'coca-colonization' of culture); the development of diseases carried across national borders by travellers (AIDS); the intermittent collapse of world markets particularly for agricultural commodities; financial meltdowns and their devastating effects upon economic and social life within particular places, especially in the developing world; the proliferation of hugely insecure, unpoliced and out of control 'wild zones' (such as former Yugoslavia, Somalia, inner-city USA); and the dependence of people upon expert systems (for travel, environmental protection, medical support, safe food and so on), which they may not trust since they contradict day-to-day social experiences and forms of lay knowledge.

With regard to global *rights*, these might be thought to include (see Held, 1995; Urry, 1995; Pierson, 1996; Castells, 1997) the right to migrate from one society to another and to stay at least temporarily with comparable rights to the indigenous population; to be able to return not as stateless and with no significant loss of rights; and to be able to carry one's culture with one and to encounter elsewhere a hybrid culture containing at least some elements of one's own culture. Global rights might also include the right to be able to buy across the globe the products, services and icons of other cultures and then to be able to locate them within one's own culture, and to be able to form social movements with citizens of other cultures to oppose particular states (such as the UK as the dirty man of Europe), sets of states (the North), corporations (Shell), general 'bads' and so on. There are also rights to be able to engage in leisure migration throughout almost all of the 200 countries on the globe and hence to 'consume' all of those other places and environments (including especially those of global significance such as UNESCO-designated World Heritage Sites); and to have access to the variety of multimedia products increasingly available across the globe. There are rights to be able to inhabit environments which are relatively free of risks to health and safety produced by both local and distant causes; to be provided with the means by which to know about those environments through multimedia sources of information, understanding and reflection; to be able to sense the quality of each environment that one encounters directly rather than to have to rely on expert systems; and for future generations to have access to these rights into the unknowable future (see Batty and Gray, 1996, p. 159).

Global duties and responsibilities could be thought to include the duty to find out the state of the globe, both through national sources of information and images but especially through sources which are internationalized (see Ohmae, 1990, on the borderless world where states are increasingly unable to control information flows). There is also the responsibility to demonstrate a stance of cosmopolitanism toward other environments, other cultures and other peoples. Such cosmopolitanism may involve either consuming such environments across the globe or refusing to consume such environments (see Bell and Valentine, 1997, on how to 'cook global' on the one hand, and how to cook 'for a small planet' on the other). There is the duty to engage in forms of behaviour with regard to culture, the environment and politics which are consistent with the various official *and* lay conceptions of sustainability which often contradict each other (Macnaghten and Urry, 1998, chap. 7). We can also point to the duties to respond to images, icons, narratives and so on which address people as highly differentiated citizens of the globe rather than as citizens of a nation, ethnicity, gender, class, generation (as in Benetton advertising the colours of the world; more generally, see Szerszynski and Toogood, 2000); and to convince others that they should also seek to act on the part of the globe as a whole which is suffering collectively, rather than in terms of shared identity interests.

Two sets of *practices*, of consumerism and of the mass media, need now be considered. Citizenship and consumerism would once have been thought to be entirely opposed practices and discourses. Citizenship was to do with service, the public, the state, while consumerism involved the private, the market, the customer. But now citizenship and consumerism increasingly overlap, and clear boundaries cannot be drawn around what is 'public' citizenship and what is 'private' consumerism. There are a number of processes which have brought this about: transformations to a post-Fordist mode of production and mode of consumption; the increasing significance of the quality of 'service' to both the private and public sectors; the increased array of 'services' which are relevant to the forming of especially the citizenship of flow; and changes in the nature of the state away from the direct provision of services to regulating services provided by many diverse private, voluntary, quasi-public and public agencies. This de-differentiation produces a major shift from public citizenship, directly provided primarily by the nation-state on the basis of compulsory taxation and insurance, to what can be termed 'consumer citizenship', provided by many diverse institutions, global organizations, nation-states, corporations, NGOs, consumer organizations, the media, voluntary groups and so on. The regulatory role of the state, aided by new computer systems, enables the monitoring of performance and the achievement of common standards irrespective of which organization actually provides the service (see Urry, 2000, chap. 8).

One consequence is that advertising is deeply implicated within contemporary citizenship rather than wholly opposed to it. There is a dedifferentiation between public information and private advertising, between education and entertainment and, most importantly, between textual information and visual imagery. Indeed, part of what constitutes contemporary citizens may not be about what services they are provided with, but about what commodities they can in fact *buy*. Elsewhere I have discussed the significance of consumerism and indeed of 'tourist shopping' in the development of citizenship rights in the later years of 'Eastern Europe' (Urry, 2000, chap. 2). The purchase of particular goods, which signified membership of the 'West', became a real component of citizenship within a number of such countries. And Burgess describes new forms of cultural politics involving purchase: 'the alliance between actors, musicians, Brazilian Indians, population music promoters, conservation organizations, the media industry and mainly young consumers who buy records to support the campaign against the destruction of the Amazonian rainforest' (Burgess, 1990, p. 144).

This relates more generally to changes taking place in what it is to be a 'member' of organizations in the emergent global age. Membership has typically been thought of as the formal joining of organizations which provide various rights and duties to their members and which are organized through a hierarchy. Trade unions have been the classic model. But what is happening is that new 'organizations' have developed which are much more *media*-ted and based upon consumption. Greenpeace is the classic example of an oppositional organization skilled at developing and handling its media images (see

Szerszynski, 1997). Although part of its appeal is through the bearing of witness and the transgressive use of theatre, metaphor and symbol, Greenpeace mainly constructs its membership as relatively passive 'supporters'. Thus while it is the bearer of ecological wisdom and virtue, its membership can get on with leading regular lives of work and family. Like other global players, Greenpeace has devoted much attention to developing its brand identity, which has 'such an iconic status that it is a world-wide symbol of ecological virtue quite above and beyond the actual practical successes of the organization' (Szerszynski, 1997, p. 46). Many young environmentalists would view themselves as citizens of Greenpeace rather than as citizens of a particular nation. This may connect to the development of a polling culture where we are interpellated as consumer-citizens through being polled about pertinent issues – we do not need to be members for the views of citizens like us to be surveyed, measured, reported in the media, consumed (see Macnaghten and Urry, 1998, chap. 3). People can imagine themselves as members (or supporters) of such organizations by being polled, acquiring various purchases, wearing the T-shirt, hearing the CD, surfing to the organization's page on the Web, buying the video of iconic figures and so on.

The second practice is that of the mass media. Citizenship has always necessitated symbolic resources distributed through various means of mass communication (see Murdock, 1992, pp. 20–1), primarily in terms of the significance of print capitalism for the development of the imagined community of the nation in the nineteenth century. Particularly important in the development of twentieth-century notions of national citizenship was the emergence of radio broadcasting, especially when publicly owned. As Murdock notes: 'Where commercial broadcasting regarded listeners as consumers of products, the *ethos* of public service viewed them as citizens of a nation state. It aimed to universalize the provision of the existing cultural institutions' (1992, pp. 26–7). In interwar Britain, particularly, the radio helped to develop the increasingly *national* ideology of Englishness, including English ruralism (Macnaghten and Urry, 1998, chap. 6). The BBC 'marginalized or repressed the situated cultural formations generated by labour, ethnicity, and locality' (Murdock, 1992, p. 29).

In the past two decades or so the global media appears to have been crucially important in generating images of many environmentally threatened localities throughout the world, for example the Amazonian rainforest which has come to represent global suffering. We can imagine ourselves sharing some of the same global problems because of media images which suggest the globalization of nature, in contrast to images of nature which are predominantly national (see Hansen, 1993). At least one precondition of global citizenship is the development of global media, and especially of images of threatened places which become partly representative of the plight of the globe as a whole. Such images may enable people to view themselves as citizens of the globe, as opposed to, or at least as well as, citizens of a nation-state.

In particular, it is images rather than information that seem to have provided the means by which nature as the environment is understood as seriously under threat. This is a non-cognitivist view of the media and also one that bypasses the conventional debates on media 'distortion'. Images of the globe, icons of nature and exemplary heroes may in fact play a central role precisely because many sources of 'information' are only weakly trusted. Both states and corporations are often viewed as lacking in trustworthiness and so, paradoxically, media images can provide more stable forms of meaning and interpretation in a culture in which 'seeing is believing', especially if those images are repeated time and time again (Macnaghten and Urry, 1998, chap. 2). Such media images connect local experiences with each other and hence provide powerful sources of hermeneutic interpretation which make sense of disparate and apparently unconnected events and phenomena.

Electronic communication is creating a global village, blurring what is private and what is public, what is frontstage and what is backstage, what is near and what is far, what is now and what is in the future. Little remains hidden from view, and this may form shared structures of social and political experience, such as a global public concerned with global environmental change (see Meyrowitz, 1985). Indeed, in the last few decades, the public *sphere*, as discussed in the older citizenship literature, is being transformed into a visible public *stage* (see Szerszynski and Toogood, 2000). In Habermas's original conception, the salon, coffee house and periodical press provided the late eighteenth century with a 'public sphere' in which private individuals could debate and resolve political issues (1989). Central to this notion (criticized not least for its gender-bias) was co-presence and dialogue between people face to face. But the 'mediated' character of contemporary social life transforms such a sphere. There are various forms of quasi-interaction that people develop through the media, via a kind of 'enforced proximity'. This produces a visual and narrative 'staging' of the public sphere as it gets transformed into a 'public stage' (Szerszynski and Toogood, 2000; Meyrowitz, 1985).

This public staging of what might otherwise remain private means that all individuals and social institutions can be put on that stage and 'shamed'. The identification within the various media of potentially shameful behaviour can happen to every person and every institution. When that behaviour transgresses norms, others express their disapproval through what Thompson terms an opprobrious discourse, and those involved have a reputation or 'name' to lose, then a scandal will ensue with the person or institution being nationally or globally shamed (see Thompson, 1997, especially on how those 'who live by the media are most likely to die by the media'). Increasingly states and corporations are subject to shaming over their environmental policies and practices. The 'good name' or the 'brand' of the state or corporation is particularly vulnerable symbolic capital that can rapidly diminish within an increasingly mediated culture of shame. Much backstage behaviour affecting the environment can be revealed, put on display, shown around the globe and re-presented over and over again (such as Shell over its environmental record in Ogoni Land in Nigeria and its alleged complicity in the hanging of the Nigerian environmental rights campaigner, Ken Saro-Wiwa, and the French for continued nuclear testing in the Pacific in the face of international opposition).

'Humans' and global citizenship

So far citizenship has been seen from the perspective of relatively abstracted individuals facing certain risks, rights and duties, and in terms of how, with 'globalization', the nature of citizenship may be consequentially reconfigured. Although various 'practices' underpin such conceptions of citizenship, global practices may be transforming what it is to be a human being. If humans 'flow' within and across societal borders, as do information, money and images, then how and why are humans worthy of their designation as *citizens*? Why should they have special rights and duties as they happen to constitute networks alongside, and equivalent to, all sorts of objects, things and environments? Further, if we increasingly think of humans as in some sense cyborgs then what is there to stop them from being programmed to undertake some or all of the duties of the global citizen (Haraway, 1991)? Perhaps so-called humans are already programmed in these ways, and what is needed is a manifesto for such 'cyborgs' (see 'Cyborg Manifesto', 1997).

More generally, should nature be conceived of as analogous to humans, as independently effectual? If nature is in some sense autonomous (in the same sense as humans), then this entails rethinking whether 'objects' can in some sense be considered as citizens. We are already familiar with certain classes of objects as possessors of rights, hence the 'rights of nature' discussed above. But do objects also possess responsibilities? This is obviously a way of conceiving of objects that runs counter to western science and its construction of the object-ness of scientific materials.

One approach to the notion that objects might have responsibilities is through the concept of 'affordances' (Gibson, 1986, chap. 8). Gibson argues that we do not encounter in the environment a set of objective 'things' that people may or may not visually perceive. Rather, different surfaces and different objects, relative to the organism in question, provide opportunities for lying on, sitting on, leaning against and so on. An affordance is neither objective nor subjective, neither part of the environment nor part of the organism. Affordances only stem from the relations between the two.

Gibson's discussion is rather limited in the examples he considers. We can consider other examples of affordances and resistances. A path may beckon us to walk along it, a rock can provide a place from which to view the lake, a wood can function as a repository of memories, a sea can engulf us with cooling water, the heat of the sun may resist our attempts to climb the mountain and so on (see Szerszynski, 1996, for a Heideggerian analysis of the 'ready-to-hand'). Objects can afford us certain possibilities even if western science would tell us that lanes cannot invite, rocks cannot provide viewing places and so on. But sometimes they do because of the particular embeddedness of people, technologies and environments. Given certain past and present social relations, particular 'objects' can afford us a range of possibilities and opportunities, and this can relate to objects of the city as well as objects of nature. We can think of nature as owing us certain affordances and consider whether nature itself has rights and duties towards humans or, indeed, towards other animals. Can we imagine a responsible nature, a nature that possesses rights but also has the duty to provide humans and other animals with appropriate affordances?

That this is counter-intuitive stems from the elision of the concepts of citizen and citizenship, as though the only entities that might be involved in citizenship are human subject/citizens. But while it would indeed be odd to describe nature as a citizen, it might not be so odd to conceptualize nature as embedded in the discourses and practices of citizenship. Michael seeks to 'draw out some of the ways in which "nice nature" interacts with the body to recover previously suppressed possibilities, where the environment ... potentially enables, rather than constrains, the movement of the body in light of the body's capacities' (1996, p. 149). 'Nice nature' is, one might say, nature demonstrating good citizenship. 'Affordance' refers to the way in which the array of surfaces and structures in the environment specify a range of possible embodied actions for the organism, and particularly for the human organism.

There are four points to note in connection with nature and citizenship in relation to 'human' organisms. First, nature provides limits to what is corporeally possible but it does not determine the particular actions humans engage in. Michael summarizes: 'there are a range of options ... implicit within a physical milieu and this implicitness is directly connected to the bodily capacities and limits of the [human] organism' (1996, p. 149). Second, the options afforded to humans should relate to the variety of senses that can be involved in their relationship to the environment and not just to the optic sense which Gibson principally examines (on the senses and nature, see Macnaghten and Urry, 1998, chap. 4). 'Nice nature' should afford experiences of touch, hearing, smell and taste, as well as vision. Third, a 'nice nature' provides affordances for humans, which enables them to resist certain modes of disciplining (Michael, 1996, p. 149). Nature acting as a good citizen opens up behavioural vistas. For human organisms, a good nature, according to Michael, expands the potential range of identities available for individuals (1996, p. 150). And finally, the 'niceness' of nature does not mean that nature is wholly enabling of short-term human practice. What should be afforded by nature in citizenship terms will often be limits upon short-term human activity, as there should be a viable longer-term or glacial time horizon built into nature's role (see Macnaghten and Urry, 1998, chap. 5, on the times of nature). Such glacially organized practices involve developing the concept of affordance, not just to individuals or to social groups, but to the human species as a whole.

Conclusion

The suggestion that we should consider affordances in relationship to the species as a whole connects to some general observations about humans and citizenship. First, the concept of the citizen seems so bound up with that of the nation-state society, such that if societies are no longer powerful entities then there would no longer appear to be citizens in the discursive and active sense of citizenship employed in this chapter. It seems that citizens require societies and states, and the mutual antagonisms that they generate. Without them in the same form it may be that we are witnessing the slow death of the citizen, just as citizenships seem to have become so widespread.

Further, many appeals in the media are concerned with developing a sense of planetary responsibility rather than responsibility for particular towns and cities. This is a relatively new notion and one that appears to distinguish humans from other species. However, previous citizenships have been based upon antagonism between those inside and those outside, upon identifying the non-citizen, the other, the enemy (as with those inside/outside city states). We can thus ask whether a conception of citizenship is emerging which does not presume an enemy, an 'other'? Alternatively, does the lack of an 'enemy' for global citizens mean that such a citizenship will never develop on any significant scale (there are few global citizens because there is nobody to be excluded)?

Or again, perhaps there *is* an enemy – the system of powerful states and global corporations, whose commitment to the globe is shamefully hesitant, hypocritical and fragmented. Or maybe the enemy, the other, of the global citizen is actually within each of us. Does widespread ambivalence mean that the enemy is in fact the enemy in each person – since global citizens are happy global consumers much of the time, caring little for the affordances of a 'nice' nature, and easily consuming, whenever possible, images, icons and commodities from towns, cities, countries and corporations across the globe.

Note

1   This chapter stems from a research project at Lancaster University on Global Citizenship and the Environment funded by the UK ESRC (grant no. R000236768). I am extremely grateful to my colleagues, Greg Myers, Bron Szerszynski and Mark Toogood. I am also grateful for the comments of Mike Michael, Eric Darieré and Sylvia Walby.

Bibliography

Albrow, M. (1996) *The Global Age* (Cambridge: Polity).
Appadurai, A. (1990) 'Disjuncture and Difference in the Global Cultural Economy', *Theory, Culture and Society*, 7: 295–310.
Batty, H. and Gray, T. (1996) 'Environmental Rights and National Sovereignty', in S. Caney, D. George and P. Jones (eds), *National Rights, International Obligations* (Colorado: Westview Press).
Beck, U. (1992) *Risk Society* (London: Sage).

Bell, D. and Valentine, G. (1997) *Consuming Geographies* (London: Routledge).

Brunn, S. and Leinbach, R. (eds) (1991) *Collapsing Space and Time: Geographic Aspects of Communications and Information* (London: Harper Collins).

Burgess, J. (1990) 'The Production and Consumption of Environmental Meanings in the Mass Media: A Research Agenda for the 1990s', *Transactions of the Institute of British Geographers*, 15: 139–62.

Castells, M. (1996) *The Rise of the Network Society* (Oxford: Blackwell).

—— (1997) *The Power of Identity* (Oxford: Blackwell).

'Cyborg Manifesto' (1997) *Cultural Values*, 1.

Eade, J. (ed.) (1997) *Living the Global City: Globalization as a Local Process* (New York: Routledge).

Falk, R. (1994) 'The Making of Global Citizenship', in B. Van Steenbergen (ed.), *The Condition of Citizenship* (London, Sage).

Featherstone, M., Lash S. and R. Robertson, (eds) (1995) *Global Modernities* (London: Sage).

Garton Ash, T. (1990) *We the People. The Revolution of '89 Witnessed in Warsaw, Budapest, Berlin and Prague* (Cambridge: Granta Books).

Gibson, J. (1986) *The Ecological Approach to Visual Perception* (New Jersey: Lawrence Erlbaum).

Gilroy, P. (1993) *The Black Atlantic: Modernity and Double Consciousness* (London: Verso).

Habermas, J. (1989) *The Structural Transformation of the Public Sphere* (Cambridge: Polity).

Hansen, A. (ed.) (1993) *The Mass Media and Environmental Issues* (Leicester: Leicester University Press).

Haraway, D. (1991) *Simians, Cyborgs, and Women* (London: Free Association Books).

Held, D. (1995) *Democracy and the Global Order* (Cambridge: Polity).

Hewitt, P. (1996) 'Social Justice in a Global Economy?', in M. Bulmer and A. Rees (eds), *Citizenship Today* (London: UCL Press).

Lash, S. and Urry, J. (1994) *Economies of Signs and Space* (London: Sage).

Latour, B. (1993) *We Have Never Been Modern* (Hemel Hempstead: Harvester Wheatsheaf).

Macnaghten, P. and Urry, J. (1998) *Contested Natures* (London: Sage).

Mann, M. (1993) *The Sources of Social Power; the Rise of Classes and Nation-states*, vol. 2 (Cambridge: Cambridge University Press).

—— (1996) 'Ruling Class Strategies and Citizenship', in M. Bulmer and A. Rees (eds), *Citizenship Today* (London: UCL Press).

Meyrowitz, J. (1985) *No Sense of Place* (New York: Oxford University Press).

Michael, M. (1996) *Constructing Identities* (London: Sage).

Murdock, G. (1992) 'Citizens, Consumers, and Public Culture', in M. Shovmand and K. Shrøder (eds), *Media Cultures* (London: Routledge).

Nash, R. (1989) *The Rights of Nature* (Madison: University of Wisconsin Press).

Newby, H. (1996) 'Citizenship in a Green World: Global Commons and Human Stewardship', in M. Bulmer and A. Rees (eds), *Citizenship Today* (London: UCL Press).

Ohmae, K. (1990) *The Borderless World* (London: Collins).

Pierson, C. (1996) *The Modern State* (London: Routledge).

Rees, A. (1996) 'T.H. Marshall and the Progress of Citizenship', in M. Bulmer and A. Rees (eds), *Citizenship Today* (London: UCL Press).

Robertson, R. (1990) 'Mapping the Global Condition: Globalization as the Central Concept', in M. Featherstone (ed.), *Global Culture* (London: Sage).

Rose, N. (1996) 'Refiguring the Territory of Government', *Economy and Society*, 25: 327–56.

Rowell, A. (1996) *Green Backlash* (London: Routledge).

Runciman, G. (1996) 'Why Social Inequalities are Generated by Social Rights', in M. Bulmer and A. Rees (eds), *Citizenship Today* (London: UCL Press).

Sachs, W. (ed.) (1993) *Global Ecology: A New Arena of Political Conflict* (London: Zed Books).

Szerszynski, B. (1996) 'Sustainable Development and Human Identity' (Lancaster: CSEC, Lancaster University).

—— (1997) 'The Varieties of Ecological Piety', *Worldviews: Environment, Culture, Religion*, 1: 37–55.

Szerszynski, B. and Toogood, M. (2000) 'Global Citizenship, the Environment and the Mass Media', in S. Allen, B. Adam and C. Carter (eds) *The Media Politics of Environmental Risks* (London: UCL Press).

Therborn, G. (1995) *European Modernity and Beyond* (London: Sage).

Thompson, J. (1997) 'Scandal and Social Theory', (Cambridge: Mimeo, SPS, University of Cambridge).

Turner, B. (1993a) 'Contemporary Problems in the Theory of Citizenship', in B. Turner (ed.), *Citizenship and Social Theory* (London: Sage).

—— (1993b) 'Outline of a Theory of Human Rights', in B. Turner (ed.), *Citizenship and Social Theory* (London: Sage).

Urry, J. (1995) *Consuming Places* (London: Routledge).

—— (2000) *Sociology Beyond Societies* (London: Routledge).

Van Steenbergen, B. (1994) 'Towards a Global Ecological Citizen', in *The Condition of Citizenship* (London: Sage).

Walby, S. (1996) 'Women and Citizenship: Towards a Comparative Analysis', *University College of Galway Women's Studies Centre Review*, 4: 41–58.

Ward, N. (1996) 'Surfers, Sewage and the New Politics of Pollution', *Area*, 28: 331–8.

Waters, M. (1995) *Globalization* (London: Routledge).

Yuval-Davis, N. (1997) 'National Spaces and Collective Identities: Border, Boundaries, Citizenship and Gender Relations', Inaugural Lecture, University of Greenwich.

4 The resurgence of the city in Europe?

The spaces of European citizenship[1]

Gerard Delanty

Introduction

The European project was founded by states. Will it be challenged by cities? European integration opens up new possibilities for cities to assert their autonomy against nation-states but it also presents great dangers, such as growing fragmentation and the abandonment of social citizenship and the guarantees of a constitutional order, the achievement of states. Until now the identity of Europe has largely been shaped by the space of the nation-state, which has overshadowed other conceptions of space that are deeply embedded in the tradition of the European city. To recover and develop these traditions is an important challenge for the project of European integration, which needs to anchor itself in a substantive kind of citizenship. This chapter proposes the concept of discursive space as a theorization of democratic space in the emergent reality of the European project of shared sovereignty.

A noticeable absence in the literature on globalization and the city is work on the implications of European integration for the city and citizenship. It may be that the absence of a concern with the city is due to the fact that the European project has been on the whole shaped by statism. The sub-national level has been relatively untouched by inter-state cooperation, at least until recently. The European Union, while having greatly undermined the sovereignty of the territorial nation-state, has been engineered by nation-states who saw in the European project the means of pursuing their own ambitions (Milward, 1992). The administration of the modern city was, on the whole, an internal affair of national governments. With the emergence of a regulatory supranational polity since the 1980s, the sub-national level is now growing in salience; regions and cities are resurfacing and becoming powerful new voices in a world in which sovereignty is shared on many levels. But exactly what are the implications of European integration for the city? Can cities become new sites of autonomy for civil society? Is the European city a dual city overwhelmed by the forces of globalization or can the human order of the *polis* assert its voice over the globalizing flows of the *cosmos*? This chapter explores these questions.

According to Claude Lefort (1986, p. 279), in modern society democracy can be defined as an empty space. It is an empty space because it is never occupied by any one person or group but is the radically open domain of discourse. This emptiness, lying at the heart of democracy, is both a space and a non-space. It is a space in the sense that it is a domain that exists in some form, but it is also a non-space in that it is never a place that is actually inhabited. In short, it is not a lived space but a domain of discourse. Lefort's emphasis on the spatial dimension of democracy is significant in the context of the identity of the city, for one of the traditions of the city is the confluence of democracy and space. The term 'discursive space' expresses this relation, which is highly pertinent to the identity of the city today, for cities have become major sites of contention and are the location of different orders of discourse and democracy (Douglas and Friedmann, 1998). My approach, then, sees cities in terms of the flow of communication and the expansion of their discursive capacity.

Resurgence of the European city? European integration and citizenship

The city in Europe, as elsewhere, is caught between the poles of autonomy and fragmentation. Therborn (1995, pp. 194–5), following Rokkan (1980) and Tilly (1992), uses two geopolitical variables in the conceptual mapping of Europe, centre formation and city network. He argues that the centre of Europe formed around a strong city belt which drew the seaward empire nations together and which was characterized by the accumulation and concentration of capital, rather than by a concentration of coercive means. For Therborn (1995, p. 195), the European Union is also in itself a 'city belt writ large' with its gravity concentrated in its cities. Tilly (1994, p. 8) argues that cities shaped the destinies of states chiefly by serving as containers and distribution points for capital; states, in contrast, he argues, operated chiefly as containers and deployers of coercive means, especially armed violence. The city can be seen as one of the driving forces in European history, constituting a kind of model of autonomy which was essential to its identity (see Benevolo, 1993; Weber, 1958). This identity became fragmented by the centralizing state from the seventeenth century onwards, and in our own time the forces of globalization are bringing about a further transformation in the identity of the European city.

However, in Europe, globalization is mediated through the internal convergence of European societies. The Union is based on a regulatory order which is not comparable to other transnational processes (Majone, 1996). In other words, the convergence of European societies is not entirely the product of a world out of control. As a regulatory order – the Union is not itself a supra-state but neither is it an open structure – the supra-state has considerable powers of regulation. The European project has brought about a unique polity in which sovereignty is shared on many different levels, most notably the regional, the national and the supra-national levels. Thus, the state is being reconfigured. The tendency is for the state to surrender aspects of regulation which it is less equipped to deal with, such as control over financial markets and trade. Yet the state apparatus is still strong and in control of many of its traditional functions. For instance, there is no realistic move to create a European welfare state. Welfare is still firmly in the hands of the national state, as is witnessed by the variety of national welfare states ranging from the British to the Swedish to the German and Spanish models. Immigration is also still firmly under the control of national governments. As already argued, the Union has brought a multi-level kind of polity, with sovereignty transferred upwards to the transnational level but also downwards to the regional, and transversally to non-territorial agencies such as social movements and organized interests (Close, 1995; Tarrow, 1995).

Let us now consider the implications for the city, taking in turn the economic, political, cultural and social spheres.

Material production

Many cities in Europe are reaping the benefits of globalization and adjusting to the conditions of post-industrialism. Local economies may be gaining as national economies weaken (Harding, 1997, p. 296). However, the rosy picture of a coming age of 'glocality' is misleading. The logic of European integration is to intensify the process of territorial competition (Cheshire and Gordon, 1995, p. 109). In any competition there are winners and losers. The winners are undoubtedly the megacities – London and Paris, with Berlin as a newcomer – and the smaller 'global' cities such as Frankfurt, Amsterdam, Barcelona, Milan, as well as the national capitals such as Dublin, Madrid, Brussels, Bonn-Köln and Vienna. The losers are the former industrial cities which are unable to adjust to the conditions of post-industrialism and to rapid growth (Burthenshaw et al., 1995; Moulaert and Scott, 1996). European cities are undergoing a process of territorial alignment and segmentation. They are becoming more and more shaped by cross-national trade, and as a consequence they are becoming disjointed from their national regional contexts, which respond in a differential way to rapid change. Cappelin writes about the emergence of a new phenomenon 'in the transformation of urban centres from a function as centres of consumer services for the regional population to a function as nodes in the network of producer services, which are exchanged at the inter-regional and international level' (Cappelin, 1991, p. 237). Access to international airports will be an important factor in urban development.

A super league of mega and global cities is emerging, with a relatively strong zone of semi-peripheral cities and the growing isolation of peripheral cities. London, Paris and Berlin are increasingly becoming detached from their national and regional contexts. The former two contenders are advantaged by the fact that they were never fully industrial cities and have therefore found it easier to make the transition to the information age. We are witnessing the emergence of a series of mini-global cities stretching from Paris and Amsterdam to Milan and Zurich. This is exacerbated by the fact that there has been a weakening of national equalization (Mayer, 1992, p. 256). Moreover, within these cities, it is frequently argued, something like a process of segmentation is occurring, with the growing polarization of social groups, a phenomenon which Castells calls the 'dual city' (Castells, 1994, p. 26). This refers to the segmentation of the urban labour force into a secure multi-skilled core and a casual labour force. However, this thesis is much disputed and there is little consensus on whether European cities are becoming polarized in the way that is alleged American cities are (for a debate, see the special section in *Urban Affairs*, 33 (4), 1998). Nevertheless, we can speak of a certain degree of fragmentation (Mingione, 1991).

In sum, then, the implication for the city in terms of economic change is ambivalent. The city is not only emerging from the centuries-old tutelage of the nation-state but is also abandoning the region. Under these circumstances it is difficult to speak of autonomy when what in fact is occurring is a process of fragmentation both within the city and in its relation to its regional environment. Unemployment continues to be a problem in the old industrial and maritime cities while others adjust to globalization. There is no universal trend towards convergence; instead, we have a picture of the diversity of structures and growing fragmentation arising out of processes of segmentation.

Power, regulation and sovereignty

Here the question of the autonomy of the city is complex since the sub-national level has been relatively untouched by European integration. The European project has mostly been a project of inter-state cooperation and it is on the level of national governance that there has been the greatest degree of convergence. We must also bear in mind that the member states have themselves a great variety of internal structures with respect to regional and municipal autonomy. Thus countries such as Germany, Belgium and Austria have institutionalized federalism, while countries such as Greece, Ireland and the UK are highly centralized, and countries such as France, Italy and Spain have degrees of provincial autonomy but no federal structures as such. Some developments, however, do point to the increasing salience of the city as a political unit. Of particular importance in this regard is the Committee of the Regions. The Maastricht Treaty obliges the Commission and the Council of Ministers to consult the Committee on certain policy questions pertaining to regions and cities. However, The Committee of the Regions is largely a pressure group – albeit one which has advisory powers – with a permanent presence in Brussels. The Committee adheres to the principle of subsidiarity which lies at the heart of the Union: that bottom-up solutions are preferable to top-heavy ones. The Committee of the Regions has been the source of proposals for regional and local democracy and is committed to a model of democracy based on participation. Apart from this semi-institutionalized committee there are a variety of more peripheral and extra-institutional movements and organizations, such as the Permanent Forum of Civil Society, which consists of over one hundred NGOs and citizens' associations. The aim of this forum is to bring about a new conception of European citizenship based on participation and a notion of a 'common good'. There is now a growing literature on the resurgence of the region in Europe, but relatively little on the implications for cities as such (see Anderson, 1994; Hooghe, 1995; Sharpe, 1993; Cooke et al., 1997; Delanty, 1996; Therborn, 1995, pp. 200–5).

There is little basis in reality for a genuine Europe of Regions, still less a Europe of Cities. This is because the foundation of the Union is the state. Even though we have moved far from the realist model of inter-state cooperation, the present regulatory state is one that is not committed to a Europe of sub-national units, be they cities or regions. There is ambiguity on the meaning of subsidiarity, which originally meant a relationship between the state and the Union but now comes to embrace all the different levels on which sovereignty is shared. We should not overstate the idea of the city ideal for another reason, too. Local and municipal governance may be significant in stimulating local economic responses to the opportunities created by globalization, but we must not neglect the fact that there is a withdrawal in the provision of public services by local governments, who allow private and semi-private bodies to take over the provision of public services. In short, cities do not have the same commitment to public services that the central and national state has traditionally had. Social citizenship has after all been a creation of the central state, which is the basis of institutional responsibility. As Marris (1998, p. 14) argues: 'In the current conservative enthusiasm for decentralization, notice that what is being decentralized – or even abdicated – is responsibility.' Decentralization is good if it is in the name of citizenship and autonomy. However, the reality of neo-liberal decentralization is precisely the opposite. Concerning the question of a citizenship of participation gaining ground, there is additionally the problem that the model of citizenship that has shaped the Union and which is codified by Maastricht is one that stresses formalistically defined rights. The rights of European citizenship are highly formalized and are derivative of national citizenship. It is difficult to see how these rights – which mostly refer to rights of mobility for capital, goods, services and labour – can be the basis of a citizenship of participation.

However, it is important to see European integration as an open-ended project with many dimensions to it. The notion of 'sustainable cities', for instance, has already made an impact on the politics of the city. Of course, much of this is unrelated to the European Union and derives from some three decades of radical environmental politics emanating from outside the established political institutions. Yet, there is some evidence to suggest that ecological sustainability is a new area of potential links between cities and the Union. The politics of the sustainable city is addressed to new kinds of problems which were not considered central to the industrial city, such as the growing recognition that cities are reaching saturation point with respect to traffic, air pollution and refuse disposal.

Meaning, identity and symbolic representation

The question of culture has recently appeared on the agenda of a programme that was previously concerned only with economic and administrative steering (Wintle, 1996). Various attempts have been made to articulate a kind of European identity that both transcends and incorporates the diversity of national identities. However, it is apparent that there is no European identity as such. Europe does not have a shared cultural community which could be the basis of a common cultural identity. There is no common language nor ethnic commonalties upon which a European identity could be built (Delanty, 1995a; 1995b; 1998). Yet there is no denying that there is a space for new constructions of meaning and identity as the nation ceases to be the dominant focus of identification. In the present context, the question is whether cities can articulate a post-national identity. European integration projects, such as 'European Cities of Culture' and the European Youth Parliament, have established the city as a core domain of symbolic representation. Cities are increasingly promoting their own heritage for the purposes of tourism.

There is a renewed interest in the culture of the European city as an urban landscape that transcends the social (Barber, 1995). In this post-modernization of the city, images of the city become detached from urban reality and become their own reality. The city becomes a cultural icon to be consumed in a visual experience, something which John Urry describes as 'aesthetic cosmopolitanism' (Urry, 1995, p. 167) or what might also be called the aesthetic mode of production. Examples of this might be museums, cultural exhibitions, films such as *The Sky Above Berlin*, and the reflexive consumption of literary discourses of the city, such as the commercializing of Joyce's Dublin. Other examples might be food, which plays a major role in defining the city's symbolic economy (Zukin, 1995), as well as cafés and music. As Sharon Zukin argues, these new discourses of the city are closely related to the construction of a new middleclass culture:

> cultural strategies that rely on visual representations attempt to create a new public culture that is both non-hierarchical and inegalitarian. Although they are often applied to populist sites – commercial streets, working-class neighbourhoods, public parts, city centres – cultural strategies use visual aesthetics to evoke a vanished civic order associated with an equally vanished or at least transformed middle-class.
>
> (Zukin, 1995, p. 274; see also Smith, 1996)

What then, we may ask, is the representational space of the European city? Is this representational space connected to civil society and the politics of citizenship? Jonathan Raban (1988), in his well-known impressionistic book *Soft City*, gives the answer: the contemporary city is culturally a 'soft' city. That is, the form and space of the city is shaped by subjectivity and an imaginative component. It is the 'soft' image that is ultimately real despite the 'hard' reality of everyday life. Thus, the representational space of the city is shifting onto the new space of flows which is bringing about a homogenized uniformity which only disguises the diversity and fragmentary forms of the city (see De Certeau, 1984). This is evident in a number of urban discourses, for instance post-modern architecture. According to Castells (1996, p. 418), the 'coming of the space of flows is blurring the meaningful relationship between architecture and society'. The result of this is the generalization of an ahistorical and acultural architecture leading, according to Habermas (1989b, pp. 17–19), to a total separation of form and function. Under these circumstances there can be no European cultural identity as such, but only a globalized one which announces the end of all systems of meaning. Against this view, however, are some developments suggesting a relinking of architecture and social identity, particularly in Central and Eastern Europe where architecture has become an important part of the negotiation of post-communist identities (Leach, 1999). More generally in Europe, and particularly in the UK where there is increased government spending on architectural designs in public buildings, architects are becoming more influential in the creation of new post-national European identities.

Another example of the representational space of cities might be the growing discourse of gentrification which counter-opposes an idealized image of white middle-class urbanity and civility to an image of an 'underclass' of otherness and violence (Gos, 1997, p. 184). Thus a discourse of 'otherness' is becoming part of the symbolic representation of cities.

European countries differ in their discourses of the city. In March 1998 an estimated quarter of a million people descended on London in what was alleged to be a 'country alliance' against the city. The state was claimed to be an urban tool of oppression which failed to understand the countryside. In Britain the discourse of the country – which is mostly itself an urban creation – is stronger than the idea of the city, as is illustrated in the growing number of people moving to live in the country. Historically, too, the countryside ideal has been stronger, suggesting an image of wealth in contrast to the decadence of the city (see Bunce, 1994). Since Rousseau, the city has traditionally been seen as unnatural and dehumanizing, the themes of famous evocations of the city, such as Engels' *The Condition of the Working Class in England* (1945), James Thompson's *City of Dreadful Night* (1874), Oswald Spengler's *Decline of the West* (1918) or T.S. Eliot's *The Wasteland* (1922). Italy might be an example of a European country where the city ideal has remained stronger. Italians do not share the British nostalgia for the countryside and as a rule prefer to live urban lives, while Germany, in contrast, might be an example of a country where regional identities are stronger than city identities, a fact that might be explained by its federalist history.

Everyday life and social relations

Cities embody not only cultural discourses but are also living places. Although enhancing the flow of commodities and the mobility of capital, European integration has not reinforced the autonomy of urban life-worlds. With respect to the social realities of cities as places where people live, European integration is strengthening the separation of space from place. This is evident in, for example, the development of a high-speed transport system which will bring about a further compression of time and space. The immediate impact of this will be the polarization of Europe around cities that fall into main transport corridors and those that are outside them. The drive to become a global city is a major challenge to citizenship. For example, in Hanover – the location of the World Exposition 2000 – there has been widespread concern over the last number of years that the provision of a new transport infrastructure and the construction of a suitable site will be detrimental to the city as a social environment.

It may be suggested that European integration is being conceived around a notion of mobility rather than one of citizenship, the fluidity of which enhances fragmentation. The drive for greater convergence is one that is achieved by bringing about the provision of possibilities for the enhanced mobility of goods, capital and labour. A societal framework that is held together by processes of mobility runs the risk of achieving convergence on some levels, at the cost of divergence on others. In this context, Castells (1996, p. 394) speaks of the imminent 'death of cities': the increasing disassociation between spatial proximity and the performance of the functions of everyday life such as work, shopping, entertainment, healthcare, education and public services. Castells (1996, p. 403) claims that, in Europe as elsewhere, 'urban space is increasingly differentiated in social terms, while being functionally interrelated beyond physical continuity'. European integration has undoubtedly increased the separation of the two spatial logics of place and space, leading to the transformation of the latter into flows which are becoming disconnected with everyday life.

However, it must be mentioned that initiatives such as the European Regional Development Fund and the European Social Fund – which are part of the Structural Funds – aim to bring about long-term socio-economic development in poor regions and to overcome some of the dislocations of a project whose overall goal is societal convergence. There is no doubt that some of these measures have been highly effective, as is illustrated in the case of Ireland, whose economy and standard of living is now comparable to the European norm. The relative prosperity of Ireland can be partly attributed to the diffusion of the Structural Funds and a positive embracing of European integration. Yet, there is some evidence to suggest the growing separation of Dublin from the rest of the country, as well as evidence to indicate the internal fragmentation of Dublin along the lines of a 'dual city'. While the thesis of the dual city applies less to European cities than to some American ones, we can speak of the fragmentation of the city.

Again, we must be cautious of exaggerating the arrival of the dual city. Taking the much-discussed question of immigration as an example, we can see that European integration has opened up new possibilities for immigrants.

Recent studies (Delanty, 1997a; Soysal, 1994; Jacobsen, 1997) stress the increasing salience of post-national membership as a domain of sovereignty that challenges the exclusivity of national citizenship. While the Union is still largely based on national citizenship, it has partially acknowledged the possibility of a citizenship based on residence. It is possible, in the not too distant future, that this will become more significant in defining European citizenship.

Conclusion: discursive space, civil society and citizenship

Following Soja (1996) and Lefebvre (1991; 1996), we can argue how conceptions of urban space have been dominated by tendentially globalizing discourses of visibility and representationality – the order of the *cosmos* – with the public and the everyday space – the human order of the *polis* – being eroded. The city has been portrayed either as a material thing – an economic structure, a class system, racial relations – which required regulation by city planners in order to give it a form, or as a cultural discourse in need of an aesthetic form, for example in architecture. These conceptions of space neglect an alternative understanding of civil society. This conception of civil society and its relation to space is one that stresses the communicative or discursive component to citizenship. The essential idea is contained in Jürgen Habermas's (1989a; 1993; 1996; 1998) celebrated notion of the public sphere. As is well known, the public sphere is theorized by Habermas as the space of civic communication, which is held to be the heart of civil society. Originally located between the private realm and the domain of the state, it has now come to mean the sphere of the discursive, the radically open space of communication. The classical model – which Habermas followed in his early work – was based on the existence of a political domain of public communication which stood against both the state and the private; later it became associated with bourgeois property relations, and today the public sphere is constituted in the plurality of spaces created by social movements of all kinds.

It seems to me that we need a new conception of public space to capture the sense in which cities can be constituted as autonomous and can recreate a unity fragmented by globalization. My contention is that the idea of discursive space fulfils this need. We are living in an age which has made it impossible to return to one of the great dreams of the project of modernity, namely the creation of a unitary principle of integration capable of bringing together the domains of economy, polity, culture and society. However, this does not condemn us to a life of fragmentation in which these domains remain divorced from each other. While none of the domains are themselves capable of establishing a principle of unity, we can still hold on to the possibility of a degree of societal integration compatible with the reality of globalization. This promise lies in the institutionalization of communication.

In order to see how communication as discursive space can open up a new model of space which would be relevant to the city, we must first of all rethink the idea of civil society. It is no longer credible to conceive of civil society in terms of the dominant models of space. Civil society is constituted not in a particular space – be it the space of the political or the economic or the cultural – but in the relations between the different parts of society. The Enlightenment model of civil society – in Rousseau and republican political theory – was constructed on the basis of the separation of civil society from the state, and later, in liberal theory, it came to designate the separation of the economy from the state. In much more recent times, civil society emerged as part of the civil opposition to Soviet statism and referred to the unity of society. Today these notions of civil society are no longer viable. Society does not exist as a self-contained domain; its space has been colonized by other forces, and the state is also no longer the unified entity it once was. In short, neither society nor state exist as opposing forces. It may be suggested that the dualism of state and society has been overtaken by new configurations of culture and economy, state and society. We must now conceive of civil society less as a particular space than as a relationship between the different parts of society. Pierre Bourdieu's concept of a 'field' – itself a spatial concept – of power captures precisely this sense of the relational and discursive constitution of discourse, and is an important corrective to Habermas's somewhat decontextualized conception (see Bourdieu and Wacquant, 1992, pp. 94–8; for a discussion, Swartz, 1997, pp. 117–42; on Habermas, see Delanty, 1997b).

The (relational) space of civil society is one that is best seen as flows of communication. This notion of flows is one that is not addressed to the post-modernist idea of symbolic capital. Communication is more than merely symbolic, it also has a cognitive and discursive component to it. In the context of the new politics of the city, what is highly pertinent is the question of discursive democracy (Blaug, 1996; Drysek, 1990; Habermas, 1996). One of the most important challenges for the city is to institutionalize new discursive spaces. I shall comment on just one dimension to this: the confluence of the cognitive and the discursive, or knowledge and democracy.

One of the most striking developments in recent times is the arrival of the knowledge society (Delanty, 1997c, 2000a, 2000b; Böhme, 1997). We are living in a society in which knowledge has become a key component in all spheres of life. The knowledge society is more than what Castells calls the 'information society', which is instrumentalized knowledge at the point of application in production. Knowledge also has a cognitive dimension and is becoming more and more the basis of politics and cultural reproduction. Ulrich Beck (1992), for instance, writes of the tendency of the 'risk society' to politicize knowledge by calling into question expert systems and received notions of knowledge as deriving from self-legitimating discourses. In the risk society, everybody is an expert. Knowledge, in short, has been released from the scientific culture of experts and has been made more discursive. The separation of expert knowledge and personal, experiential knowledge is declining. It is possible to suggest that the politics of the twenty-first century will be about knowledge: its status, its application, its accessibility. In the levelling of the distance between knowledge and society on the one side, and the release of politics and culture from the nation-state on the other, we are witnessing a confluence of knowledge and democracy. Both knowledge and democracy are becoming more and more discursive. Knowledge is steadily losing its identification with expert systems and democracy is likewise losing its connection with the state. With the opening up of knowledge to the critical scrutiny of the public, democracy as a discursive process takes on a new relevance.

A crucial dimension to the future of the city may be the creation of discursive spaces in which cities can articulate a wider range of voices than those of experts and capitalists. The city of modernity was one which celebrated the eye; the city as an urban form has yet to give expression to the voice as a medium of cognitive experience. This perspective stresses the shared dimension of knowledge. In a hopelessly fragmented world which cannot reverse societal complexity, the only possibility for recovery of a point of unity is in communication. Cities must give expression to as many voices as possible. This model of discursive space is in fact also deeply embedded in the history of the European city, which was originally built around a square that served as an *agora* or forum. Historians of the city such as Lewis Mumford (1961) and Paul Chaval (1984, pp. 33–4) have recognized that these squares, which had a communicative function, constituted one of the common traits of European cities.

In conclusion, as far as European integration is concerned, the future of the city is an open agenda. It is indeed an open question whether a project that was created by states will be challenged by cities. It is true that European integration has moved far beyond the early statist project and has brought new notions of shared sovereignty into existence. However, the regulatory order that has now been created is not one that gives a central place to sub-national mobilization. The main changes have been in the relation of the state to the supra-state. It is my view, given the fact that the state is going to remain the foundation of the Union, that the best chance for the city is to adapt to the conditions of multiple orders of sovereignty, to strike up new relations with the state and the supra-state, and to do so both vertically and horizontally. One of the challenges of the city in the age of European integration might be to become an active agent in the emerging knowledge society, thereby giving a real basis to a discursive democracy of participation. Perhaps this could be the city's challenge to the state.

Note

1   I am grateful to Engin Isin, Heidi Granger and Tracey Skillington for helpful comments on an earlier draft.

Bibliography

Anderson, P. (1994) 'The Invention of the Region, 1945–1990', EUI Working Paper no. 94/2 (Florence: European University Institute).
Barber, S. (1995) *Fragments of the European City* (London: Reaktion Books).

Beck, U. (1992) *The Risk Society* (London: Sage).

Benevolo, L. (1993) *The European City* (Oxford: Blackwell).

Blaug, R. (1996) 'New Theories of Discursive Democracy: A User's Guide', *Philosophy and Social Criticism*, 22 (1): 49–80.

Böhme, G. (1997) 'The Structures and Prospects of the Knowledge Society', *Social Science Information*, 36 (3), pp. 447-68.

Bourdieu, P. and Wacquant, L. (1992) *An Introduction to Reflexive Sociology* (Chicago: Chicago University Press).

Bunce, M. (1994) *The Countryside Ideal* (London: Routledge).

Burthenshaw, D., Bateman, M. and Ashworth, G. (eds) (1995) *The European City: A Western Perspective* (London: David Foulton).

Cappelin, R. (1991) 'International Networks of Cities', in R. Camagni (ed.), *Innovation Networks: Spatial Perspectives* (London: Belhaven).

Castells, M. (1994) 'European Cities, the Informational Society, and the Global Economy', *New Left Review*, 204: 18–32.

—— (1996) *The Rise of the Network Society* (Oxford: Blackwell).

Chaval, P. (1984) 'Reflections on the Cultural Geography of the European City', in J. Agnew, J. Mercer and D. Sopher (eds), *The City in Cultural Context* (London: Allen and Unwin).

Cheshire, P. and Gordon, I. (1995) 'European Integration: The logic of Territorial Competition and Europe's Urban System', in J. Brotchie et al. (eds), *Cities in Competition* (London: Longman).

Close, P. (1995) *Citizenship, Europe and Change* (London: Macmillan).

Cooke, P., Christiansen, T. and Schienstock, G. (1997) 'Regional Economic Policy and a Europe of Regions', in M. Rhodes, P. Heywood and V. Wright (eds), *Developments in West European Politics* (London: Macmillan).

De Certeau, M. (1984) *The Practice of Everyday Life* (Berkeley, CA: University of California Press).

Delanty, G. (1995a) *Inventing Europe: Idea, Identity, Reality* (London: Macmillan).

—— (1995b) 'The Limits and Possibility of a European Identity: A Critique of Cultural Essentialism', *Philosophy and Social Criticism*, 21 (4): 15–36.

—— (1996) 'Northern Ireland in a Europe of Regions', *Political Quarterly*, 67 (2): 127–34.

—— (1997a) 'Models of Citizenship: Defining European Identity and Citizenship', *Citizenship Studies*, 1 (3): 285–303.

—— (1997b) 'Habermas and Occidental Rationalism: Moral Learning, The Politics of Identity and the Cultural Limits of Ethical Universalism', *Sociological Theory*, 15 (1): 30–59.

—— (1997c) *Social Theory in a Changing World* (Cambridge: Polity).

—— (1998) 'Redefining Political Culture Today: From Identity to the Politics of Identity', in U. Hedtoft (ed.), *Political Symbols, Symbolic Politics: Europe between Unity and Fragmentation* (Aldershot: Ashgate).

—— (2000a) *Modernity and Postmodernity: Knowledge, Power, and the Self* (London: Sage).

—— (2000b) *Citizenship in a Global Age* (Buckingham: Open University Press).

Douglas, M. and Friedmann, J. (eds) (1998) *Cities for Citizens* (Chichester: Wiley).

Drysek, J. (1990) *Discursive Democracy: Politics, Policy and Political Science* (Cambridge: Cambridge University Press).

Gos, J. (1997) 'Representing and Re-presenting the Contemporary City', *Urban Geography*, 18 (2): 180–8.

Habermas, J. (1989a) *The Structural Transformation of the Public Sphere* (Cambridge: Polity).

—— (1989b) 'Modern and Post-modern Architecture', in *The New Conservatism* (Cambridge: Polity).

—— (1993) 'Further Reflections of the Public Sphere', in C. Calhoun (ed.), *Habermas and The Public Sphere* (Cambridge, MA: MIT Press).

—— (1996) *Between Facts and Norms: A Contribution to a Discursive Theory of Law and Democracy* (Cambridge: Polity).

—— (1998) *The Inclusion of Others: Studies in Political Theory* (Cambridge, MA: MIT Press).

Harding, A. (1997) 'Urban Regimes in a Europe of the Cities?', *European Urban and Regional Studies*, 4 (4): 291–314.

Hooghe, L. (1995) 'Subnational Mobilization in the European Union', *West European Politics*, 18: 175–98.

Jacobsen, D. (1997) *Rights Across Borders: Immigrants and the Decline of Citizenship* (Baltimore: Johns Hopkins University).

Leach, N. (ed.) (1999) *Architecture and Revolution: Contemporary Perspectives on Central and Eastern Europe* (London: Routledge).

Lefebvre, H. (1991) *The Production of Space* (Oxford: Blackwell).

—— (1996) *Writings on the City*, E. Kofman and E. Lebas (eds) (Oxford: Blackwell).

Lefort, C. (1986) *The Political Forms of Modern Society*, E. Kofman and E. Lebas (eds) (Cambridge: Polity).

Majone, G. (1996) *Regulating Europe* (London: Routledge).

Marris, P. (1998) 'Planning and Civil Society in the Twenty-first Century', in M. Douglas and J. Friedmann (eds), *Cities for Citizens* (Chichester and New York: Wiley).

Mayer, M. (1992) 'The Shifting Local Political System in European Cities', in M. Dunford and G. Kafkalas (eds), *Cities and Regions in the New Europe* (London: Belhaven).

Milward, A. (1992) *The European Rescue of the Nation State* (London: Routledge).

Mingione, E. (1991) *Fragmented Societies: A Sociology of Economic Life beyond the Market Paradigm* (Oxford: Blackwell).

Moulaert, F. and Scott, A. (eds) (1996) *Cities, Enterprises and Society on the Eve of the 21st Century* (London: Pinter).

Mumford, L. (1961) *The City in History* (New York: Harcourt, Brace and World).

Raban, J. (1988) *Soft City* (London: Collins Harvill).

Rokkan, S. (1980) 'Eine Familie von Modellen für die vergleichende Geschichte Europas', *Zeitschrift für Sociologie*, 9 (2).

Sennett, R. (1990) *The Conscience of the Eye* (London: Faber).

Sharpe, L. (ed.) (1993) *The Rise of the Meso Government in Europe* (London: Sage).

Smith, N. (1996) *The New Urban Frontier: Gentrification and the Revanchist City* (London: Routledge).

Soja, E. (1996) *Third Space: Journeys to Los Angeles and Other Real- And-Imagined Places* (Oxford: Blackwell).

Soysal, Y. (1994) *Limits of Citizenship: Migrants and Postnational Membership in Europe* (Chicago: Chicago University Press).

Swartz, D. (1997) *Power and Culture: The Sociology of Pierre Bourdieu* (Chicago: Chicago University Press).

Tarrow, S. (1995) 'The Europeanisation of Conflict: Reflections from a Social Movement Perspective', *West European Politics*, 18 (2): 223–51.

Therborn, G. (1995) *European Modernity and Beyond: The Trajectory of European Societies, 1945–2000* (London: Sage).

Tilly, C. (1992) *Coercion, Capital and European States, AD 990–1990* (Oxford: Blackwell).

——— (1994) *Cities and the Rise of States in Europe* (Boulder, CO: Westview).

Urry, J. (1995) *Consuming Places* (London: Routledge).

Weber, M. (1958) *The City* (New York: Free Press).

Wintle, M. (ed.) (1996) *Culture and Identity in Europe* (Aldershot: Avebury).

Zukin, S. (1995) *The Culture of Cities* (Oxford: Blackwell).

Part II

Government, virtue, power

5 Governing cities, governing citizens[1]

Nikolas Rose

The city, for at least two centuries, has been both a problem for government and a permanent incitement to government. Modern cities are not so much entities but more like accidental agglomerations of forces, sedimented layers and fractures overlaid through time and space, seeping out at the edges, impossible to reduce to any single principle or determination except that illusion of unity and stability conferred by the proper name. Hence it is not surprising that the recurrent visions of the administered city have always been quickened by a sense of crisis, of the nefarious activities and mobile associations within urbanized territories that elude knowledge and escape regulation. For the first half of the twentieth century, the government of urban existence in the face of such anxieties was always inspired, explicitly or implicitly, by a utopian dream: a dream of the perfect rational city planned in such a way as to maximize the efficiency, tranquillity, order and happiness of its inhabitants while minimizing crime, disorder, vice, squalor, ill health and the like. This implicit utopianism that took the city as a whole as its object has largely been abandoned. Rather than 'planning the city', today, there appears to have been a pluralization of the problematizations of life that take an urban form, and a pluralization of the ways in which programmes have been designed to address them. These seek new ways of harnessing the forces immanent within urban existence: they dream of a city that would almost govern itself.

The active city and the active citizen

In Britain and America in the 1980s it became fashionable to interpret the new strategies that were emerging for governing cities in terms of the rise of 'neo-liberalism'. But subsequent events have shown that these shifts in the rationalities and technologies of government cannot be understood in terms of the temporary dominance of a particular political ideology. What we are seeing here, in my view, is the emergence of a way of thinking about government and its enactment that we can consider as an 'advanced' form of liberalism: one that underpins the programmes and policies set out by forces of almost all political persuasions. These new urban governmentalities are liberal not simply in that they stress the importance of political rule respecting the boundaries of certain zones that are out of its reach, such as markets, communities, private life. Rather, they are liberal in that they reawaken and revitalize the scepticism of classical liberalism of the nineteenth century over the capacity of political action, informed by political reason and political calculation, to act so as to bring about the good of individuals, populations and the nation at large. This is not a recipe for political inaction: as we know, nineteenth century liberal government, as it actually took shape, entailed a whole array of interventions in order to shape and discipline the freedoms and liberties upon which it depended, much to the irritation of liberal philosophers. One of the achievements of the philosophers of 'new liberalism' in the early decades of the twentieth century was to find a way, at a conceptual level, of reconciling the need for state activism with the classical liberal imperatives of autonomy, freedom and individual responsibility. Similarly, the new advanced forms of liberalism that took shape in the last decades of the twentieth century in Europe, Australia, New Zealand, Canada, America and Great Britain – and which were exported elsewhere by such organizations as the World Bank and the IMF – did not preach policies of political withdrawal and abstention. It is true that they attacked 'big government': bloated bureaucracies and civil services; complacent and patronizing professionals; the fostering of tutelage and dependency; the belief that the state could maximize economic, social and individual well-being through policies of 'tax and spend'. But they did not demand a return to the minimalist 'night-watchman' state imagined by the neo-liberal gurus of the 1970s and 1980s. Rather, they sought a new role for the political apparatus as merely one partner in government, facilitating, enabling, stimulating, shaping, inciting the self-governing activities of a multitude of dispersed entities – associations, firms, communities, individuals – who would take onto themselves many of the powers, and the responsibilities previously annexed by 'the state'.

The characteristics of contemporary strategies for 'reinventing politics' are familiar: downsizing the state, decentralizing decision-making, devolving power to intermediate bodies such as trusts or associations, privatizing many functions previously part of the state machinery and opening them up to commercial pressures and business styles of management, introducing managerialism and competitive pressures into the residual state apparatus, displacing the substantive knowledge of the welfare professionals by the knowledge of examination, scrutiny and review undertaken by accountants and consultants. In relation to urban politics, these have entailed something of an assault on the old democratic enclaves of local government, now represented as hidebound by bureaucracy and riddled with nepotism. The tendency is to bypass the traditional democratic mechanisms of the periodic vote for an elected representative with all manner of newer democratic techniques – consultations, surveys, opinion polls, citizens juries, focus groups, tele-democracy and the like. Functions of 'democratic' local government – from street cleaning to urban regeneration – have been devolved to a multiplicity of private firms or public-private partnerships. This simultaneously pluralizes the agencies and entities involved in governing, involves regulation through the techniques of the 'new public management', and transforms political control, which now operates 'at a distance' through setting budgets, targets, standards and objectives, all overseen by the ubiquitous techniques of monitoring and audit. These strategies thus involve the generation of autonomy plus responsibility. They multiply the agencies of government while enveloping them within new forms of control. The autonomy of political actors is to be shaped and used to govern more economically and more effectively. This is thought to require a reduction in the scope of direct management of human affairs by state-organized programmes and technologies, and an increase in the extent to which the government of diverse domains is enacted by the decisions and choices of relatively autonomous entities – whether these are firms, organizations such as hospitals, professionals such as doctors, community bodies and associations, or individuals themselves – in the light of their own assessment of their interests, needs and desires and the ways in which they may be advanced in a particular environment of rewards and sanctions.

These 'advanced' liberal strategies conceive of citizens, individually and collectively, as ideally and potentially 'active' in their own government. The logic of the market, in which economic agents are viewed as calculating actors striving to realize and actualize themselves through their choices in a lifeworld, according to the information that they have at their disposal, are generalized to areas previously thought immune – to all the decisions individuals and groups make about their lives in relation to the education of their children, the disposal of their income for housing or for pleasure, the investment of their energies in law-abiding enterprise or in crime, and indeed their choices about who should govern them and how. These new forms of government through freedom multiply the points at which the citizen has to play his or her part in the games that govern them. But, inescapably, they also multiply the junctures where these games are opened up to uncertainty and risk, and to contestation and redirection.

I follow James Tully here in thinking of citizenship games as practices, with certain implicit or explicit rules, that make certain actions thinkable, possible and meaningful, and in doing so actually constitute the players, or shape what it is to be a citizen (Tully, 1999). There are, of course, different ways of taking this metaphor of games and rules. One way of thinking about these games implies that the rules are fixed, given, closed, imposed, impervious to change. Those who want to play at all must obey them, because not to obey is to be excluded from the game. Some games of citizenship make themselves more or less resistant to modification, and some forms of contestation actually confirm the rules of the game. But while such aspects are clearly present in our contemporary games of citizenship, they are less closed than this implies: their rules are open to modification by the players themselves and the games can be played to many different ends. Contemporary games of citizenship, especially those that make up urban existence, contain multiple possibilities for modification: in the way in which they are played one can see the ways in which certain individual or collective lines of flight can challenge, subvert or modify the rules, can introduce something new.

Despite their celebrated 'individualism', the games of citizenship promoted by the right-wing versions of advanced liberalism located the autonomy of the individual within a set of 'natural' relations of concern and commitment – counterpoised to the 'artificial' bonds supposed to exist between individuals and their society – embodied most clearly in the family and kinship but also extending to less immediate communities of allegiance such as those of religion, voluntary associations and 'nation'. These imaginary bonds of allegiance have been accentuated even further in our contemporary games of urban citizenship. The citizens who are imagined here are not the social citizens who formed the final stage of T.H. Marshall's tale of the evolution of citizenship. Citizenship is understood as formed by allegiance to something closer, something more natural, arising out of the lived experience of modern existence: community. This is not a relation of citizen and community in terms of blood, descent, lineage, tradition, fixity, mechanical solidarity and the like, but a relation of identification. Citizens are here imagined as bound to communities through ties of allegiance, affinity and mutual recognition, and as acquiring their identities – thought of as a complexity of values, beliefs, norms of conduct, styles of existence, relations to authority, techniques of self-management, ways of resolving dilemmas and coping with fate – in and through these identifications. Note that community, here, includes the values of love, care, emotion, solidarity, sharing, self-sacrifice and so forth, which some feminist philosophers mistakenly think have been excluded or marginalized by a rationalistic patriarchal world. Community here is construed as natural: unlike 'society', it is not a political fabrication. But community also must be built, must be made real, must be brought into being by campaigns of consciousness raising, by pressure groups and community activists, and increasingly by acts of political government themselves.

Advanced liberal forms of government rest in new ways upon the activation of the powers of the citizen. In doing so, they involve new ways of recognizing those who are citizens. As Tully suggests, this involves a number of things: binding them into the games as players of certain types (for example, active citizens); generating novel forms of exclusion of those who cannot meet the criteria for recognition (for example, the underclass or 'three strikes and you are out', as citizenship has to be earned by certain types of conduct); generating new practices of reformation to turn recalcitrant subjects into recognizable citizens (for example, citizenship education, reconstruction of the will); and stimulating new formations of the demands for recognition as citizens capable of playing the games, or as requiring a modification of the games to allow certain identities to be included (for example, gay marriages). Crucially, the citizen as member of a community is to be made responsible for his or her fate as well as for that of family, kin and neighbours. Here we see all the arguments for reviving the community: Etzioni-style communitarianism as political cure-all; Fukuyama-style community as trust relations for economic success;

Himmelfarb/Gingrich-style community as neo-conservative politics of the remoralization of America; multicultural-style demands for communities of identity to be recognized; and the emphasis on 'social capital' in the policies from those of the World Bank to those of the British proponents of the Third Way. Government is to work in partnership with citizens to enhance the levels of civic engagement in all manner of urban activities – from residents groups to churches, Parent-Teacher Associations, drop-in centres for the homeless and choral societies – thus promoting the networks, norms, trust and relationships within which citizens cooperate for mutual benefit, and so generating the public engagement necessary to overcome poverty, reduce crime and violence, enhance solidarity, boost economic development and much more.

The urban politics of citizenship today

Of course, city and citizenship have long been linked. The origin of the public sphere wherein modern citizenship took shape has been traced to the specific form of civility brought into existence by the intercourse among free burghers made possible by the towns; and in the eighteenth century, coffee houses, newspapers and popular literature produced both a certain form of public persona and a certain form of private subjectivity. Critical theorists in particular have mourned the transformation and potential liquidation of the public sphere with the rise of a mass media, of public opinion pollsters and of a variety of other ways of manipulation to produce pseudo-participation (Habermas, 1989; Koselleck, 1988, p. 66). While the limited forms of citizenship in the nineteenth century stressed the moral proprieties of the few, the universalistic citizenship of social welfare societies over the first half of the twentieth century was to be solidaristic and responsible, with social duties matching individual rights. Over the past two decades, however, we have seen the emergence of a novel way of imagining the citizen and the links between private subjectivities and will and the public good. Citizenship – ceasing to be a kind of 'possession' or simple right of persons – has taken on a relational form. Citizenship is as much a capacity to act in relation to the particular circumstances of one's environment, as well as in relation to others, as it is a 'right' conferred by the state. If the city is again central here it is in that – as with the Ancient Greeks – the city can be imagined as a field of competitive relations between individuals in the context of a specifiable environment; and also in that – insofar as it is a concrete, localized space – the city can take over from the state as the primary reference point of citizenship. This transformation from citizenship as possession to citizenship as capacity is embodied in the image of the active and entrepreneurial citizen who seeks to maximize his or her lifestyle through acts of choice, linked not so much into a homogeneous social field as into overlapping but incommensurate communities of allegiance and moral obligation.

The multiple projects of contemporary urban government work with these presuppositions about urban citizenship in terms of activity and obligation, entrepreneurship and allegiance, in which rights in the city are as much about duties as they are about entitlements. Each tries to govern through a certain kind of citizenship game. Each, by virtue of its dependence on an active practice of citizenship, opens the possibilities for a certain agonism. This political agonism is not a traditional politics of the party, the programme, the strategy for the organized transformation of society or the claim to be able to implement a programme of better government. Rather, these minor practices of citizen formation are linked to a politics of the minor, of cramped spaces, of action on the here and now, of attempts to reshape what is possible in specific spaces of immediate action, which may connect up and destabilize larger circuits of power. Strategies of governing through citizenship are inescapably risky because what they demand of citizens may be refused, or reversed and redirected as a demand from citizens for a modification of the games that govern them, and through which they are supposed to govern themselves. Four brief examples may clarify this argument.

Healthy cities

The city has long been imagined as a threat to health: an agglomeration of dangers and hazards to be governed in order to prevent or minimize the harms immanent to urban forms of human and inhuman associations. But in recent decades, a new image of the city has come to dominate the urban imagination. For the planners of the first half of the twentieth century, the city could, in its optimum form, be constructed, almost *ab initio*, as a machine for health. But more recently, a new image of the healthy city has emerged: the city as a network of living practices of well-being. This is not a matter of imposing some rational, sterile, planned diagram of sanitary existence. Rather, the aim is to configure the forces immanent to urban life, to shape the ecology of the city in order to maximize the processes that would enhance the well-being of its inhabitants individually and in their 'communities', and to minimize those that would threaten them. All aspects of urban life are now understood as factors that can be instrumentalized in the name of a norm of maximized health: health now appears, simultaneously, as a maximization of the values of community, public safety, economic development, family life. Roads, traffic and pollution, zoning, the design of buildings and open spaces, the organization of shopping locales, and other elements of 'urban design' are to be suffused with this 'ecological' concern for health. Further, the activities of health profession-als, as well as the media, local politicians, trade unions, educationalists, representatives of non-governmental organizations, local community 'grassroots' organizations and others are brought into an alliance that would perceive and act upon all aspects of urban existence – jobs, housing, environ-ment, public safety, diet, transport – not just to ward off sickness but to promote well-being.

In the name of well-being, urban communities are to be empowered such that they are collectively and individually made responsible for their own healthiness. In other words, health is not simply a value in its own right, but rather a resource within a whole spiral of positive values that can be made to breed and spread in the urban ecology. In this vision of urban health, the very idea of disease in the city has been transformed. It is no longer imagined in epidemic form – the invasion of the urban milieu by cholera or typhus, putting its inhabitants at risk of infection. Rather, disease, and ill health more generally, are imagined in terms of activities – diet and coronary heart disease, smoking and lung cancer, obesity and all manner of threats to health – and relationships – unsafe sex and HIV, rave parties and drugs. We no longer have the sick on the one side of a division, the healthy on the other – we are all, actually or potentially, sick, and health is not a state to be striven for only when one falls ill, it is something to be maintained by what we do at every moment of our everyday lives. Threats to well-being are immanent to the life of the active individual: they result from a breakdown of controls on conduct, the failure to develop a healthy lifestyle, to eat properly, to manage stress. But threats to well-being also inhere in the relations of individuals to their environment, which can exacerbate or minimize the risks, not merely because of the levels of pathogens – physical and psychological – circulating within it, but also because of the styles of living which are promoted within particular communities.

The healthy citizen exercises active self-responsibility in a health-conscious community. This is not only because one can only be held responsible on the condition that one possesses the good health to exercise one's responsibility, but also because the health field has itself become an arena of responsibility. The domain of health has become a novel and paradigmatic kind of civic space, where the exercise of a popular ascetic of self-control will be implanted and augmented through a community politics of healthy living, by stress clinics, and exercise centres, by healthy diets in factory canteens and local health promotion campaigns. The imperative of health thus becomes a signifier of a wider – civic, governmental – obligation of citizenship in a responsible community. The healthy city is not a city of minimal disease and social contentment, it is an active organic striving for its own maximization against all that which would threaten it, including the threats that it secretes as part of its very existence. But as the individual aspirations of citizens to their own health are enhanced, their complaints, disaffections and demands achieve a new significance, and new points of application and leverage develop within the practices that seek to govern their conduct in the name of health.

Risky cities

Since the nineteenth century, the criminal character of urban space has been charted by the police forces of each nation through the collection, classification and presentation of the statistics of crime. Perhaps this always gave rise to an image of the city in terms of zones of danger and safety, and to a way of living in the city informed by a perception of the relative riskiness of particular zones. Riskiness, of course, was not merely a negative value: risk-taking in the city is a matter not only of an awareness of hazards of assault and robbery, but also of an active pursuit of the prospects of excitement, sexual gratification, debauchery, licence, gambling and the like. But our current image of the criminogenic city governmentalizes risk as a spatialization of thought and intervention. Using techniques pioneered by the commercial demands of insurance, and based on informatics and postcode mapping, this spatialization is now at the molecular level of urban existence. The contemporary city is thus visualized as a distribution of risks: one of those maps with coloured overlays where each layer marks out a particular breed of riskiness – of street crime, of sexual assault, of burglary, of car theft, of beggars and marginal persons, of single-parent families and ethnic minorities. Unlike the moral topographies of urban space developed in the mid-nineteenth century, the contemporary urban topography of risk indicates less a concrete statistic attached to a locale, and more a factor calculated through the amalgamation of a concatenation of 'indicators' to each of which may be attached a certain probability of a less than optimal outcome of an activity – shopping, parking a car, buying a house, walking to the shops. Risk is thus as much a feature of spatialization itself as it is of the particular 'characteristics' of people that inhabit certain zones. It is to be governed through the continual monitoring and assessment of risk in relation to urban space and place, and through the active adoption of strategies of risk reduction by authorities, communities and individuals.

One vision for urban risk reduction is animated by the dream of a new separation of the virtuous and the vicious, a new and clear spatialization of danger into safe zones and risk zones. Fictional representations of urban life capture this well: such as in the so-called 'Blade Runner' scenario, in which a division is attempted – and always threatened – between the safe spaces of civility – in certain secured zones, policed buildings, civilized communities with broad boulevards, watered gardens, elegant interiors and the like – and the space lying outside the limits of these secure spaces, full of threat, chaos and danger but also excitement, seduction, glamour, glitter, drugs, sex and 'real life', 'the glop', the 'sprawl'. This fictional representation is imitated in real life in a defensive spatialization that has come to shape city space: shopping malls and shopping centres with their own internal security systems, guarded at their perimeters and monitored by close circuit TV; and, 'contractual' communities with walls around them and entrances controlled by security guards, as in the so-called gated communities that have arisen from Istanbul to Islington. Mike Davis is right in one respect to regard these developments as entailing the *death* of the city: for what would be marked by such developments would be the death of a particular kind of *liberal* dream of the city as an open, civilized and civilizing habitat for the existence of free citizens (see also Davis, 1988, p. 87).

Hence it is not surprising that this image of government of risk through spatial separation is increasingly coming under challenge by another, in which security is not thought of in absolute terms. In this image, there can be no inherently safe locales or activities and, in addition, there must be no 'no-go' zones where law-abiding citizens will not venture and where the innocent are effectively held hostage by criminal anti-citizens. Risk reduction is to form part of the moral responsibility of urban citizens themselves. This brings into alignment a whole array of discrepant issues within a single programmable domain – from domestic violence to street crime, from burglary to car theft, from routes for travel to arrangements for children's play areas. Safer Cities initiatives, Neighbourhood Watch and other community safety programmes work by enrolling citizens in the practices of crime reduction: planning our travel arrangements, securing our homes and property, instrumentalizing our daily activities in the name of our own security, guided by police, community safety officers and a host of other experts of risk. But they also seek to reawaken in citizens their own moral responsibilities to the policing of conduct, in particular, through the popularity of such notions as 'zero tolerance' and the 'broken windows thesis' – the argument that toleration of minor breaches of civility sows the seeds of a more dangerous and insidious criminal culture.

This new image of citizenship must be understood in relation to that which opposes it, a kind of anti-citizen that is a constant enticement and threat to the project of citizenship itself. The emergence of the notion of exclusion to characterize those who previously constituted the social problem group defines these non-citizens or anti-citizens not in terms of substantive characteristics but in relational terms; that is, it is a question of their distance from the circuits of inclusion into virtuous citizenship. The 'excluded' might make it into citizenship if they can only be connected up to the right networks of community and the requisite channels of enterprise. Exclusion is imagined in a spatial form, in the form of excluded and marginal spaces within the urban fabric itself, enclosures where the lines of virtuous inclusion have somehow become disconnected and failed to flow: not so much a ghetto, more a precise localization of the marginal which is given the name of an estate, a housing project, an urban enclave, for example Spitalfields, Broadwater Farm. In these enclaves, the links of citizenship and community have turned against themselves, and all those things which would connect individuals into the networks of inclusion have instead produced negative feedback: family life, welfare solidarity and state education are all seen as machines for disconnection rather than for connection. Hence the need to reawaken in these zones the dormant moral energies of those who exist within them: in neighbourhood-based schemes for the reclamation of the streets from drug dealers and prostitutes; in estate-based schemes for regeneration which target the anti-social, name and shame them, refuse to be terrorized by their immoral and criminal conduct, and so forth. Once more, government of risk is to proliferate at a molecular level through the enrolment of the capacities and commitments immanent to citizens themselves.

Cities of enterprise

In contrast to the classical liberal diagram, the economic salience of the city has ceased to be thought of simply in terms of a space or a milieu: it is a node within pathways of mobility, a matrix of flows, a point of connection and rebranching of lines of activity which connect persons, processes and things. No doubt mercantilism, capitalism, colonialism, imperialism were always matters of flows over distance and concentrations in space: cities as economic concentrations of raw materials, labour power, wealth, a local market; trade routes, exports, imports, competition and so forth as economic networks into which each was integrated to a greater or lesser degree. But the contemporary images of globalization and localization spatialize economic activity in new ways. A growing literature argues that the route to economic success lies in the establishment of entrepreneurial localities with fluid and flexible internal economic arrangements dependent upon physical proximity, and competing with one another on a world market. The idea of a 'local economy' informs economic policy at the regional level and, increasingly, within urban government itself. As the boundaries and unity of national economies are thought to be breached by flows of goods, money, information, expertise, profit and labour, and around global networks, 'local economies' are understood as almost the only geographical zones where capital, labour, raw materials and expertise can be captured and acted upon. Perhaps more significantly, their novelty lies in the relations established between previously nomadic forces, in the attempt to connect the restless energy of the entrepreneur with more than simply the pursuit of maximum profit. The relation of capital to the urban should be more than that of a raiding party with its prey: it should take a stake in the shaping and destiny of the urban itself, in the reshaping of its decayed docklands and abandoned factories into shopping malls and waterfronts, in the rebuilding of its concrete and windswept wastelands into malls and markets, in the reconstruction of its estates so that they shift from spaces for the residential storage of labourers at maximum density into communities of homes that activate the dreams of possession and self-improvement necessary to bind the energies of young men and women into the regimes of civility.

There are, of course, different versions of this new economic localism. It can have a left-wing, corporatist formulation, as in some arguments on the governmental requirements and inter-agency relations necessary to promote the interaction, trust, cooperation and mutual obligation necessary for flexible specialization. Or it can have an entrepreneurial form: the city is an entity to be made entrepreneurial in and through acting upon the enterprising capacities of different 'partners' or 'stake-holders', stimulating their competitiveness, their rivalry, their capacity to meet the challenge of economic modernization in a harsh ecology full of Pacific tigers and other voracious beasts in an economic struggle for the survival of the fittest in which cities, rather than nations, are the key actors. It is in these terms that it has now been possible to render the city as an economic subject, not a favourable geographical location on coast, river, trade routes, nor as a milieu within which some prosper and some strive and all benefit from their enterprise, but as itself an economic actor in the world economy of cities, such that one can talk about the remarkable revival of Glasgow, the decline of Sunderland, or the reawakening of Baltimore. In each case what is declining or reviving is a kind of ethico-economic character of enterprise imbuing a city as a whole by virtue of the motivation, the sense of pride and competitiveness, the installation of a relentless rivalry between cities and regions mobilized by means of the enterprise of each and of all (see also Sassen, 1991; Knox and Taylor, 1995; King, 1990).

The urban economy, here, has a kind of quasi-organic life of its own: it can be in health, decline or recovery, it can be regenerated by calculated means of intervention, it is in competition with other 'local economies', and it must therefore have its own peculiarities and advantages that will provide it with a niche within this competitive ecology of local economies – its labour force, its transportation systems, its rates of local tax and subsidy, its skill levels and so on – in order to attract inward investment and the like. Increasingly, and perhaps surprisingly, economic regeneration at this local level is itself understood in terms of new games of citizenship. On the one hand, this is a matter of entrepreneurship, of acting upon the dependency culture fostered in the heart of industrial urban decline, the lack of entrepreneurship which is the legacy of an age of mass factory employment now past. But on the other hand, it is a matter of recreating communities of obligation and allegiance within these zones. The recent upsurge of interest in trust relations as a condition of economic health, the communitarian emphasis upon civic commitment as a key factor in economic development, the arguments of social capital theorists that very local features of moral relations – networks, norms, trust and so forth – facilitate coordination and cooperation, minimize transaction costs, serve as vital sources of economic information and so on – all these make economic regeneration a matter of local economic citizenship. The immanent productive capacities of the city are to be released by action upon the subjects and agents who make up its economy. A whole range of initiatives for economic regeneration have taken shape, which operate through action on the culture of enterprise within cities, seeking simultaneously to maximize the enterprise of these constituents of the labour force now thought of in terms of their location and residence, and to maximize the relations of obligation which they feel to others, not in a society or a nation, but in a localized and particular network of commitment, allegiance and reciprocal responsibility.

Cities of pleasure

From at least the nineteenth century, the city has been represented, in literature and in documentary descriptions, as promoting a certain type of mentality and sociality. These analyses have usually had a negative tone. First, perhaps, it was a matter of the production of certain degenerate characters within the city: Baudelaire's rag-pickers, Mayhew's costermongers, Booth's forgotten classes, Engels' proletariat – in short, misbegotten peoples who have little in common beyond their poverty, exclusion and the territory they inhabit, and little to lose but their misery. The city becomes a site for investigation of these strange underclasses or non-classes; an unknown territory like 'darkest

Africa' to be exposed by intrepid explorers, a laboratory for investigations into 'unknown England' (see also Stallybrass and White, 1986). The urban reportage of the nineteenth century sought to capture these forms of debased subjectivity secreted by the urban. But it also represented, for its proponents, a kind of work upon the self, a search for sensation which was made possible by urban existence itself: this is why the urban explorers are so often to be seen taking a walk.

Hence the other side of urban sociality which is so often written about: the city as the place for the chance encounter, as, in Judith Walkowitz's terms, the *City of Dreadful Delight* (Walkowitz, 1992). In one version of this argument, the city produces a kind of *alienated* sociality in the city dweller. Urban existence sunders social bonds and replaces them by a mass of impersonal relations; the city is the place where there are masses in close, almost paranoiac, contiguity, yet where interpersonal relations are cold and artificial. And, at the same time, the city subjects the human psyche to shocks, sensations, impressions and experiences that are overwhelming, simultaneously exciting and enervating the character of the urban dweller and producing a particular urban mentality. But, from Walter Benjamin to the contemporary post-modern romances of the urban *flâneur* and *flâneuse*, of department stores, shopping malls and the 'public sphere', another version has been made popular – the city as a site of a peculiarly civilized array of pleasures. It is the site of the quintessentially civic pleasure of the bohemian promenade, of public life and the encounter of one with another in the civilized spaces of the city centre street with its window displays, its pubs and clubs, its museums and galleries. And it is the site of the transgressive pleasure that escapes the governmental dream of a purified, hygienic, moral space inhabited by a well-regulated population: it is the opaque, excessive, ungoverned city, a fecund, heterogeneous, spontaneous, dangerous, promiscuous warren of 'other spaces' where pleasure is spiced with danger, and where desire can run free in alleyways, tenements, clubs, bars, theatres, music halls and gambling dens (see also Donald, 1992).

But pleasure has not evaded the networks of capture that filiate the advanced liberal city: transgression is itself to be brought back into line and offered up as a package of commodified contentment. The city of pleasure celebrated in poetry, novels, films and systematized in social theory has itself been fed into the programmatic imagination, in an alliance between city politics and commercial imperatives. A multitude of projects, in almost all major cities, seek to reshape the real city according to this image of pleasure, not least in order to enter into the competitive market for urban tourism. In these programmes and projects, the image of urban space as providing a multitude of spontaneous encounters, of sudden glimpses of architectural oddities and esoteric markets, of bustling yet safe public spaces, this urban experience, seen by its celebrants as arising out of the intersection and accumulation of thousands of spontaneous histories and schemes, has been transformed into calculated, rationalized and repetitive programmes for reshaping waterfronts and port areas, sites of old buildings, palaces, warehouses, piers, vegetable markets and the like into tourist attractions and urban theme parks, each more hyper-real than real. Disused wharves become craft markets. Victorian structures that accommodated carcasses of sheep and cows on their way to butchers, sacks of potatoes and cauliflower on their way to corner shops are now filled with trendy boutiques and cafes. Sectors of space once occupied, for specifiable economic and other reasons, by people of Chinese extraction become 'Chinatown' and are proclaimed by street signs and with elaborate and publicly funded festivals to mark the start of the Chinese year of a particular animal. Each 'conservation area', each 'heritage trail' is populated, not by the spontaneous movements of the urban inhabitants, but by those transported by tour coaches, clutching guidebooks, video cameras and postcards. The city becomes not so much a complex of dangerous and compelling spaces of promises and gratifications, but a series of packaged zones of enjoyment, managed by an alliance of urban planners, entrepreneurs, local politicians and quasi-governmental 'regeneration' agencies. But here, once more, urban inhabitants are required to play their part in these games of heritage, not only exploiting them commercially through all sorts of tourist-dependent enterprises, but also promoting their own micro-cultures of bohemian, gay or alternative lifestyles, and making their own demands for the rerouting of traffic, the refurbishment of buildings, the mitigation of taxes and much more in the name of the unique qualities of pleasure offered by their particular habitat.

A new political diagram?

Since at least the nineteenth century, the urban has been the site par excellence of the politics of plural forces, of philanthropists, pressure groups, localities, neighbourhoods, local business interests and the like; and the urban politics of the twentieth century is a tangle of alliances, conflicts, stand-offs, incorporations, bribes and corruptions in the relations between these local forces and the aspirations of local politicians. In the second half of this century, between the territorializing ambitions of municipalism and the work of *interessement* undertaken by the indigenous tribes of the urban space – residents, entrepreneurs, traders, construction firms, utility suppliers and carpetbaggers – one saw a new plane of activity, the work of a thousand agencies operating in the name of urban renewal on educational enrichment, housing action, crime prevention, drug education, community responsibility and so on. Hence the creativity of the new diagram of urban politics should not be overdramatized, nor seen as essentially characterized by reaction. The plethora of associations, forums, regeneration agencies, enterprises, partnerships, stakeholders and the like brought into existence by these novel forms of urban government and its games of citizenship are not novel because they pluralize and fragment a previously organized set of political forces traversing urban space. Of course in part their novelty lies in the well-explored disenchantment with representative democracy at the local level and the invention of new forms of accountability, from those of the contract to those which seek to re-engineer community associations as agencies of regulation. But more significant, in my view, is the displacement of an earlier notion of social space by the micro-moral territory of the community, and the emergence of new games of citizenship that operate in terms of the relations between community and subjectivity, between collective responsibilities and an ethic of personal obligation.

It is in terms of this new ethical space of the community – the ways of understanding it, the passions that motivate it, the pathologies that inhere in it, the potentials that it offers up – that all our new forms of urban governmentality operate. At its most general, in contemporary games of citizenship, citizenship is no longer primarily realized in a relation with the state. Indeed, the idea that it was is probably a false path opened up by T.H. Marshall's famous essay on citizenship. Nor does citizenship inhere in participation in a single 'public sphere', even if this is understood as a diversified 'civil society'. What we have are a set of dispersed and non-totalized practices within which games of citizenship must be played. Games of citizenship today entail acts of free but responsible choice in a variety of private, corporate and quasi-public practices, from working to shopping. The citizen as consumer is to become an active agent in the regulation of professional expertise. The citizen as prudent is to become an active agent in the provision of security. The citizen as employee is to become an active agent in the regeneration of industry. The citizen as consumer is to be an agent for innovation, quality and competitiveness. The citizen as inhabitant is to enhance economic development through his or her intimate knowledge of the economic environment, through networks of trust and reciprocity. The citizen is to enact his or her democratic obligations as a form of consumption through new techniques such as focus groups and attitude research. In these contemporary 'post-political' games of citizenship, and in the new expectations and hopes attached to the ethical comportment of citizens, new agonistic possibilities open up. It is in this respect that we can see, in the new urban activism, the signs of a new radical politics of urban citizenship.

Note

1 This chapter is largely drawn from a piece authored jointly with Thomas Osborne and published as 'Governing cities', in E. Isin, T. Osborne and N. Rose, 1998, *Governing Cities: Liberalism, Neoliberalism and Advanced Liberalism*, Urban Studies Working Paper no. 19, York University, Toronto, Canada.

Bibliography

Davis, M. (1988) 'Urban Renaissance and the Spirit of Post-modernism', in E.A. Kaplan (ed.), *Post-modernism and its Discontents* (London: Verso).

Donald, J. (1992) 'Metropolis: The City as Text', in R. Bocock and K. Thompson (eds), *Social and Cultural Forms of Modernity* (Cambridge: Polity).

Habermas, J. (1989) *The Structural Transformation of the Public Sphere*, trans. T. Burger and F. Lawrence (Cambridge: Polity).

King, A. (1990) *Global Cities* (London: Routledge).

Knox, P. and Taylor, P. (1995) *World Cities in a World System* (Cambridge: Cambridge University Press).

Koselleck, R. (1988) *Critique and Crisis: Enlightenment and the Pathogenesis of Modern Society* (Oxford: Berg).

Sassen, S. (1991) *The Global City: New York, London: Tokyo* (Princeton, NJ: Princeton University Press).

Stallybrass, P. and White, A. (1986) *The Politics and Poetics of Transgression* (London: Methuen).

Tully, J. (1999) 'The Agonic Freedom of Citizens', *Economy and Society*, 23 (2).

Walkowitz, J. (1992) *City of Dreadful Delight: Narratives of Sexual Danger in Late-Victorian London* (London: Virago).

6 Imagining democratic urban citizenship[1]

Janine Brodie

Introduction

This chapter explores the potential for the invention of an urban citizenship in a globalizing era. It argues that the linkages between democracy, citizenship rights and national sovereignty have been dislocated by the multiple processes of globalization. They have shifted political power up to the transnational, out to the private sector and down to the local. These shifts have led some to reconsider the local, particularly the city, as the place to revive democratic citizenship in a globalizing era. The possibilities for an urban citizenship, however, have been insufficiently interrogated, especially with respect to the current transformation of the local through the interlocking processes of decentralization, privatization and individualization. The chapter concludes that the local is a potential, although not obvious, site for citizenship politics in the third millennium. This outcome is dependent on a sustained campaign to reinvent the very idea of the public and to expand the terrain of democratic citizenship.

As we enter the twenty-first century, social scientists, political activists and citizens alike find themselves deeply implicated in a prolonged process of fundamental change, or as Soja puts it, 'a significantly different order and configuration of social, economic and political life' (Soja, 1989, p. 159). After over two decades of restructuring to meet the imperatives of a globalizing international political economy, there is a widespread sense of rupture and disorientation. Most of the organizing signposts of the postwar period have either disappeared or lost their initial intent and meaning – among them, state sovereignty, liberal-democratic citizenship rights, especially social citizenship rights, and collective political identities and alliances. The latter are said to have become 'decentred, dislocated and fragmented' (Hall, 1996, p. 596).

At the same time, it is not obvious what kind of state or politics will take their place. The foundational building blocks of the Keynesian welfare state have been 'hollowed out', stripped of their promise of political emancipation and collective well-being, while the very spaces for liberal democratic politics are no longer particularly apparent or efficacious. Indeed, Mouffe goes so far as to suggest that what is at stake for citizens is politics itself and the distinct possibility of its elimination (Mouffe, 1993, p. 1). Similarly, Turner argues that current changes in global systems have rendered some aspects of postwar liberal-democratic citizenship redundant, if not obsolete (Turner, 1992, p. 58).

Of course, the content and practice of citizenship are neither fixed nor finite. Across the history of liberal democracies, the state has been charged with the codification and enforcement of quite distinct citizenship regimes – a term which entails complex and historically negotiated institutional and discursive underpinnings. Any construction of citizenship assumes an amalgam of compatible political institutions, policy-making practices and patterns of political representation (Jenson, 1997, p. 631). The concept of citizenship, then, includes much more than the idea of formal membership in a national community. It is the object of ongoing political struggle and a pivotal component of a broader historical matrix of governance. In particular, the content of citizenship defines the relation between the state, civil society and the individual.

Over time, citizenship has been associated with different technologies of power, different spaces for political engagement and claims-making on the state, and different webs of inclusion and exclusion. As in the current period, the imperative to 'rethink citizenship' usually coincides with, and in fact is precipitated by, deep ruptures in the prevailing economic, social and political orders. The ascendance of the industrial bourgeoisie out of the ashes of mercantile capitalism, the politicization of a large industrial working class, the feminist and civil rights movements, and postwar decolonialization all brought, in different ways, to different countries, a refashioning and expansion of citizenship rights.

The revised conception of citizenship arising in the West out of the ravages of the Great Depression of the 1930s and the Second World War is particularly germane to the current debate about the meaning of citizenship in an era of globalization. The western postwar citizenship regime was firmly cast within the liberal-progressivist (meso-) discourse of the welfare state (Brodie, 1997, p. 232; Lipietz, 1994). This discourse held that the market should be regulated politically in order to maximize economic stability and collective welfare, that the state should provide social welfare for all of its citizens as a right of citizenship, and that state practices should be guided by a commitment to formal equality and impersonal procedures (Young, 1990, p. 67). In addition to civil and political rights, citizens became bearers of social rights which, in turn, were linked to broader conceptions of progress, rationality, social planning, centralized bureaucratic control and equality (Lipietz, 1994, p. 353).

After a generation of profound upheaval and horrendous experimentation in governance, there was a widespread postwar consensus that finally the right governance formula had been found. The economic, social and political grew together in tandem, each depending on the other, in what some call the 'virtuous circle'. The state took command of the national economy, through fiscal and monetary policy and regulation, to maintain a healthy investment climate, redistribute income, generate demand and provide for the basic needs of its citizens. Class conflict was 'democratically negotiated' through elections, collective bargaining and the protection of workers' rights, thus heralding the 'end of ideology'.

T.H. Marshall's influential story of the evolution of liberal-democratic citizen-ship rights perhaps best illustrates postwar thinking. He argued that citizenship rights evolved from state recognition and protection of civil rights to political rights and, finally, to social rights. In fact, Marshall argued that social citizenship rights, delivered through the welfare state, were a prerequisite for the effective exercise of civil and political rights. For him, social stability and cohesion in modern industrial societies, and the health of democracy itself demanded social rights (Marshall, 1950). It was inconceivable that there would be any turning back from the extension and elaboration of citizenship rights. The personal tragedies of the Great Depression simply could not be revisited.

The postwar conception of citizenship was consistent with the dominant modernization paradigm in the social sciences of the period. This evolution-ary tale of citizenship and its celebration of progress has been criticized for being, among other things, linear, ahistorical, phallocentric and Eurocentric. There is another assumption, however, which has become critical to our understanding of citizenship in an era of globalization. The concept of social citizenship was universalized and decontextualized from the international political economy and the place of the nation-state within it. The postwar guarantee of social rights depended on the complementary interaction of a matrix of historically specific economic, social and political factors and, as any survivor of matrix algebra will attest, the displacement of only one term changes the meaning of all others, shifting the entire logic, coherence and functioning of the ensemble. Globalization, in all its complexity, represents just such a displacement. One of its consequences – the erosion of state sovereignty – has immediate consequences for the exercise of citizenship rights precisely because liberal-democratic citizenship was built around the sovereign nation-state. Globalization has skewed the historical coincidence between national territory, national economy, state sovereignty, citizenship rights and democratic politics. Consequently, 'the very processes of govern-ance seem to be escaping the categories of the nation-state' (Held, 1996, p. 338).

Our present understanding of democracy and citizenship rights seems to be set adrift, lost in space, precipitating a nostalgic search to reground them elsewhere, at the level of either the global or the local. The quest to cultivate citizenship at the level of the local, however, is rife with ambiguity about the point of reference. What is the 'local' in the present context of a globalizing political economy? As discussed below, the multiple ways in which the local itself is now being reconstructed and incorporated into the emerging governing matrix of globalization have not been sufficiently interrogated.

Deterritorialization, reterritorialization and citizenship

Globalization and deterritorialization

Globalization is quickly becoming one of the most overused and least understood words in the English language. The ambiguity surrounding this term has significant political consequences, opening some avenues for political contestation and closing others. Liberal economists and other supporters of global capitalism, for example, tend to define it in narrow market terms. From this perspective, globalization represents progress – the opening of borders and new markets, the end of political interference in the economy, the unencumbered flow of finance and industrial capital, the efficiencies of new communication technologies and transnational corporate organization, and so on. This definition obviously discounts globalization's social and political dimensions and thereby attempts to deflect the idea that the new global economy has concrete and distinct social and political manifestations, or that it requires political surveillance or regulation.

Of course, neo-liberal fundamentalism is profoundly political. It rests on an economic determinism which attempts to trump the very ideas of democratic choice and political intervention. After years of being rehearsed by such mentors as the International Monetary Fund (IMF) and the World Trade Organization (WTO), most of us can recite the mantra by memory. We begin with the religious conviction that all markets, including the international market, are neutral mechanisms which, if left alone, produce competitive and efficient outcomes which eventually 'trickle down' to all. Second, we recall that the emergence of the global economy puts the same demands on all governments. They must maximize exports, reduce spending on social programmes, curtail regulation of business, and facilitate the integration of national economies into regional and international markets (Friedman, 1991, p. 35). As Margaret Thatcher first pronounced, 'there is no alternative'.

Less invested observers, however, depict globalization as a key word for a still unfolding process which involves critical shifts in the spatial organization of political power and social relations (Giddens, 1990), a new discursive formation driving the restructuring of the state, civil society, the political economy and popular culture (Gill, 1995, p. 405), and a new form of state and philosophy of governance (Brodie, 1997). Jan Aart Scholte, in particular, argues that globalization represents an ontological shift from territorial reference points to deterritorialized ones, which, in turn, have transformed the capacities, constituencies and policies of the postwar state. In contrast to those who argue that globalization is not new but simply more of interdependence, internationalization and trade liberalization, Scholte claims that globalization represents the transcendence of social relations from a territorial framework to a 'supra-territorialization' which is increasingly detached from our lived experience of geographic space. The emergence of this deterritorialized political space marks, among other things, the end of sovereign statehood, the construction of supra-territorial political constituencies and the impracticability of achieving democratic governance through the nation-state (Scholte, 1997, pp. 23, 25).

Globalization has changed the policy agendas of western governments, regardless of partisan stripe. The question of who holds the reign of *government* has become increasingly irrelevant with respect to what governments do. This is because globalization has been accompanied by a transformation in the fundamentals of liberal-democratic *governance* – here defined as 'the complex of mechanisms, processes, relationships and institutions through which citizens and groups articulate their interests, exercise their rights and obligations and mediate their differences' (UNDP, 1997b, p. 9). The erosion of state sovereignty is the vexing lynchpin in current debates about the continued vitality of liberal democratic governance. Democratic theory, political practices and alignments and citizenship rights have all been premised upon the foundational assumption of state sovereignty. In the early twenty-first century, however, governments are losing their capacity to shape the contours of the national economy and polity, and national electorates are increasingly at a loss as to how to hold their governments accountable. In a recent publication of the Canadian federal government, the problem was posed in the following way.

> Canada's sovereignty ... is increasingly circumscribed by multilateral arrangements and diluted by the decentralization of knowledge and decision-making. By negotiating away Canadian sovereignty in some key areas, albeit for important reasons, we constrain our ability to make effective domestic decisions in economic and social policy and elsewhere. Harmonization, convergence, labour and capital mobility will increasingly make those decisions for us.
>
> (Canada, Privy Council Office, 1996, p. 4)

Persky muses that now big decisions 'are made outside of all national boundaries, even as they shape lives within all such entities. It is as if global capitalism was headquartered somewhere off the globe' (1992, p. 187).

Globalization and reterritorialization

Students of globalization point out that the state has not disappeared but, instead, has lost, often relinquished, its sovereignty by passing it elsewhere: sideways to the market through privatization, deregulation and self-orchestrated attrition; upwards to international regulatory bodies and binding regional trade agreements; and downwards to the local through decentralization and individualization (Crook et al., 1992, p. 97). In the process, the so-called 'post-sovereign' (Scholte, 1997), 'performative' (Yeatman, 1994), 'competitive' (Cerney, 1990) or 'neo-liberal' (Brodie, 1997) state is fashioning itself as a market player rather than as the purveyor of public goods or as the instrument of democratic will. The neo-liberal state increasingly rejects the idea that the provision of certain goods and services defies the logic of the market and, therefore, must be the purview of the collective, the public. Instead, it measures its own performance by its capacity to commodify and displace public goods and services onto either the market or the individual and home. In other words, the neo-liberal state embraces the ascendancy of the market both *over* the state and *inside* the state. It closes political space, privatizes the postwar political agenda and further marginalizes the already marginalized (Brodie, 1997). Citizens at the millennium are constrained by a very narrow conception of democracy which effectively means voting in and out sets of elites with similar biases toward market provision and private ownership and profit. As Bessis explains, the late twentieth century world has been gripped by the reign of a *pensée unique* – 'a single acceptable way of viewing things'. Neo-classical economics is considered by 'its proponents as being universally valid in both its premises and assumptions' (Bessis, 1995, p. 7).

Later, this chapter argues that the survival of liberal-democratic citizenship in the twenty-first century depends on the contestation of the shift in state sovereignty sideways to the private from the public. Students of globalization, however, have more actively engaged with the political consequences of shifts in state power on the vertical axis, either upwards to the international/transnational or downwards to the local. Globalization, it is argued, is characterized by two seemingly contradictory movements – the simultaneous power shift away from the national to transnational institutions *and* to regional and local bodies (Jessop, 1994, p. 271; Turner, 1992, p. 58). Thomas goes further to suggest that the current situation is characterized by the globalization of economics and the localization of politics (1997, p. vii). Both movements – to the global and to the local – according to Gill, have to be theorized in their own right (1995, p. 404). Social science journals are now swelling with analyses of the multiple manifestations of globalization but, as Held rightly observes, democratic theory's exploration of the global–local problematic is still in its infancy (1996, p. xii).

To date, much of the literature on the democratic implications of globalization has focused on the international dimension. This is understandable given the plethora of international institutions and agreements which now assume primacy over the nation-state: the WTO, the IMF, the European Union (EU), the North American Free Trade Agreement (NAFTA) and the temporarily stalled Multilateral Agreement on Investment (MAI) are obvious examples. This expansion of transnational political space has lead some to argue for a complementary expansion of transnational democracy and democratic institutions. The United Nation's 1992 *Human Development Report*, for example, argues that 'Human society is increasingly taking on a global dimension. Sooner or later it will have to develop the global institutions to match' (UNDP, 1992, p. 78).

Others have focused on the relationship between the expansion of transnational political and economic power and the restructuring of the postwar welfare state. Robert Cox, among others, identifies binding and extensive international institutions and agreements as defining marks of the politics of globalization as well as of the transformation of the postwar state. The argument goes that the state has not had its sovereignty usurped as much as it has surrendered it in response to the 'perceived exigencies' of the new international political economy. Governments are willingly forfeiting their role as managers of national economies and, instead, are facilitating the integration of national spaces into new models of regional and transnational governance. In the process, nation-states themselves have become internationalized (Cox, 1991).

Stephen Gill calls the result the 'new constitutionalism'. This emerging and ever more pervasive regulatory regime emphasizes market efficiency and discipline, while constraining, in critical ways, the terrain of national autonomy and democratic accountability. The new constitutionalism mandates 'the insulation of key aspects of the economy from the influence of politicians or the mass of citizens by imposing, internally and externally, "binding constraints" on the conduct of fiscal, monetary, trade and investment policies' (Gill, 1995, p. 410; Brodie and Smith, 1998). The new constitutionalism, Gill argues, 'confers privileged rights of citizenship and representation on corporate capitalism, whilst constraining the democratization process that has involved struggles for representation for hundred of years' (1995, p. 411). Only to underline this point, documents such as the NAFTA and the proposed MAI refer to the public sector as 'non-conforming measures'. Moreover, both documents make it virtually impossible for its signatories to expand the public sector without paying staggering monetary settlements to private interests. Recently, the head of the OECD, Donald Johnston announced that the approval of the MAI (which limits the actions of all levels of government with respect to capitalist investment and enables corporations to sue democratically elected governments) is a question of 'when and not if'. He explained that the MAI had fallen into trouble because 'you don't conduct negotiations of any agreement in public' (*Globe and Mail*, 26 May 1998, p. B4). These and other factors put flesh on Touraine's bold pronouncement that 'there are no grounds for identifying democracy with the globalization of the economy' (1997, p. 195).

It is perhaps the enormity and evasiveness of the idea of democratizing the global that have led others to explore the possibilities and constraints of reinventing liberal-democratic citizenship at the level of the local. The popular slogan of 'thinking globally and acting locally' conveys the message that many Davids, usually through individual consumption choices of the everyday, can indeed defeat the global Goliath. This prescription has some strategic merit within the current context of globalization. Urban governments have become increasingly important players in the global economy. In contrast to their previous role as an administrative extension of the welfare state and as the most proximate infrastructural and social service providers, local governments have gained relevance as a focus for proactive economic development strategies (Mayer, 1994, p. 317). Increasingly, national populations are concentrating in cities, which, in turn, are being integrated into global capillaries of power and production, frequently bypassing national governments (and sub-national governments in the case of federations). Cities now differentiate themselves as either 'world-class' cities that are integrated as nodes in the new global order or as the local others. In addition, it is also argued that the local is gaining importance because it has become a site of resistance to the process of globalization (Hall, 1996, p. 619). Finally, others suggest that the decline of class politics has given impetus to civic initiatives as a relevant and effective form of political mobilization (Crook et al., 1992, p. 222).

Caroline Andrew argues that all of these factors have encouraged an optimistic scenario about the democratic potential of the local in an era of globalization – that globalization has opened up new political spaces for local actors, collective action and the possibility of innovative connections between local political actors and municipal governments (Andrew, 1997, p. 139). Despite the growing importance of the local, however, the literature is frequently unclear about what, in fact, is meant by the term. Is it an opposition to the national and global, a community, a discursive field, a level of government, the city?

The 'local' and other imagined political spaces

Anderson's commentary on communities also applies to current thinking about the local. Communities, he writes, 'are to be distinguished, not by their falsity/genuineness, but by the style in which they are imagined' (Anderson, 1991, p. 6). The local is imagined in many ways, often as an opposition on a duality such as local/national-global, community/individual, concrete/abstract, near/far and democratic/bureaucratic. At the heart of these distinctions are the notions of physical space and proximity. Consider, for example, Magnusson's recent assessment of the municipality in his aptly titled book *The Search for Political Space*. 'The political space of the municipality', he writes, 'is much more akin to the political space of the world in which we live than is the artificial construction of the state.' 'The municipality', he continues, 'is designed to provide an *enclosure for popular politics*' (1996, p. 10, emphasis mine). This sentiment is echoed by Young in her discussion of the publicity of the city. 'Cities provide important public spaces – streets, parks, plazas – where people stand and sit together, interact and mingle.' Moreover, she contends, politics 'critically depends on the existence of *spaces and forums* to which everyone has access' (Young, 1990, p. 240, emphasis mine). These pronouncements are echoed in international policy circles with respect to the advantages of decentralization. The United Nations Development Program, for example, urges 'governments everywhere' to decentralize in order 'to make them more responsive to global economic changes and to the demands of citizens'. 'Political decentralisation', it continues, 'gives more political clout in decision-making to citizens and their elected representatives, and is usually associated with representative government, citizen participation and democratisation' (UNDP, 1997a, pp. 29–30).

These arguments for the reterritorialization of politics at the level of the local reflect the growing spatial disorientations associated with globalization.

The local connotes a sense of place that is concrete, familiar and bounded, seemingly more compatible with the everyday concerns of citizens (Giddens, 1990, p. 18; Young, 1990, p. 227). It advances the ideas of community as opposed to individualism, of shared space, of common interests, of the public – all those things which seem under siege in this period (Fraser, 1993). The local also conjures up images of active citizenship, whether in terms of the folklore of the town-hall meeting and direct democracy or, in more academic terms, Arendt's insistence that citizenship requires public spaces where citizens can interact, talk and persuade. Public meeting places, as Bauman underscores, are the places where norms are debated, values are confronted and clashes negotiated (1998, p. 25).

It would be mistaken, however, to imagine the local as public space, let alone Arendt's public space. She was insistent that, instead of physical 'public' space, it was the discursive elements interacting within that space which deemed it public. Arendt's space of appearance required the rebirth (or perhaps birth) of the rational civic-minded individual who was capable of speech, persuasion and collective action. These actions differentiated public space from private space. 'Wherever people gather together', Arendt writes, '[the public sphere] is potentially there, but only potentially, not necessarily and not forever' (1958, p. 199). As D'Entreves further explains, the existence of the public sphere is realized 'whenever actors gather together for the purpose of discussing and deliberating about matters of public concern, and it disappears the moment these activities cease' (1992, p. 147).

Unfortunately, much of the current literature on the local conflates the idea of local space with the practices of governance within that space. Magnusson, for example, suggests that the local has a pre-discursive affinity with the public and the practice of democratic citizenship. He imagines the municipality as a 'political space', a place 'intended' for 'ordinary people to participate in the business of the state'. If the municipality has not acted as an incubator for democratic citizenship in the past, it is because it has been 'displaced and repressed' and awaits its reclamation as a 'space of political freedom' (1996, pp. 8, 11, 301). Students of urban government continue to debate whether local governments ever performed the idealized democratic functions that are often attributed to them (Graham et al., 1998, p. 93). In fact, studies consistently conclude that local government is biased in favour of property interests (Lightbody, 1995). Regardless, the point to be emphasized here is that there is no necessary or obvious linkage between the local and the democratic.

The idea that the local has a democratic essence and has been denied its political mission derives, in large part, from its imagined opposition to the postwar welfare state. Critics on both the right and left denounced it for being too bureaucratic, alienating, centralized and distant (Rose, 1996, p. 332). The local, in contrast to this, was imagined to be more immediate, more responsive and more porous to the demands and participation of citizens. The disappearance of the welfare state, however, does not now mean that the local has been liberated from the repressive hand of its overly bureaucratic big brother. The passive 'managerial' local state of the postwar years was very much an extension of the welfare state – an integral part of its governing matrix. The local did not rest outside of the postwar system of governance but was an integral component of it. There are no grounds for assuming that the local can rest outside the process of globalization or the governing matrix of the neo-liberal state.

This is precisely why Robertson prefers the term 'glocal' when contemplating the local in a globalizing era. He contends that imagining the local as a form of opposition or resistance to the global is not a productive, analytic or interpretative point of departure. Instead, he contends that the local is very much included within the global. Indeed, the process of globalization involves 'the invention of locality' (Robertson, 1995, pp. 29, 35). Amin and Robbins underscore this point. They argue that globalization means that the local 'can only be seen as a node within the global' and that it has no 'meaningful existence outside this context' (1990, p. 28; Jessop, 1994, p. 271). Rather than standing in opposition to the global, the glocal allows us to reconceptualize processes of economic globalization as concrete economic, social and political forms 'situated in specific places' (Sassen, 1998, p. x).

Imagining the glocal performative state

While social theorists and political activists contemplate the municipality as a site of revived citizenship, the local is rapidly being refashioned to mesh with the governing philosophy of the neo-liberal state form. Neo-liberal governance rests on three foundational ideals: (1) decentralization; (2) privatization; and (3) individualization (Brodie, 1997). These governing instruments place severe constraints on the idea of a local 'public' and, thus, on the (re)birth of local democratic citizenship.

One of the critical shifts associated with the neo-liberal governance has been decentralization, within the public sector to lower levels of government and quasi-autonomous government bodies, or to the private sector, or to the community, family and individual. Decentralization, in its simplest terms, transfers government responsibilities and accountability from a single centre to smaller multiple units (Crook et al., 1992, p. 97). Some of these units are more easily identified than others and many are not subject to direct democratic control or accountability. Decentralization is generally applauded among neo-liberal circles on the grounds that it enhances democratic accountability, policy innovation and administrative efficiency. It is presented as a corrective to the worst excesses of the welfare state. As Leslie puts it,

> it makes sense to decentralize certain functions of government because doing so creates a public sector that will respond more adequately and sensitively to voter preferences … that will adapt public policies to regionally varying needs and conditions; that will experiment with different approaches … and that can be expected to achieve relative administrative efficiency.
>
> (Leslie, 1993, p. 10)

Decentralization is often justified in the name of subsidiarity, a term first advanced by Pope Pius XI in *Quadragesimo anno*, 1931. Subsidiarity promotes the philosophic premise that 'it is an injustice, a grave evil and a disturbance of right order for a larger and higher organization to arrogate to itself functions which can be performed efficiently by smaller and lower bodies'. Stripped of its papal roots, the principle is entrenched in the Maastricht Treaty, was an operating principle in the restructuring of the economies of the former Soviet Union and has been informally and incrementally implemented in federations such as Canada. Subsidiarity, it is claimed, advances the goal of democratic governance. As the UNDP argues, 'a highly centralized system of government is less democratic than one in which there is a network of local and regional authorities ... when units are small enough for ordinary people to feel that they count' (UNDP, 1997a, p. 23).

While there is little empirical evidence to support this glowing rhetoric, it is a classic example of how the glocal is being reconstructed within neo-liberal discourse out of previous imaginations of the local. Throughout the 1960s and 1970s, equality-seeking groups demanded more control in the design and delivery of social services and for more integrated community-based programmes. These demands were premised on two assumptions: first, that social citizenship rights would continue to be respected; and, second, that local control would be democratic and inclusive. These assumptions clearly are not part of the current decentralization agenda. There are many different ways to decentralize, some of which have more democratic potential than others. Ideally, central governments can decentralize on a vertical axis downward to local levels of government and thereby potentially enhance the local as a site for democratic participation and accountability. The transfer of functions to a local or provincial state is often termed *devolution*. Governments can also decentralize through *deconcentration*, the relocation of decision-making from central to sub-national units within a central government agency, or through *delegation*, the shift of responsibility from a central government to semi-public agencies or the private sector (UNDP, 1997a, p. 29).

The experience of Canada and elsewhere, however, suggests that the democratic potential of devolution can be quickly offset by fiscal and other constraints. In the Canadian case, the rhetoric of decentralization has masked a demolition derby – a scurry of fiscal off-loading onto newly designated 'shock absorbers'. The federal government, for example, recovered its fiscal bottom line largely by off-loading the costs of social programmes on the provinces, which, in turn, have off-loaded on municipalities. The first 'revolutionary' budgets of the newly elected neo-liberal governments in Alberta and Ontario, for example, exacted the largest cuts to municipalities (in the range of 40 per cent), followed by 20 per cent cuts to social assistance. But, the impact of decentralization on municipalities has not been uniform. Some cities, caught in a global competition to attract and maintain investment, are reluctant to increase taxes in order to maintain social services. Instead, they have turned to the voluntary sector, user fees and privatization to deliver services. Urban centres also vary in their ability to adapt to off-loading. Some have little alternative other than to both increase taxes and cut services.

Rather than promoting accountability and innovation, then, vertical decentralization combined with fiscal restraint can result in a number of highly 'inefficient' outcomes. Most municipalities have insufficient resources to deliver on social programmes or cope with dips in the business cycle over which they have little control. The result is an acceleration in the process of urban decay and tax-flight to the suburbs, both of which increase the demand for social services in the core. These and other factors increase the pressure on local governments to attract investment and, thus, to become more susceptible to the power of both local and global capital. The drive to integrate local economies into global networks has led local governments to hold down wages and taxation, create Enterprise Zones, deregulate, curtail local planning to improve the urban environment for people and privatize essential services to open up new investment opportunities of corporate capital (Broomhill, 1995, p. 32). Subsidiarity, within the context of neo-liberal governance, may simply underwrite shopping and social dumping among corporations and the affluent few. Instead of being the incubator for a new urban democratic citizenship, the city becomes a container of the economic, environmental and social costs of globalization, and the home of those marginalized by an increasingly polarized polity.

The grounds for a new democratic urban citizenship are further eroded by delegation. Governments have also decentralized downward to smaller units, and outwards, either to quasi-autonomous agencies, the market or to the community, home and individual (Crook et al., 1992, p. 97). Government restructuring in Alberta, one of Canada's richest provinces, provides an interesting case study in the different ways in which this double movement – downward and outward – can occur. First elected in 1993, the Klein government was the vanguard of the neo-liberal revolution in Canada. Almost immediately after taking office, the Klein government followed a two-tiered decentralization strategy. The first was a straightforward transfer down and out or delegation to the private sector of, among others, liquor sales, registrations, licensing and provincial parks.

The second strategy was deconcentration – the creation of non-elected regional bodies in the healthcare bureaucracy, so-called Regional Health Authorities (RHAs). Their creation reflects the government's vision of 'revitalizing communities' so that 'government assumes less responsibility and individuals, families and communities assume more' (Alberta, 1996, pp. 9, 15, 16, 41). More tangibly, this has meant that RHAs now compete among themselves for healthcare dollars, thereby promoting inter-city resentment, the uneven provision of critical healthcare services and the privatization of public sector jobs. A similar decentralized and privatized model for the provision of child welfare services is currently being implemented. It bears repeating that none of this is particularly empowering, democratic or responsive to local needs and demands. The World Bank, itself an enthusiastic advocate of decentralization, confirms this point. Indeed, decentralization can 'increase regional income disparities, accentuate macro-economic stability and encourage corruption' (Prud'homme, 1995, p. 206).

Others have argued persuasively that the idea of subsidiarity may be quite counterproductive, especially with respect to the protection of social citizenship entitlements in an era of globalization. Deacon, for example, contends that 'the more states have the autonomy to determine what and how social needs might be met ... the less the guarantee they will be met'. He goes on to suggest that the regime shopping and social dumping associated with capital mobility may very well indicate that the transnational rather than local is the best place to ensure social provision and redistribution (Deacon et al., 1997, p. 19). Regardless, the relationship between democratic citizenship and decentralization hinges less on whether or not to decentralize but, instead, on the *how* to decentralize in order to promote transparency, accountability, capacity and citizen participation.

Decentralization often goes hand in hand with privatization, which is decidedly incompatible with democratization and citizenship rights. Privatization shifts power from the public to the private spheres. By definition, it atrophies the public and reduces the terrain of democratic citizenship. But it also involves much more than simply removing things from the public basket and placing them on the market. The things that are privatized are themselves transformed into something qualitatively different. As services and responsibilities are shifted from the public to the private, they become differently encoded, constructed and regulated (Brodie, 1995, p. 54). Citizens become consumers, public spaces are commodified, and urbanity becomes narrowly redefined as a consumption experience available to some and not others (Christopherson, 1994, p. 413). The very idea of a public space itself has been radically altered in the glocal. As Flusty explains, 'traditional public spaces are increasingly supplanted by privately produced (though often publicly subsidized), privately owned and administered spaces of consumption. ... Access is predicated on the ability to pay' (quoted in Bauman, 1998, p. 20).

The marketized 'public' spaces of the glocal do not constitute democratic communities, norms or consensus, but instead inculcate the tastes and identities of global consumer culture. In the process, the local loses its uniqueness: there is little room for the notions of locality or local opinion as such (Bauman, 1998, p. 26). Once inside a shopping mall or a multi-billion dollar sports facility, geographic locality means little. It could be Dayton, Edmonton or a suburb of any city where consumers engage in the global market. In fact, the ability of some consumers to buy particular global products, such as Tommy Hilfiger clothing or a Mazda Miata, are often more important markers of who we are than our place of residence or our 'so-called' community. As Christopherson points out, 'when the celebration of consumer values is combined with a limited domain of discussion in the public sphere, the result is a limited sphere of public action for larger social purposes' (1994, p. 418). Privatization constructs relationships between individual consumers and a market which is detached from physical space. A necessary component of community – the ideas of shared space and fate – lose their cohesive potential.

Neo-liberalism's reinvention of the concept of community cannot be separated from this process of deterritorialization and atomization. Although western political theory has traditionally defined community and individualism as opposites, increasingly these terms have become conflated. The work of Nikolas Rose is particularly insightful in this regard. He argues that the terrain of the social and thus social policy have been tied to an enclosed national territory. Social citizenship rights, for example, were part of being a member of a national community. With globalization and the decline in importance of national economies and nation-states, however, the idea of 'community has become a new spatialization of government' (1996, p. 327).

This movement has encouraged the conflation of the local, community and the city. But the emerging conception of community has little to do with political jurisdictions or citizenship rights. Increasingly, the discursive construction of community is being deterritorialized, referring instead to ascriptive categories into which individuals are fit. Community, in other words, has become a dividing practice and a mode of governance (Rose, 1996, p. 335). The so-called gay community, the business community, the women's community, the immigrant community and so on are increasingly becoming the relevant categories for the governance of the individual who, in turn, is responsible for his or her community and self. This neo-liberal redefinition of community from shared space to individual attributes has significant implications for the generation of an urban citizenship. It recasts the individual, the citizen and ultimately, the community in the abstract and decontextualized language of neo-classical economics and liberalism. Government policy turns from the concept of collective well-being and community-building to the problems of particular 'communities' that require regulation, surveillance and discipline. They are 'targeted' as being outside the community.

The idea of targeting is fully consistent with decentralization and privatization. Its overt rationale is that universality is no longer the best way to attend to the 'local' or the 'individual'. Instead, the collective is best served when limited government resources are used to reform those who, for whatever reason, do not measure up to the abstract, self-sufficient individual. Obviously, this means of governance pathologizes the targeted as 'the problem', as arbitrary statistical and administrative categories that require some sort of therapeutic intervention. In the process, there is a systematic erasure of consideration of structural factors in the formation of social policy as well as in the formation of political identities and political alliances. The urban poor, for example, are no longer part of the community or, for that matter, the global political economy. They are outside, individualized and responsible for their own plight. Similarly, women, aboriginals and other marginalized groups become personally responsible for the consequences of systemic sexism and racism. As Rose puts it, 'the economic fates of citizens are uncoupled from one another and are now understood and governed as a function of their own particular levels of enterprise, skill, inventiveness and flexibility' (1996, p. 339).

The new philosophy of governance represents a tidal shift in thinking, from communitarian and collective values to the enforcement of individual responsibility. The central operating principle is that it is up to individuals and vaguely defined communities to look after themselves, and that it is up to governments to make sure that they do. More and more people who have been displaced by globalization find that they are ineligible for government assistance. Cut-backs in healthcare mean that families are increasingly responsible for the comfort and care of hospitalized loved ones. Grandmothers assume responsibility for the childcare of working mothers. The list of responsibilities for the self-reliant individual grows daily. Haltham and Kay call this new construction of the citizen a 'market model based on economic individualism'. They argue that it 'gives rise to a political model based on economic individualism ... [which] provides public services which are of an inadequate standard, inefficiently managed and inequitably distributed'. In the process, there are decreasing incentives to think about broader conceptions of the collective and of community (Haltham and Kay, 1994, p. 11).

These observations draw us to a final point about the potential for urban citizenship in a globalizing era and that is how globalizing processes have changed our relationship with locality and community. After two decades of neo-liberal governance, social scientists and policy-makers have identified three persistent and vexing problems in the glocal social structure. These are increasingly high levels of structural unemployment among identifiable groups, particularly those in the inner city core, increasing levels of poverty, and the dualization or polarization of incomes and life chances. Put simply, the ability of individuals to become self-reliant increasingly depends on their position in the global international economy. Those 'affiliated' with the global economy belong to the community of self-reliant citizens while all others are marginalized, indeed often deprived of some of the most fundamental rights of citizenship (Rose, 1996; Brodie, 1999). Workfare, 'snitch-lines', finger-printing and the extraordinary surveillance of welfare recipients point to the differential citizenship rights accorded to citizens on the basis of income source. As important, those iterated into the global economy are, in many ways, detached from local physical space. Their communities are mobile, global, virtual and corporate. The marginalized, in contrast, are tied to local space. The homeless man cuddled to a heating grate for warmth, the welfare recipient without sufficient means to pay for bus fare to seek out employment or the single mother unable to leave the home because there is no alternative childcare are obvious examples of the degree to which the economically marginalized are fixed in the physical space of the home, street and city. Some now argue that globalization has forced a new and uncompromising pattern of social stratification which is less amenable to the redistributive policies of the postwar welfare state. Large proportions of the population have become excluded from the global economy, creating what Bessis calls an 'economic apartheid' that is most visible in urban spaces (Bessis, 1995, p. 19).

Recently, Bauman has pursued the notion that this fixedness to the local is a measure of social stratification and marginalization from the global. He argues that globalization processes are both space-liberating and space-fixing. In an era of globalization, 'mobility climbs to the rank of the uppermost among the coveted values – freedom to move, perpetually a scarce and unequally distributed commodity, fast becomes the main stratifying factor of our late-modern or post-modern times'. He continues, 'Some of us become fully and truly "global" ... [while others] are fixed in their "locality". ... Being local in a globalized world is a sign of social deprivation and degradation' (Bauman, 1998, p. 2). The different proximity of individuals, who may live side by side, to the global is itself a challenge to the possibility of local democratic citizenship. The ideas of commonality and community are even more illusory when local citizens do not share the same political space and potential for political participation, influence and alliances.

Conclusion

> Globalization divides as much as it unties; it divides as it unites – the causes of division being identical with those which promote the uniformity of the globe.
>
> (Bauman, 1998, p. 1)

Contemporary politics is increasingly marked by new contradictions, spatial dislocations, social fragmentation and political disorientation. National sovereignty, democratic accountability and citizenship rights all appear to have been cast adrift from their modernist and territorial moorings. Current thinking about the rebirth of the local citizen in a glocal urbanity reflects one potential response to these dislocations. In a sense, we are all creatures of geographic space, increasingly urban space, and will remain so in the imaginable future.

At the same time, we must be attentive to the ongoing reconstruction of the very concepts of the citizen, the local and the public. The ideal of modern democratic citizenship was grafted onto the nation-state but political territory is not now the most relevant space underlying the creation of citizenship rights. While some explore the potential of the local for a revived citizenship in an era of globalization, current governing discourses are rapidly transforming the very idea of the local. It is becoming detached from its shared geographic moorings. The potential for an urban citizenship, then, depends first on a struggle for space – public space. It is the fleeting but essential condition for democratic citizenship: the discursive space attributed to the public sphere. It helps us interpret our social lives and institutions, what we consider to be a social problem and its appropriate remedies, where the sphere of political negotiation begins and ends, and who we believe ourselves to be. Throughout the history of liberal democracy, workers, women and other marginalized groups have struggled to expand the terrain of the public and, in so doing, make citizenship rights more encompassing and inclusive. Now, as then, the vitality of democracy depends less on questions of location than on content. The critical issues of democracy and citizenship in the twenty-first century cannot be strategized without an intensive interrogation and contestation of the many ways in which globalization is transforming civil society at the level of the local, the city and the individual. As Held rightly argues, for democracy to flourish today, it has to be reconceived as a double-sided process – the reform of state power and the restructuring of civil society (Held, 1996, p. 316). As with the progressive social movements of a century ago, citizens will again have to assert their will – that there is a place for substantive equality and collective provision, that some things are simply incompatible with marketization, and that other things must be protected from the risk of market failure. Without the terrain of the public, citizenship will forever be lost in space.

Note

1   I wish to thank Engin Isin, Linda Trimble and, most especially, Malinda Smith for their helpful comments on an earlier draft of this chapter.

Bibliography

Alberta (1998) 'New Roles, New Frameworks-Rebuilding the Alberta Public Service: A Discussion Paper', April.

Amin, A. (1994) 'Post-Fordism: Models, Fantasies and Phantoms of Transition', in A. Amin (ed.), *Post-Fordism: A Reader* (London: Blackwell).

Amin, A. and Robbins, K. (1990) 'The Re-emergence of Regional Economies?', *Environment and Planning D: Society and Space*, 9.

Anderson, B. (1991) *Imagined Communities* (London: Verso).

Andrew, C. (1997) 'Globalization and Local Action', in T. Thomas (ed.), *The Politics of the City: A Canadian Perspective* (Toronto: IPT Nelson).

Arendt, H. (1958) *The Human Condition* (Chicago: University of Chicago Press).

Barlow, M. and Campbell, B. (1995) *Straight Through the Heart: How the Liberals Abandoned the Just Society* (Toronto: Harper).

Bauman, Z. (1998) *Globalization* (New York: Columbia University Press).

Bessis, S. (1995) 'From Social Exclusion to Social Cohesion: A Policy Agenda', paper presented at the Roskilde Symposium (Denmark: University of Roskilde).

Brodie, J. (1995) *Politics on the Margins: Restructuring and the Canadian Women's Movement* (Halifax: Fernwood Publishing).

—— (1997) 'Meso-Discourses, State Forms, and the Gendering of Liberal-Democratic Citizenship', *Citizenship Studies*, 1 (2): 223–42.

—— (1999) 'The Politics of Social Policy in the 21st Century', in D. Broad (ed.), *Citizenship and Social Policy: Neo-Liberalism and Beyond* (Halifax: Fernwood Publishing).

Brodie, J. and Smith, M. (1998) 'Regulating the Economic Union', in L. Pal (ed.), *How Ottawa Spends – 1998–1999* (Ottawa: Carleton University Press).

Broomhill, R. (1995) 'Globalization, Neo-Liberalism and the Local State', in J. Spoehr and R. Broomhill (eds), *Altered States: The Impact of Free Market Policies on the Australian States* (Adelaide: Centre for Labour Studies and Social Justice).

Canada, Privy Council Office (1996) *Canada 2005: Global Challenges and Opportunities* (Ottawa: Privy Council Office).

Cerney, P. (1990) *The Changing Architecture of Power* (London: Sage).

Christopherson, S. (1994) 'The Fortress City: Privatized Spaces, Consumer Citizenship', in A. Amin (ed.), *Post-Fordism: A Reader* (London: Blackwell).

Cox, R. (1991) 'The Global Political Economy and Social Choice', in D. Drache and M. Gertler (eds), *The New Era of Global Competition: State, Policy and Market Power* (Montreal, McGill-Queen's University Press).

Crook, S., Pakulski, J. and Waters, M. (1992) *Post-modernization: Change in Advanced Society* (Newbury Park, CA: Sage).

Deacon, B., with Hulse, M. and Stubbs, P. (1997) *Global Social Policy: International Organizations and the Future of Welfare* (London: Sage).

D'Entreves, M. (1992) 'Hannah Arendt and the Idea of Citizenship', in C. Mouffe (ed.), *Dimensions of Radical Democracy* (London: Verso).

Fraser, N. (1993) 'Rethinking the Public Sphere: A Contribution to the Critique of Actually Existing Democracy', in B. Robbins (ed.), *The Phantom Public Sphere* (Minneapolis: University of Minnesota Press).

Friedman, H. (1991) 'New Wines: New Bottles: The Regulation of Capital on a World Scale', *Studies in Political Economy*, 36.

Giddens, A. (1990) *The Consequences of Modernity* (Stanford, CA: Stanford University Press).

Gill, S. (1995) 'Globalization, Market Civilization and Disciplinary Neo-Liberalism', *Millennium: A Journal of Interdisciplinary Studies*, 24 (3): 399–423.

Graham, K., Phillips, S. and Maslove, A. (1998) *Urban Governance in Canada: Representation, Resources and Restructuring* (Toronto: Harcourt Brace).

Hall, S. (1996) 'The Question of Cultural Identity', in S. Hall, D. Held, D. Hubert and K. Thompson (eds), *Modernity* (London: Blackwell).

Haltham, G. and Kay, J. (1994) 'The Assessment: Institutions of Policy', *Oxford Review of Economic Policy*, 10 (3).

Held, D. (1996) *Models of Democracy*, 2nd edn, (Stanford, CA: Stanford University Press).

Jenson, J. (1997) 'Fated to Live in Interesting Times: Canada's Changing Citizenship Regimes', *Canadian Journal of Political Science*, 30 (4).

Jessop, B. (1994) 'Post-Fordism and the State', in A. Amin (ed.), *Post-Fordism: A Reader* (London: Blackwell).

Leslie, P. (1993) 'The Fiscal Crisis of Canadian Federalism', in P. Leslie, K. Norrie and I. Ip (eds), *A Partnership in Trouble* (Toronto: C.D. Howe Institute).

Lightbody, J. (1995) *Canadian Metropolitics: Governing Our Cities* (Toronto: Copp Clark).

Lipietz, A. (1994) 'Post-Fordism and Democracy', in A. Amin (ed.), *Post-Fordism: A Reader* (London: Blackwell).

Magnusson, W. (1996) *The Search For Political Space* (Toronto: University of Toronto Press).

Marshall, T.H. (1950) *Citizenship and Social Class* (Cambridge: Cambridge University Press).

Mayer, M. (1994) 'Post-Fordist City Politics', in A. Amin (ed.), *Post-Fordism: A Reader* (London: Blackwell).

Mouffe, C. (1993) *The Return of the Political* (London: Verso).

Persky, S. (1992) 'City Without Citizens', in M. Wyman (ed.), *Vancouver Forum: Old Powers, New Forces* (Vancouver: Douglas McIntyre).

Prud'homme, R. (1995) 'The Dangers of Decentralization', *The World Bank Research Observer*, 10 (2).

Robertson, R. (1995) 'Glocalization: Time-Space and Homogeneity-Heterogeneity', in M. Featherstone, S. Lash and R. Robertson (eds), *Global Modernities* (London: Sage).

Rose, N. (1996) 'The Death of the Social? Re-figuring the Territory of Government', *Economy and Society*, 25 (3): 327–56.

Sassen, S. (1998) *Globalization and Its Discontents* (New York: The New Press).

Scholte, J.A. (1997) 'Global Capital and the State', *International Affairs*, 73 (3): 427–52.

Soja, E. (1989) *Post-modern Geographies* (London: Verso).

Thomas, T. (1997) 'Introduction', in T. Thomas (ed.), *The Politics of the City: A Canadian Perspective* (Toronto: ITP Nelson).

Touraine, A. (1997) *What is Democracy?* (Boulder: Westview).

Turner, B. (1992) 'Outline of a Theory of Citizenship', in C. Mouffe (ed.), *Dimensions of Radical Democracy* (London: Verso).

UNDP (United Nations Development Programme) (1992) *Human Development Report* (New York: Oxford).

UNDP (Regional Bureau of Europe and the CIS) (1997a) *The Shrinking State: Governance and Sustainable Human Development* (New York: UNDP).

UNDP (Management Development and Governance Division) (1997b) *Reconceptualising Governance: Discussion* (New York: UNDP).

Yeatman, A. (1994) *Post-modern Revisionings of the Political* (New York: Routledge).

Young, I.M. (1990) *Justice and the Politics of Difference* (Princeton, NJ: Princeton University Press).

7 Cosmopolitan virtue

Loyalty and the city

Bryan S. Turner

Introduction

The city and citizenship have in the modern world been powerful agencies for shaping and forming individual identities. Citizenship is primarily a political category relating to individuation but it in turn confers a juridic identity on individuals. In sociological and historical terms, the juridical identity of citizens has evolved according to the larger political context, because citizenship has been necessarily housed within a definite political community, such as the nation-state. City and citizenship are also linked to a number of other terms which have had an honorific status in shaping and forming the western consciousness – civilization, civility and civic virtue. This chapter provides a short historical sketch of this development from the city-state to the nation-state and then to the contemporary global system. Currently the problem for the development of contemporary forms of citizenship is that global society is not (as yet) a definite political community.

The development of these juridic identities is not, however, an evolutionary process. There was certainly a transformation of the Enlightenment and revolutionary ambitions for cosmopolitanism (in, for example, Kant's notion of world history) into exclusionary nationalist paradigms of citizenship with the development of the nation-state. Friedrich Meinecke's notion of cosmopolitanism as a critique of Prussian nationalism is a case in point. In the twentieth century, the critics of cosmopolitanism were, generally speaking, also critics of liberalism. Carl Schmitt and Leo Strauss were clearly hostile to liberalism as a philosophy and liberal democracy as a political system. Straussian political theology may well be equally hostile to multiculturalism.

This historical sketch is partly motivated by the concept of the civilizing process in the sociology of Norbert Elias. In Elias's processual sociology, feudalism required certain formations of the warrior identity that were relevant to the militarized pattern of land settlement in the Middle Ages. With the evolution of court society, aristocratic identities were forged around the role of the courtier, whose ritualized manners exercised control over strong and violent emotions. The rise of the bourgeoisie represented yet a further development of civilized identities; bourgeois educational institutions became key elements in this social and psychological transition. There is a further possibility regarding the emergence of a global citizen whose lifestyle requires a new pattern of social restraint and self-formation, a pattern which we may call cosmopolitan virtue. Can the worldly intellectual be a carrier of cosmopolitan values? Cosmopolitan virtue is defined by irony, emotional distance, scepticism, secularity and an ethic of stewardship.

In trying to pull together a debate about identities and ethics, on the one hand, and the political history of citizenship and liberalism on the other hand, attention is drawn to the obvious historical and etymological connections between the concepts of civil society and citizenship, civility and civilization, the city and the citizen. The concept of 'civil society' (*bürgerliche Gesellschaft*) owes its origin to a particular pattern of historical development. A *Bürger* was originally a person who defended a castle (*Burg*), and from around the twelfth century the term referred simply to a city dweller. It has also retained its association with the French *bourgeois* (from *bourg* or borough); Hegel used *citoyen* to indicate the citizen of a state. Thus in *bürgerliche Gesellschaft* we have a combination of 'civic' and 'bourgeois'. Now *Gesellschaft* is from *Geselle*, or somebody who shares a dwelling place as one's companion. This civil society is not a *Gemeinschaft* (community) but an association of citizens. For Hegel, civil society is a distinctive area of ethical life that stands between the family and the state (Inwood, 1992, p. 53). This connection between civil society and citizenship is retained in many European languages, as in the Dutch *Burgerma-atschappij* and Hungarian *allampolgar*. Only in Russia, where the walled city did not fully evolve as a centre of urban immunities, did the concept of citizen diverge significantly. The Russian *grazhdanin* indicates that the citizen belongs to the state, not the city.

In this European tradition, the cultured citizen is somebody whose lifestyle and mentality has been cultivated by a process of discipline and education, because, in addition to being constituted around a juridic identity, the citizen is also somebody whose personality has been, in ideal terms, moulded by a civil culture, which this chapter refers to simply as 'virtue'. These virtues of the citizen are typically described within a framework of obligations and duties, which stand alongside the rights and immunities that are enjoyed by the citizen. Within a republican tradition for example, the 'good citizen' is somebody who undertakes certain duties and responsibilities, not because they have a market value, but because they contribute to the common good.

By recognizing this historically close relationship between the development of the institutions of citizenship and the growth of urban culture, we see the possibility that the growth of the global city may provide that definite political community which is a necessary adjunct of citizenship. There has to be a political agency that is able to deliver the rights and immunities to which citizens are entitled, and to anticipate the obligations, duties and loyalties that underpin these rights. In short, citizenship has to correspond to some definite form of sovereignty, and this political shell is also the arena within which certain mentalities, identities and cultures are housed.

Earlier sociologists have argued that the plural and cosmopolitan cities of Europe in the late and early twentieth century produced, in the terminology of Georg Simmel, new identities or mentalities which were characterized by the blasé attitude of the stranger or, in the work of Walter Benjamin, by the lifestyle of the *flâneur*. Following post-modern theory, an orientation towards irony dominates cosmopolitan virtue. There is an elective affinity between post-emotional distance, cosmopolitan irony and the multicultural tensions of global city cultures. Traditionally, expressions like 'blasé attitude', or 'the urban flâneur' or 'ironic criticism' carry a certain negative quality, but these cosmopolitan characteristics should be developed as the virtues of a global city.

The Marshallian legacy

This introduction to an analysis of citizenship identities in the post-modern, global city provides an overview of the contemporary debate on culture and citizenship. My purpose is to take the Marshallian legacy and forge it to the analysis of identities, entitlements and citizenship in the modern city. It is thus, in part, an extended commentary on the legacy of T.H. Marshall, although an adequate understanding of the issues surrounding citizenship in modern societies must go well beyond the Marshallian framework. Citizenship is a particular case of social rights in which there are tensions between social and human rights. Marshall (1950) developed a theory of postwar societies through an analysis of the relationships between social class, welfare and citizenship; his approach to the citizenship debate proved to be seminal, but the Marshallian tradition is particularly deficient as a perspective on ethnically diverse societies.

Citizenship can be defined as a collection of rights and obligations which give individuals a formal legal identity; these legal rights and obligations have been put together historically as sets of social institutions, such as the jury system, parliaments and welfare states. Citizenship has traditionally been a fundamental topic of philosophy and politics, but, from a sociological point of view, we are interested in those institutions in society that embody or give expression to the formal rights and obligations of individuals as members of a political community. This approach is 'sociological' because political interpretations of citizenship typically have a sharper focus on political rights, the state and the individual. From a sociological point of view, we are interested in how citizenship shapes identity and how it functions to influence the distribution of resources in a society.

It is conceptually parsimonious to think of three types of resources: economic, cultural and political. Alongside these resources, we typically find three forms of rights: economic rights, which are related to basic needs for food and shelter; cultural rights, which include both access to welfare and access to education; and finally, political rights, which cover the conventional area of liberal concern such as individual freedoms and rights to expression through political means such as parliaments. These rights may be collectively referred to as 'social' rights, as distinct from human rights, because they typically presuppose membership of a nation-state. At a more fundamental level, cultural resources include the special identities which people enjoy as citizens.

The first thing to emphasize about citizenship is that it controls access to the scarce resources of society and hence this allocative function is the basis of a profound conflict in modern societies over citizenship membership criteria. The process of and conditions for naturalization and denaturalization tell us a great deal about the character of democracy in society because these processes relate fundamentally to the basic values of inclusion and exclusion (Brubaker, 1992). French colonialism typically involved a notion of a *mission civilisatrice*, in which metropolitan culture attempted to impose a uniform identity on its dependent regions, and in the nineteenth century colonization required cultural assimilation (Aldrich and Connell, 1992), but these inclusionary and exclusionary processes are obviously not merely about cultural identity.

In this account of the transformation of modern politics, we need to consider an ancient problem of cultural diversity and political power. Let me emphasize the word 'ancient', since it can be argued that fear of diversity in classical Greece was in fact the condition that produced political theory in the first instance (Saxonhouse, 1992). Although this problem of cultural diversity within the framework of the city-state has a long history in political thought, there are some new ingredients within the contemporary context. The essence of these new circumstances is, first, the globalization of economic and cultural relationships and, second, the post-modernization of cultural phenomena. In reality, these are the same issues, because the post-modernization of culture is closely related to the development of hybridization, and hybridity is a function of cultural globalism. The question then is: how can citizenship exist in such a context of staggering diversity? How can citizens be committed to some political community (the city or the state) when social and cultural fragmentation makes the possibility of solidarity unlikely? Generally speaking, the response to this circumstance has been somewhat apologetic and typically nostalgic. The point of my chapter is to try to celebrate diversity and to do so through the development of a notion of cosmopolitan virtue. Here again, the ancients and the moderns cannot be kept apart, because it was after all the Stoics who, in response to the anxieties of diversity, created the notions of cosmopolitanism and universal order as a suitable ethic for the imperial city (Wolin, 1961).

It is important to distinguish the notions of post-modernity and post-modern theory (Turner, 1990a). The former means a social condition of advanced societies in which cultural and social relations are transformed by new modes and methods of communication and information storage, especially by electronic means of delivery. Post-modern society is the product of the transformations of communication systems as described initially by theorists such as Marshall McLuhan (1964). By contrast, post-modern theory means a way of theorizing society in which the principal mode or style of theoretical analysis is ironic, employing textual devices which signify the constructed and malleable forms of reality representation, and which indicate a certain distance from the object of analysis or signification. In short, post-modern theories question grand narratives (Lyotard, 1984) or, in the words of Richard Rorty, the ironist is somebody who profoundly doubts the authority of any final vocabulary about reality, including their own final vocabulary (Rorty, 1989). Since democracy can be regarded as the grand narrative of the modern state, post-modern theory would appear to be incompatible with much conventional political philosophy. Post-modern theory, with its sensitivity to simulation, metaphor and artificiality, describes or attempts to describe the condition of post-modernity. Post-modern theory is thus an effect of and response to a social world that is increasingly complex and differentiated, and to a culture which is increasingly reflexive and sceptical about its own sources of authority. Questions about the status and role of authors in post-modernity are invariably questions about authorization, that is about authority. Who has authority to speak in a context of competing cultures? This chapter attempts to describe the emergence of a mode of political identity in a global post-modern society and to describe these social changes within the paradigm of an ironic theory of social relations, but my purpose is to go beyond description in order to prescribe a response to the erosion of nationalistic citizenship.

The next important aspect of citizenship is that it confers, in addition to a legal status, a particular cultural identity on individuals and groups. The notion of the 'politics of identity' indicates an important change in the nature of contemporary politics. Whereas much of the struggle over citizenship in the early stages of industrialization was about class membership and class struggle in the labour market, citizenship struggles in early twenty-first-century society are more commonly about claims to cultural identity and cultural history. These struggles have been about sexual identity, gay rights, gender equality and aboriginality. Most debates about citizenship in contemporary political theory are, as a result, about the question of contested collective identity in a context of radical pluralization (Mouffe, 1992). When political scientists therefore refer to 'citizenship', they are not merely thinking about access to scarce economic and political resources, they are concerned ultimately with questions about identity in civil society and civic culture. In formal political philosophy, the notion of citizenship contains a clear notion of the civic virtues that are regarded as necessary for the functioning of a democracy. The word 'citizenship' (*citézein*) itself indicates a connection with the rise of bourgeois society and in particular with the tradition of civil society (*die bürgerliche Gesellschaft*). For the Scottish political economists such as Adam Smith and Adam Ferguson, civil society was contrasted with the barbarism of primitive society; citizenship was seen to be connected with *civilitas* (Bobbio, 1989). In Germany, the idealists merged the idea of the Greek *polis* with the tradition of independent German towns with their distinctive educational cultures (in the virtues of the *Bildungs* tradition) to produce a defence of individual rights against both the militarized aristocracy and proletarian vulgarity. The high point of this tradition was in

Fichte's Kantian statement of the intersubjectivity of rights (Ferry, 1990). The values of citizenship were merged with those of civilization and hence Weber was to argue that citizenship as a uniquely western institution had its origin in the peculiar structures of the occidental city. However, for Weber the basis of 'democratization is everywhere purely military in character; it lies in the rise of disciplined infantry' (Weber, 1981, p. 324). The decline of the noble cavalry marks the rise of the urban militia, the autonomous city, civil society and citizenship. The status of citizenship was part of the process of civilization wherein the virtues of the knight-at-arms were transferred to the arena of the royal court with its effeminate courtiers and its ideology of courtesy, and later to the disciplined asceticism of the bourgeois household. These social conditions also indicate the rootedness of the concept of obligation as the cornerstone of bourgeois responsibility (to family and occupation), bourgeois morality with respect to the public/private division, and bourgeois versions of civil republicanism. This politico-moral configuration was also the origin of Karl Marx's hostility to the 'possessive individualism' of the English utilitarians such as Bentham and Mill, and to the narrow, uni-dimensional development of the 'political' in classical liberalism. With the rise of economic rationalism in the twentieth century, interest once more returned to the analysis of the market in relation to egotistic individualism, indifference to strangers and hostility to welfare dependency among the economically marginalized. Citizenship and civic virtues are once more seen to be an essential ingredient of a civilized and pluralistic democracy. This concern for the political threat to civic culture in a market society has been associated with a reappraisal of Mill's liberalism (Bobbio, 1987), the importance of pluralism (Hirst, 1989) and the role of voluntary associations in democracy (Cohen and Rogers, 1995). The cultural dimension of citizenship is now an essential component of citizenship studies, especially in a context where there is political ambiguity around the analysis of cultural fragmentation and simulation brought about by post-modernization.

The final component of this sociological model of citizenship is the idea of a political community as the basis of citizenship; this political community is typically the nation-state. When individuals become citizens, they not only enter into a set of institutions that confer upon them rights and obligations, they not only acquire an identity, they are not only socialized into civic virtues, but they also become members of a political community with a particular territory and history. In order to have citizenship one has to be, at least in most modern societies, a bona fide member of a political community. Generally speaking, it would be highly unusual for people to acquire citizenship if they are not already a national member of a political community, that is a nation-state. One should notice here an important difference between human rights and citizenship. Human rights are typically conferred upon people as humans irrespective of whether they are Australian, British, Chinese, Indonesian or whatever, but, because human rights legislation has been accepted by the nations of the world, people can claim human rights even where they are stateless people or dispossessed refugees. In general, citizenship is a set of rights and obligations that attach to members of formally recognized nation-states within the system of nations, and hence citizenship corresponds to legal membership of a nation-state. Citizenship identities and citizenship cultures are national identities and national cultures. Since nations are, following Benedict Anderson (1983), 'imagined communities', and since nations are created (James, 1996), the communal basis of citizenship has to be constantly renewed within the collective memory by nostalgic festivals, public ceremonies of national struggle and effervescent collective experience. National culture has all the characteristics of a civil religion, and hence modern citizenship is a form of social solidarity.

These reflections on the growth of citizenship suggest a model of western evolution. Citizenship evolves out of the notion of a denizen of an urban space, but it is replaced by a stronger notion of citizenship in the autonomous city-state of medieval society. This conception is the basis of Weber's model of city politics. Within Marshall's model, this notion of political citizenship is expanded through the welfare state into social citizenship. Finally, the globalization of contemporary society indicates a growing importance in terms of general human rights regardless of nationality.

We cannot however take the cosy or comforting view that modernization is painless or uniformly enlightened; the spread of urban citizenship, because it required the extension of the nation-state as its political shell, also involved the exclusion and in many occasions the destruction of local, traditional, tribal cultures. The marginalization and exclusion of the 'Celtic fringe' in Great Britain was historically a classic example of the growing dominance of the Westminster model of citizenship founded on an assumption of ethnic and religious homogeneity (Hechter, 1975). Citizenship is necessarily a contradictory force, because it creates an internal space of social rights and solidarity, and thus an external, exclusionary force of non-membership. This inclusionary and exclusionary dynamic is one explanation of continuing ethnic violence in Central Africa where the modern boundaries of nationalistic states do not correspond with ancient boundaries between such ethnic communities as the Tutsis and Hutus. One mechanism for the genocidal conflict has been the fact that the Banyarwanda have been stripped of citizenship by Zaire.

If citizenship is the politico-cultural expression of the successful growth of the nation-state through the nineteenth and twentieth centuries, then citizenship is an incomplete or unfinished version of universalistic rights that are embraced, for example, in United Nations legislation on *human* rights. Globalization involves politically the growing importance of human rights over nation-state citizenship rights. Human rights and citizenship rights often collide in the modern state, where those who suffer from state legislation will appeal to a 'higher' court. The global advocacy of indigenous rights by humanitarian agencies presents the paradox of particular or local claims being expressed against state citizenship structures.

Although he was not particularly interested in the question of political identity, Marshall's analysis of citizenship still provides a useful route into the discussion of political identity and contemporary citizenship (Marshall, 1964). Marshall's silence on this issue is, however, instructive, because it points to a period in British history in which, at least in public debate, the problem of identity politics had not fully emerged. Marshall's argument is well known. He claimed that citizenship evolved through three stages of legal, political and social rights from around the middle of the seventeenth century to the creation of the welfare state in the middle of the twentieth century. This evolution of citizenship has to be seen against the background of the emergence of antagonistic social classes in the urban context of industrial capitalism. The growth of capitalist markets was accompanied by the emergence of class-based urban communities characterized by a high level of class consciousness and class conflict. Traditional sources of solidarity and legitimacy in rural communities, which had been partly held together by Christian rituals and beliefs, were challenged by the class-based ideologies of the working-class movement, namely by socialist ideas of working-class cooperation. Old status relations were being replaced by the solidarities of class. 'Class', which in traditional political economy was an impersonal association of individuals with the same relationship to economic relations of ownership, began to assume characteristics normally associated with community or *Gemeinschaft* (Holton and Turner, 1989).

Citizenship took different forms depending on the historical circumstances of its formation (Mann, 1987). It is possible to distinguish between active and passive forms of citizenship, which arise from variations in the relationship between the subject and the state. Thus, radical social movements expand citizenship rights through a process of political conflict, while the more passive forms of citizenship are the effect of the political strategies of the dominant political elite (Turner, 1990b). In England there has been a tradition of passive citizenship which followed the 'Glorious Rebellion' and political settlement of 1688, and which was enshrined in John Locke's justification of the constitution in social contract theory in his *Two Treatises of Government* in 1690. The absence of a genuine revolutionary working-class confrontation in the eighteenth and nineteenth centuries contributed further to this history of 'gradualism'. It has often been argued in the Halevy thesis that the Methodist Revolution was, as it were, a substitute for a socialist revolution and that Methodism created the conditions for social mobility of individuals out of the working class, but that at the same time the inherent political conservatism of Wesleyan theology promoted an ideology of acceptance (Halevy, 1962). The English citizen evolved as a 'subject' of the monarchy, which remained largely unchallenged in political terms. The nature of citizenship in different European societies varies according to the specific history of its class formation, the impact of warfare and the peculiar features of its political history. It is this specificity of the historical constitution of class relationships which determines the peculiarities of the national combination of rights, obligations and immunities within citizenship (Janoski, 1998).

National citizenship: rights and obligations

The rise of modern citizenship in the nineteenth and twentieth centuries was primarily associated with the growth of nation-states and with nationalism as the principal political ideology of nation-state building.[1] To be precise, modern citizenship dates from the Treaty of Westphalia in 1648, which launched the modern system of nation-states as the principal actors within the world system. National identity and citizenship identity became fused in the late nineteenth century around the growth of nation-states characterized by the dominant ideology of nationalism. In many societies this juridic identity was given strong racist characteristics in the creation of such notions as 'the British people' or 'the German folk'. The growth of national citizenship was associated with occidentalism (as an adjunct of orientalism), creating strong notions of Otherness as the boundary between the inside and outside world. National citizenship became crucial to the building of loyalties and commitments around the nation-state.

Citizenship in this framework can be seen as (1) an inclusionary criterion for the allocation of entitlements, and (2) an exclusionary basis for building solidarity and creating identity. In this sense, national citizenship is constructed around institutionalized racism because it excludes outsiders from access to entitlements, characteristically on the basis of a racial or national identity. The creation of the nation-state based upon citizenship involved various levels and degrees of 'ethnic cleansing' because the exclusionary principle of citizenship was structured around a juridic and racial identity. As nation-states were challenged from within by class division and from without by warfare and imperial struggle, there was an enhanced requirement for a strong basis of loyalty in the national community.

Following these arguments, we can analyse citizenship as a system for the allocation of entitlements, obligations and immunities within a political community. These entitlements are organized around a number of principles which describe the specific types of contributions which individuals have made to society, such as war service or reproduction or work. People can achieve entitlements by the formation of households and families that become the sites for the reproduction of society through the birth and maintenance of children. These services to the state via the family provide entitlements to both men and women as parents, that is as reproducers of the nation-state (Yuval-Davis, 1997). These entitlements become the basis for family security systems, various forms of support to mothers and health, and educational provision for children. Questions of justice as a result become closely tied to principles of cross-generational responsibilities for the management and conservation of environment and society (Barry, 1977). Second, entitlements can be achieved through the production of goods and services, namely through work which has been the most significant basis for the provision of superannuation and pension rights, but these entitlements also include rights to safety at work, insurance schemes relating to health and employment, and various provisions for retirement. It is for this reason obviously that the entitlements of men have been more significant than entitlements for women in societies where values relating to work in the formal economy form the core of the value system as a whole. Finally, service to the state through warfare generates a third range of entitlements for the soldier-citizen. War-time service typically leads to various pension rights, health provisions, housing and other entitlements for returning servicemen.[2] Here again the entitlements of men dominate entitlements for women, who may be able to claim rights indirectly as war widows. These routes to entitlement (family, work and war) also generate particular types of identity such as the soldier-citizen, the working citizen and the parent-citizen.

Within the Marshallian framework, these are the basic structures of entitlement, but perhaps we can identify a fourth figure – the citizen as national intellectual. In many historical patterns of the formation of a national culture of citizenship, the intellectual has played an important part in shaping national consciousness, often through his or her contribution to the protection of a national language or a national system of mythology. The cases which come to mind are Hugh McDiarmid's contribution to Scottish national consciousness through his poetry, the contributions of the writings of W.B. Yeats and James Joyce to Irish historical consciousness, the place of Van Dale's dictionary of the Dutch language, or the role of ethnographers in the maintenance of Finnish identity through the recovery of the epic tradition. It is possible to argue that the intellectuals enjoyed an entitlement by virtue of their contributions to the shaping of national consciousness and national identity.

The erosion of entitlement

In contemporary society, these routes to citizenship entitlement are becoming weaker and less reliable as guarantees or conditions for resource allocation and identity formation. For example, in the advanced industrial societies warfare has become, in the postwar period at least, far less common and therefore the soldier-citizen has become less significant as an identity and as a mode for distributing entitlement. In general terms, compulsory service has become less common in the industrial capitalist West and military activities have become a profession for an elite rather than a requirement of all able-bodied men. We can also argue that in many circumstances the use of mercenary soldiers is a way of 'outsourcing' the need for military service to minority communities such as hill tribesmen. As warfare becomes more technical, so the employment of mass troops becomes less important, thereby closing off a traditional avenue for the working class into welfare provision. The traditional tie between the militia and the citizenry has been partially broken, although in America through various gun clubs the association between a citizenship militia and the individual right to carry arms has perverted a tradition of active citizenship.

Second, following the work of Ulrich Beck and Elizabeth Gernsheim-Beck (1990), there has been a significant erosion of the classical nuclear family as a social location of reproduction. Levels of reproduction have declined with an increase in life-expectancy, the mass availability of contraceptive methods and changing value systems. The classical S-shaped demographic revolution means that the advanced industrial societies are characterized by a rapid process of ageing and by either declining or stationary populations. Many European societies now depend heavily on migration as a method of reproducing the nation-state in demographic terms. Hence one can expect that there will be an erosion of family-based rights and entitlements relating to reproduction. At the very least, the notion that there is a crisis in the family as an institution of modern societies will continue to grow in intensity. Many states in the industrial societies have withdrawn from direct welfare provisions for the family in the wake of fiscal rationalism, and depend increasingly on third-sector provision. These forms of privatization also weaken the overt link between parenthood and citizenship.

Finally, with the transition of the economy from Fordism to post-Fordism, there has been a profound restructuring of the occupational system, with a growth in the service sector, a decline in industrial manufacturing and an increase in the number of jobs relating to communication and the leisure industries. My picture of the economy is influenced by the work of Robert Reich (1991) in his *The Work of Nations*, which predicts a significant growth in the importance of the symbolic analyst – the managers and controllers of information and knowledge systems. To some extent Reich's view of the economy follows the earlier work of Daniel Bell (1974) in the now famous discussion of the post-industrial society, with its emphasis on the importance of knowledge and the university system as crucial components of economic production. However, the long-term problems associated with structural unemployment and under-employment, and the decline of large-scale manufacturing industries are worrisome. It is difficult to see how young workers in the twenty-first century will find sufficient employment to provide them with entitlements within the welfare state. The indications are that work will become increasingly scarce, typically short-term and casual, and normally unpredictable. For many, the absence of work threatens the traditional access to superannuation benefits and other retirement schemes. This economic scenario is a recipe for significant industrial and social unrest in which struggles will be frequently based on generational rather than class conflicts. Paradoxically, 'the death of class' may also parallel the death of citizenship (Lee and Turner, 1996). Class conflict was a motor of interest formation in which the social rights of citizenship expanded because the state was forced to respond to industrial unrest. The erosion of class loyalties and identities signals the decline of a mass labour market.

While the traditional labour markets of the capitalist West have contracted, there has been a cultural and ethnic diversification of labour through migration in the world economy. The consequences of the globalization and post-modernization of society are an erosion of national loyalties and identities based upon a traditional racial homogeneity because the growth of a global labour market has increased the number of migrant workers in the industrialized modern societies with a consequent growth in the heterogeneity of those economies. Alongside this growing ethnic diversity and multiculturalism, there is a weakening of the sovereignty of the nation-state as the state is drawn into global political relations.

These developments are clearly uneven, and globalization is typically followed or accompanied by powerful forces of localization as communities attempt to protect themselves from global cultures. These global changes raise questions about the stability and integration of citizenship identities based upon traditional modes of loyalty and commitment. There has already been an erosion of entitlements within the modern welfare state and citizenship entitlements. The twenty-first century will be characterized by a growing scarcity of work (hence a decline in the traditional employment route into citizenship entitlement) and a corresponding decline of loyalty and solidarity within the nation-state. How can the state secure the loyalty of younger generations who are under-employed or unemployed, who will never serve in a national army, and who may not form families either because of personal sexual preference or because they may not be able to afford children and support a family? They are citizens only in a superficial and formal sense by being in possession of a passport; in fact we may give them the title of 'quasi-citizens'. We can anticipate that the loyalties of these marginalized groups may be 'artificially' sustained by creating in them a fear of outsiders and foreigners who are 'stealing' their jobs, their homes and their girlfriends. Their alienation may eventuate paradoxically in an increased patriotic loyalty that targets strangers as the cause of their misery. Nationalist and fascist revivals in the former regions of East Germany and racial unrest in France are indications of these fears. The traditional mixture of youth unemployment, racial antagonism and political alienation is providing a fertile basis for xenophobic politics in contemporary Europe.

The erosion of the citizen-intellectual has taken place through processes that were described in Bauman's notion of the separation of the state from the legitimation of the national culture. As the state has retreated from the protection and evaluation of culture, markets have been more important in shaping the order of values. However, with the growth of new global communication systems, intellectuals can of course play a global role in shaping the world of symbolic analysis. Intellectuals may find new roles as mediators between local and global cultures. What will be the shape of their loyalties?

These conclusions look rather pessimistic, especially in terms of the growth of racial conflict among the poor urban white working class of Europe and North America. But perhaps there could also be more positive outcomes, namely a reduction in the intensity of national commitment to the state and a greater willingness to support multicultural policies and the creation of identities that are not simply focused on a narrow racial basis. The argument here is that cosmopolitan virtue would be initially a mentality and morality characteristic of globalized intellectuals (in the broad sense), but, following Elias's model, there may be a trickle-down effect.

The post-modernization of identity

We can think of these two dimensions (political loyalty to the state and social solidarity) in terms of a typology defined on the one hand by the notion of hot/cool loyalty (following the work of Marshall McLuhan) and thick/thin solidarity which indicates the depth and strength of the forms of inclusion.[3] This typology enables us to develop an ironic theory of loyalty and solidarity in modern society. Thick solidarities very well describe the type of social involvement of, for example, the Arunta tribe in Emile Durkheim's analysis of mechanical solidarity in his *The Elementary Forms of the Religious Life* (Durkheim, 1954). The Arunta world involved the closed communities of a quasi-nomadic life of hunter-gatherer tribalism. Their social relations were largely permanent, emotional and solid, and their belief systems were not regularly challenged. By contrast, modern societies are organized around the marketplace of anonymous strangers, where these strangers are mobile and disconnected. The distinction between hot/cool loyalties is taken from McLuhan's analysis of modern communication; for example, the telephone offers a uni-dimensional communication with high definition. It is a cool medium, while the tribal mode of communication of tradition by oral and ritualistic means is hot. This distinction in McLuhan's theory of the media is redeployed in this chapter to talk about modes of loyalty in the modern state.

Here post-modern or cosmopolitan citizenship will be characterized by cool loyalties and thin patterns of solidarity. Indeed we could argue that the characteristic mode or orientation of the cosmopolitan citizen would in fact be one of (Socratic) disloyalty and ironic distance. An ironist always holds her views about the social world in doubt, because they are always subject to revision and reformulation.[4] Her picture of society is always provisional and she is skeptical about grand narratives, because her own 'final vocabulary' is always open to further inspection and correction. Her ironic views of the world are always 'for the time being'. If the cosmopolitan mentality is cool, the social relationships of the ironist will be thin; indeed e-mail friendships and electronic networks will constitute the new patterns of friendship in a post-modern globe.

These post-modern cool loyalties will be characteristic of the global elite of symbolic analysts who are geographically and socially mobile, finding employment in different global corporations in different parts of the world. These mobile symbolic analysts are quite likely to enjoy multiple citizenships, several economic identities, and various status positions within a number of blended families. They are inclined toward reflexivity because they get the point of hermeneutic anthropology – namely that the world is a site of contested loyalties and interpretations. The post-modern citizen is only moving on. By contrast, those sections of the population which are relatively immobile and located in traditional employment patterns (the working class, ethnic minorities and the under classes) may in fact continue to have hot loyalties and thick patterns of solidarity. In a world of mounting unemployment and ethnic tensions, the working class and the inhabitants of areas of rural depopulation may well be recruited to nationalist and reactionary parties. Their worldview, rather than being ironic, becomes associated with reactionary nationalism. The third possibility would be characteristic of the liberal middle classes and professional groups who have relatively cool loyalties to the nation-state, but are involved in a dense network of voluntary associations and other institutional links within society, and therefore have thick solidarity. These ethnic patriots resemble the neo-tribalism described by Michel Maffesoli (1996) as a subterranean *Gemeinschaft* in contemporary societies. Their affective world will revolve around social spectacle, particularly the gladiatorial struggles between national football teams.

Cosmopolitan virtue

While these post-modern commitments and disloyalties are often described in a negative fashion, they are perfectly functional in a world where the rigidities of the nation-state with its thick solidarities are collapsing in the face of globalized economies and societies. Citizenship within a multicultural environment will have to be understood through a framework that requires sophisticated forms of tolerance, in which thick moralities may prohibit the evolution of inter-civilizational agreements over moral codes (Walzer, 1994; 1997). Cosmopolitanism within this Rortian world can be justified morally, because hot loyalties and thick solidarities are more likely to be points of conflict and violence in post-modern, ethnically diverse labour markets. Indifference and distance may be useful personal strategies in a risk society where ambiguity and uncertainty reign. In a more fluid world, the ironic citizen needs to learn how to move on, how to adjust and adapt to a world of cultural contingency. Because historically we have learned to respect the virtues of loyalty and duty, we find it difficult to embrace the suggestion that the next century will not be able to afford strong nationalist commitment in a global community where hybridity and diversity have all but obscured the stable world of nineteenth-century nationalism. It was the political environment of loyalty to the state and trust in political leaders which at least contributed to twentieth-century authoritarianism on both the left and the right. The ironic citizen of the global city may hopefully be less likely to give her undivided support to whatever government happens to be in power. We need an ideology of membership, therefore, which will celebrate the uncertainty of belonging where our 'final vocabularies' are never final. A pragmatic philosophy does not, according to this argument, rule out political commitment or serious intellectual engagement. On the contrary, it requires a careful commitment to improving the lot of ordinary people without any rigid identification with conventional ideologies of the cultural left (Rorty, 1998).

It is interesting, finally, to connect this discussion of movement with the origins of social contract theory in the late sixteenth century. In the little known work of Simon Stevin, a native of Bruges who was born in 1548, on the life of the citizen (*Het Burgherlick Leven*) of 1590, there is the interesting idea that, before becoming the citizen of a particular place, individuals have a right to travel in order to study the civil societies and constitutions of different lands (Romein-Verschoor, 1955). Before giving their loyalty to a particular state through a social contract, citizens had to be well informed about their options; travel and mobility were thus essential preconditions for loyalty and commitment. This view of peripatetic citizenship was a consequence of Stevin's own experiences of political uncertainty and conflict in the 'low countries' of that time. There is however, in this early version of contractarianism, an important lesson for us that psychological and political distance may be necessary conditions for any subsequence and conditional identity with the polity. Uncertain loyalties and contingent identities may become virtues of a postmodern society.

The components of cosmopolitan virtue are as follows: irony both as a method and as a mentality; distance and reflexivity (coolness); scepticism (towards grand narratives); care for other cultures (arising from an awareness of their precarious condition) and acceptance of hybridization; post-emotionalism; 'presentism' as opposed to nostalgia; and secularity or an ecumenical appreciation of other religions and cultures.

Cosmopolitan virtue in a post-emotional city

We can of course find precursors of this idea of ironic distance in, for example, the idea of the other-directed personality. It is helpful to illustrate the characteristics of cosmopolitan virtue through the idea of a post-emotional society. Stjepan Mestrovic's *Postemotional Society* is self-consciously a tribute to David Riesman's *The Lonely Crowd* of 1950, which analysed American society around the distinction between the inner-directed and the other-directed personality. Riesman, who provides a brief foreword to the book, is a figure who provides a linking theme throughout this argument. The book was a critique of the impact of advertising and opinion-formation on the lives and mentalities of the professional middle class in urban America. The theory of the lonely crowd was part of a larger critique of American commercial culture and its impact on the psychology of the upwardly mobile lower middle and middle classes. Whereas the Protestant founding fathers, according to Max Weber, built America on the basis of inner-worldly asceticism and personal discipline, the other-directed business executives of the 1950s were consumed by the need for approval through favourable opinion. They had lost all sense of self-direction and personal worth. In post-emotional society, the other-directed personality becomes a 'powerless inside-dopester' whose emotional life ranges from ineffectual indignation to being nice. These emotional responses are, however, also packaged; in the new etiquette books, being nice becomes ritualized and routinized.

Mestrovic, who is generally hostile to post-modern theory, reconceptualizes emotions through the lens of Jean Baudrillard's analysis of the simulacra. In *Cool Memories* (1990) and *America* (1989), Baudrillard provides a far-reaching critique of American society as a culture that is recycled, and simulated through advertising. Disneyland is America, because the endless circulation of empty signs has destroyed the division between the real and the fake. Baudrillard's study of America is a reflection on Alexis de Tocqueville's historical study of American democracy. For de Tocqueville, the cultural emphasis on egalitarianism threatened to undermine individualism and self-reliance. In Baudrillard's work, the empty signs of commercialism undermine authentic experiences, but ironically America is a success. Europe is a society of failed revolutions and thwarted political aspirations; America is a successful commercial cornucopia (Rojek and Turner, 1993).

Thus, to summarize, modern society is post-emotional because (1) it is over-emotional or hyper-emotional; (2) emotions are manufactured and simulated as tokens of social relationships, thus replacing primary relationships; (3) they are recycled through a nostalgic paradigm of the authentic past, which (re)presents contemporary realities through the simulated icons of past ages; and finally (4) they are customized through a process of cultural standardization. Post-emotional society is 'a concrete world of rooted fictions saturated with emotions that are *displaced*, misplaced and manipulated by the culture industry' (Mestrovic, 1997, p. 39).

Apart from this passive conclusion, Mestrovic's position is open to two important criticisms, which we should consider. First, the formulation of a contrast case is important in convincing us that the phenomenon at hand is adequately defined, and more importantly that it exists. If post-emotional society exists, what would emotional society look like? Where and when did it exist? One answer might be that, before the rise of a mass consumer society, real emotions were placed in a natural context and could function alongside reason as guides to action. Authentic emotions thus exist in traditional societies before the rise of simulation and McDonaldization. Perhaps the work of Norbert Elias might provide some historical verification of the notion that, for example, western societies, before the dominance of bourgeois civility, permitted and valued the display of raw emotions in public. The civilizing process (Elias, 1978) thus contributed to the transformation of emotions. Civility brought about a sophistication of emotional life, in which people had to learn techniques of emotional control. In turn, this urban civility permitted the idea that civilized people could display or create appropriate emotional gestures and responses.

My final problem is that, given the complexity and the hybridization of the global city, there is no convenient place for real or hot emotions (Turner, 1998). Inter-cultural sensitivities and the need to interact constantly with urban strangers promote irony as the most prized norm of wit and principle of taste. Irony is sensitive to the simulation which is necessary for interaction in global, multicultural societies (Rorty, 1989). In such a world, ironic distance is functionally compatible with globalized hybridity because we have all become strangers in the Simmelian city. Hot emotions and thick solidarities are dysfunctional to social intercourse, which has to take place on a purely superficial and artificial plane. The difficulty for Mestrovic's condemnation of the Artificial City is that post-emotionalism may be functionally necessary for modern society to exist. Hence, he has difficulty in finding a remedy to accompany the diagnosis.

Conclusion: irony, stewardship and cosmopolitan virtue

By describing the intellectual as ironic, the intellectual may be taken to be indifferent to ethical issues. Cosmopolitan virtue does not mean moral indifference. One could imagine that cosmopolitan virtue could take on a more active engagement with cultural issues such as (1) the protection of so-called primitive cultures and aboriginal communities which are clearly threatened by globalization, and (2) responsibility for advocacy in a world of collapsing environments and endangered languages. Perhaps it is not too fanciful to believe that, precisely because of exposure to global concerns and global issues, the urban ironists might, in recognizing the ubiquity of hybridization, reject all claims to cultural superiority and cultural dominance. Precisely because we are exposed to global forces of post-modernization, the ironists should welcome a stance which supports post-colonial cultures and celebrates the teeming diversity of human cultures. In their awareness of the tensions between local cultures and global processes, cosmopolitan virtue might come to recognize a stewardship over and for cultures that are precarious.

Notes

1 Elsewhere (Turner, 1990b, 1997) I argued that the concept of citizenship was primarily a modern political notion, namely a concept of political relations that dated from the French and industrial revolutions. It charts the history of the growth of bourgeois civil society, that is a public space of opinion formation in relation to democratic institutions. Any use of the concept with respect to Athens or Greece is misleading, because the very existence of the modern concept indicates the decline of slavery and feudalism. I do not wish to depart radically from that view, except to note here that the Treaty of Westphalia recognized a necessary precondition for such a development, namely the creation of an international system of nation-states.

2 There is an important, but somewhat neglected, argument that warfare is a fundamental force in the modern creation of national citizenship. Richard M. Titmuss (1963) argued that war had contributed significantly to the creation of social security schemes. The theme was taken up by Marshall and further elaborated as a cause, along with migration and social movements, of the expansion of social rights in *Citizenship and Capitalism* (Turner, 1986). Perhaps the point to stress, however, is that warfare also creates a cultural identity in which the individual fortunes of service men and women are tied to the self-image of the nation-state as an historical actor.

3   This model of solidarity was first presented as a public lecture to celebrate the fiftieth anniversary of the Department of Sociology at Lund in a symposium on 'Sociology Facing the 21st Century'. The paper was published as a research report (Isenberg, 1998).
4   This use of gendered terminology is consciously employed here to reflect Rorty's use of 'her' in describing the attitudes of the modern ironist (Rorty, 1989).

Bibliography

Aldrich, R. and Connell, J. (1992) *France's Overseas Frontier* (Cambridge: Cambridge University Press).

Anderson, B. (1983) *Imagined Communities: Reflections on the Origin and Spread of Nationalism* (London: Verso).

Barry, B.M. (1977) 'Justice between Generations', in P.M.S. Hacker and J. Raz (eds), *Law Morality and Society: Essays in Honour of H.L A. Hart* (Oxford: Clarendon Press).

Baudrillard, J. (1989) *America* (London: Verso).

—— (1990) *Cool Memories* (London: Verso).

Beck, U. and Gernsheim-Beck, E. (1990) *Das ganz normale Chaos der Liebe* (Frankfurt: Suhrkamp).

Bell, D. (1974) *The Coming of Post-industrial Society* (New York: Basic Books).

Bobbio, N. (1987) *The Future of Democracy*, trans. R. Griffin (Cambridge: Polity Press).

—— (1989) *Democracy and Dictatorship: The Nature and Limits of State Power*, trans. P. Kennealy (Oxford: Polity).

Brubaker, R. (1992) *Citizenship and Nationhood in France and Germany* (Cambridge: Harvard University Press).

Cohen, J. and Rogers, J. (1995) *Associations and Democracy* (London: Verso).

Debord, G. (1987) *The Society of the Spectacle* (London: Rebel Press).

Durkheim, E. (1954) *The Elementary Forms of the Religious Life* (London: Allen and Unwin).

Elias, N. (1978) *The Civilizing Process: The History of Manners* (Oxford: Basil Blackwell).

Ferry, L. (1990) *Political Philosophy* (Chicago: University of Chicago Press).

Halevy, E. (1962) *A History of the English People in the Nineteenth Century*, 2 vols, 2nd edn (London: Benn).

Hechter, M. (1975) *Internal Colonialism: The Celtic Fringe in British National Development, 1536–1966* (Berkeley, CA: University of California Press).

Hirst, P.Q. (ed.) (1989) *The Pluralist Theory of the State: Selected Writings of G.D.H. Cole, J.N. Figgis and H.J. Laski* (London: Routledge).

Holton, R.J. and Turner, B.S. (1989) *Max Weber on Economy and Society* (London: Routledge).

Inwood, M. (ed.) (1992) *A Hegel Dictionary* (Oxford: Blackwell).

Isenberg, B. (ed.) (1998) *Sociology and Social Transformation* Lund University Research Report.

James, P. (1996) *Nation Formation: Towards a Theory of Abstract Community* (London: Sage).

Janoski, T. (1998) *Citizenship and Civil Society: A Framework of Rights and Obligations in Liberal, Traditional and Democratic Regimes* (Cambridge: Cambridge University Press).

Lee, D. and Turner, B.S. (eds) (1996) *Conflicts about Class: Debating Inequality in Late Industrialism* (London: Longman).

Locke, J. (1690 [1884]) *Two Treatises of Government* (London: Routledge).

Lyotard, J-F. (1984) *The Post-modern Condition: A Report on Knowledge* (Manchester: University of Manchester Press).

McLuhan, M.(1964) *Understanding the Media: The Extension of Man* (Toronto: McGraw-Hill).

Maffesoli, M. (1996) *The Time of the Tribes: The Decline of Individualism in Mass Society* (London: Sage).

Mann, M.(1987) 'Ruling Class Strategies and Citizenship', *Sociology*, 21: 339–54.

Marshall, T.H. (1950) *Citizenship and Social Class* (Cambridge: Cambridge University Press).

—— (1964) *Class, Citizenship and Social Development* (Chicago: University of Chicago Press).

Mestrovic, S.G. (1997) *Postemotional Society* (London: Sage).

Mouffe, C. (1992) *Dimensions of Radical Democracy: Pluralism and Citizenship* (London: Verso).

Reich, R. (1991) *The Work of Nations: Preparing Ourselves for 21st Century Capitalism* (New York: Random House).

Rojek, C. and Turner, B.S. (eds) (1993) *Forget Baudrillard?* (London: Routledge).

Romein-Verschoor, A. (1955) *Civic Life by Simon Stevin* (Amsterdam: Swets and Zeitlinger).

Rorty, R. (1989) *Contingency, Irony and Solidarity* (Cambridge: Cambridge University Press).

—— (1998) *Achieving our Country: Leftist Thought in Twentieth-Century America* (Cambridge: MA, Harvard University Press).

Saxonhouse, A.W. (1992) *Fear of Diversity: The Birth of Political Science in Ancient Greek Thought* (Chicago and London: University of Chicago Press).

Titmuss, R.M. (1963) *Essays on 'The Welfare State'* (London: Unwin University Books).

Turner, B.S. (1986) *Citizenship and Capitalism: The Debate over Reformism* (London: Allen and Unwin).

—— (ed.) (1990a) *Theories of Modernity and Post-modernity* (London: Sage).

—— (1990b) 'Outline of a Theory of Citizenship', *Sociology*, 24 (2): 189–217.

—— (1997) 'Citizenship Studies: A General Theory', *Citizenship Studies*, 1 (1): 5–18.

—— (1998) 'Post-modernisation of Political Identities: Solidarity and Loyalty in Contemporary Society', in B. Isenberg (ed.), *Sociology and Social Transformation*, Lund University. Research Report.

Walzer, M. (1994) *Thick and Thin Moral Argument at Home and Abroad* (Notre Dame: University of Notre Dame Press).

—— (1997) *On Toleration* (New Haven, CT: Yale University Press).

Weber, M. (1981) *General Economic History*, trans. F.H. Knight (New Brunswick, NJ: Transaction Books).

Wolin, S.S. (1961) *Politics and Vision: Continuity and Innovation in Western Political Thought* (London: George Allen and Unwin).

Yuval-Davis, N. (1997) *Gender & Nation* (London: Sage).

8 Governing cities without government[1]

Engin F. Isin

Introduction

Since 1953 Metropolitan Toronto has been synonymous with effective regional government. When, in 1997–98, both the constituent municipalities and the government of Metropolitan Toronto were abolished and consolidated into a single-tier city of Toronto by the conservative government, which was swept into power in 1995, it unleashed both a province-wide and, in some circles, nation-wide debate and activism over the nature, purpose and function of local government in particular, and local democracy in general. Many students of local government drew parallels with the abolishment of the Greater London Council (GLC) by the Thatcher government in 1986. This chapter attempts to situate the consolidation within the broader aims of the government as an instance of even broader transformation of mentalities of government that have become dominant in the last two decades in liberal democracies in Europe, North America, Australia and New Zealand. 'Governing without government' implies a shift in both (the aims and instruments of government,) in that within the new mentalities of government the focus is less on governmental institutions and more on the strategies and technologies of government, a shift that has been captured by the increased usage of the term 'governance' in fields as diverse as local government studies and international relations. The perspective from which the assessment of the formation of the new city of Toronto is undertaken in this chapter is not, however, one of 'governance' but 'an analytics of government' (Rose, 1999, pp. 15–20; Dean, 1999, pp. 20–7). Before examining the changes brought about and resisted in Toronto, I briefly outline the development of the currently dominant advanced liberal form of government and its implications for 'governing the local'.

An analytics of local government

Typically, analyses of government centre upon the state as the source of authority and take state institutions as their objects. 'Government' in such analyses means both the government in power and its activities sanctioned by a parliament or legislature. More recently, a literature on government following the studies by Michel Foucault (1977; 1979), suggested a shift in focus. Rather than taking the state and law as its centre, it is suggested, we can define government as a general activity or practice of conduct of conduct. This shift in emphasis, while drawing attention to both the activities and consequences of governing, resulted in various studies of 'governmentality' exploring how specific mentalities constitute different practices as their object and subject of government (Dean, 1999; Rose, 1999). Government is thus defined as any more or less calculated and rationalized activity, undertaken by a multiplicity of authorities and agencies, employing a variety of techniques and forms of knowledge, which seeks to shape conduct by working through the desires, aspirations, interests and beliefs of both those who govern and those who are governed (cf. Dean, 1999, pp. 11–16).

From this perspective an analysis of government is concerned with the means of calculation, both qualitative and quantitative, the type of governing authority and agency, the form of knowledge, techniques and other means employed, the objects of government and their conceptualization, the ends sought, and the outcomes and consequences. The focus is therefore on regimes or practices of government, insofar as governmental institutions, procedures or rules are studied. An analytics of government examines the conditions under which regimes or practices of government arise, are maintained and transformed. These regimes of government embody institutional practices in the sense that they are routinized and ritualized in specific manners. This entails a focus on regimes of government as organized practices that become relatively durable and enduring aspects of governing. An analytical approach to these practices is useful precisely because it begins to reveal the invented, strategic or programmatic character of otherwise taken-for-granted and relatively enduring practices of government.

> An analytics of a particular regime of practices, at a minimum, seeks to identify the emergence of that regime, examine the multiple sources of the elements that constitute it, and follow the diverse processes and relations by which these elements are assembled into relatively stable forms of organization and institutional practice.
>
> (Dean, 1999, p. 21)

To secure and maintain institutionalization and routinization of practices, regimes of government depend upon professional and expert forms of knowledge to monitor, enact, evaluate and reform both the subjects and objects of government. Regimes of government thus develop a programmatic character by adopting deliberate and relatively systematic forms of thought that continuously reform their practices. An analytics of government often commences analysis by examining aspects of regimes of practices, which are thus called into question or problematized. It thus seeks to discover the intrinsic logic or strategy of a regime of practices via exploration of its characteristic forms of visibility, and ways of seeing and perceiving as embodied in particular locales, milieux and documents. When doing so it takes special care to emphasize that these characteristic ways (logics and strategies) are intentional but not subjective in the sense that while they are articulable, they are not reducible or attributable to the opinions, views, desires, ideas and claims of any one agent or any group of agents. 'The critical purchase of an analytics of government often stems from the disjunction between the explicit, calculated and programmatic rationality and the non-subjective intentionality that can be constructed through analysis' (Dean, 1999, p. 22).

In short, an analytics of government focuses on (1) characteristic forms of visibility, ways of seeing and perceiving; (2) distinctive ways of thinking questioning, relying on definite vocabularies and procedures for the production of knowledge; (3) specific ways of acting, intervening and directing, embodying specific types of rationality and relying upon various mechanisms, techniques and technologies; and (4) characteristic ways of forming and addressing subjects, selves, persons or agents. This is a very different focus from studying governmental institutions, norms, procedures, legislation and policies as intentional *and* subjective instruments. That an analytics of government focuses on the intentional but non-subjective character of the regimes or practices of government makes it possible to link these practices with broader and wider mentalities of rule, and to trace out their connections, deployment and dissemination – their genealogies, if you like.

If we follow these principles, we cannot consider local government merely as practices engaged and services delivered by municipal governments with specific territorial jurisdiction. Rather, local government can be considered as the multiplicity of authorities and agencies that seek to shape conduct within specific fields that are substantively deterritorialized but territorially organized. Recently, the shift of focus in local government studies from government to governance signifies the recognition of the trend that municipal governments have become entangled with a variety of authorities in governing the local (Andrew and Goldsmith, 1998; Wilson, 1998). There is a growing recognition that local government is accomplished through multiple actors and agencies rather than a centralized set of state apparatuses. Some argue that many of the practices considered to be new, such as quangos, have long been an essential aspect of local government and that their novelty is exaggerated (Imrie and Raco, 1999). Nevertheless, it is undeniable that there has been a fundamental shift in local government in the last two decades (Aulich, 1999; Eisinger, 1998; Johnston and Pattie, 1996; Lewis and Moran, 1998; Loughlin, 1996; Marshall, 1998; Stoker, 1996a). There has been a paradoxical double movement where, on the one hand, central governments have increased their control over local authorities via new techniques and technologies, such as auditing, monitoring, appointing, measuring and regulating, and where, on the other hand, they have increasingly devolved, downloaded, contractualized, marketized and entrepreneurialized local governmental functions via a plethora of agencies, quangos and partnerships. It is this double movement of centralization of control and decentralization of function, and the techniques and technologies by which it is accomplished, that is new and requires new theoretical perspectives and empirical analyses.

Yet so far the tendency among students of local government has been to invoke broad substantive theories such as regulation or regime theory to 'explain' or interpret this double movement (see Clark, 1997; Goodwin and Painter, 1996; Isin and Wolfson, 1999; Jones, 1998; Mayer, 1996; Purcell, 1997). Those who recognize these shifts still remain focused on institutions and agencies, whether it be quangos or partnerships, rather than regimes of local government.

The value of studies on governmentality is precisely their refusal to start with general theories or a set of non-negotiable substantive theoretical principles. An analytics of government allows bracketing out of theoretical questions and focuses on questions of how different agents are assembled with specific powers, how different domains are constituted as authoritative and powerful, and how these regimes connect up with broader mentalities of rule. By so doing it allows disjunctive interpretations, rather than over-determining transformations by evaluating them with older categories. This is no more obvious than with regard to the idea of local democracy. While some argue that the neo-liberal forms of government eradicated local democracy, others argue that they have made local governments more democratic by empowering consumers (Beetham, 1996; King and Stoker, 1996; Stoker, 1996b; Teune, 1995). There is certainly an analytical and political need to bracket out values of local democracy and cast a critical eye on both its valorizations and devalorizations. There is obviously no space here to elaborate upon the political and theoretical strengths and weaknesses of such a perspective on local government. Rather, this chapter aims to contribute both to the rethinking of government in local government studies and to governing the local in studies on governmentality by focusing on a specific regime of government that emerged in Toronto in the second half of the 1990s.

Liberalism and municipal government

Since the nineteenth century the liberal conception of municipal government has constituted the city as a simultaneous space of government and liberty, which was captured by perhaps one of the most revealing phrases of liberalism – 'local self-government' or 'local democracy'. This concept embodied two seemingly contradictory movements. First, it expressed autonomy exercised by municipal governments, where cities were accorded powers to manage their 'local' affairs. It was a political space in which the bourgeois *man*, as owner of property and head of the household, learned how to participate in the democratic process, practice his citizenship and develop his virtues, civics and loyalty. Second, the municipality was constituted as a space of government in which subjects as members of specifically targeted 'groups' were subjected to discipline via requirements placed upon municipal government. Hospitals, prisons, schools, policing and correctional institutions were operated and maintained by municipal governments. There is a telling symbolism in the fact that de Tocqueville came to America to study the penitentiary system and wrote an influential book about the need for local self-government (de Beaumont and de Tocqueville, 1964; de Tocqueville, 1945). With the celebration of individual liberty in the nineteenth century, there arose a bewildering array of practices that governed the conduct of individuals as members of groups. It seems as if liberty was really the emancipation of bourgeois *man* from the shackles of aristocracy, but it also meant a new tangled web of obligations for groups of individuals, which the bourgeoisie depended upon. While the nineteenth century is replete with the talk of the liberty of bourgeois *man* (never specified but always universalized), an immense machinery of regulation was put in place that acted upon the conduct of 'dangerous' groups. For labouring men and women, children, youth, the poor, destitute and mentally ill, the world of freedom was as abstract as the brave new world of wealth, colonialism and imperialism. It is in this sense that liberty and order were not contradictory but interdependent realities. The exercise of liberty, constituting oneself as a civil man meant the constitution of the city as an ordered space with its norms, patterns, regularities and properties.

In Canada, France, Germany, Britain and America resolving this conflict or tension between the two 'contradictory' principles of liberty and order within liberal rationalities of government followed different trajectories. While municipal government in America showed the most entrepreneurial zeal in addressing the conflict and in creating spaces of liberty and order simultane-ously by building up a massive disciplinary infrastructure layered upon the autonomous space of expression and investment, in France and Britain the relics of past municipal governments required the heavier hand of states to introduce legislation and open up new spaces of discipline *and* freedom.[2]

How did liberalism assemble various practices of government into a specific mentality of government, a manner of governing?[3] Nikolas Rose has suggested that in responding to a series of problems about the governability of individuals, families, markets and groups, regimes of truth emerged about these problems as problems of conduct solvable by action at a distance rather than violence or force (Rose, 1996b). The rise of expertise in the sense of authority arising out of a claim to knowledge, to neutrality and efficacy, came to provide a number of solutions to the tension between liberty and order. By a sheer explosion of statistical and other forms of knowledge, the governing authorities described in detail how the lifestyles of various groups (for example, the mentally ill, immigrants, hysterical women, unruly children) and working classes departed from expected and useful norms. The rise of sites for correcting such departures such as hospitals, correctional facilities, prisons, housing projects and other institutions marked the characteristic form of liberal government. What made liberalism governmental rather than philosophical was its wish to make itself practical, to connect itself up with various procedures and apparatuses of correction, inculcation and disposition.

There is certainly an affinity between liberalism as regimes of truth and assemblages of practices and the regimes of accumulation in nineteenth-century capitalism. With the rise of factory, workshop and market as fundamental mechanisms of a new regime of accumulation, there was certainly the question of transforming the dangerous classes into working classes. That said, however, liberalism as an assemblage of governing practices cannot be read off from 'interests' of capital accumulation or dictates of capitalism. To assume a straightforward causal homology between liberalism and capitalism overlooks the fact that governing practices embody their own histories and develop their own rationalities which may or may not link up with economy. As much as capitalism needed liberalism as a series of technologies of government, the rise of liberalism as a regime of government also made capitalism possible. Well before the rise of factory discipline, for example, the early modern workhouses made a major contribution to the discipline of the working classes. The labouring men and women were not simply found in cities looking for jobs; they were made into a class by technologies of power. Liberalism relied on strategies, techniques and procedures through which different state authorities sought to enact programmes of government in relation to different groups and classes, and the resistances and oppositions anticipated or encountered (Burchell, 1996; Rose, 1996b, 1996c). These technologies of power did not derive from a formula but were invented throughout the late eighteenth and nineteenth centuries in Europe and America. The more there was talk about the liberty of the bourgeois *man*, the more there was a proliferation of such techniques. The constitution of the self as an object of regulation was linked up with the constitution of groups as objects of discipline.

An aspect of the 'governmentalization of the state' that both Foucault and subsequent studies neglected was that the tension between order and liberty – between the necessity of making individuals conducive to a moral order and opening up a space of freedom in which individuals govern themselves – was clearly connected with the problem of municipal government. Nineteenth-century liberalism inherited a conception of municipal government that followed the principles of state sovereignty: municipality was a site of absolute exercise of power over groups of individuals. For example, through the sixteenth- and seventeenth-century poor laws, beggars, vagabonds and other groups were subjected to brutal and punitive power, and cities were ruled by self-perpetuating oligarchies drawn from aristocracy (Isin, 1992a, 1992b). The governing of cities in early modern Europe became a major target of reform for liberalism. For example, in England, on the one hand the bourgeoisie lacked representation in cities, and, on the other cities had not yet become technologies of power to target the working classes. However, a series of liberal reforms including the Reform Act (1832) and the Municipal Corporations Act (1835) dramatically altered the conception of municipal government that liberalism inherited. These acts, and a plethora of commissions, reports and surveys associated with them, were clearly concerned about governing cities. While the fundamental aspects of local government remained intact throughout the nineteenth and early twentieth centuries, there were also significant changes that locked local government into a network of governing practices. By the second half of the twentieth century, with the rise of the welfare state and expansion of government services, municipal government increasingly played a more significant role in the provision and delivery of these services. In addition to policing, education, hospitals and prisons, welfare and housing were the most important functions that cities assumed. The introduction of metropolitan or regional governments to co-ordinate, rationalize and provide new soft and hard services such us public transportation, housing and social services became a widely used experiment within the liberal rationalities of government (Magnusson, 1981). Municipal government was subsumed under the welfare state.

Advanced liberalism, new groups and municipal government

In the late twentieth century and early twenty-first century, from Canada to New Zealand, we have witnessed the rise of new rationalities of government. The primary focus has been to 're-engineer' the welfare state: the privatization of public utilities and welfare functions in the opening up of health services, social insurance and pension schemes to markets; educational reforms to introduce competition between colleges and universities; the introduction of new forms of management into the civil service modelled upon an image of methods in the private sector; new contractual relations between agencies and service providers, and between professionals and clients; and a new emphasis on the personal responsibilities of individuals, their families and their communities for their own future well-being as well as their own obligation to take active steps to secure this. In other words, we are seeing the emergence of a new 'governmentality' – the deliberations, strategies, tactics and devices employed by authorities for making up and acting upon a population and its constituents to ensure effective governance (Isin et al., 1998; Rose, 1996a, 1996c).

The rise of a new regime of governmentality has been called 'advanced liberalism', and its tactics, strategies and rationalities have been called 'neo-liberal'. Consistent with the view that considers liberalism a philosophy, neo-liberalism has been defined by its fiscal conservatism, by the reduction of budget deficits that have been the hallmark of the activist welfare state and hence by the reduction of the role of government in markets. The problem with this definition is that it focuses upon justifications rather than practices. Some studies have shown, for example, that despite severe cutbacks in the public sector, government spending as a percentage of gross domestic product has actually continued to increase (Carpenter, 1995; Hardt and Negri, 1994). If, however, we consider neo-liberalism as a series of technologies of power, this apparently paradoxical empirical record may assume a different meaning. In other words, it can be argued that neo-liberalism has not been about less government but about shifting the techniques, focus and priorities of government.

Although various neo-conservative regimes have been elected in Britain, America, Canada and New Zealand since the 1970s, it would be misleading to suggest that these regimes had a clear political ideology or programme at the outset, which they then implemented. Rather, these regimes initially sought to solve some perceived and real problems associated with finance, services and capital accumulation. But gradually, these diverse experiments were rationalized within a relatively coherent rationality of government that can be described as advanced liberalism. Despite all the rhetoric of the reduction of government and the rollback of the state, advanced liberalism has not abandoned its will to govern but merely shifted its focus and, more importantly, rationalized some old techniques as well as invented some new techniques of government. Therefore the state in liberal democracies is perhaps stronger and more effective in more sectors than it was in the 1970s. And yet the image that persists is the decline of the state, if not its death. This stems from the fact that many associate the state with its institutions rather than considering it a field of governmental practices in which the government is one agent among others.

Considering the rise of advanced liberalism as an invention of new technologies of power rather than as a decline of the state, three characteristic shifts have been suggested. The first shift concerns a new relationship between expertise and politics. While in liberalism knowledge had come to occupy a central role in government by virtue of its ability to raise claims to truth and validity in fields such as education, health and cities, the legitimacy and authority of new knowledges do not derive from their truth and validity, but from their ability to gauge performance. Accordingly, there has been a shift from the older occupations of law, medicine and academics to newer occupations of expert consultancy, accountancy and audit (Rose, 1996b; Starr, 1987). If the modes of circulation of knowledges that animated liberal technologies of power were verity, validity, reliability, the new modes of circulation are enumeration, calculation, monitoring and evaluation. With this shift from older occupations to new ones, there is also a shift in the sites where education, training and certification take place. Universities that traditionally educated and trained cadres of public sector professionals in law, medicine and administration are now pressured to shift to new occupations. In addition the new occupations shift their focus from the patient, the ill and the poor to the client and consumer, who are constituted as autonomous individuals capable of making the right choices (Brint, 1994). Risk reduction has become an individual responsibility rather than a collective or state responsibility. Neo-liberalism therefore constitutes the individual not as a subject of intervention but as an active agent of decision and choice. This is a significant shift in the production of subjectivities in that, instead of disciplines, the field of choice and its structure become a contested arena of political struggle.

A second shift concerns the proliferation of new technologies of power. Evidenced by the rise of quasi-autonomous 'non-governmental' organizations, the new technologies arise out of the shifting of responsibilities from govern-mental agencies and authorities to organizations without electoral accountabil-ity and responsibility, for example, the 'privatization' of 'public' utilities, civil service, prisons, insurance and security. Again, with the proliferation of these technologies neither government nor its will to govern (nor its size) declines. Rather, this shift is about the manner in which individuals are constituted as subjects of government and about the agents who are invested with the responsibility of governing.

A third shift concerns a new specification of the subject of government. The rise of the powers of the individual as client or customer of services specifies the subjects of government in a new way. Individuals are now constituted as active purchasers and enterprisers in pursuit of their own choices: vouchers in education, housing and other services replace 'paternal' forms of distribution. Just as avoiding risk is the responsibility of individuals as authors of their own destiny, ill-fate and misfortune have also become their responsibility: the unemployed, homeless and poor are constituted as responsible for their own condition. Effective governance of such people does not necessarily require governmental intervention, but rather a new subjectification.

Just as there were some affinities between the rise of liberalism and capital-ism, there are also affinities between neo-liberalism and the rise of new groups and classes and different forms of capital in the late twentieth century. This has been associated with the rise of new classes variously described as the 'new class', the professional class or the information bourgeoisie. Sociologists such as Gouldner and Bourdieu have argued that the rise of new groups and classes based on the accumulation of cultural capital (skills and expertise) has considerably transformed political arrangements and institutions in liberal democracies (Bourdieu, 1987; 1991; Clement and Myles, 1994; Gouldner, 1979; Szelényi and Martin, 1990; Wright, 1997). The widespread adoption of neo-liberal technologies of power undoubtedly favours private sector professionals. Harold Perkin (1989), for example, has argued that the main conflict in liberal democracies today is between public sector and private sector professionals (see also Rose, 1996a). Many aspects of the various neo-liberal technologies shift responsibilities from the *paternalistic* state or public professions such as law, medicine and academe toward *entrepreneurial* professions that emphasize client and consumer control: subjects become consumers who are invested with capacities for making choices and agents are no longer state officials exercising authority over them, but experts assisting subjects in making these choices. Again, much of the shift toward privatization does not really cost less in terms of delivering government services but shifts control to these new professions. Brint has characterized this shift as that from 'social trustee professionals' to 'expert professionals' (Brint, 1994). In short, in advanced liberalism, while the agents of power undergo alteration and begin to deploy new technologies of power, the exercise of power shifts from government as an authority to governance practices that operate throughout the social body – hence governance without government.

What role does municipal government assume under advanced liberalism? How does advanced liberalism constitute local government? Amidst much debate over liberty, markets and consumerism, there is an increasing and parallel emphasis on communities as means of government: Rose argues that, consonant with the emphasis of neo-liberalism on conceiving individuals as active participants in their own government, the relations of obligation have shifted from citizens and society mediated and regulated by the state to relations between active individuals and their immediate communities of allegiance and care. The interesting thing about the increasing emphasis on community in the neo-liberal grammar of government and politics is that the term itself originated as a critique of bureaucratic and rational government. Nonetheless, it has been now incorporated into a neo-liberalism that constitutes various communities, such as moral (religious, ecological, feminist), lifestyle (taste, style and modes of life) and activist. Such communities are construed as heterogeneous, overlapping and multiple, commanding unstable and ephemeral allegiance and existing 'only to the extent that their constituents are linked together through identifications constructed in the non-geographic spaces of activist discourses, cultural products and media images' (Rose, 1996a). From the point of view of this new conception of community, the subject is addressed as a moral individual with bonds of obligation and responsibilities for conducts that are assembled in a way that traverses and criss-crosses fixed territorial boundaries, including those of cities. Thus, rights are not only given today to municipal governments but to groups that define their own moral and geographic boundaries – ones that do not match the fixed boundaries of municipal governments (see also Frazer, 1996).

Modern municipal government does not fit the image of deterritorialized communities that are spread across boundaries and interconnected via a variety of geographic and non-geographic links. Municipal governments with fixed boundaries and self-enclosed spaces of regulation are unable to meet the new specification of the subject and its government. In other words, municipal government becomes one agent among other technologies of power. As we have seen, many of the functions of *modern* municipal government, such as housing, hospitals, prisons, schools and correctional institutions, have either already shifted to the senior levels of government or have been privatized. *Modern city government is increasingly like an empty shell whose territory marks out the once-meaningful boundaries of the political.* Elsewhere the rise of this new urban space was called the 'cosmopolis' (Isin, 1996a, 1996b, 1997). All those who argue for local democracy and seeking political and institutional arrangements are perhaps trying to impose a solution to a problem that has already disappeared from neo-liberal thought.

In the last two decades, in Anglo-American states, municipal government reforms converged on a few elements: forcing reduction in municipal expenditures via a combination of controls on municipal budgets and reduction in transfers; downloading and decentralizing services via enabling municipal governments to privatize or forcing them to establish partnerships with private companies; reforming and consolidating property tax by centralizing its control; radical education reforms introducing central control and abolishing local control; radical public health reforms to centralize control; forcing municipal governments to abandon services such as housing and sell local authority owned dwellings; the formation of a plethora of special purpose bodies or quangos (quasi-autonomous non-governmental organizations); forcing local governments toward user fees as a resource of revenue; and centralizing and/or privatizing correctional and punitive institutions. Admittedly, each of these elements has worked out rather differently in each jurisdiction. Nevertheless, to varying degrees, each neo-liberal regime has sought to implement these measures, and in a very quick manner (Loughlin, 1996). In the debate over local government in Anglo-American states, it has become customary to describe this shift as a transformation from local government to local governance (Andrew and Goldsmith, 1998; Johnston and Pattie, 1996; Wilson, 1998). What is meant by this is that local government is now merely an agent of government in a multiplicity of agents and quangos that are vested with various governmental authorities and powers. While some are sceptical about whether this shift is from local government to local governance or merely a deepening of local government, the general trend of more direct central engagement with the local and the proliferation of local bodies is agreed upon (Imrie and Raco, 1999). Another debate is over whether this shift from local government to local governance increases the possibilities of local democracy or circumvents its established procedures, and whether this shift expands the boundaries of the political or eradicates them (Beetham, 1996; Jones, 1998). Adequately resolving these issues, however, requires placing the transformations in local government within broader transformations in rationalities of government (advanced liberalism) and economy (advanced capitalism) because, taken together or in any combination, these transformations go far beyond 'municipal restructuring', as they constitute a radical restructuring of government.

More recently, these rationalities were at work in various governments in Canada, notably the conservative governments in Alberta and Ontario and the 'left' governments in Quebec and British Columbia. In Ontario, these rationalities found their expression in a remarkable small document that was initially ridiculed by many on the left but which became the campaign platform for the Progressive Conservative Party in the 1995 provincial election: the Common Sense Revolution (CSR). Although arguments were made that the CSR had not made promises for restructuring municipal government or even amalgamation, an examination of its premises reveals that the massive legislation the Harris government introduced in the first two years of its mandate (1995–7) stemmed from its determination to implement the CSR, a neo-liberal programme.

Governing Toronto: citizens for local democracy

It is against the background of these broad transformations of liberal regimes of government and the rise of advanced liberalism that the creation of the new city of Toronto must be understood. The amalgamation of the constituent municipalities of Metropolitan Toronto has sharpened and brought to the fore the main political fault-lines in the city. The inner city constituency of public sector professional-managerial groups reacted defensively, invoking a grammar of local democracy and citizenship. By contrast, immigrant groups, visible minorities and working classes largely watched the debate with relative indifference, perhaps corroborating my earlier suggestion that modern city government is increasingly like an empty shell whose territory marks out the once-meaningful boundaries of the political. These groups remained on the sidelines during the opposition against amalgamation, and during the subsequent election in November 1997 they actively forged ahead with a different agenda – new voices for the new city – which saw amalgamation as an opportunity to secure rights for immigrant groups. This was a major defeat for the public sector professional-managerial groups that coalesced under the banner of Citizens for Local Democracy – affectionately known as C4LD – coming at the end of an arduous fight to stop amalgamation.

At first C4LD appeared to be heading for success. There were two reasons for this. First, when the proposed amalgamation of the constituent municipalities of Metropolitan Toronto was announced in October 1996, the opposition against the Harris government had been building in Ontario for more than sixteen months. Beginning with the swearing-in ceremony on 26 June 1995, the Harris government had been greeted with protests by various social justice groups such as the Ontario Coalition Against Poverty and Metro Network for Social Justice. These protests were widened by the labour movement via a series of 'days of action' in Ontario cities such as London, Hamilton, Kitchener-Waterloo, Peterborough and, finally, Toronto. Massive one-day demonstrations and strikes in these cities were unprecedented in Ontario history. Although downplayed by the government, as expected, the impact of these demonstrations and strikes was beyond doubt, at least in raising the profile of opposition in the media. Although organized labour remained sceptical of municipal politics and kept its distance from C4LD, when C4LD began its agitation to organize, it was addressing already-politicized Torontonians.

Second was the class composition of C4LD. Like its counterparts in other Anglo-American states, particularly in Britain, the Harris government was conceived right from the beginning as a movement against public sector professionals, social interest groups, public sector unions who staffed provincial and municipal bureaucracies, and professionals in education, the arts, media and government – essentially groups that are concentrated in the large cities of the province. Toronto is the largest and the most concentrated city of the new class.[4] The Harris government targeted the public sector segment of the new class from the day it gained power. Not only did it pass legislation to reduce dramatically the provincial government workforce, which led to the first-ever strike by the

union of provincial employees in February to March 1996, but it also systemati-
cally targeted lawyers and doctors, although with limited success. While the
government opened these fronts all at once, these groups had not coalesced until
the very city in which they lived became the target. The proposed amalgamation
of the city with its postwar suburbs would potentially unleash an intellectual
assault of an intensity that few democratic governments had probably ever
endured. More than 500 deputants of the hearings on Bill 103 (the City of
Toronto Act) included the critical voices of prominent urbanists such as Jane
Jacobs, as well as artists, historians, constitutional experts, economists, political
scientists, sociologists, planners, journalists and very eloquent, not-so-ordinary
citizens. Although expecting, in fact almost revelling in, opposition, there is no
doubt that the Harris government was still startled by the depth, sophistication
and strength of all this uproar.

A 'rebellion' march, as well as the referendum and its incredible skills in
commanding symbolic capital throughout February and March made it look as
if perhaps the Harris government was about to lose its first battle and suffer
humiliation at the hands of the very class that it targeted. The government had
looked quite powerful until that moment, at which point even its public
relations officials complained that they were unable to get their message across.
To counteract the symbolic domination of the public sector professionals, the
Harris government itself embarked upon an embarrassing and desperate media
campaign. The downloading, the privatization and the indifference of the
government to democratic procedures and deliberation was suddenly clearly
and forcefully exposed.

Yet C4LD lost the battle. As much as C4LD achieved a certain political
mobilization in the city of Toronto, its grammar of politics based upon liberal
citizenship and democracy and its tactics also failed as a movement. At one
level, its failure was obvious: despite all the activities of C4LD, the Harris
government pressed on with its agenda with little alteration and little concern
for the resistance and opposition. The City of Toronto Act passed in April 1997
with little change, and the government continued its 'downloading' of services
to the municipalities across the province. It also moved ahead with its other
policies, including the centralization of the property taxation system and the
take-over of the education system. Finally, in April 1999, it won a second
majority in the provincial legislature. Meanwhile, C4LD not only became
tangled up in a futile citizens' legal challenge to Bill 103 (led by a smaller
group), but it shrank back to a handful of citizens, who became increasingly
despondent. Finally, C4LD politics failed to make any appreciable impact on
the next election, in which the Harris government won a resounding victory
and a second term.

On another level, the failure had been even deeper. From the beginning,
C4LD appealed to and was led by the new class, which was, compared to
Toronto's ethnic, racial and class profile, astonishingly homogenous. Although
it was not expected that C4LD would appeal to organized labour – which
remained sceptical not only of C4LD but also of other social movements –

there was a real expectation or hope that it would appeal to the 'new social movements'. Instead, the movement for local democracy and citizenship failed to appeal to the mass of ethnic, immigrant, low-income service workers and tradesmen, and other political groups that are spread around Metropolitan Toronto. Accordingly, C4LD and its grammar of politics were increasingly interpreted as the voice of the self-interested professional class in the inner city of Toronto, who had little regard for its 'suburban' counterparts. In addition, while it attempted somewhat to align with other groups on issues of social welfare and social justice, their interests were often too far apart. The supporters of the government used this to their advantage.

To declare C4LD as a failure may be considered a harsh judgement. The movement against the Harris government that was accelerated by the amalgamation of Toronto and joined by the province's teachers and unions against Bill 136 (which attempted to roll back the right to strike) would appear to have won certain concessions from the government, at least in making it pause, even if only for publicity and re-election reasons. The role of C4LD in this broader movement should not be underestimated. Nevertheless, the grammar of politics that revolved around local democracy and citizenship failed to stir imagination and was ineffective in achieving concrete results or concessions from the government, or in attracting broader groups. The liberal interpellation of subjects into enacting as 'citizens' failed because the majority of Torontonians were caught between enacting themselves either as clients and consumers or as a variety of other identities, such as youth, homeless, workers, squeegees or immigrants, which the universal category of citizenship did not capture. This lesson was painfully brought home during the municipal elections in which the 'suburban' vote brought Mel Lastman, a politician held in contempt and ridiculed by the city elite, into power. Yet, his message, 'freeze the taxes', was heard loud and clear by the groups that surround the city. This was not because these groups were well-off suburbanites 'who liked their lawns', as the city elite portrayed them, but because they were predominantly the groups, made up of immigrants, refugees, the working poor, non-unionized and low income service workers and tradesmen, who had felt the most adverse impacts of the declining real wages in Ontario in the previous decade. It was these groups that the old City of Toronto's new class had perhaps never understood.

Advanced liberalism, movements, resistance

Although there are several specific and contingent reasons behind the amalgamation of Toronto, it must nevertheless be understood against the background of a shift towards advanced liberalism. The Harris government displayed very little affinity for local democracy or local government, not because it was 'anti-democratic' but because the rationalities it represented were those of advanced liberalism, with its emphasis on rationalization, privatization, marketization and centralization. There is no doubt that the

Harris government reached its conclusion to amalgamate Toronto as a result of its broader policies to centralize property taxation, restructure and centralize education, rationalize and download services, and force municipalities to reduce expenditures and privatize (Isin and Wolfson, 1999). Much has been said about the fact that the introduction of the amalgamation of municipalities was inconsistent with traditional Tory philosophy. This view misses the fact that local government has a very limited role in neo-liberal programmes. The new city of Toronto has so few powers that it is really nothing other than a board of the provincial government. At any rate, 'explaining' the reforms enacted in Ontario local government and specifically in Toronto is not the aim of this chapter. However, given these considerations, should seeking new powers for municipal government be the aim of progressive politics?

With advanced liberalism, the focus of urban politics has shifted from local government as a locus of power to diverse spaces of power such as private and non-governmental provision and delivery of services. The new subjects of government – clients, customers, consumers, users – govern themselves everyday in the face of growing complexity and uncertainty, seeking the best possible alternatives and choices. This has resulted in a growing polarization in the distribution not only of economic capital but also of social and cultural capital. While there are those who are increasingly at liberty to create options in terms of where they live, work, play and seek health and educational services for themselves and their children, there are those for whom such choices are becoming ever more limited. To participate in the game of 'conduct of conduct' requires not only economic capital but also social and cultural capital in the form of linguistic ability, educational resources and social competence. In fact, the lack of cultural and social capital often limits access to economic capital. The aim of progressive politics must be, while questioning the formation of subjects as merely customers, clients and consumers, to seek new group rights for those unable to compete in the market due to lack of economic, social and cultural capital, who increasingly find themselves under oppressive conditions. If the city is the space of the struggles for these rights, the state still remains as the source and grantor of them.

The state is neither dead nor omnipotent. There is evidence that the state has become larger, stronger and more effective under advanced liberalism. Every political regime that has been associated with neo-liberalism in Britain, America, Europe and Canada has passed more legislation and regulation than its predecessors have.[5] The irony that should not be lost on anyone is that neo-liberal regimes have enacted more legislation and regulation than social democratic regimes. But neo-liberalism has also shifted the emphasis and priorities of government. The will to govern has not diminished but it has become more widespread and embedded. There is, then, a need to rethink ways in which the state can be invoked as an agent of a new series of social, cultural, political and group rights (Albo et al., 1993). Rather than seeking rights *for* municipal government as territorial polities, deterritorialized group rights must be taken into consideration. As Warren Magnusson has recently argued, one of the promising aspects of the new social movements in the last twenty years is to have opened up new political spaces other than the self-enclosed spaces of municipal government (Magnusson, 1996). Magnusson has illustrated how the municipality has been reclaimed by various social movements (a category which Magnusson retains despite some concerns), such as feminism, environmentalism and that of the First Nations. Magnusson has convincingly argued that the municipality is neither an apparatus of the state nor an autonomous (sovereign) entity. Rather, it is a liminal or marginal space where identities are contested, negotiated and remade through the flow of ideas, practices and struggles. The municipality is thus neither a self-enclosed nor a self-sufficient space, but an open space of flows. As such, it has been the site and incubator of the most critical and progressive movements in the last two decades, ranging from the sanctuary movements to nuclear-free zones, from local socialism to aboriginal claims.

Being narrowly focused on municipal government as a container of politics, C4LD has fashioned an ineffective style of politics for newly emerging realities. While the Harris government simply regarded the current municipal institutions at best irrelevant and at worst an impediment to implementing the CSR, C4LD increasingly relied on a liberal grammar of politics that invoked 'democracy', 'due process', 'citizenship' and 'public good'. The Harris government realized that it was not simply implementing a revolution that was forged in the back rooms, but that it was giving a programmatic form to technologies, techniques, mentalities and rationalities that have been emerging in the social body along with the new alignment of groups and classes. The Harris government knew well who its constituency was – the rising new professional and quasi-professional groups in the non-public sectors of the economy, largely in managerial, executive, new media, high-technology, technical service industries, whose lives are already ordered in a different way and who accept the technologies of neo-liberal government as rational and necessary. As consumers and customers, they constitute themselves as active purchasers of services in the market. The Harris government presented itself effectively as the voice of a new rationality on the side of history.

For progressive movements, two avenues would be mistaken. The first is to assume that a new provincial 'government' would do things differently. The Harris government has already managed to forge a second term, and the revolution it has initiated will by and large remain. This has also happened in Britain, America, and New Zealand. Moreover, the 'left' governments that replaced the radical right governments have continued with neo-liberal programmes with even more success (Schwartz, 1997). The second is to refuse to delineate the new technologies of power in all their precision and exactitude. Governing Toronto without government means that neo-liberal technologies of power are not invented and implemented in a top-down hierarchical way and implemented via government but are rationalizations of emerging practices throughout the social body. The left rhetoric of 'corporate or global agenda' is far too simplistic to capture this complex change under way (Gill, 1995).

Advanced liberalism is neither an ideology nor a worldview, but it is the name *we* give to a way of thinking about the objects, targets, mechanisms and limits of government. It has been assembled from a variety of sources over the last three decades and has incorporated, invented, appropriated and deployed numerous technologies of government that have changed what it means to govern. Just as nineteenth-century struggles revolved around and arose from specific ways of thinking about government, at the dawn of the twenty-first century, we find ourselves presented with the problem of how to govern ourselves and others in a different way. It is fairly obvious that what it means to 'govern the local' or 'govern through the local' has also undergone dramatic change. The ways of thinking about the objects, targets and mechanisms of local government have changed. Modern city or municipal government, with its self-enclosed, territorial jurisdiction, has dispersed into manifold spaces of power in which municipal government is one actor among others. By an emphasis on breaking dependence on the public professions, and its attack on at least certain fields of professional expertise, advanced liberalism has also changed our ways of thinking about the subjects of government: we are unable to think about the poor, youth, homeless, welfare recipients and criminals as victims in the way that we used to do. A new grammar of politics, a new set of tactics and strategies are needed to work our way through these new objects and subjects of government. Those who want effectively to resist the policies of the Harris government, which aim to eliminate various labour, gender, ethnic and other group and class rights, must not seek to reconstitute these groups as victims or as other fixed and solid identities. How a new progressive politics would work through the formation of deterritorialized group identities (youth, students, immigrants, visible minorities, jobless) as active forces by creating platforms and forums for their articulation, proliferation and recognition, without slipping into essentialism or nihilism, is one of the questions we face.

Notes

1   An earlier version of this chapter appeared in *Studies in Political Economy* (Summer 1998). I am grateful to Evelyn Ruppert, Greg Albo, Warren Magnusson, Myer Siemiatycki and Frances Frisken for providing critical comments on earlier drafts. I am indebted to Warren Magnusson for pointing out to me the symbolism in de Tocqueville's works. I would also like to acknowledge that the data on social classes used for this chapter are drawn from a large-scale research project on urban citizenship and immigration in the Greater Toronto Area. I would like to thank my co-researcher Myer Siemiatycki and the Centre of Excellence for Research on Immigration and Settlement (CERIS) for their support.

2   There is a tradition of historiography that explores how the municipal corporation was reinvented in the modern era to contain these two seemingly contradictory principles – a history traversed by Gierke and others. See Black (1984); Frug (1980); Gierke (1900); Gierke (1990); Isin (1992b); Williams (1985).

3   Following Michel Foucault's work on governmentality, a number of authors have suggested a rather different usage based on the idea of a liberal mode of government. See (Barry et al., 1996; Burchell et al., 1991). The term government follows Foucault in that it does not refer simply to governing institutions, and less so to the party in power, but to different modes through which individuals affect the conduct

of other individuals. In this view of government, the rules and principles that regulate a household, neighbourhood, municipality or state all embody government. In this usage, then, liberalism refers not to a political ideology or doctrine but to the assemblage of techniques, rationalities, methods and instruments of government that constitute individuals and influence their conduct.

4 See Caulfield (1994); Ley (1996). In 1991, Statistics Canada began collecting data on occupations based on a new national occupational classification system (NOC). The two major attributes of jobs, which were used as classification criteria in developing the NOC, were skill level and skill type. Other factors, such as industry and occupational mobility, were also taken into consideration. Skill level is defined generally as the amount and type of education and training required to enter and perform the duties of an occupation. Four major categories of NOC are: A, *professional* occupations requiring university degree including bachelor's, master's or postgraduate; B, *para-professional and technical* occupations requiring two to three years of post-secondary education at community college or institute of technology, or two to four years of apprenticeship training, or three to four years of secondary school and more than two years of on-the-job training, training courses or specific work experience; C, *routine* occupations requiring one to four years of secondary school education; up to two years of on-the-job training, training courses or specific work experience; D, *manual* occupations requiring up to two years of secondary school and short work demonstration or on-the-job training; and M (*managerial* occupations). These groups roughly correspond to major classes. See Ben-David (1964); Bradley (1996); Burris (1995).

5 Loughlin (1996, p. 383) argues that in their effort of rationalization and reducing the role of government in social, political and economic life, the Thatcher governments ironically embarked on massive efforts of legislation, which Loughlin calls the juridification of central-local relations. Between 1979 and 1992 the Thatcher governments sought to marginalize, undermine or bypass the administrative networks and procedures, and to govern by way of central direction. The then existing legal framework, however, not having been drafted for such purposes, simply contained too many gaps and ambiguities to be susceptible to conversion into an instrument of centralized regulation. The scale of this programme is highlighted by the fact that in this period 143 Acts having a direct application to local government in England and Wales were enacted, of which fifty-eight contained major changes. The scale and complexity of this governmental programme seeking to establish a more precise legal framework regulating local government have imposed major strains on parliamentary procedures. The exigencies of time, in conjunction with the complexity of the task of drafting directive rather than facilitative legislation, have caused governments regularly to use parliamentary procedures primarily for the purpose of tidying up the rough drafts of legislation which were introduced as government bills (Loughlin, 1996, p. 387). This tendency to legislate through drafts became a particularly noticeable feature of local government legislation. In 1987/8, for example, the government promoted some 1,259 amendments to three bills on local government. In the following session, there were 606 amendments made to the Local Government and Housing Bill alone (Loughlin, 1996, p. 388).

Bibliography

Albo, G., Langille, D. and Panitch, L. (eds) (1993) *A Different Kind of State? Popular Power and Democratic Administration* (Toronto: Oxford University Press).

Andrew, C. and Goldsmith, M. (1998) 'From Local Government to Local Governance – and Beyond?', *International Political Science Review*, 19, (2): 101–17.

Aulich, C. (1999) 'From Convergence to Divergence: Reforming Australian Local Government', *Australian Journal of Public Administration*, 58, (3): 12–23.

Barry, A., Osborne, T. and Rose, N. (eds) (1996) *Foucault and Political Reason* (Chicago: University of Chicago Press).

Beaumont, G. de and Tocqueville, A. de (1964) *On the Penitentiary System in the United States and its Application in France* (Carbondale: Southern Illinois University Press).

Beetham, D. (1996) 'Theorising Democracy and Local Government', in D.S. King and G. Stoker (eds) *Rethinking Local Democracy* (Basingstoke: Macmillan), 28–49.

Ben-David, J. (1964) 'Professions in the Class System of Present-Day Societies', *Current Sociology*, 12: 247–330.

Black, A. (1984) *Guilds and Civil Society in European Political Thought from the Twelfth Century to the Present* (Ithaca: Cornell University Press).

Bourdieu, P. (1987) 'What Makes a Social Class? On the Theoretical and Practical Existence of Groups', *Berkeley Journal of Sociology*, 32: 1–18.

—— (1991) *Language and Symbolic Power* (Cambridge, MA: Harvard University Press).

Bradley, H. (1996) *Fractured Identities: Changing Patterns of Inequality* (London: Polity).

Brint, S. (1994) *In an Age of Experts: The Changing Role of Professionals in Politics and Public Life* (Princeton, NJ: Princeton University Press).

Burchell, G. (1996) 'Liberal Government and Techniques of Self', in A. Barry, T. Osborne and N. Rose (eds), *Foucault and Political Reason* (Chicago: University of Chicago Press).

Burchell, G., Gordon, C. and Miller, P. (eds) (1991) *The Foucault Effect: Studies in Governmentality* (Chicago: University of Chicago Press).

Burris, V. (1995) 'The Discovery of the New Middle Classes', in A.J. Vidich (ed.), *The New Middle Classes: Life-Styles, Status Claims and Political Orientations, Main Trends in the Modern World* (New York: New York University Press).

Carpenter, J. (1995) 'Regulation Theory, Post-Fordism and Urban Politics', in D. Judge, G. Stoker and H. Wolman (eds), *Theories of Urban Politics* (London: Sage).

Caulfield, J. (1994) *City Form and Everyday Life: Toronto's Gentrification and Critical Social Practice* (Toronto: University of Toronto Press).

Clark, D. (1997) 'Local Government in Europe: Retrenchment, Restructuring and British Exceptionalism', *West European Politics*, 20, (3): 134–63.

Clement, W. and Myles, J. (1994) *Relations of Ruling: Class and Gender in Postindustrial Societies* (Montreal: McGill-Queen's University Press).

Dean, M. (1999) *Governmentality: Power and Rule in Modern Society* (London: Sage).

Eisinger, P. (1998) 'City Politics in an Era of Federal Devolution', *Urban Affairs Review*, 33, (3): 308–25.

Foucault, M. (1977) *Discipline and Punish* (New York: Vintage).

—— (1979) 'On Governmentality', *Ideology & Consciousness*, (6): 5–21.

Frazer, E. (1996) 'The Value of Locality', in D.S. King and G. Stoker (eds), *Rethinking Local Democracy* (Basingstoke: Macmillan), 89–110.

Frug, G.E. (1980) 'The City as a Legal Concept', *Harvard Law Review*, 43 (April).

Gierke, O. (1900) *Political Theories of the Middle Age*, trans. F.W. Maitland (Cambridge: Cambridge University Press).

—— (1990) *Community in Historical Perspective*, trans. M. Fischer, ed. Antony Black (Cambridge: Cambridge University Press).

Gill, S. (1995) 'The Global Panopticon? The Neo-liberal State, Economic Life, and Democratic Surveillance', *Alternatives*, 20 (1): 1–49.

Goodwin, M. and Painter, J. (1996) 'Local Governance, the Crises of Fordism and the Changing Geographies of Regulation', *Transactions, Institute of British Geographers*, 21, (4): 635–48.

Gouldner, A.W. (1979) *The Future of Intellectuals and the Rise of the New Class* (New York: Oxford University Press).

Hardt, M. and Negri, A. (1994) *Labor of Dionysus: A Critique of State-Form* (Minneapolis: University of Minnesota Press).

Imrie, R. and Raco, M. (1999) 'How New is the New Local Governance? Lessons from the United Kingdom', *Transactions of the Institute of British Geographers NS*, 24: 45–63.

Isin, E.F. (1992a) 'Cities and Canadian Federalism: A Colonial Legacy', in H. Lustiger-Thaler (ed.), *Political Arrangements: Power and the City* (Montreal: Black Rose Books).

—— (1992b) *Cities Without Citizens: Modernity of the City as a Corporation* (Montreal: Black Rose Books).

—— (1996a) 'Global City-Regions and Citizenship', in D. Bell, R. Keil and G. Wekerle (eds), *Global Processes, Local Places* (Montreal: Black Rose Books).

—— (1996b) 'Metropolis Unbound: Legislators and Interpreters of Urban Form', in J. Caulfield and L. Peake (eds), *City Lives and City Forms: Critical Urban Research and Canadian Urbanism* (Toronto: University of Toronto Press).

—— (1997) 'Who Is the New Citizen? Toward a Genealogy', *Citizenship Studies*, 1, (1): 115–32.

Isin, E.F., Osborne, T. and Rose, N. (1998) *Governing Cities: Liberalism, Neo-liberalism, Advanced Liberalism* (Toronto: Urban Studies Programme Working Paper, no. 19, York University).

Isin, E.F. and Wolfson, J. (1999) *The Making of the Megacity: An Introduction* (Toronto: York University).

Johnston, R.J. and Pattie, C.J. (1996) 'Great Britain New Local Government Structures', *Geography Review*, 9, (5): 27–32.

—— (1996) 'Local Government in Local Governance: The 1994–95 Restructuring of Local Government in England', *International Journal of Urban and Regional Research*, 20, (4): 671–96.

Jones, M. (1998) 'Restructuring the Local State: Economic Governance or Social Regulation?', *Political Geography*, 17, (8): 959–88.

King, D.S. and Stoker, G. (eds) (1996) *Rethinking Local Democracy*, (Basingstoke: Macmillan).

Lewis, N. and Moran, W. (1998) 'Restructuring, Democracy, and Geography in New Zealand', *Environment and Planning C: Government and Policy*, 16, (2): 127–53.

Ley, D. (1996) *The New Middle Class and the Remaking of the Central City* (New York: Oxford University Press).

Loughlin, M. (1996) *Legality and Locality: The Role of Law in Central-Local Government Relations* (Oxford: Clarendon Press).

Magnusson, W. (1981) 'Metropolitan Reform in the Capitalist City', *Canadian Journal of Political Science*, 14 (September): 557–77.

—— (1996) *The Search for Political Space: Globalization, Social Movements, and the Urban Political Experience* (Toronto: University of Toronto Press).

Marshall, N. (1998) 'Reforming Australian Local Government: Efficiency, Consolidation – and the Question of Governance', *International Review of Administrative Sciences*, 64, (4): 643–62.

Mayer, M. (1996) 'Post-Fordian Urban Politics: New Forms of Regulation in Local Politics and Planning', *Zeitschrift für Wirtschaftsgeographie*, 40: 20–7.

Perkin, H. (1989) *The Rise of Professional Society: England since 1880* (London: Routledge).

Purcell, M. (1997) 'Ruling Los Angeles: Neighborhood Movements, Urban Regimes, and the Production of Space in Southern California', *Urban Geography*, 18, (8): 684–704.

Rose, N. (1996a) 'The Death of the Social? Re-figuring the Territory of Government', *Economy and Society*, 25 (3): 327–56.

—— (1996b) 'Governing "Advanced" Liberal Democracies', in A. Barry, T. Osborne and N. Rose (eds), *Foucault and Political Reason* (Chicago: University of Chicago Press).

—— (1996c) 'Government, Authority and Expertise in Advanced Liberalism', *Economy and Society*, 22 (3): 283–99.

—— (1999) *Powers of Freedom: Reframing Political Thought* (Cambridge: Cambridge University Press).

Schwartz, H.M. (1997) 'Reinvention and Retrenchment: Lessons from the Application of the New Zealand Model to Alberta, Canada', *Journal of Policy Analysis and Management*, 16 (3): 405–23.

Starr, P. (1987) 'The Sociology of Official Statistics', in W. Alonso and P. Starr (eds), *The Politics of Numbers* (New York: Russell Sage Foundation).

Stoker, G. (1996a) 'Introduction: Normative Theories of Local Government and Democracy', in D.S. King and G. Stoker (eds) *Rethinking Local Democracy* (Basingstoke: Macmillan), 1–27.

—— (1996b) 'Redefining Local Democracy', in L. Pratchett and D. Wilson (eds) *Local Democracy and Local Government* (Basingstoke: Macmillan), 188–209.

Szelényi, I. and Martin, B. (1990) 'The Three Waves of New Class Theories and a Postscript', in C.C. Lemert (ed.), *Intellectuals and Politics* (Newbury Park, CA: Sage).

Teune, H. (1995) 'Local-Government and Democratic Political Development', *Annals of the American Academy of Political and Social Science*, 540: 11–23.

Tocqueville, A. de (1945) *Democracy in America* (New York: Alfred A. Knopf).

Williams, J.C. (1985) 'The Invention of the Municipal Corporation: A Case Study in Legal Change', *American University Law Review*, 34: 369–438.

Wilson, D. (1998) 'From Local Government to Local Governance: Re-casting British Local Democracy', *Democratization*, 5, (1): 90–115.

Wright, E.O. (1997) *Class Counts: Comparative Studies in Class Analysis* (Cambridge: Cambridge University Press).

Part III
Difference, identity, city

9 Citizenship, territoriality and the gendered construction of difference

Nira Yuval-Davis

What is citizenship? In the many articles written in the British press about Princess Diana's death and the radical changes as a result of public pressure which followed it in the behaviour of the royal family, one sentence kept on being repeated as an explanation of the change – 'the people behaved as citizens and not as subjects'. This concept of citizenship has very little to do with the right to vote or even to carry a passport of a specific state. It has to do instead with people's sense that they are members of a specific community and polity, and have a say in what the leaders of that community do and say. The French word *citoyen*, which emerged so powerfully after the French Revolution, has tended to express that meaning of citizenship most commonly.

In the ideology of the French Revolution and in the majority of literature on citizenship in political theory, either liberal or social democrat, the notion of citizenship is bound to that of the 'nation-state', as the state is the collective expression of the 'will of the people'. There is an automatic assumption that the boundaries of 'the people', 'the nation' or 'civil society' overlap the boundaries of the state. In the political reality at the beginning of the twenty-first century this is not true in the case of virtually all states, if it was ever true before. T.H. Marshall, the most important British theoretician on citizenship and the welfare state (1950; 1975; 1981), has defined citizenship as 'a full membership in the community' including rights and responsibilities. While Marshall did identify 'the community' with the 'nation-state', this definition can also be useful when we recognize that these days people are usually members in more than one community and polity – local, ethnic, national, state and cross/supra-state.

Elsewhere (Yuval-Davis, 1991; 1997; 1999) I have developed the notion of 'the multi-layered citizen', which follows such a recognition. Very often people's rights and obligations to a specific state are mediated and largely dependent on their membership of a specific ethnic, racial, religious or regional collectivity, although very rarely are they completely contained by it. At the same time, the development of ideologies and institutions of 'human rights' means that, ideologically at least, the state does not always have full control of the construction of citizenship's rights, although usually it is left for states to carry them out. It is important to remember that in this respect people are not positioned equally within their collectivities and states, collectivities are not positioned equally within the state and internationally, and states are not positioned equally with other states. However, citizenship is not just a question of being or not being a member in communities. Different social attributes would construct the specific positioning of people within and across the communities in certain social categories. The liberal/communitarian debate notwithstanding (Avineri and De Shalit, 1992; Daly, 1993; Mouffe, 1993), what follows is that citizenship cannot be analysed as either a completely individual or a collective phenomenon.

This chapter examines the territorial/spatial nature of contemporary citizenships and how these relate to ethnic/national collectivities, global cities and the construction of difference. In exploring these relationships the chapter explores the roles of women as symbols of collectivities, as symbolic border guards and as the bearers of 'the private' domain.

States, nations and territoriality

The state can be defined as 'a body of institutions which are centrally organized around the intentionality of control with a given apparatus of enforcement (juridical and repressive) at its command and basis' (Anthias and Yuval-Davis, 1989, p. 5). The reason we included the word 'intentionality' is that, although states claim to be the only legitimate power in control, very often this intention is not realized because smaller or larger parts of the state's territory include other polities which do not accept partially or wholly the legitimacy of the authority of the state (Joseph, 1993). In many Third World countries the state's penetration of its periphery would be partial at best, and although to a certain extent modern means of transportation and communication have increased central control, and there are probably no more *totally* isolated communities in the world (Lowenhaupt Tsing, 1993), there *are* communities in jungles or in the mountains organized by traditional tribes which have not been incorporated into the civil society of the state. Such territories may also be controlled by revolutionary guerillas attempting to establish a competitive social and political order in the state and/or drug barons.

However, communities which are not governed by the state do not necessarily have to be territorially remote. There are many cases of warlords in shanty towns or religious and other cults who are to a greater or lesser extent able to establish an alternative social and political order to that of the state, without the latter being able or willing to challenge them. Sometimes it is even desirable to those who control the state that there are enclaves within the state's territory which are to some extent outside their direct control: examples include the Bantustans in South Africa under apartheid, and the West Bank supposedly under the control of the Palestinian National Autonomy, where more than 70 per cent of the land belongs to the Israeli government.

In many other cases, a more or less centralized regional or federal regime does exist and central and local government share in the control of the territory. And in many other cases, as remnants of older political orders in the post-colonial, postwar world, as well as part of the new world order, one or more superpowers and/or UN forces have extra-territorial rights to use territory as military bases for their own strategic goals, as buffers between warring polities, and as facilities for the work of international agencies (Enloe, 1993).

If states do not always control their own territories, the relationships between nations and states is even more complicated. Gellner has defined nationalism as a

> theory of political legitimacy which requires that ethnic boundaries should not cut across political ones, and in particular, that ethnic boundaries within a given state ... should not separate the power holders from the rest ... and therefore state and culture must now be linked.
>
> (Gellner, 1983, pp. 1, 36)

Today there is virtually nowhere in the world in which such a 'pure' nation-state exists, if it ever did, and therefore there are always settled residents (and usually citizens as well) who are not members of the dominant national collectivity in the society. The fact that this automatic assumption about the overlap between the boundaries of the state citizens and 'the nation' still exists is one expression of the naturalizing effect of the hegemony of one collectivity and its access to the ideological apparatuses of both state and civil society. This constructs minorities into assumed deviants from the 'normal', and excludes them from important power resources. This, in turn, has crucial implications for the relations to space and territory of minorities as well as to states, and will be discussed again later on in this chapter.

Both ethnic and national collectivities are constructed around boundaries which separate the world into 'us' and 'them'. As such, both are the Andersonian 'imagined communities' (Anderson, 1983). Depending on the objectives of different ethnic and national projects involving members of the same collectivity, or people outside it, the boundary lines of these collectivities can be drawn in very different ways. One example, of course, is the debate over whether the English and the Scots or the 'Anglo' and the 'Francophone' Canadians are/should be members of the same nation. Another is the difference between the Jewish Bund which saw itself as the national liberation movement of the Jews – but related only to the Jews of Eastern Europe – and the Zionist movement who included (in principle) in the boundaries of its imagined community Jews from all over the world.

What is specific to the nationalist project and discourse is the aim of a separate political representation for the collective. This often – but not always – takes the form of a claim for a separate state and/or territory, although some states are based on bi- or multinational principles (for example, Lebanon or Belgium) and some supra-state political projects like the European Union can, at specific historical moments, develop more state-like characteristics. Nationalist demands can also be aimed at establishing a regional autonomy rather than a separate state – such as in the case of Wales or Catalonia – or they can be irredentist, advocating joining a neighbouring state rather than establishing one of their own – such as the republican movement in Northern Ireland or the Kashmiri movement for unification with Pakistan. Although state and territory have been closely bound together, there have been cases of nationalist movements which called for the state to be established in a different territory than that in which they were active. Both the Jewish Zionist movement (which established the state of Israel) and the Black Zionist movement (which established Liberia) called for the mass emigration of their members from the countries in which they lived. Others have not articulated any specific territorial boundaries for their national independence. It is the demand for political sovereignty which separates the 'Black Nation' from other 'Black community' activists, and which separates those who call for the 'Khalipha', the global nation of Islam, from other committed Muslims. The Austrian Marxist Otto Bauer (Bauer, 1940; Nimni, 1991; Yuval-Davis, 1987a) called for the separation of nationalism and the state as the only viable solution to the hopeless mix of collectivities in the territories which constituted the Austro-Hungarian empire, and this might be the only viable long-term alternative to 'ethnic cleansing' in contemporary ethnic fundamentalist movements that have emerged with the fall of the Soviet empire and in many other places in the post-colonial world (for example, in Rwanda).

The separation of nationality and the state also takes other forms. In many parts of the world there exist immigrant communities which are culturally and politically committed to continue to 'belong' to their 'mother country' – or more specifically to the national collectivity from which they, their parents or their foreparents, have come. The rise of these 'committed diasporas' has been co-determined by several factors. First, technological advances in means of international travel and in media and communication, have made the preservation of links with the 'homeland' much easier, just as they have made inter-generational cultural and linguistic reproduction easier. 'Ethnic videos', for example, is one of the largest video markets and is aimed at people who have very little or no access to the mass media of the countries where they live. Cable systems or satellite dishes have enabled, for many, direct access to their own national and ethnic media, as well as established new defused ethnic collectivities (for example, of an international South-Asian community).

At the same time, as a result of certain successes of the anti-racist and civil rights movements, there has been a certain shift in national ideologies in many western countries, and multiculturalism has, until recently, become an hegemonic ideology which, with all its problems, has somewhat eased the pressures on immigrants to assimilate. This has been aided by the fact that in the post-colonial world there are many ongoing nationalist struggles in which different collectivities compete not just for access to their states' powers and resources, but also over the constitutive nature of their states. One cannot imagine the continued nationalist struggles of the IRA, for instance, without the financial, political and other help of the Irish diaspora communities, especially in the USA. In the case of the Jewish diaspora – the oldest 'established' diaspora – the hegemony of Zionism has meant that many have transformed Israel into a 'post-factum homeland' even if they have never been, let alone lived, there, and international Jewish support has played a crucial role in the establishment and development of Israel (Yuval-Davis, 1987b). As Anderson has commented (1983), not enough recognition is given to the role of diaspora communities in contemporary nationalist struggles, although recently Robin Cohen (1997), for instance, has started to carry out such research.

However, the connections between diasporas and homelands or between associated diasporas do not solely depend on means of communication and political and economic assistance. The exchange of brides, which Levi-Strauss has seen as the basic cement of social cohesion (1969), is one of the major ways in which the close connections and the management of inclusionary relations within the imagined national community continue to operate between diasporas and homelands. This points to the important roles gender relations play in the construction of ideological and emotional attachments between territories, states and nations.

Women as embodiments and border guards of 'the nation'

The mythical unity of national 'imagined communities' which divides the world between 'us' and 'them' is maintained and ideologically reproduced by a whole system of what Armstrong (1982) calls symbolic 'border guards'. These 'border guards' can identify people as members or non-members of a specific collectivity. They are closely linked to specific cultural codes of style of dress and behaviour, as well as to more elaborate bodies of customs, religion, literary and artistic modes of production, and, of course, language. Because of the central importance of social reproduction to culture, gender relations often come to be seen as constituting the 'essence' of cultures as ways of life to be passed from generation to generation. The construction of 'home' is of particular importance here, including relations between adults and between adults and children in the family, ways of cooking and eating, domestic labour, play and bedtime stories, etc. Constructions of manhood and womanhood, as well as sexuality and gendered relations of power, need to be explored in relation to these processes (Yuval-Davis, 1997).

A figure of a woman, often a mother, symbolizes in many cultures the spirit of the collectivity, whether it is Mother Russia, Mother Ireland or Mother India. In the French Revolution its symbol was *La Patrie*, a figure of a woman giving birth to a baby, and in Cyprus a crying woman refugee on roadside posters was the embodiment of the pain and anger of the Greek-Cypriot collectivity after the Turkish invasion. In peasant societies, the dependence of the people on the fertility of 'Mother Earth' has no doubt contributed to this close association between collective territory, collective identity and womanhood. However, women also symbolize the collectivity in other ways. As

Cynthia Enloe (1990) has pointed out, it is supposedly for the sake of the 'womenandchildren' that men go to war. Women are associated in the collective imagination with children and therefore with the collective, as well as the familial, future. But this does not only happen during wars. For instance, in the riots which flared among Muslim youth in Bradford, during the mid-1990s, one of the participants clarified the motivation behind their actions to the *Guardian* reporter: 'It's not about prostitution or unemployment or about all that nonsense of the Chief Constable. It's about the way two police officers treated one of *our* women' (Travis, *The Guardian*, 18 June 1995).

The 'burden of representation' on women for the collectivity's identity and future destiny has also brought about the construction of women as the bearers of the collectivity's honour. Manar Hasan (1994) describes how many Palestinian women have been murdered by their male relatives because in their behaviour they brought 'shame' on their families and community. Women, in their 'proper' behaviour, their 'proper' clothing, embody the line which signifies the collectivity's boundaries. Other women in many other societies have also been tortured or murdered by their relatives because of adultery, flight from home, and other cultural breaches of conduct which are perceived as bringing dishonour and shame on their male relatives and community (see Chhachhi, 1991; Rozario, 1991). A weaker version of retaliation against women who betrayed the collective honour was the mass shaving of women's heads in different European countries after the Second World War. These women were accused of befriending the occupying Nazi armies during the occupation (Warring, 1996). The flip-side of this is the use of systematic rape during war as a way of shaming the collective enemy. It is not incidental that, until the success of the feminist campaign in the 1994 UN conference on human rights, the Geneva Convention would not consider rape a war crime or a mode of torture by 'crime against honour' – the honour not being that of the woman alone (Pettman, 1996; Zajovic, 1994).

The centrality of women in nationalist discourse is even more apparent when we examine their roles in national liberation struggles both pro-and anti-modernist. 'Women's emancipation' or 'women following tradition' (as has been expressed in various campaigns for and against women's veiling, voting, education, military service and employment) has been at the centre of most modernist and anti-modernist nationalist struggles.

Chatterjee (1986) observed that cultural decolonization has anticipated and paved the way for political decolonization – the major rupture which marked the twentieth century. This process involved not so much going back to some mythical golden age in the national past but rather a growing sense of empowerment, a development of a national trajectory of freedom and independence. A central theme in this process of cultural decolonization has been the redefinition and reconstruction of sexuality and gender relations. Franz Fanon (1952) encapsulated it for the black man to 'reclaim his manhood'. As Ashis Nandy (1983) has argued, the colonial man has been constructed as effeminate in the colonial discourse, and the way to emancipation and empowerment is seen as the negation of this assertion. In many cultural systems, potency and masculinity seem to be synonymous. Such a perspective has not only legitimized the extremely 'macho' style of many anti-colonialist and black power movements, it has also legitimized the secondary position of women in these national collectivities.

And yet the 'emancipation of women' has come to signify much wider political and social attitudes towards social change and modernity in a variety of revolutionary and decolonization projects, whether in Turkey, India, Yemen or China (Kandiyoti, 1991). As Chatterjee (1989) has pointed out, because the position of women has been so central to the colonial gaze in defining indigenous cultures, it is here that symbolic declarations of cultural change have taken place. It has been one of the important mechanisms in which ethnic and national projects have signified – inwardly and outwardly – their move towards modernization. Similarly, the inclusion of women in the national liberation armies of countries such as Nicaragua, Eritrea and Lybia has been a signifier not only of the incorporation of women as citizens of the nation, but also, if not more importantly, as the incorporation of the nation as a whole in the populist armed struggle. However, these changes did not lack ambivalence because at the same time they had to signify modernization and national independence. The process of mimicry was limited at best.

Because the hegemony of the modern nation state in the post-colonial world has often been very limited, being mostly confined to urban centres and the upper classes, the use of cultural and religious traditions as symbolic border guards has to a large extent enabled the continued co-existence of a 'modern' centre with pre-modern sections of society. At a later period, it has also enabled, in many cases, the rise of a new generation of leaders who could turn to those very customs and traditions and develop ethnic and national projects of a very different kind. In these projects, what formerly symbolized progress and modernity was now constructed as European cultural imperialism. As an alternative, a fundamentalist construction of 'the true' cultural essence of the collectivity has come to be imposed. These constructions, however, are often no more similar to the ways people used to live historically in these societies than the previous modernist 'national liberation' ones, nor have the fundamentalist projects abandoned modernity and its tool, whether it be modern media or high-tech weaponry (Sahgal and Yuval-Davis, 1992).

Once again, women occupy an important role in these projects. Rather than being seen as the symbols of change, women are constructed in the role of the 'carriers of tradition'. The symbolic act of unveiling which played centre stage in the emancipatory projects is now being surpassed by the campaigns of forced veiling, as happened, for example, in post-revolutionary Iran. Even practices such as Sati in India can become foci of fundamentalist movements which see in women following these traditions the safeguard of the national cultural essence, operating as a mirror mirage to the colonial gaze which focused on these practices to construct Otherness (Mani, 1989; Chhachhi, 1991).

Cultures, however, are not fixed essential entities. As the slogan of Southall Black Sisters and Women Against Fundamentalism challenged, when they chanted in anti-domestic violence demonstrations in Southall and in countering the Islamist anti-Rushdie demonstration, 'Women's tradition – resistance, not submission!'

Rather than a fixed and homogenous body of tradition and custom, 'cultural stuff', therefore, needs to be described as a rich resource, usually full of internal contradictions, which is used selectively by different social agents in various social projects within specific power relations and political discourses in and outside the collectivity. Gender, class, membership in a collectivity, stage in the life cycle and ability all affect the access and availability of these resources and the specific positions from which they are being used.

Urban space and the construction of difference

Migrant labourers and refugees, unless bound in particular labour contracts to particular geographical locations, tend to settle in metropolitan urban areas. This is where labour markets would be the largest and the most flexible (Castles and Miller, 1993). Familial and ethnic networks of support would develop so that later waves of immigration would tend to settle, if possible, near those who came earlier, and the growth of community religious and cultural services would reinforce this tendency. Sometimes, as happened in the Southall area in London, the high concentration of communal services and networks of support might counter-balance the attraction of upwardly mobile suburbs, and even people who could afford to move to more affluent areas would not do so, or would sometimes return after a period of moving out. Overall, however, like most other strata of population, the more settled and upwardly mobile the immigrant community, the more it transfers itself gradually from the inner city to suburbia, resisting the racism and other modes of exclusion which originally make such a move problematic.

Territorial concentrations in inner cities are almost never ethnically homogeneous, unless this is decreed by law, as in the case of the Jewish ghettos under the Nazi regime. Socio-economic class factors such as prices of housing, places of work, transport facilities, etc. would tend, in the last instance, to determine the population character of a particular neighbourhood. Public housing policies would operate in similar ways.

Sharing public space in housing estates and neighbourhood streets does not necessarily break down boundaries. Phil Cohen (1997), for instance, has shown how male youth gang cultures develop in order to mark the territoriality of one 'community' in certain public spaces, with the tacit – and sometimes not so tacit – support of the older generations. Control of the behaviour and mode of dress of women and girls of the community is a major occupation of such gangs when they are not fighting (Patel, 1990).

Even when communal boundaries are not marked by open 'warfare', urban space is not considered to be 'a safe home', as there are no proper defences in it from the intrusion of 'the stranger'. Verity Staffulah Khan (1979) carried out a comparative study on women's purdah in Bradford in the UK and in Bangladesh in the villages from which the Bradford immigrants had come, and found the practice of purdah to be much more extreme and rigid in Bradford than in Bangladesh. This is but one facet of a more general defensive rigidity and 'freezing' of cultures which tends to take place in diasporic communities.

This is important, because the classical studies on 'the stranger' (Schutz, 1976; Simmel, 1950), have tended to consider the immigrant, the newcomer as 'the stranger'. But, of course, as John Berger (in his famous *The Seventh Man*) has pointed out, for 'the stranger', all the locals are strangers as well! As Therese Wobbe (1995, p. 92) has shown, the fear of the stranger is often specifically gendered. She argues that the gendered challenge that the stranger presents constitutes a physical-affective dimension which is central to the understanding of racist violence. It is structured around the common stereotype of the male stranger harassing, threatening or actually raping 'our women', whose honour has to be defended. On the other hand, she also argues that the constructed collectivity boundaries 'between "us" and "them" also indicates the limits and intersections of social obligations and social norms'. This is a central dimension in the understanding of actual racist violence and violence against women in everyday life, as the absence of social responsibilities towards the Others often implies the freedom to violate and attack. The targets for such attacks could be not only 'their' women, but also 'traitors', such as wives from mixed marriages.

Multiculturalism and its dangers

The doctrine of multiculturalism has developed as an attempt to neutralize this sense of mutual threat and the exclusions and violence which develop as a result of it. Trin-Min Ha has commented (1989, pp. 89–90) that there are two kinds of social and cultural differences: those which threaten and those which do not. Multiculturalism is aimed at nourishing and perpetuating the kind of differences which do not.

Carl-Ulrik Schierup (1995) has claimed that multiculturalism is an ideological base for transatlantic alignment whose project is the transformation of the welfare state. It has been developed as a major form of accommodation to the settlement of immigrants and refugees from ex-colonial countries, the institutionalization of ethnic pluralism and the preservation of the cultures of origins of the ethnic minorities as legitimate parts of the national project. Multiculturalism, however, is problematic in several ways. As Andrew Jakubowicz concluded in relation to Australian policies of multiculturalism: 'Multiculturalism gives the ethnic communities the task to retain and cultivate with government help their different cultures, but does not concern itself with struggles against discriminatory policies as they affect individuals or classes of people' (Jakubowicz, 1984, p. 42).

A controversial, related question is the extent to which the conservation of collective identities and cultures is important as a goal in itself or has only become so as a result of collective will. John Rex (1995) argues that both are true, but this implies a homogeneous construction of both cultures and collective wills, and assumes that the attitudes of all members of a specific ethnic community to its 'culture' would be the same.

Moreover, it would be a mistake to suppose that those who support multiculturalism assume a civil and political society in which all cultural identities would have the same legitimacy. In all states in which multiculturalism is an official policy, there are cultural customs (such as polygamy, using drugs, etc.) which are considered illegal as well as illegitimate, giving priority to cultural traditions of the hegemonic majority. At the same time, in multicultural policies, the naturalization of the western hegemonic culture continues while the minority cultures become reified and differentiated from normative human behaviour.

The whole debate on multiculturalism stumbles on the fact that the boundaries of difference, as well as the boundaries of social rights, are determined by specific hegemonic discourses, perhaps using universalistic terminology, but definitely not universal. And universalist discourses which do not take into account the differential positionings of those they refer to often cover up racist (and one can add sexist, classist, ageist, disablist, etc.) constructions.

The construction of 'the community' in multiculturalism assumes a unified cultural or racial voice for each community. These voices are constructed to be as distinct as possible (within the boundaries of multiculturalism) from the majority culture in order to be able to be 'different'; thus, within multiculturalism, the more traditional and distanced from the majority culture the voice of the 'community representatives' is, the more 'authentic' it is perceived to be within such a construction. Such constructions do not allow space for internal power conflicts and interest differences within the minority collectivity, for instance conflicts along the lines of class, gender politics and culture. Moreover, they tend to assume collectivity boundaries which are fixed, static, ahistorical and essentialist, with no space for growth and change. When such a perspective becomes translated into social policy, 'authenticity' can become an important political resource with which economic and other resources can be claimed from the state as being the representative of 'the community' (Cain and Yuval-Davis, 1990). As Yeatman observes:

> It becomes clear that the liberal conception of the group requires the group to assume an authoritarian character: there has to be a headship of the group which represents its homogeneity of purpose by speaking with the one, authoritative voice. For this to occur, the politics of voice and representation latent within the heterogeneity of perspectives and interests must be suppressed.
>
> (Yeatman, 1992, p. 4)

This liberal construction of group voice, therefore, can collude with fundamen-talist leaderships who claim to represent the true 'essence' of their collectivity's culture and religion, and who have high on their agenda the control of women and their behaviour (Sahgal and Yuval-Davis, 1992).

Multiculturalism can often have very detrimental effects on women in particular, as often 'different' cultural traditions are defined in terms of culturally specific gender relations and the control of women's behaviour (in which women themselves, especially older women, also participate and collude) is often used to reproduce ethnic boundaries (Yuval-Davis and Anthias, 1989). An example of such collusion, for instance, is the case in which the judge refused a request for asylum to an Iranian woman who had to escape Iran after refusing to be veiled because 'this is their culture' (case recounted by the solicitor Jacqui Bhabha). Another example is that of a young Muslim girl who fled her parents' home because of their restrictive control of her, and who was placed by the social services in another Muslim home, even more pious, against the wish of the girl and the advocacy of the Asian Women's Refuge (case recounted by the workers of Southall Black Sisters).

As Stuart Hall (1992; 1996) points out, cultural identities are often fluid and cross-cutting. Even more importantly, perhaps, they are not only multiple, but they are multi-layered. This does not mean only that boundaries of certain identities are by definition wider and inclusive of other more specific identities (local, regional, national, racial, etc.) but also that some identities which have no pre-fixed cohesion or assumption of common origin or even common destiny may co-exist within individual or communal subjective narratives. Those hyphenated identities have been theorized as hybrid identities located within the symbolic border (or, rather boundary) zone (Bhabha, 1990; 1994; Anzaldua, 1987).

Hybrids have been celebrated in post-modernist literature as the symbol of the time, and are seen as both evoking and erasing the 'totalizing boundaries' of their adoptive nations. Located within the context of globalization, hybrids, nomads (Bradiotti, 1993) and other 'travelling identities' have been celebrated by writers like James Clifford and Rosi Bradiotti. Talal Assad (1993, pp. 9–10), for instance, contrasts James Clifford's (1992) celebration of 'the widening scope of human agency that geographical and psychological mobility now afford' with the deep pessimism of Hanna Arendt (1951), herself a refugee from the Nazis, who spoke of 'the uprootedness and superfluousness which has been the curse of modern masses'. The difference, of course, is embedded in the construction of the notion of free agency versus what Amrita Chhachhi calls 'forced identities' (1991). Whoever watched the terrible sight of Rwandan refugees being taken back to Rwanda from Zaire would question the global validity of the celebration of the nomad.

The problems with the notion of 'the politics of border' and its associated constructions of the nomad, the hybrid and 'travelling cultures', are twofold (Brah, 1996; Welchman, 1996). First, its image of crossing boundaries, travelling and miscegenation relies upon a fixed notion of location and culture which brings back essentialism through the backdoor. Second, in the process of concentrating on the imagery, the signifier, the agency, all too often questions of political economy disappear. As a result, there is not enough attention to the differential power relations between the different cultures and locations which are supposedly hybridized or travelled. Carl-Ulrik Schierup (1995) and Aleksandra Ålund have called this mode of analysis and politics 'culturization' in which 'the cultural has colonized the social' (Ålund, 1995, p. 319).

The conflation of (territorial) borders and (identity) boundaries can have important political consequences. The politics of diaspora illustrate these particularly well. It is important to differentiate between what Avtar Brah calls the 'homing desire' and the 'desire for homeland' (1996, p. 180), as well as between 'diaspora communities' (Brah, 1996; Lavie and Swedenburg, 1996; Lemelle and Kelley, 1994) and political exiles. Political exiles are usually individuals or families who have been part of political struggles in the homeland and their identity and collectivity membership continues to be directed singularly, or at least primarily, towards it, with the aim of 'going back' the moment the political situation changes. For diaspora communities, on the other hand, participation in the national struggles in the homeland, including sending ammunition to Ireland or 'gold bricks' to build the Hindu temple in place of the Muslim mosque in Ayodhya which was burned in December 1992, can be done primarily within an ethnic rather than a nationalist discourse, as a symbolic act of affirmation of their collective identity. Their destiny is primarily bound up with the country in which they live and their children are growing up, rather than with their country of origin. Nevertheless, such acts of symbolic identification can have very radical political and other effects in the 'homeland', a fact which might often be of only marginal interest to the people of the diaspora. I came across this very clearly when I was speaking in the early 1970s in the USA on the effects American Jewry's support had had on the continued occupation by Israel of the territories after the 1967 war, and the resulting violations of human rights by Israel. I was speaking before a synagogue audience known for its liberal politics concerning Vietnam and civil rights in the USA, trying to dissuade them from continuing to send money to Israel as a means of pressure on Israel to end the occupation. 'You don't understand,' a woman from the audience explained to me. 'I'm not interested in what Israel is doing – for me the most important thing is that I support Israel because Israel is part of me.' The sentiments are not always so extremely clear-cut, but this is definitely one illuminating example of the danger of under-emphasizing the difference between mythical desires for home and actual political realities, as well as the conflation of identification and participation (i.e. membership in the community, citizenship).

This example highlights the crucial importance of incorporating differential spatial relationships into the notion of citizenship and the ways in which living in the diaspora, living in metropolitan urban centres in the 'homeland' or living on the land might affect modes of participation in ethnic and national collectivities.

The domains of the public and the public

When discussing issues of citizenship, space and gender relations vis-à-vis the spatial division of 'the private' and 'the public' as gendered and ethnocized, it is crucial also to discuss the spatial dichotomy which has been underwritten as the basis of the relationship of gender and citizenship – the domains of 'the private' and 'the public'.

The private/public dichotomy has been central to the theorization of gender relations (Pateman, 1988; Vogel, 1994; Lister, 1997) as well as political theory, citizenship and the state (Turner, 1990, Jayasuriya, 1990). Feminist theory has challenged this dichotomy in several different ways, claiming that 'the personal is political'; that 'the public' social/political 'contract' cannot be understood without including 'the private', 'sexual contract' into the story; and that the dividing line between 'the public' and 'the private' is itself politically, culturally and gender specific. Moreover, as I have argued elsewhere (Yuval-Davis, 1997), there has been a high degree of inconsistency in the ways in which different authors discuss the public/private boundary and its relationship to other concepts such as political and civil society, the family, the economy, the voluntary sector, etc.

In the way in which feminists such as Carol Pateman (1988), Rebecca Grant (1991) and Ursula Vogel (1991), for instance, talk about the public and the private spheres, it is clear that the public sphere is identical in their writings to the political sphere, while the private sphere relates primarily to the family domain in which women are mainly located. In contrast to this construction of the private as the domain of the family, in Jayasuriya's writings (1990), the private domain is that which is not financed and/or controlled by the state and includes, for example, religious institutions. Bryan Turner (1990) uses the public/private dichotomy as one of the axes for his typology of citizenship, and includes in the private domain self-enhancement and other leisure, as well as spiritual activities. Sylvia Walby (1994, p. 383) criticizes him for adopting 'the male viewpoint' by conflating two meanings of 'private' – one which relates to the autonomy of the individual, and one which relates to freedom from the interventions of the state. She argues that while the family can or cannot be free from the intervention of the state, it is not an autonomous and free space for women, nor has it a unitary set of interests because husbands and wives (and children and other relatives in cases of extended families) have different social positionings, powers and interests within the family.

If we accept the meaning of 'private' as that in which the individual is autonomous, then this can be exercised to a lesser or greater extent in all social spheres, in which people – and not just women – can act both as part of social structures and collectivities, with all the constraints these provide, and as autonomous individual agents, whether it be in the family, in the civil or in the political domain. Similarly, depending on people's preferences and hobbies, leisure and self-enhancement activities can be spent with the family or other personal friends, with a trade-union, church or ethnic sports association, or as a councillor in the local government in the political domain. At the same time, especially in the modern welfare state, there is no social sphere which is protected from state intervention. Even in cases where there is no direct intervention, it is the state which has usually established, actively or passively, its own boundaries of non-intervention. In other words, the construction of the boundary between the public and the private is a political act in itself. Political power relations with their own dynamics exist in each social sphere. The most important contribution of feminism to social theory has been the recognition that power relations operate within primary social relations as well as within the more impersonal secondary social relations of the civil and political domains.

There is another meaning of 'the private', one which Sylvia Walby does not explore. This relates to the hidden, the unmarked, the anonymous. In the context of 'the global city', real and virtual, the visible and the invisible play particularly important roles. At the same time the imaginary geography of contemporary media and IT technologies has also helped to transform notions of intimacy, individual and collective.

Anonymity and visibility are context-dependent. The veiling of women in Muslim societies has been aimed at maintaining their anonymity in the public domain of the street. However, in western countries in which most women do not veil themselves or wear a headscarf, wearing one has the opposite effect of making one invisible – it makes a public statement about one's identity and usually (unless one is forced to this by others) one's identification with a particular cultural tradition, as part of a specific ethnic/political project. In the public debates about the 'headscarf affair', both in France and in Britain, newspaper articles continuously commented on the fact that the girls who insisted on wearing headscarves to school were anything but meek and subdued (Silverman and Yuval-Davis, 1997).

Ethnic, sexual and other minorities tend to gravitate to large metropolitan cities. Such cities can often offer two contradictory/complementary attractions relating to the private and the public. As Jeffrey Weeks explains:

> It was the growth of the city, with its physical density and moral anonymity, which provided the possibilities for lives lived at odds with the norms and values of the culture, both private in that they expressed personal needs and desires, and often had to be protected from the threat of exposure and possible social disgrace, and public in that new social spaces offered the chance for different ways of life.
>
> (Weeks, 1995, p. 147)

Here Weeks speaks of 'culture' in generic terms, but it is important to emphasize that the anonymity of the city can offer protection not only for those who 'deviate' from the hegemonic culture. It can also offer, probably even more so, the opportunity for members of ethnic minorities and other minority culture communities to escape from gendered social controls enacted upon them in efforts to reproduce the boundaries of their community of origin. Their 'deviancy' can be constructed in terms of assimilation into the hegemonic culture as well as in other urban subcultures.

Moreover, the sheer size, density and heterogeneity of human populations in global cities often also ensures that people in search of new social spaces can find others who share with them facets of identity and culture, such as the same myth of common origin, language etc., and with whom the anxiety and risk of facing the unknown, of often being doubly excluded from the hegemonic majority and from the established minority community, can be shared and mutually supported (examples include Jewish gays and lesbians, black feminists, Christian AIDS sufferers, etc.). At the same time the urban space can offer fluidity and temporality to these comings together, and people are freer to move on from these closures than in other social settings. Moreover, the involvement of people in the city in such communities on the marginal matrix of society (Evans, 1993) can be partial and can often remain detached from other facets of their lives at work and in the family.

Even more partial and hidden can be the membership of people in virtual communities, based on e-mail and the internet. However, as a transsexual Labour councillor explained recently to an interviewer on BBC Radio 4, such hidden communities can become invaluable sources of support and empowerment when those in the immediate physical spatial environment do not share, or have strong views against, people of particular social categories, identities or political views.

Conclusion

Physical and imaginary territories and boundaries construct the spaces in which citizenship practices and struggles are being carried out. As the boundaries of countries, nations and states do not usually overlap with each other, and as the individual boundaries of each country or nation are often contested, citizenship needs to be seen as a multi-layered construct, because people's membership in communities and polities is dynamic and multiple.

Ethnic, class and gender differences play particularly important roles in constructing and delineating the spaces, especially the urban spaces, in which the theatre of citizenship is taking place on a daily basis. One imaginary boundary whose tenacity is particularly vulnerable in such a context is the boundary between the private and the public.

New technologies, global markets and the changing international political context all affect specific constructions of citizenship. However, these effects are mediated via the specific gender, ethnicity, class and other intersecting categories of the social positioning from which people view the world, as individuals and as members in multi-layered communities.

Bibliography

Ålund, A. (1995) 'Alterity in Modernity', *Acta Sociologica*, 38: 311–22.

Anderson, B. (1983) *Imagined Communities* (London: Verso).

Anthias, F. and Yuval-Davis, N. (1989) 'Introduction', in N. Yuval-Davis and F. Anthias (eds), *Woman-Nation-State* (London: Macmillan).

Anzaldua, G. (1987) *Borderlines/La Frontera* (San Francisco: Spinsters/Aunt Lute Books).

Arendt, H. (1951 [1975]) *The Origins of Totalitarianism* (New York: Harcourt Brace Janovitch).

Armstrong, J. (1982) *Nations Before Nationalism* (Chapel Hill: University of North Carolina Press).

Assad, T. (1993) *Genealogies of Religion* (Baltimore: Johns Hopkins University Press).

Avineri, S. and De Shalit, A. (eds) (1992) *Communitarianism and Individualism* (Oxford: Oxford University Press).

Bauer, O. (1940) *The National Question*, in Hebrew (Hakibutz Ha'artzi).

Berger, J. (1982) *The Seventh Man: A Book of Images and Words about the Experience of Migrant Workers* (London: Writers and Readers).

Bhabha, H. (ed.) (1990) *Nation and Narration* (London: Routledge).

—— (1994) *The Location of Culture* (London: Routledge).

Bradiotti, R. (1993) 'Nomads in Transformed Europe: Figurations for Alternative Consciousness', in R. Lavrijsen (ed.), *Cultural Diversity in the Arts* (Amsterdam: Royal Tropical Institute).

Brah, A. (1996) *Cartographies of Diaspora: Contesting Identities* (London: Routledge).

Cain, H. and Yuval-Davis, N. (1990) 'The "Equal Opportunities Community" and the Anti-Racist Struggle', *Critical Social Policy*, 29: 5–26.

Castles, S. and Miller, M.J. (1993) *The Age of Migration: International Population Movements in the Modern World* (New York: Guilford).

Chatterjee, P. (1986) *Nationalist Thought and the Colonial World: A Derivative Discourse* (London: Zed Books).

—— (1989) 'The National Resolution of the Women's Question', in K. Sangari and S. Vaid (eds), *Recasting Women, Essays in Colonial History* (New Delhi: Kali for Women).

Chhachhi, A. (1991) 'Forced Identities: the State, Communalism, Fundamentalism and Women in India', in D. Kandiyoti (ed.), *Women, Islam and the State* (London: Macmillan).

Clifford, J. (1992) 'Travelling Cultures', in L. Grossberg, T. Nelson and P. Treichler (eds), *Cultural Studies* (New York: Routledge).

Cohen, P. (1997) *Rethinking the Youth Question* (London: Macmillan).

Cohen, R. (1997) *Global Diasporas: An Introduction* (London: UCL Press).

Daly, M. (1993) *Communitarianism: Belonging and Commitment in a Pluralist Democracy* (Belmont, CA: Wadsworth).

Enloe, C. (1990) ' "Women and Children": Making Feminist Sense of the Persian Gulf Crisis', *The Village Voice* (25 September).

—— (1993) *The Morning After: Sexual Politics At the End of the Cold War* (Berkeley, CA: University of California Press).

Evans, D.T. (1993) *Sexual Citizenship: The Material Construction of Sexualities* (London: Routledge).

Fanon, F. (1952 [1986]) *Black Skin, White Masks* (London: Pluto Press).

Gellner, E. (1983) *Nations and Nationalism* (Oxford: Basil Blackwell).

Grant, R. (1991) 'The Sources of Gender Bias in International Relations Theory', in R. Grant and K. Newland (eds), *Gender and International Relations* (Bloomington, IN: Indiana University Press).

Hall, S. (1992) 'New Ethnicities', in J. Donald and A. Rattansi (eds), *"Race", Culture and Difference* (London: Sage).

—— (1996) 'Who Needs "Identity?" ', in S. Hall and P. du Gay (eds), *Questions of Cultural Identity* (London: Sage).

Hasan, M. (1994) *The Murder of Palestinian Women for Family "Honour" in Israel*, MA dissertation, Gender and Ethnic Studies, University of Greenwich.

Jakubowicz, A. (1984) 'State and Ethnicity: Multiculturalism as an Ideology', *Australia and New Zealand Journal of Sociology*, 17 (3).

Jayasuriya, L. (1990) 'Multiculturalism, Citizenship and Welfare: New Directions for the 1990s', paper presented at the 50th Anniversary Lecture Series, Department of Social Work and Social Policy, University of Sydney.

Joseph, S. (1993) 'Gender and Civil Society', *Middle East Report*, 183: 22–6.

Kandiyoti, D. (1991) 'Identity and its Discontents: Women and the Nation', *Millennium*, 20 (3): 429–44.

Lavie, S. and Swedenburg, T. (eds) (1996) *Displacement, Diaspora and Geographies of Location* (Durham, NC: Duke University Press).

Lemelle, S. and Kelly, R. (eds) (1994) *Imagining Home: Class, Culture and Nationalism in the African Diaspora* (London: Verso).

Levi-Strauss, C. (1969) *The Elementary Structures of Kinship*, ed. R. Needham, trans. J.H. Bell and J.R. von Sturmer, 2nd edn (Boston: Beacon Press).

Lister, R. (1997) *Citizenship: Feminist Perspectives* (London: Macmillan).

Lowenhaupt Tsing, A. (1993) *In the Realism of the Diamond Queen* (Princeton, NJ: Princeton University Press).

Mani, L. (1989) 'Contentious Traditions: The Debate on Sati in Colonial India', in K. Sangari and S. Vaid (eds), *Recasting Women, Essays in Colonial History* (New Brunswick, NJ: Rutgers University Press).

Marshall, T.H. (1950) *Citizenship and Social Class* (Cambridge: Cambridge University Press).

—— (1965 [1975]) *Social Policy in the Twentieth Century* (London: Hutchinson).

—— (1981) *The Right To Welfare and Other Essays* (London: Heinemann Educational Books).

Mouffe, C. (1993) 'Liberal Socialism and Pluralism: Which Citizenship', in J. Squires (ed.), *Principled Positions* (London: Lawrence and Wishart).

Nandy, A. (1983) *The Intimate Enemy: Loss and Recovery of Self Under Colonialism* (Oxford: Oxford University Press).

Nimni, E. (1991) *Marxism and Nationalism* (London: Pluto Press).

Patel, P. (1990) 'Southall Boys', in Southall Black Sisters (eds), *Against the Grain* (London: SBS).

Pateman, C. (1988) *The Sexual Contract* (Cambridge: Polity).

Pettman, J.J. (1996) *Worlding Women: A Feminist International Politics* (London: Routledge).

Rex, J. (1995) 'Ethnic Identity and the Nation State: The Political Sociology of Multicultural Societies', *Social Identities*, 1 (1).

Rozario, S. (1991) 'Ethnic-Religious Communities and Gender Divisions in Bangladesh: Women as Boundary Makers', in G. Bottomley, M. de Lepervanche and J. Martin (eds), *Intersexions: Gender/Class/Culture/Ethnicity* (Sydney: Allen and Unwin).

Sahgal, G. and Yuval-Davis, N. (eds) (1992) *Refusing Holy Orders: Women and Fundamentalism in Britain* (London: Virago Press).

Schierup, C-U. (1995) 'Multiculturalism and Universalism in the USA and EU Europe', paper for the workshop 'Nationalism and Ethnicity', March, Bern, Switzerland.

Schutz, A. (1944 [1976]) 'The Stranger: An Essay in Social Psychology', in A. Brodersen (ed.), *Alfred Schutz: Studies in Social Theory, Collected Papers II* (The Hague: Martinus Nijhoff).

Silverman, M. and Yuval-Davis, N. (1997) *Racialized Discourses on Jews and Arabs in Britain and France*, research report submitted to the ESRC.

Simmel, G. (1950) 'The Stranger', in K.H. Wolff (ed.), *The Sociology of George Simmel* (New York: Free Press).

Trin-Min Ha (1989) *Woman, Native, Other* (Bloomington, IN: Indiana University Press).

Turner, B.S. (1990) 'Outline of a Theory of Citizenship', *Sociology*, 24 (2): 189–217.

Vogel, U. (1991) 'Is Citizenship Gender Specific?', in U. Vogel and M. Moran (eds), *The Frontiers of Citizenship* (Basingstoke: Macmillan).

—— (1994) 'Marriage and the Boundaries of Citizenship', in B. van Steenbergen (ed.), *The Condition of Citizenship* (London: Sage).

Walby, S. (1994) 'Is Citizenship Gendered?', *Sociology*, 28 (2): 379–95.

Warring, A. (1996) 'National Bodies: Collaboration and Resistance in a Gender Perspective', paper presented at the *Women and War* session at the European Social Science History Conference, May, The Netherlands.

Weeks, J. (1995) *Invented Moralities: Sexual Values in an Age of Uncertainty* (Cambridge: Polity Press).

Welchman, J.C. (ed.) (1996) *Rethinking Borders* (Basingstoke: Macmillan).

Wobbe, T. (1995) 'The Boundaries of Community: Gender Relations and Racial Violence', in H. Lutz, A. Phoenix and N. Yuval-Davis (eds), *Crossfires: Nationalism, Racism and Gender in Europe* (London: Pluto).

Yeatman, A. (1992) 'Minorities and the Politics of Difference', *Political Theory Newsletter*, 4 (1): 1–11.

Yuval-Davis, N. (1987a), 'Marxism and Jewish Nationalism', *History Workshop Journal*, 24.

—— (1987b) 'The Jewish Collectivity and National Reproduction in Israel', *Khamsin*, special issue on *Women in the Middle East* (London: Zed Books).

—— (1991) 'The Citizenship Debate: Women, the State and Ethnic Processes', *Feminist Review*, 39 (Autumn): 58–68.

—— (1997) *Gender and Nation* (London: Sage).

—— (1999) ' "The Multi-layered Citizen": Citizenship at the Age of "Glocalization" ', *International Feminist Journal of Politics*, 1 (Autumn).

Yuval-Davis, N. and Anthias, F. (eds) (1989) *Woman-Nation-State* (London: Macmillan).

Zajovic, S. (ed.) (1994) *Women for Peace* (Belgrade, Women In Black).

10 Multicultural citizenship

The politics and poetics of public space

Robert J. Holton

An important feature of recent discussions of citizenship is the more explicit discussion of cultural difference. The emergence of multicultural citizenship as a focus of inquiry is one highly significant manifestation of this. Such developments are in part the reflection of a wider unease with the foundational precepts of what might be called the classical liberal tradition in political philosophy. This unease is to be found among feminist and post-colonial as much as multicultural critics of liberalism. But debates over multicultural citizenship are also a reflection of rethinking and revision within liberal traditions in response to late twentieth century social change. Liberalism is not so unitary or static as many of its critics seem to believe.

Even so, the force of the critique of liberalism's handling of cultural issues has become a matter of practical politics and social planning as much as intellectual disputation. In Canada, Australia and many other nations, the current legacies of a variety of historic processes such as imperial conquest, enslavement, genocide and colonization now intersect with the contemporary trajectories of globalization and culturally diverse international migration. Conflicts over the politics of culture have emerged at the heart of social life.

This chapter explores debates over multicultural citizenship as they have arisen in critical engagements with liberalism. My interest is in the relationship between moral philosophy, sociology and history in such debates. My argument is, first, that strictly philosophical disputation about the foundational characteristics and weaknesses of liberalism has been eroded by increasing recourse to analyses of the social and historical contexts within which the politics of culture takes place. The second part of my argument is that debates over the cultural politics of multiculturalism have an excessive preoccupation with politics rather than poetics. One consequence of this is continued insistence on a public/private divide within which rational debate over public policy displaces a concern with the poetics of emotion, feeling and cultural representation. Conceptions of multicultural citizenship thereby exhibit an excessively macro- or structural focus that has inhibited understanding of what it means to live with difference.

Liberalism and culture

One of the major contemporary criticisms of liberalism, in its various utilitarian and republican formulations, is that it is blind to culture, or at least blind to the often subtle ways in which cultural presuppositions enter into and vitiate liberal constructions of citizenship rights. Liberal ideals of political and legal equality grounded in notions of individual rights claim universality on the grounds that such rights are equal and equivalent for each individual regardless of status. The minimum requirements made of the individual citizen are, first, the capacity to exercise rationality and, second, the capacity to exercise freedom from all forms of dependency that fundamentally impair individual autonomy. The equality underlying the structure of political rights elaborated by liberalism is said to be of a procedural rather than substantive kind, in that no individual's objectives are privileged over and above those of any other individual. Rather, procedural rights mean equality of access and treatment within the constitutional, legal and political institutions of the nation-state. The good life, inasmuch as it involves interpersonal engagement, thereby rests not on social control over the ends of action, but rather on a procedural equality of rights such as the right to vote, or to be equal before the law.

The theory is a familiar one, and so is the set of objections that have arisen over time. This chapter does not rehearse them in any comprehensive manner. Rather, it emphasizes those criticisms that raise issues of cultural difference and citizenship and shows how such criticisms have advanced by bridging the gap between moral philosophy and empirically grounded social inquiries.

Liberal claims to universalism have been critically received within two broad types of counter-argument. The first deconstructs the core presuppositions of the liberal universe. The liberal ideal of the autonomous individual citizen has been criticized, for example, on the grounds that it privileges a particular kind of dispassionate public rationality and specific forms of individual autonomy, characteristic of the public culture of males, from which women have typically been excluded. In Iris Young's (1989) critique, for instance, unacknowledged cultural presuppositions to do with masculinity are built into liberal citizenship, insofar as the rational citizen is constructed from a 'specifically masculine experience: militaristic norms of honour and homo-erotic camaraderie; respectful competition and bargaining among independent agents; discourse framed in unemotional tones of dispassionate reason' (Young, 1989, p. 253). In this way, so the argument continues, dominant forms of masculinity became identified with public reason, while femininity became associated with the residual apolitical spheres of sentiment and desire.

Similar critiques of liberal social contract theory and liberal jurisprudence have been mounted, respectively by Carole Pateman (1988) and Martha Minow (1990). Each demonstrates how various categories of 'others' are constructed so as to justify exclusion from membership of the supposedly universal liberal polity. Others may include those regarded as incapable of exercising reason, such as children, the insane or, in a number of historical contexts, women and supposedly inferior races. They may equally include those regarded as lacking free-standing autonomy, for example slaves, children and women subject to patriarchal authority. Neglect of the needs of such diverse groups has allowed a liberal theory of need to emerge in which needs are universalized to a standard format (for example, the right to vote or *habeas corpus*) that glosses over difference.

At stake here, then, is the very image of the autonomous individual citizen to whom rights are allocated. It would be a caricature of liberalism to suggest that this image is entirely abstract. Much has been made of its historic roots in the urban environments of the ancient *polis* and the medieval urban communes of Western Europe. The adage 'urban air makes free' is one normative legacy of this tradition. Another is the tendency to position perceived pathologies of the modern city and polity as deviations from myths of a golden civic republican past. Such associations have also reinforced cultural contrasts between the west and a range of eastern or orientalized Others. This entire historical construction is nonetheless highly problematic both in terms of historical plausibility (Holton, 1986), and in terms of its neglect of the uncomfortable normative association of civic humanism with slavery, imperialism and exclusionary patriarchy.

While images of the autonomous citizen make gestures towards history, they make few if any gestures towards cultural difference. Until recently this image has been taken as effectively culture-free by proponents of liberal universalism. Its universalism is felt to reside in the accessibility in principle of all individuals to citizenship, regardless of status or status group membership. It is further felt to be a merit of liberalism that it ignores, and even transcends, different social ends or values in the name of the public interest or general will.

One crucial element here is the liberal emphasis on rationality and self-government. These qualities, characteristic of what it means to be an autonomous individual, are valorized as preconditions for an effective liberal polity, the centre point of the good life. Their centrality occurs at the expense of expressive and affectual qualities which are marginalized or demeaned as public virtues. It may also clash with communitarian cultural formations which penalize individual autonomy in favour of group norms.

None of these criticisms necessarily unsettle the moral values associated with liberalism, but they do challenge the idea that liberalism somehow offers within its foundational presuppositions a universalistic culturally neutral way of accommodating cultural difference. For some reformers of liberalism such as Charles Taylor, this means that liberalism's universalism claims cannot be sustained, even though the political values at stake remain culturally worthwhile to many social groups. Liberalism, in his view, 'is not a possible meeting ground for all cultures, but is the political expression of one range of cultures, and quite incompatible with other ranges ... all this is to say that liberalism can't and shouldn't claim complete cultural neutrality' (Taylor, 1994, p. 62).

Debates over cultural difference and the conceptual structure and foundational presuppositions of liberalism may therefore lead in different directions. What participants share, at the very least, is scepticism towards liberal claims to universality. This scepticism usually combines political and legal philosophy with a kind of speculative and conjectural sociology or social history. Within such parameters, liberal political philosophy has to pass a general social and political realities test – if not a historical complexity test. Put another way, critics seek to identify the general social foundations of the liberal political utopia and the broad interests it serves, marginalizes or silences. The critical argument here is that liberal polities are indeed skewed to the interests of groups such as white middle-class males or western nations in contrast to those of the Third World.

One of three political responses follows: the first, by reformers of liberalism, is to seek the inclusion of those excluded or marginalized, through extensions of citizenship rights. The American civil rights movements of the 1950s and 1960s, promoting the inclusion of Afro-Americans, are an important example of this response. More recent Australian policies of access and equity in social programmes for indigenous peoples, women and non-English-speaking background migrants are another. In all such cases, inclusion is thought of in terms of the sets of individuals that comprise the groups concerned, rather than the groups as such. One strength of this position, deriving from T.H. Marshall (1950), is that the structure of citizenship rights over the last two hundred years has permitted extension to members of hitherto excluded groups. One problem with it is that it still leaves the discursive presuppositions and socio-cultural biases of liberalism intact.

An alternative, more radical approach is to claim group rights for the excluded or marginalized. These have been justified in several ways. First, they address pre-existing inequalities of power built into the status quo, somehow matching or balancing the pre-existing group advantages of privileged groups. Second, they address the so-called 'paradox of democracy', whereby equal citizenship still ends up privileging those who are most articulate or who possess the cultural capital to dominate discourses of rationality (Young, 1989, p. 259).

Within this framework, it is important to define exactly what is meant by a group, and how groups are seen as relating one with one another. The criteria typically used focus on a range of political and cultural rather than demographic characteristics. The idea of minorities, for example, refers not so much to demographic size, but rather to political vulnerability in the face of dominant structures of power held by the majority, on the basis of shared cultural characteristics perceived or claimed by the minority group in question. In the case of women, who are of course a majority, group characteristics focus upon subordinate social status by virtue of gender, associated with forms of oppression, marginalization and violence experienced as women.

The major strength of this response is that it makes cultural difference an irreducibly important issue in discussions of citizenship. By treating the foundational characteristics of liberalism as culturally skewed to particular modes of life, this response identifies types of political and psycho-social exclusion that are incompatible with norms of equality and justice. A way of widening access is required such that different voices and different kinds of voices may emerge. A major difficulty with this approach has to do with problems in the institutionalization of group rights. Who, for example, is to determine which groups are to be recognized, and what is to prevent group rights from leading to the 'fixation and homogenization of identity' (Castles, 1997, p. 12) in ways that are oppressive to individuals or sub-groups within recognized groups?

One area of confusion in discussions of group rights involves the relationships that are posited between groups and ideals of the good society. Are groups to be understood in *Gemeinschaftlich* ways, binding individuals to a strong sense of community norms, or are they to be seen in more *Gesellschaftlich* ways as associations of choice and affinity? Liberal critics of group rights express particular concern about the former option, insofar as it is perceived to constrain the individual autonomy of group members. In addition, a polity of group rights creates the spectre of a society of warring tribes, in which groups jealously guard their exclusive privileges, undermining any sense of commonality. Iris Young, however, has argued that group rights need not be constituted in this manner, but may be modelled on the moral philosophical idea of 'city life' as 'the being together of strangers' (Young, 1990, p. 237). Groups, in her view, mediate the potential atomism of this world of strangers, in the form of 'supportive social networks and subcultural communities' (1990, p. 238). The normative ideal here is one of social differentiation without exclusion from enjoyment of urban space.

The problem remains, nonetheless, as to how to get from the ideal to its effective social implementation. While the norm of 'the being together of strangers' may be created out of the urban experience, it is not immediately apparent how we move from a world of co-existing urban residents and urban subcultures to the construction of culturally-inclusive polities, be they national, regional or local. The politics of Australian multiculturalism, to take one example, is characterized by conflicts between the sectional ambit claims of those who speak for ethnic groups, and a sectional counter-politics by opponents of multiculturalism around the perceived neglect of Anglo-Australians, including poor whites. This may be interpreted positively as opening up debate about the basis of cultural difference, but the reality seems rather different, namely the perpetuation of stereotypical myths about 'ethnic', 'indigenous' or Anglo-Australian 'Others'. What passes for 'debate' over cultural difference is usually closer to diatribe.

This raises the issue of how far Iris Young's 'being together as strangers' is sufficient as a social basis for the achievement of social differentiation without exclusion. This approach is undoubtedly very useful as a way of addressing citizenship and cultural difference, a way that lies beyond conventional choices between liberal individualism and Rousseauist communitarianism. Its rejection of communitarianism may however be premature, insofar as some kind of moral sympathy and reciprocity is necessary to prevent group rights from degenerating into institutionalized sectionalism. The second part of this chapter will return to this point where it discusses the micro-sociology of interculturalism.

A third response to the issue of liberalism and cultural difference seeks to reconcile a liberal political tradition ostensibly founded on individual rights with particular notions of group rights. This position starts out with the presumption that the orthodox liberal position of benign neglect towards the different interests of component parts of the polity is not compatible with rights to justice or dignity. This option is especially evident in Canadian debates about multicultural citizenship involving Charles Taylor and Will Kymlicka.

Taylor's well-known essay on 'the politics of recognition' attempts to distinguish between fundamental rights of universalistic application that are essential to a liberal society (for example, *habeas corpus*) and cases for non-uniform treatment based upon the wish that particular groups have for cultural survival. As an example of the latter, he cites the collective goal of many francophones living in Quebec to preserve the French language. His support for this goal is not derived from the normative principle that all cultures are worthy of respect. It arises rather from a sense that cultural recognition is somehow central both to personal identity, and to interpersonal respect between the different cultural groups that make up Canada and, by extension, many other nation-states. Dignity in short requires more than the capacity to exercise rational autonomy in goal-setting and purposive social action. It also requires social arrangements and conditions under which different 'ways of belonging' associated with different identities are made possible.

Kymlicka's attempt to reconcile liberalism and cultural difference also picks up the centrality of identity formation and the social conditions which underpin it. This is set within a broader historical framework, deriving in part from William McNeill's approach (1986), in which most human societies are seen as culturally diverse and multi-ethnic. While cultural difference has not featured explicitly within philosophical discussions of liberalism until recently, Kymlicka makes the important point that it has nonetheless been an implicit element in the political practice of liberal nation-states. This is evident in several senses.

First, the association of citizenship with the nation-state has in effect created a system of nationally differentiated group rights based on nationality. The effect of this becomes evident when one considers the position of those such as refugees, who are denied citizenship rights within their nation of origin, but excluded by immigration and naturalization restrictions from participation as citizens in potential nations of refuge. Judged against the yardstick of global liberal norms, nationally differentiated citizenship rights erect group-based barriers so as to deny justice and equality for many members of the world's population.

We might note in passing that this has led some analysts, including Bryan Turner (1993), to see human rights rather than nationally focused citizenship rights as a more appropriate framework for effective rights under globalized cross-border conditions of population and resource mobility. This is an important point, although it is not clear that global human rights regimes are necessarily able to promote minority rights. This is primarily because human rights are generally couched in universalistic terms which are not easy to apply in any straightforward way to the particular needs of specific groups.

Kymlicka goes on to discuss several additional ways in which liberal polities have implicitly recognized group rights. These include historical treaties in which different cultural groups have been incorporated into emergent nations (such as the French territories incorporation into the Canadian Confederation in 1867). They are also evident in the ways in which electoral boundaries are typically drawn and redrawn, reflecting concerns over the *de facto* political representation of particular groups such as farmers or religious communities. Cultural difference and distinction is also evident at a symbolic level in the symbols of state and nationhood, including the symbolism of public buildings and the rationale for public holidays. This interest in muted symbolic modes of national expression has been explored more fully in Michael Billig's recent (1996) study, *Banal Nationalism*.

By surfacing implicit issues in political practice, Kymlicka wants to draw attention to the ways in which concern with personal autonomy has not necessarily ruled out concern for cultural difference. He uses this kind of historical precedent, then, as licence to investigate the terms upon which concern with cultural groups may be integrated within a liberal polity. The argument here is that generalized recourse to citizenship or human rights does not assist in resolving either constitutional choices over optimal modes of representation, or political choices over questions such as which languages have official status or how cultural difference is incorporated within the educational curriculum.

Kymlicka goes on to identify three cases for the recognition of group rights (1995, p. 108). These are, very briefly, the equality argument, the historical argument and the cultural diversity argument. The equality argument seeks to address existing inequalities in the status quo, which discriminate in favour of disadvantaged groups, even if only temporarily. The historical argument refers back to historic treaty rights which recognize groups, and which may well remain relevant in the present. Finally, the cultural diversity argument refers to the positive public benefits that flow from encouragement and public support for groups. Each may be consistent with liberal principles, insofar as they enhance the capacity of polities to effect greater equality between groups, or to meet specific needs that would not otherwise be attained through the generalized application of abstract liberal principles.

In delineating excluded or marginalized groups, discourses about citizenship, gender, race and multiculturalism, have drawn on sociological and historical argument. This move is necessary to elaborate exactly who has been excluded or marginalized, when, and on the basis of which kind of rationale, and with what kind of consequences. Within this endeavour, the macro-sociology of large structures such as property rights or racist discourse has begun to be combined with a micro-sociology of personal experience and interpersonal identity. This in turn necessarily requires involvement in historical analysis of the ways in which particular groups became incorporated into particular nation-states, with or without citizenship rights, or the effects of denial of cultural recognition on identity, and forms of resistance in the politics of culture. The net effect has been to erode the abstract context-free discourses of moral and political philosophy with a sense of the actual social conditions under which particular groups, individuals and societies function, conflict with each other and articulate various notions of citizenship rights.

The debates over the cultural adequacy of liberalism indicate a move beyond strictly philosophical discourse. In one sense, the recent cultural critique of liberalism has begun to follow the broad intellectual trajectory of Karl Marx, whose neo-Hegelian philosophic critique of liberal citizenship led from the abstract to the concrete. This evolution proceeded in increasingly political economic and historical materialist directions, grounded in analyses of actual conditions of social life and their implications for competing theories of human emancipation. In another sense, the use of conjectural sociology within cultural critiques may be regarded as an instance of contemporary trends which blur distinctions between moral philosophy and sociology.

There is nonetheless a distinction to be made between critique of liberalism that bolsters philosophical argument with conjectural sociology, and critique that is empirically grounded in an explicit way in time and space. A second route by which liberal claims to universalism have been critically assessed arises then within sociology, anthropology, geography and social history.

Here the analysis centres upon social interaction, conflicts and solidarities as they affect particular social groups, cities and nations. The concern is less with the underlying logic and adequacy of citizenship rights as a system of thought, and more with material and symbolic features of social life, including those mediated through citizenship and those located in terms of cultural difference. Such conflicts may take place over urban planning and the use of public space, over land rights for indigenous peoples, or in relation to language policy and the educational curriculum. Citizenship in this second idiom is something that is performed and acted out in cultural as much as political or legal processes. It is also important for this idiom to determine exactly how specific conflicts over culture and citizenship are historically situated in terms of processes that may include imperial conquest and the dispossession of indigenous peoples, mass migration and the creation of ethnic minorities, or economic globalization and the restructuring of public space.

Much writing in this second idiom is concerned with social and political struggles around structural changes connected with economic globalization and their impact upon the city. Kay Anderson's work (1991; 1993) on Chinatowns in both Canada and Australia is an example. The focus here is on the growth of what are called 'ethnic precincts' within Australian and Canadian cities. Here a variety of architectural and urban planning schemes have set out to differenti-ate the symbolic character of streetscapes in terms of a range of commercial and policy-driven objectives. Chinatowns, in particular, have been reinvented, not as organic cultural expressions of ethnicity based on residential settlement, but as socially constructed images of a benign otherness that are designed to further popular consumption of orientalized commodities.

An important theoretical move behind such analyses is the synthesis of work by David Harvey (1989) on late capitalism, with that of Edward Said (1978) on the discursive construction of difference. Anderson seeks to integrate the political economy of urban renewal with a cultural economy of racialized and orientalist urban social geography. This occurs through a linkage of state and capital, as globalized development capital interacts with state policies of multiculturalism. The critical edge to this analysis is directed in part at the economic liberalism of global capital flows that undermine democratic planning processes. But it is also directed at the co-option of the political liberalism of multicultural policies, promising an enhancement of the social status of migrants, into discourses of otherness. The denouement of this process within contemporary Australia is the revival of a populist racism led by the Pauline Hanson, One Nation party. This has revived images of Asian 'ghettos' seen as locations of pathological difference, crime and moral disorder. The shallowness of official multicultural discourses on cultural difference has thereby created a two-edged sword. Recognition of difference may be a first step towards a cultural democracy, yet it may equally reinforce cultural stereotypes that reinforce racism and prejudice.

The engagement of sociology, geography and social history with citizenship, cultural difference and the city has, of course, always been heavily laden with normative concerns. These are sometimes transposed into the voices of social actors seeking alternatives to top-down planning initiatives, or intercultural ways of being in festivals, carnivals and other forms of popular culture. But they are equally evident in critiques of the way that social arrangements limit active voice and encourage passivity. One such occasion is to be found in the concluding chapter of Richard Sennett's (1994) book *Flesh and Stone*. Here the spectre is raised of the multicultural city, be it New York or some other, in which cultural difference is mediated through the passive 'gaze' rather than through intercultural engagement, communication and exchange. Sennett's story is not one of the search for radical political subjects within emergent social conflicts over rights to the city. His interest, at least in part, is in the moral challenges of living with difference, and especially of the possibility of arousing moral sympathy with the other. This concern encourages us to think in terms of the interpersonal as much as the structural, that is with the micro- as much as the macro-sociology of multicultural citizenship.

The theme of activity and passivity within the multicultural city seems to me to be unresolved. One way of pursuing this theme further in a way that does justice to micro-level and psycho-social dimensions, alongside the political economy, is to focus on cultural agency, and on the poetic as much as the political. The anthropologist Gillian Bottomley (1992) speaks of the poetic through a concern with the expressive and affectual as much as with the cognitive. In this sense the poetic has a generic significance within but also beyond poetry, dance, music or literature as such. The poetic in this larger sense is about what Italo Calvino (1982) refers to as the inner as well as the outer world. Put another way, it is like an ear that can hear things beyond the understanding of the language of politics; it is like an eye that can see beyond the colour spectrum perceived by politics.

One problem with conventional accounts of citizenship is that they are typically silent on most questions of emotion and feeling. The idealized citizen, therefore, not only lacks gender and culture, but is never humiliated or marginal, never wants for self-esteem or a sense of personal dignity or worth, is never angry, and of course rarely, if ever, admits to emotionality in public. To do so would be an embarrassment. All of this reflects an underlying emphasis on Stoic qualities of self-mastery and self-control, qualities built into dominant modes of masculinity.

If expressive qualities are admitted at all, they relate not so much to personal emotions and feelings as to symbols of virtue derived from public life. These include the majesty of royalty or presidential status, the fortitude of the explorer in the struggle with nature, the courage of the soldier in war, the earnestness of the political reformer, the pedagogic wisdom of the thinker, or the hubris of the successful entrepreneur. The statues that abound in the public spaces of cities are generally of this kind, and may certainly evoke feelings, whether of pride and respect or cynicism and disgust. Yet the range of representations is a limited and exclusive one, inasmuch as the stories represented are generally skewed to the powerful and the successful.

Some recent writing on cultural representations within museums and exhibitions consolidates this line of argument, connecting representation with imperial, colonial and racialized forms of discursive power. Jan Nederveen Pieterse (1997), in reviewing this current, notes the historic function of ethnological museums in constructing stories of the West's 'triumphant evolutionary attainments', but also emphasizes how this role has shrunk under the corrosive impact of post-colonial and multicultural challenges. Different voices and different angles of vision have been opened up by oppositional movements seeking cultural self-representation, and some of these have been represented in new kinds of museums and exhibitions.

Such changes are important, although the continuing reproduction of older exclusionary representations into contemporary urban spaces should not be under-emphasized. The city of Adelaide in the state of South Australia, where I live and work, was founded in 1836 by reforming religious dissenters, and has strong traditions of humanist liberalism and social democracy. Nonetheless, within the central public precinct of Adelaide that contains art galleries, libraries and two universities, the official representation of indigenous peoples has until very recently been located within a museum, surrounded by taxonomic presentations of flora and fauna. The atmosphere was one of physical anthropology and the nineteenth-century epoch of scientific racism. Cultural difference was represented as being as natural as the difference between species of marsupials.

The alternative to this, several blocks away is Tandanya, a centre of aboriginal arts, popular with tourists for the artifacts that it sells. This centre is, in contrast to the museum, both self-managed by aboriginal people and a place where living artistic creativity in a number of visual arts may be practised. There is thus some aboriginal presence within the city's urban space. Simultaneously, the historic record within the museum has now been transformed to represent aboriginal agency and culture. But for the most part, and within the city's mainstream public spaces, representations of indigenous peoples and the experience of invasion, humiliation and abjection or white shame are notably absent. This is partly a matter of official cultural exclusion and neglect, an exclusion perpetuated even after the gaining of formal citizenship rights by indigenous peoples in 1967. But it is also, in part, a reflection of different symbolic spaces within which aboriginal peoples understand the history of their colonization, linked above all else with the land. Cities, then, have no particular significance as such, only as impositions on an earlier landscape with an entirely different set of symbolic markers, centred around sacred places and dreamtime narratives.

Immigrants, by contrast, have a more integral part in the city's central precinct within a separate place, the Migration Museum. Here migrants are represented as social actors, not as natural exhibits. The active voice of the various migrant groups is also recognized in a series of exhibitions which remember the history and settlement of ethnic groups through multimedia displays. The emotions of pathos are evoked as much as hubris. This contrasts with the ways in which indigenous peoples are represented, but also with the more commercially driven ethnic precinct of Chinatown.

These contrasts are important, in part, because some of the literature on cultural representation and the city is too deterministic, and insufficiently subtle. One cannot easily read off the complexities of representation simply by invoking the cultural logic of late capitalism, the historic legacy of racism or the contemporary dominance of economic rationalism.

In her own work on the poetics of Greek migrants in Australia, Gill Bottomley (1992) pursues a micro-approach to settlement experience, through notions of *xenitia*, which means the experience of exile and its association with humiliation. She notes how *xenitia* has reappeared as a major theme in Greek culture in light of the mass international migrations of the last two hundred years. Loss of place or home, and the search for a new order, informs the work of migrant Greek writers. Popular activities, such as dance, remain ways of working through issues of continuity and change, though younger generations may turn against all that is represented as 'ethnic'. They are, in this sense, the site of 'the small politics of everyday life' (Bottomley, 1992, p. 80).

What, then, has all this to do with citizenship? Dance, after all, has been caricatured as a cultural folkway, and the emblem of the apolitical face of multiculturalism, which is easiest to accommodate, but which does nothing to address political exclusion or economic inequality. Such folkways, it is said, are private rather than public, matters of which a liberal polity need take no note.

Even if this devaluation of the politics and poetics of everyday life is rejected, it remains to be established how bridges may be built between the poetics of different groups. Such challenges are made harder by limits to the micro-sociology of interpersonal relations, which has focused mostly on intra-group relations, rather than interculturalism *per se*. Bottomley's reference to poetics is, for example, specific to Greeks.

Poetics, politics and citizenship

Robert Frost once remarked that poetry may be defined as that which cannot be translated. Does this render the expansive metaphorical use of poetics explored here liable to issues of incommensurability between the experience of different groups? How, in other words, do ideals of multicultural citizenship assist in clarifying how we might live with difference?

There is a connection, it seems to me, between the small politics or poetics of everyday life, and larger issues to do with citizenship and multiculturalism. The case for such a connection depends in part on deficiencies in the foundational presuppositions of liberal political philosophy. Critique of such presuppositions has led to an expanding interest in the social conditions under which effective citizenship becomes possible. It does, however, require an enlarged view of what is meant by 'social conditions' for any kind of micro-focus on citizenship to emerge. This enlargement takes us into the realms of affective and expressive as well as cognitive and moral concerns. From this perspective, questions such as the historical and contemporary experience of humiliation, abjection, demoralization and loss of esteem are as significant obstacles to effective citizenship as material poverty or economic exploitation. Similarly, moral feelings such as love, care and solidarity may be assets in the work of constructing a multicultural citizenship of difference.

Neither constitutional change to enshrine formal legal rights, nor welfare rights to a decent living standard, significant though they may be, are enough then to encompass interculturalism. Political liberalism and social democracy are both inadequate in responding to Sennett's haunting question, namely the issue of how to live with difference in a manner that is based on active moral sympathy, rather than passive distance, and a minimal and fleeting residue of respect. Here the vision is not so much one of political bargaining and conflict between groups with rights, as some kind of inclusive intercultural reciprocity, grounded in difference. But what exactly is meant here by moral sympathy? Is this grounded in sympathy with particular others, with some kind of generalized other, or in some kind of combination of the two? This is, of course, the issue at stake in debates over Habermas's conception of the politics of communicative action (1984; 1994), involving Seyla Benhabib (1986), Iris Young (1989; 1990) and many others.

Such debates, it seems to me, have been faced with the conundrum that all claims to represent the generalized other cannot escape their historic origins in the life experience and moral horizons of particular groups, while all claims to work outwards from the life experience of particular groups cannot explain how dialogue and emotional engagement with others is possible outside shared norms of some kind. A more sociological way of putting this, which derives from the work of Roland Robertson (1992), is that universalism and particularism are mutually constitutive of the human condition, especially under conditions of globalization. Generality and particularity are inescapably intertwined. They cannot be separated either through the search for trans-contextual transcendent universals, whether individualist or communitarian, or through recourse to relativistic accounts of the good life, based on the simple valorization of difference for its own sake.

An analogous way of understanding the difficulties in grounding a politics and poetics of multicultural citizenship is in terms of the problem identified by Martha Minow as the dilemma of difference (1990, pp. 20–2). This may be stated as follows: treating people the same is likely to be insensitive to the differences between them, but treating them as different may equally stigmatize or hinder them on the basis of that difference. Minow sees this dilemma as arising from the social construction of difference, and the way that individuals are assigned to categories. Assertions of difference are thus statements of relationships. They also constitute and distribute power, including the power to name. Movement beyond this dilemma does not consist in reframing the structure of rights, to include new categories, for these will still be liable to negative stereotyping.

Minow's alternative 'social relations' approach calls rather for the recursive scrutiny of all arguments about difference in terms of the voices present or absent in such arguments, as well as the choices about human society and social institutions that they embody. From this perspective notions of multicultural citizenship or group rights must be scrutinized for their particular context-bound social assumptions and consequences, just like any more conventional form of liberal citizenship. There is, in other words, no transcendent trans-contextual universalistic form of sociological objectivity through which the dilemma of difference might be resolved. Sociology cannot resolve the dilemma of difference but it can assist value clarification, human choice and social emancipation by addressing Minow's admonition to 'resist abstraction … demand context' (1990, p. 216).

Bibliography

Anderson, K.J. (1991) *Vancouver's Chinatown: Racial Discourse in Canada* (Kingston and Buffalo: McGill-Queens University Press).

—— (1993) 'Otherness, Culture and Capital: Chinatown's Transformation Under Australian Multiculturalism', in G.J. Clark, D. Forbes and R. Francis (eds), *Multiculturalism, Difference and Post-modernism* (Melbourne: Longman Cheshire).

Benhabib, S. (1986) *Critique, Norm, and Utopia* (New York: Columbia University Press).

Billig, M. (1996) *Banal Nationalism* (London: Sage).

Bottomley, G. (1992) *From Another Place: Migration and the Politics of Culture* (Cambridge: Cambridge University Press).

Calvino, I. (1982) *The Uses of Literature* (San Diego: Harcourt Brace Jovanovitch).

Castles, S. (1997) 'Multiculturalism and Citizenship: A Response to the Dilemma of Globalization and National Identity', *Journal of Intercultural Studies*, 19 (1): 5–22.

Habermas, J. (1984) *The Theory of Communicative Action*, vol. 1 (London: Heinemann).

—— (1994) 'Struggles for Recognition in the Democratic Constitutional State', in A. Gutmann (ed.), *Multiculturalism: Examining the Politics of Recognition* (Princeton, NJ: Princeton University Press).

Harvey, D. (1989) *The Condition of Post-modernity* (Oxford: Blackwell).

Holton, R. (1986) *Cities, Capitalism, and Civilization* (London: Allen and Unwin).

Kymlicka, W. (1995) *Multicultural Citizenship* (Oxford: Clarendon Press).

McNeill, W.H. (1986) *Polyethnicity and National Unity in World History* (Toronto: University of Toronto Press).

Marshall, T.H. (1950) *Citizenship and Social Class and Other Essays* (Cambridge: Cambridge University Press).

Minow, M. (1990) *Making All the Difference: Inclusion, Exclusion, and American Law* (Ithaca: Cornell University Press).

Pateman, C. (1988) *The Sexual Contract* (Stanford: Stanford University Press).

Pieterse, J.N. (1997) 'Multiculturalism and Museums: Discourses about Others in the Age of Globalization', *Theory, Culture and Society*, 14 (4): 123–46.

Said, E. (1978) *Orientalism* (New York: Vintage Books).

Sennett, R. (1994) *Flesh and Stone: The Body and the City in Western Civilization* (London: Faber and Faber).

Robertson, R. (1992) *Globalization: Social Theory and Political Culture* (London: Sage).

Taylor, C. (1994) 'The Politics of Recognition', in A. Gutmann (ed.), *Multiculturalism: Examining the Politics of Recognition* (Princeton, NJ: Princeton University Press).

Turner, B.S. (1993) 'Outline of a Theory of Human Rights', *Sociology*, 27 (3): 489–512.

Young, I.M. (1989) 'Polity and Group Difference: A Critique of the Ideal of Universal Citizenship', *Ethics*, 99: 250–74.

—— (1990) *Justice and the Politics of Difference* (Princeton, NJ: Princeton University Press).

11 Women's rights to the city

Gendered spaces of a pluralistic citizenship[1]

Gerda R. Wekerle

In cities throughout the world, women are invoking the language of rights and citizenship in making a multiplicity of collective claims on the city for the fulfilment of basic needs, space and inclusion. Within the same city, different groups of women may be simultaneously engaged in making multiple claims in different arenas and spaces. For poor and marginalized women, survival issues may be paramount; while other women may focus on democratic participation or equity. Women's urban movements are examples of an 'insurgent citizenship' (Holston, 1998): resistance and mobilization from below that provide us with alternative models of urban citizenship rooted in women's multiple identities of class, race, ethnicity and sexual orientation. This 'militant particularism', to borrow David Harvey's (1998) phrase, this embeddedness of local political action, challenges globalization and restructuring by articulating an alternative story of citizen resistance and alternative practices within civil society.

A closer examination of women's claims to rights in the city contributes to our understanding of the relations between citizens, civil society and the local state. These cases, often based in one locality, articulate new forms of governance rooted in the politics of everyday life. At the same time, there is an extension of the local into the global as women's claims to rights in the city draw upon international human rights discourse, applying it to new policy arenas. Women in cities are located at a critical juncture in the ongoing remaking of civil society that is occasioned by forces of globalization in the economic sphere, but also by shifts in discourse at the international level related to the expansion of human rights to focus on moral rights and human dignity.

A new dimension of women's claims in cities in the last decade has been their positioning within a discourse of human rights; particularly women's rights as human rights. Such claims, framed in terms of a language of moral rights and human dignity, represent an expansion of human rights talk to focus on collective rather than individual rights. In an environment of globalization in which formal membership in a political community entitles citizens to fewer and fewer necessities of daily life, citizens have shifted to a discourse on rights as a protection against neo-liberal states in industrialized countries that are imposing policies such as the elimination of social welfare and equity legislation and the implementation of workfare. In particular, poor and marginalized women in cities of the South are framing their demands in terms of moral claims for justice and for fundamental human rights that ensure the necessities of human survival as structural adjustment policies erode the bases of livelihood.

International women's movements have sought to broaden the interpretation of women's rights by reframing women's rights as human rights through a series of international agreements and covenants. Starting in the 1970s, women's movements in North America and Europe made claims for women's equality and formulated rights claims in the courts. However, this initial focus on equal rights and comparisons with men tended to limit the development of women-centred perspectives or the use of such claims for collective empowerment (Schneider, 1990, p. 238). In the 1990s, the focus shifted to framing human rights as an international moral vision. Through a series of international conventions and UN conferences, women's NGOs (non-governmental organizations) pushed the boundaries of human rights interpretations from an emphasis on the individual as a free agent to a focus on 'substantive equality', which deals with the causes and consequences of exclusion (Lamarche, 1995, p. 12). According to Charlotte Bunch (1990, p. 493), reframing women's rights as human rights involved four approaches: counting women's rights as political and civil rights; including socio-economic rights, such as rights to food, shelter, healthcare and employment; emphasizing women's rights and the law; and taking into account 'a woman-centred stance'.

The development of an international women's rights movement, initially through networks in Latin America, Asia and Africa, has expanded the scope of human rights, the sphere of state responsibility, and the power of international mechanisms to monitor government actions and omissions related to women's human rights (Schuler, 1995, p. 3). Significant milestones have been the International Convention on Economic, Social and Cultural Rights (ICESCR) passed in 1963, which focuses on material conditions and recognizes the right of every human being to nurturance (Day and Brodsky, 1998, p. 47); the Convention on the Elimination of all Forms of Discrimination Against Women (1979); The Vienna Declaration on Human Rights (1993); the Declaration on the Elimination of Violence Against Women (adopted by the UN General Assembly in 1994); and the Beijing Platform (1995).

The Vienna Declaration on Human Rights (1993) first acknowledged that women's rights are human rights (Schuler, 1995, p. xi) by integrating the human rights of women and the equal status of women. The Vienna Declaration states (para. 18) that

> the human rights of women and of the girl child are an inalienable, integral and indivisible part of universal human rights. The full and equal participation of women in political, civil, economic, social and cultural life at the national, regional and international levels, and the eradication of all forms

of discrimination on the grounds of sex are priority objectives of the international community.

(Schuler, 1995, p. 1)

It targeted violence against women as a human rights violation (but not social, cultural, economic, sexual and reproductive rights) (Schuler, 1995, p. 8). A special Rapporteur on Violence Against Women was named within the UN human rights system, and, in fall 1993, the UN General Assembly passed a Declaration on the Elimination of Violence Against Women.

The Beijing Conference on Women (1995) integrated gender and development and a human rights focus. This conference bridged the gap between basic needs and basic rights, and developed a new paradigm focusing on women's needs as opposed to women's equality with men (Schuler, 1995, p. 8). The Beijing Platform for Action asserted that women's civil and political rights are indivisible from economic, social and cultural rights, including women's right to education, food, health, freedom from violence and exercise of citizenship (Bunch et al, 1995, p. 10).

These international agreements established the principle that women's rights are not separable from human rights; that human rights are indivisible; that civil and political rights cannot be separated from the economic, social and cultural rights of women. Based on these international agreements, signed by national governments, women's movements argue that human rights cannot be constrained or revoked by nation-states. Instead of relying on individual legal claims within nation-states, women's organizations have shifted to making collective claims on behalf of groups of women whose rights are alleged to have been abrogated. The cumulative impact of these shifts in the boundaries of human rights agreements has created an environment in which women's grassroots movements reframe their issues in terms of rights and, most importantly, draw upon the resources and experiences of women's groups in other parts of the world to inform their oppositional discourse and practices.

Women's movements globally have been central to a rethinking of concepts of citizenship and rights. In response to the decline of the will of national governments to challenge the corporate sector, women's movements have focused on the dignity of human life as a moral imperative. These shifts in ways of thinking about human well-being are often framed as a discourse on rights which focuses on civil society as the testing ground for new forms of democracy and citizenship. It represents a shift from equality-based legislation to the global political arena and active participation by citizens in the drafting and monitoring of international and transnational agreements on human rights. Through global politics and movements, a feminist discourse on rights has begun to be articulated that is collective rather than individual in its focus. This is particularly important for marginalized and racial minority women as it provides a political tool for challenging globalization and its impacts from below.

Pluralistic citizenship and women's standpoint

Political theorists, including Warren Magnusson (1996, p. 63) and John Friedmann (1998, p. 20), argue that we are experiencing a revival of civil society. Civil society is defined variously: by Magnusson (1996, p. 63), drawing upon Arendt, as the place for 'public spirited action', a place apart from both the state and the market; by Friedmann (1998, p. 21) as 'those social organizations, associations and institutions that exist beyond the sphere of direct supervision and control by the state'; and by Laclau and Mouffe (1985) as the space for political mobilization and active resistance. As women are forced by global economic restructuring to bear the burdens of meeting human needs, from their position on the margins, they are actively engaged in remaking civil society and rethinking what it means to be a citizen of the city, the nation and the globe.

Citizenship is also undergoing re-examination. The notion that 'citizen rights derive from full membership in a distinct political community' (Friedmann, 1998, p. 25) has been contested by feminist theorists (Pateman, 1988) who argue that women have frequently been excluded from such membership. Further, when formal membership in a political community entitles a member to fewer and fewer necessities of daily life, there is a new emphasis on broadening the concept of citizenship to include 'the life space of daily life' (Friedmann, 1998, p. 27).

Savarsy and Siim (1994, p. 250) suggest that it is easier to understand women's politics and the variety of forms that women's grassroots mobilizations take if we adopt a notion of 'pluralistic citizenship'. This would include the recognition that women participate in a variety of areas of public life – neighbourhoods, organizations, political institutions and social movements; that such participation occurs at a number of different formal levels; that the category 'women' includes a diversity of identities, interests and ideologies; and that each woman has a number of different roles and identities. According to Savarsy and Siim,

> The strength of a feminist version of pluralistic citizenship is that it proposes to use difference both to analyze unequal power relations that impede an inclusive politics of diversity and to give voice to those who are usually underrepresented.
>
> (Savarsy and Siim, 1994, p. 254)

The concept of 'women's standpoint', defined by feminist theorist Dorothy Smith (1998; 1987) as a standpoint that is rooted in time, place and the body, the local and the everyday, has become an important theoretical underpinning for women's claims in cities. This translates into arguments that people are 'the experts of their own lives and local practices' and that citizenship must be broadened to include 'the life spaces of daily life' and 'the connections between the actualities of their daily lives and what is going on in the economy or polity' (Smith, 1998, pp. 106–8). The emphasis on women's standpoint has required a shift in our view of what constitutes legitimate knowledge and the basis for a liberatory praxis. Greater attention is paid to the use of stories and direct experience as a form of resistance and to learning from the lived experience of women of colour, working-class women and their everyday acts of resistance.

The concepts of a pluralistic citizenship and women's standpoint suggest that we look at the ways in which women make multiple claims for equality and inclusion, claims often based on their roles as mothers, community guardians and urban citizens, and that we pay attention to the politics of everyday resistance, as well as the institutionalized politics of the public sphere.

Friedmann and Douglass (1998, p. 2) characterize the expanded demands of citizenship as interconnected claims for rights to voice, difference and human flourishing. A new development is that small locality-based women's urban movements have attempted to link human rights to their claims to urban citizenship.

Pluralistic citizenship and standpoint are expressed through rights claims that have different targets and take diverse forms: maternalist claims for resources to meet basic human needs; claims for spatial-temporal spaces that support everyday life; claims for more participatory, inclusive structures of urban governance; and rights claims to international bodies by women's urban movements.

The rights of mothers and the political resource of motherhood

In cities throughout the world, the restructuring of the economy has resulted in the withdrawal of states from responsibility for providing basic services and an erosion of accountability to citizens. In the North as well as the South, women who are responsible for the caring work in society, are expected to be the shock absorbers of restructuring by managing poverty and the essential needs of family and community. All over the globe, women have been making claims to 'fundamental human rights' – to food, shelter, health and peace – the necessities for human survival (Kaplan, 1997, p. 8).

Feminist philosopher Sara Ruddick (1989) argues that maternal thinking, reflected in 'strategies of protection, nurturance and training' is a feminist standpoint that generalizes caring labour to society as a whole. She argues that

> a women's politics of *resistance* is composed of women who take responsibility for the tasks of caring labour and then find themselves confronted with policies or actions that interfere with their right or capacity to do their work. In the name of womanly duties that they have assumed and that their communities expect of them, they resist.
>
> (Ruddick, 1989, p. 223)

In cities of the South, particularly in Latin America, as well as in cities in North America, poor, marginalized and racialized women are asserting their moral right to the basic necessities of human life. Women's standpoint is often expressed as a maternalist discourse, as mothers' claims to the resources to meet the needs of their families. In cities such as Lima, Peru, for example, women engaged in mutual aid, built their family home and confronted the government to consolidate land claims (Jelin, 1990, p. 188). 'Mothers clubs' organized collective kitchens which represented a new form of female organization and public activity.

Women's urban movements in Latin America force political recognition of the public face of reproduction, according to Elizabeth Jelin (1990, p. 192). They attempt to recover the public and political dimension of women's domestic role and try to change the social forces that create the private sphere (Jelin, 1990, p. 187). A critical element is the emphasis on empowerment. Women's urban movements in Latin America shatter the passive image of women by establishing gender organizations to take control of their own destiny (Jelin, 1990, p. 193). What is new, according to historian Temma Kaplan, is that ordinary women, women from working classes and subordinated ethnic and racial groups, make claims for justice and challenge the rights of private property and unfettered markets. They integrate social and economic demands into their conceptualizations of human rights and make 'broad claims about human needs and rights according to an interpretation of justice that they themselves are developing through their actions' (Kaplan, 1997, p. 7).

An indication of the linkages among transnational movements is the way in which food security as a mobilizing issue has moved from cities of the economic South to cities of the North. In Toronto, for example, Food Share, a community agency, has developed political strategies based on the right to food as resistance to neo-liberal cutbacks. Visits to Peru's community kitchens and Brazilian cities' involvement in wholesale food markets, meal programmes and community gardens (Field, 1997) inspired Food Share to establish community kitchens, a Field to Table Program to link small farmers directly to consumers, a Food Training Program for low income women that has led to a multicultural Catering Company, and community gardens that produce organic produce within the city. An agency with female leadership, Food Share has reframed a traditional 'women's issue' – access to nutritious food – into a discourse on 'the right to food'.

The struggles of mothers often arise around access to food, shelter, urban safety and the right to employment (Susser, 1982; Leavitt and Saegert, 1990; Hardy-Fanta, 1993; Rabrenovic, 1995) in low-income and ethnocultural neighbourhoods. Groups such as the Mothers of Love Canal and the Mothers of East Los Angeles have become well known for their engagement in toxic waste struggles (Gibbs, 1981; Pardo, 1990). Based in the 'resource of motherhood' (Krauss, 1993), their mobilizations have extended the boundaries of what it means to be a mother in working-class and ethnic minority communities that often provide very limited public roles for women.

However, there are limits to the mobilization potential of maternalism. Such mobilizations occur more frequently out of necessity than choice, and not all mother's movements are progressive or emancipatory. When mothers are called upon to shoulder a triple burden – as mothers responsible for the welfare of their families, as breadwinners and, increasingly, as organizers of the survival of the community – women bear heavy costs. Moreover, feminist scholars have argued that the focus on maternalism and women's caring as the basis for a politics of resistance is essentialist and more delimiting than political action grounded in women's role as citizens. Dietz (1985) argues that feminist political consciousness must draw upon the potentiality of women-as-citizens and their historical reality as a collective and democratic power, not upon the 'robust' demands of motherhood.

Citizenship and the life spaces of daily life

Women are also making rights claims as gendered subjects who demand spatial-temporal spaces that support everyday life. They argue that their standpoint and gendered experiences have been excluded and denied by decision-makers, politicians and corporations that shape cities as growth machines, or the global nodes for the accumulation and flow of international capital. In European cities, women are asserting their rights as citizens to reshape public space and services in cities by redefining sustainability from women's standpoint. Over the past two decades, groups of feminist planners and architects have been engaged in realizing the utopian vision of the non-sexist city which has been articulated by women civic reformers and theorists since the nineteenth century (Hayden, 1984; Cott, 1989). An initiative of Nordic women, the 'everyday life approach' has developed alternative visions of housing and the organization of neighbourhoods based on the needs of women and children, with special attention to the social reproduction of people and nature (Horelli and Vepsa, 1994, p. 203). Through funding from the European Community, the project supports local and regional infrastructures that integrate dwelling, care and work in space and time, through the enrichment of life at the neighbourhood level and a focus on the informal economy (Horelli and Vepsa, 1994, p. 207).

In the Nordic countries there has been a focus on planning cities from the standpoint of women's everyday life by applying the experiential knowledge of women to create sustainable communities. This has resulted in new gendered plans for mobility and urban safety and designs for the intermediate spaces of cities that better integrate employment, family life and services. These projects have moved beyond utopian dreaming to actual projects on the ground. For example, in Göteborg, Sweden, the city council has developed a new neighbourhood based on gender planning principles (Eurofem, 1996, p. 9).

In Italy and Germany, much attention has been devoted to 'time planning', or 'Zeitpolitik' as it has been called in German (Eurofem, 1996). This means reorganizing daily activities in urban space and time, coordinating the schedules of shops, government offices, schools and workplaces. Invoking the phrase, 'Citizens time the city', women have linked the rights of citizens to the reorganization of daily life and have articulated alternatives to the 24-hour globalized city. These are examples of civil society working through the local state, with the resources of the state, to create models for new ways of living in the city through projects that seek to reorganize space and time to define women's urban citizenship rights.

Whose city? Women's rights to voice and inclusion

Citizenship as a democratization of politics, particularly as this relates to the social production of space, has been a key element of women's rights claims to cities. The emphasis on 'spaces of democratic practice' has taken two directions: demands for changes in the process of planning to accommodate women's voices based on 'women's ways of knowing'; and demands for inclusion through the creation of institutionalized structures to mainstream a gendered perspective within municipal governance. These claims for voice and inclusion are often framed in struggles over space in the city. A poster produced by the Women's Office of Frankfurt am Main, Germany, exemplifies this dual theme. The central image, a bright red boxer's glove, is aggressive and 'male' in its connotations. The caption, 'Frauen nehmen sich die Stadt', translates as 'Women take the city for themselves'. This is a play on 'Take Back the Night Marches' institutionalized in many cities of the North since the 1970s as women's demands for urban safety. But the Women's Office of Frankfurt and the women's movements in the city were not content with the night; they claimed the city and developed a month long series of workshops and public events to educate and engage citizens throughout the city in rethinking how the city could be made more women-friendly. Special attention was devoted to eliciting the voices of a multiplicity of women: children and youth, immigrants and refugees, housewives and professional women. Co-sponsorship by the Women's Office and women's movements in the city signalled a partnership between the local state and civil society.

Women's claims to urban citizenship often take spatial and territorial forms as women map out place-based strategies in opening up new political spaces in cities. Priority issues are identified as mobility, urban safety, housing and urban services (OECD, 1995; Commission of the European Communities, 1994; Eurofem, 1996). But it is spatial planning with a difference: viewed from the life space of subaltern, marginalized and culturally diverse citizens, it involves questioning urban regimes of accumulation in the global city from the standpoint of everyday life.

A report sponsored by the Equal Opportunities Commission of the European Communities (1995), *The European Charter for Women in the City*, has set the agenda for many European projects on women and the city by articulating twelve goals for promoting an active citizenship from the bottom up. A primary emphasis is to increase women's participation in decision-making processes, particularly in urban planning and settlement. Demands are for participation in decision-making that is more inclusive, diverse and equitable.

Holston (1998, p. 48) suggests that sites of insurgent citizenship are created when citizens introduce to the city new identities and practices that disturb the status quo. Women in cities often engage in insurgent planning practices. They question the modernist discourse of planning by challenging the reliance on experts and the relegation of citizens to consumers. Instead, they argue that women are the experts of their own lives and should also be engaged in shaping urban space.

In challenging traditional planning practice, women have simultaneously employed new frameworks and participatory planning tools. For example, the focus on urban safety in North American, European and British cities has generated detailed studies of fear of crime, as well as the development of new planning approaches, including ethnographic safety audits, focus groups, storytelling, drama and design with young children (Wekerle and Whitzman, 1995). In Barcelona the whole city mobilized to focus on women's rights to the city in 1996 to 1998. A project sponsored by a union foundation, the city government and the European Union, conducted consultations on women's needs in each electoral area and made recommendations on how to reorganize the city to better suit women. Based on two-day workshops throughout the city that focused on women's needs at the scale of the body, home and public sphere, women made recommendations on housing, urban space and planning, mobility, access, security and decision-making (Eurofem, 1996; Bofil, 1998).

Women's groups have also questioned who develops cities and on what basis. Pointing out that only a tiny minority of architects and engineers are women, organized groups of women architects and planners in Germany, Austria and Switzerland have produced submissions to design competitions which provide alternative models of how to live in cities. In 1992, Vienna sponsored a model suburban residential neighbourhood of 350 housing units that would be based on gender-sensitive design. Women architects, who had never been shortlisted for tenders in Vienna, were encouraged to apply, and the jury was composed mainly of women architects and landscape planners. Designed by a woman architect, the project includes a variety of units, a range of public open spaces, and living streets designed for children's play. As a consequence, women architects now regularly appear on the shortlists for competitions, and development plans submitted to the city are assessed in terms of gender equity (Kail, 1998).

Institutionalizing women's demands for the rights to inclusion in cities has been dependent on urban regimes and their agendas. These efforts have taken diverse forms, including the establishment of women's departments within local government (for example, Frankfurt and Hamburg); women's committees or commissions within local government (in the UK and the USA); special committees of municipal government focused on violence against women or women's housing; gender planners within planning departments of cities (Frankfurt and Hamburg); or the creation of national planning standards that incorporate a gender perspective (Germany). These attempts to institutionalize some form of gender planning by working through the local state vary in the resources that are made available and in the extent to which these initiatives are advisory only or are supported by the full weight of the local state. In the cases of both Frankfurt and Hamburg, women's movements have gained greater visibility and influence within the context of red–green coalitions that form the city government.

Political opportunities wax and wane as regimes change in cities. This has been the case in the UK, where women's committees of local government established in the 1980s are being 'mainstreamed', i.e. eliminated as stand alone units in favour of gender sensitivity throughout all departments (Little, 1994). In the context of downsizing and continuing restructuring of urban governance, instead of expanding the boundaries of women's citizenship, women are fighting a rearguard action in many cities.

At the same time, the emergence of transnational networks among women and city projects means that successful models are picked up and adapted by other cities even if political opportunities are shut down for gender planning in one city. Through networks such as Eurofem, which links gender planning and community development projects throughout Europe (Eurofem, 1996) through regular conferences and the development of a toolkit of successful projects, innovative ideas and social movement strategies continue to be disseminated beyond their localized origins. Such networks ensure that the flow of ideas and good practice in cities are not limited by institutional politics but continue to be nurtured within civil society.

Transnational appeals for rights in the city

A recent development has been the appeal by women engaged in specific local struggles in cities to international agencies. They seek to call governments to account and force compliance with international agreements and minimum standards, or, at the least, to embarrass national governments on the international stage and in their competition for global capital. As Temma Kaplan notes in her discussion of women's urban movements in Latin American cities (1997, p. 14), 'commitments to international platforms set a moral standard, providing NGOs with leverage they can use on their own governments, and enabling grassroots activists to organize across borders to compel governments to comply'.

The way in which Canadian women's groups have extended human rights discourse into new arenas demonstrates how strategies developed at the level of the nation-state may be extended as appeals to international bodies. The Canadian Charter of Rights and Freedoms was enshrined in the Constitution in 1982. Section 15 guarantees 'equal benefit of the law'; Section 15 (2) authorizes laws, programmes or activities designed to ameliorate conditions of disadvantage for members of disadvantaged groups, including women. In response to massive cutbacks in the welfare state instituted by a neo-liberal provincial government in Ontario, elected in 1995, women instituted Charter challenges against the repeal of equity legislation and cuts in social assistance on the grounds that they violated basic human rights (Vincent, 1996; Monsebraaten, 1995). When these legal challenges were unsuccessful, a new strategy was to turn to the human rights agreements signed by the federal government.

The Ontario Association of Interval and Transition Houses (OAITH) is a local women's advocacy organization that has resisted welfare state cutbacks by mounting an international human rights complaint. After the province of Ontario cut back funding to Violence Against Women Initiatives in the fall of 1995, OAITH documented the impacts of cutbacks on women's daily lives. OAITH (1995, p. 23) argued that 'Under the Canadian Charter of Rights and Freedoms (Section 7) life, liberty and physical and psychological security of women are guaranteed.' The dismantling of programs to provide protection and support to abused women and their children contravenes this legislation. Moreover, it contravenes the Declaration on the Elimination of Violence Against Women, adopted at the UN General Assembly in February of 1994, of which Canada is a participating member. The Declaration obliges countries to develop prevention approaches that promote protection of all women against all forms of violence, and guarantees the establishment of specialized services. After receiving no response from the provincial or federal governments, OAITH submitted its report to the UN Special Rapporteur on Violence Against Women in Geneva in November 1996. The Rapporteur replied that the information from OAITH on cutbacks to violence against women programmes would be included in future reports. In addition, OAITH included its report as part of the National Action Committee on the Status of Women (NAC) NGO report to the UN regarding Canada's compliance with CEDAW. In its yearly report, CEDAW expressed concerns about Canada's responses in meeting its international commitments to improving women's equality and freedom from violence.

In a second case, a small locally based organization of single parents in Toronto, Low Income Families Together (LIFT), coordinated a campaign by social justice groups to document the ways in which cutbacks in social welfare undermine human rights. This local agency prepared a report, *The Real Ontario UN Report: Holding Government Accountable to Human Rights Agreements*, which was presented to the UN Committee on Economic, Social and Cultural Rights to inform its regular review of Canada's record of performance under the international covenant. In response, the Committee has forwarded a list of priority concerns to the government of Canada, including concerns about discrimination on the basis of income or social condition, the institution of workfare, changes in social assistance schemes, homelessness, equal pay, employment insurance changes, the right to an adequate standard of living, the right to health and human rights legislation (UN website www.unhchr.ch/tbs/doc.nsf; *Toronto Star*, 1998).

In US cities, welfare rights organizations have also developed UN-focused campaigns. For example, geographer Melissa Gilbert (1998), is engaged in ongoing research on a welfare rights organization in Philadelphia, KWRU, which organized a march of predominantly African-American women to the

UN in the summer of 1997, to protest the absence of jobs at living wages as a human rights violation. In the summer of 1998, the organization held Human Rights Tribunals throughout the US and will forward this documentation to the UN. According to Gilbert, using a human rights frame as an organizing tool has allowed a local welfare rights group to take an international route to publicizing local welfare rights abuses.

These examples, drawn from Toronto and Philadelphia, are cases of particular localized struggles that are universalized by their rootedness in a discourse of human rights that is framed as a moral right. Perhaps it is a measure of the desperation of local movements that they are appealing to remote and bureaucratically cumbersome UN agencies. Such measures seek primarily to embarrass national governments concerned with international reputations, since lack of enforcement mechanisms, limited budgets and timetables for compliance mean that UN human rights agreements are weak instruments for social movements.

At the same time, human rights complaints to international bodies by small locally based agencies located in civil society that have exhausted domestic remedies represent an appeal to a vision of the dignity of human life and resistance to the neo-liberal agenda that has become pervasive in countries of the North and the South. Building upon the international women's human rights movements, such strategies contribute to the growth of a civil society that is both rooted in the local and without borders.

Conclusion

At the end of the twentieth century, we see a convergence of the interests of movements of resistance and a new focus on the daily practices of survival and resistance (Mohanty, 1991, p. 39). Women in industrialized cities are beginning to connect their local struggles for survival with the struggles of women in the economic South who experience 'the simultaneity of systemic forms of domination and oppression: racism, sexism, colonialism, imperialism, and monopoly capital' (Mohanty, 1991, p. 4). Transnational networks, often developed among women's city projects, diffuse participatory planning approaches and successful practices. Susan Smith (1989) argues that globalization is always experienced through a locality. The way a given locality responds to globalization pressures and who wins and who loses in this process becomes critical. Political theorists, including Magnusson (1992, p. 75), argue that the globalization of the economy and the neo-liberal advance of state policies have resulted in an 'erosion of the privileges of citizenship'. It is within this framework that a wider discourse on citizenship and the restructuring of human rights has emerged. Women's rights claims have highlighted the ongoing tensions between discourses on the global city and an emphasis on everyday life. By focusing on an alternative politics that is pragmatic and rooted in daily life, they seek to counter a moral order based on universal human rights to a focus on the global economic order. Renewed attention within the social movement literature to mothers' movements shows them as not purely defensive and survivalist. By creating conditions within civil society to meet the everyday survival needs of families and communities, they also challenge existing social priorities and the political order. Arguing from the standpoint of everyday life, women's initiatives in cities of the economic South and in the North have documented particularistic circumstances and universalized them to focus on human well-being and the spatial-temporal order that would support this.

In the course of many localized struggles, citizenship is being redefined from a common political identity to 'ethical norms or norms of justice' (Jones, 1994, p. 258). Increasingly, the emphasis is on a more pluralistic and diversified practice of citizenship. Jones (1994, p. 260) suggests that citizenship can be 'understood as an *action* practised by people of a certain *identity* in a specifiable *locale*'. In extending citizenship beyond national borders, she argues that:

> Feminist commitment to a politics of diversity and, at the same time, to structural transformations of a world political economy that continue to systematically deprive most of the world's women and men of adequate food, clothing, and shelter suggests a desire both to repudiate conceptions of citizenship and to situate citizenship as civic-minded world transformation within the context of justice, responsibility, and care.
>
> (Jones, 1994, pp. 268–9)

These debates are often framed as women's rights to the city; they are expressed as claims to space and to inclusion in the political spaces of city-making.

Note

1 Linda Peake has shared with me her insights on various ideas presented in this chapter in its previous incarnations and I am grateful for her suggestions. Leonie Sandercock, John Friedmann and David Harvey commented on an earlier, and quite different, version of this chapter and I thank Engin Isin for his assistance and support.

Bibliography

Bofil, A. (1998) Personal interview.

Bunch, C. (1990) 'Women's Rights as Human Rights: Toward a Re-vision of Human Rights', *Human Rights Quarterly*, 12: 486–98.

Bunch, C., Dutt, M. and Fried, S. (1995) 'Beijing '95: A Global Referendum on the Human Rights of Women', *Canadian Woman Studies*, 16: 3, 7–14.

Commission of the European Communities Equal Opportunities Unit (1994) *Proposition for a European Charter for Women in the City* (Brussels: Commission of the European Communities Equal Opportunities Unit).

Cott, N. (1989) 'What's in a Name? The Limits of "Social Feminism", or, Expanding the Vocabulary of Women's History', *Journal of American History*, 76: 809–29.

Day, S. and Brodsky, G. (1998) *Women and the Equality Deficit: The Impact of Restructuring Canada's Social Programs* (Ottawa: Status of Women Canada).

Dietz, M. (1985) 'Citizenship with a Feminist Face: The Problem of Maternal Thinking', *Political Theory*, 13: 19–37.

Eurofem (1996) 'Gender and Human Settlements', *Proceedings from the Third Working Meeting*, Aosta, Italy.

Field, D. (1997) 'As Food Share Sees It', *Food Share's Food Action* (August): 2.

Friedmann, J. (1998) 'The Political Economy of Planning: The Rise of Civil Society', in: M. Douglass and J. Friedmann (eds) *Cities for Citizens* (New York: John Wiley and Sons).

Friedmann, J. and Douglass, M. (1998) 'Editors' Introduction', in M. Douglass and J. Friedmann (eds), *Cities for Citizens* (New York: John Wiley and Sons).

Gibbs, L. (1981) *Love Canal: My Story* (Albany: State University of New York).

Gilbert, M. (1998) Presentation at Panel on Human Rights, American Association of Geographers, Boston.

Hardy-Fanta, C. (1993) *Latina Politics, Latino Politics: Gender, Culture and Political Participation in Boston* (Philadelphia: Temple University Press).

Harvey, D. (1998) 'Seven Steps to Planning Heaven', *Plurimondi Workshop*, Perugia, Italy.

Hayden, D. (1984) *Redesigning the American Dream* (New York: W.W. Norton).

Holston, J. (1998) 'Spaces of Insurgent Citizenship', in L. Sandercock (ed.), *Making the Invisible Visible: A Multicultural Planning History* (Berkeley, CA: University of California Press).

Horelli, L. and Vepsa, K. (1994) 'In Search of Supportive Structures for Everyday Life', in I. Altman and A. Churchman (eds), *Women and Environments* (New York: Polonium).

Jelin, E. (ed.) (1990) *Women and Social Change in Latin America* (London: Zed Books).

Jones, K.B. (1994) 'Identity, Action and Locale: Thinking about Citizenship, Civic Action and Feminism' *Social Politics*, 1, 3: 256–71.

Kail, E. (1998) Personal interview.

Kaplan, T. (1997) *Crazy for Democracy: Women in Grassroots Movements* (New York: Routledge).

Krauss, C. (1993) 'Women and Toxic Waste Protests: Race, Class and Gender as Resources of Resistance' *Qualitative Sociology*, 16: 247–62.

Laclau, E. and Mouffe, C. (1985) *Hegemony and Socialist Strategy: Towards a Radical Democratic Politics* (London: Verso).

Lamarche, L. (1995) 'Women's Social and Economic Rights: A Case for Real Rights', in M. Schuler (ed.), *From Basic Needs to Basic Rights: Women's Claim to Human Rights* (Washington, DC: Institute for Women, Law and Development).

Leavitt, J. and Saegert, S. (1990) *From Abandonment to Hope: Community-Households in Harlem* (New York: Columbia University Press).

LIFT (Low Income Families Together) (1997) *The Real Ontario UN Report: Holding Government Accountable to Human Rights Agreements* (Toronto: LIFT).

Little, J. (1994) *Gender Planning and the Policy Process* (Oxford: Elsevier Science).

Magnusson, W. (1992) 'The Constitution of Movements Versus the Constitution of the State: Rediscovering the Local as a Site for Global Politics', in H. Lustiger-Thaler (ed.), *Political Arrangements: Power and the City* (Montreal: Black Rose Books).

—— (1996) *The Search for Political Space* (Toronto: University of Toronto Press).

Mohanty, C.T. (1991) 'Introduction: Cartographies of Struggles: Third World Women and the Politics of Feminism', in C.T. Mohanty, A. Russo and L. Torres (eds), *Third World Women and the Politics of Feminism* (Bloomington: Indiana University Press).

Monsebraaten, L. (1995) 'Welfare Recipients Push to See Secret Paper', *Toronto Star* (7 November).

OAITH (Ontario Association of Interval and Transition Houses) (1995) *Home Truths* (Toronto: OAITH).

OECD (1995) *Women in the City: Housing, Services, and the Urban Environment* (Paris: OECD).

Pardo, M. (1990) 'Mexican American Women Grassroots Community Activists: "Mothers of East Los Angeles" ', *Frontiers: A Journal of Women Studies*, 11: 1–7.

Pateman, C. (1988) *The Sexual Contract* (Palo Alto: Stanford University Press).

Rabrenovic, G. (1995) 'Women and Collective Action in Urban Neighbourhoods', in J. Garber and R. Turner (eds), *Gender in Urban Research* (Thousand Oaks, CA: Sage).

Ruddick, S. (1989) *Maternal Thinking: Toward a Politics of Peace* (Boston: Beacon).

Savarsy, W. and Siim, B. (1994) 'Gender, Transitions to Democracy, and Citizenship', *Social Politics*, 1: 249–55.

Schneider, E.M. (1990) 'The Dialectic of Rights and Politics: Perspectives From the Women's Movement', in L. Gordon (ed.), *Women, the State and Welfare* (Madison: University of Wisconsin Press).

Schuler, M.A. (1995) 'Introduction', in M.A. Schuler (ed.), *From Basic Needs to Basic Rights: Women's Claim to Human Rights* (Washington, DC: Institute for Women, Law and Development).

Siim, B. (1994) 'Engendering Democracy: Social Citizenship and Political Participation for Women in Scandinavia', *Social Politics*, 1, 3: 287–305.

Smith, D. (1987) *The Everyday World as Problematic: A Feminist Sociology* (Boston: Northeastern University Press).

Smith, D. (1998) 'Consciousness, Meaning and Ruling Relations: from Women's Standpoint', in J.L. Abu-Lughod (ed.), *Millennial Milestone: The Heritage of Sociology in the North American Region, Proceedings* (Madrid: International Sociological Association).

Smith, S. (1989) 'Society, Space and Citizenship: A Human Geography for the New Times', *Transactions of the Institute of British Geographers*, 14: 144–56.

Susser, I. (1982) *Norman Street: Poverty and Politics in an Urban Neighbourhood* (New York: Oxford University Press).

Toronto Star (1998) 'Canada Faces UN Scrutiny' (28 September).

United Nations Committee on Economic, Social and Cultural Rights, http://www.unhchr.ch/tbs/doc.nsf.

Vincent, D. (1996) 'Tories Violated Charter, Judge Told in Equity Case', *Toronto Star* (27 November).

Wekerle, G.R. and Whitzman, C. (1995) *Safe Cities: Guidelines for Planning, Design and Management* (New York: Van Nostrand Reinhold/John Wiley).

12 Associational rights-claims, civil society and place

Raymond Rocco

Introduction

Much of the recent work on rights and citizenship has been a response to the dramatic consequences of the related processes of globalization and transnationalism on the complex relationship between the nation, identity, community, territory and the state.[1] Rapid and large-scale migrations of people from Asia, Latin America and Africa to European and US megacities, their impact on cultural, economic and political relationships, and the construction, interpretation and representation of these as perceived threats to the maintenance of the cultural ground of national identity, have altered the basic institutional configuration of these societies to such a degree that the discourses of modern citizenship, with conceptual roots in the seventeenth century, have been unable to satisfactorily address the range of issues that have resulted.[2] Yet, despite the fact that the need to rethink citizenship arises from changes in institutional relations, political theorists addressing the issue have focused remarkably little attention on the issue of how to conceptualize the linkage between the theoretical and philosophical parameters of citizenship and its institutional embeddedness.[3] This chapter proposes a particular formulation of the relationship between rights-claims, civil society and place as a strategy for responding to this concern.

Theorizing rights-claims

The foundational assumptions of long-standing conceptions of the nature of rights, as well as the relation between the modern 'subject' and the 'subject of rights' have been challenged on different grounds by the recent works of rights' scholars.[4] Somers, for example, argues that the underlying basis of the conceptions of citizenship developed in most traditions tend to define citizenship as a status or attribute of a category of persons.[5] This leads to static analysis, which in turn makes it extremely difficult to understand the ways in which citizenship practices emerge and the fact that they are dependent on the particular and historically specific articulation of several institutional relationships related to citizenship. She considers citizenship as an instituted process, as a set of institutionally embedded social practices (Somers, 1993, p. 589).

Thus, citizenship is reconceptualized as the outcome of political, legal, and symbolic practices enacted through universal membership rules and legal institutions that are activated in combination with

> the particularistic political cultures of different types of civil societies. As such, citizenship practices are also a source of political identity – the translation of this identity into a rights-based positive citizenship identity depends entirely on the contexts of activation. ... Quasi-democratic citizenship rights can emerge only in certain institution-specific relational settings and only in the context of particular social practices, namely practices that support popular public spheres. ... Theorizing about citizenship must ... include a sociology of public spheres and their relationships to the associational practices of civil society.
>
> (Somers, 1993, p. 589–90)

The institutional sites of civil society are most effectively construed, Somers contends, in terms of a 'relational/network and institutional analysis', in which institutions are understood as 'organizational and symbolic practices that operate within networks of rules, structural ties, public narratives, and binding relationships that are embedded in time and space', and in which the relational approach 'disaggregates social categories and reconfigures them into institutional and relational clusters in which people, power, and organizations are positioned and connected' (Somers, 1993, p. 595). Instead of using the concept of 'society' to frame the issue of citizenship, Somers proposed the term *relational setting*, which she defines as

> a patterned matrix of institutional relationships among cultural, economic, social, and political practices. ... A relational setting has no governing entity according to which the entire setting can be categorized; it can only be characterized by deciphering its spatial and network patterns and its temporal processes.
>
> (Somers, 1993, p. 595)

This approach generates a different way of linking citizenship to the dimensions of subjectivity and agency. Instead of 'categorical' attributes being the source of legal and political standing and action, 'identity' becomes the axis for conceptualizing the source of political action. Identities are

> not derived from attributes imputed from a stage of societal development (e.g., pre-industrial or modern) or a social category (e.g., traditional artisan, factory laborer, or working-class wife), but by actors' places in the multiple relationships in which they are embedded. ... It is no longer

assumed that a group of people has any particular relationship to citizenship simply because one aspect of their identity is categorized as the
'working class'. 'Social categories' presume internally stable properties such
that, under normal conditions, entities within that category will act appro-
priately, whereas 'identities' embed the actors within relationships and
stories that shift over time and space. Social action thus loses its categorical stability, and class embeddedness becomes more important than class
attributes. Thus, citizenship identities are investigated by looking at actor's
places in their relational settings.

(Somers, 1993, p. 595)

Somers argues instead that rights-claims must be understood within specific and
local institutional relations, and that these relations mediate between the state
and civil society, i.e. they constitute the articulations between state and civil
society. As such, the framework provides a way to assess at least in a general
way, the degree to which various social and cultural practices, or, more
specifically, 'associational practices', within civil society might be claims to
rights. The forms and modalities of activities and practices that express claims
to citizenship depend on the institutional mix of factors, so it allows for the
possibility (and likelihood) that there are different forms and expressions of
making these claims. Somers focuses primarily on the set of practices that
constitute the 'public sphere', understood as 'a contested participatory site in
which actors with overlapping identities as legal subjects, citizens, economic
actors, and family and community members, form a public body and engage in
negotiations and contestations over political and social life' (1993, p. 589). She
thus establishes the theoretical basis for linking the various dimensions of civil
society to the institutional axis of citizenship.

Like Somers, McClure argues that our understanding of and discourses on
citizenship and civil society must be historically and institutionally grounded
(McClure, 1992). But her emphasis is more focused on historicizing the
intersection of our notions of the 'subject' who makes rights-claims and the
claims of sovereignty on which the state rests, and on situating this within the
problematic of the 'new' pluralism, more often known as multiculturalism.
McClure argues that modern political theory since the rise of the nation-state
has privileged both the 'sovereign subject' as political agent and the state as the
legitimate locus of political action. What this obscures is the actual historical
development of rights-claims which is characterized by 'the displacement of a
range of diverse and contradictory localist and participatory constructs by
centralized national and statist codifications of legal discourse. Thus the
modern form of the 'subject of rights' can itself be understood as an effect of the
practical and discursive struggles of modern constitutionalism 'under very
specific historical and geopolitical conditions' (McClure, 1992, p. 111; Rocco,
forthcoming b).

Now the emergence of new social actors making political claims on the basis
of race, gender, sexuality and ethnicity in the current period has challenged

established notions of the subject, identity and agency.[6] In particular, the notion of a 'sovereign subject' has been critiqued as a contingent construct masquerading as a universalist category, which then obviously undermines any universalist notion of a 'subject of rights' or citizen. But these challenges do not necessarily signal the disappearance of the 'subject of rights'. Instead the 'subject of rights' is reconstituted in such a way that the issues and questions regarding political identity and agency are reconfigured. Thus, as McClure argues,

> we might question rather than presume its ["subject of rights"] relation to contemporary assertions of rights on the terrain of "differences", for these may themselves significantly transform or exceed the conventional figuration of the subject, especially as this has taken the formal character of individual citizenship in the modern state.
>
> (McClure, 1992, p. 112)

In historical situations where the emergence of these 'differences' are closely related to transnational or non-national primary linkages and solidarities, what this calls into question is the degree to which existing discourses and practices of citizenship, limited by modernist conceptions that assume the coincidence of the boundaries of state, territory, nation, sovereignty and citizenship, are capable of providing either theoretical or institutional spaces that can respond effectively to the new basis of rights-claims.

While there are a number of scholars rethinking the problematic of citizenship within the context of the new terrain of difference and multicultural societies, the most well-known effort is the series of arguments put forth by Kymlicka (1995a; 1995b). His work seeks to provide a way to bridge the two major seemingly irreconcilable perspectives on citizenship and advance a theory of citizenship that can account for the reality of multiculturalism. The first of these positions, the liberal approach, is organized around the primacy of individual rights, and citizenship is construed in terms of the individual as the bearer of these rights. These rights insure that private individuals can pursue their self interests through the protection of the state, whose primary function is to mediate conflict and regulate activities. The opposing view is that proposed in the communitarian formulation, and although there are several versions of this approach, what is common to each of these is the conception of rights as a function of membership in a historically specific society, community or state, as well as the emphasis on the formative role that cultural context plays in defining the nature and significance of claims to rights. It is only within the context of the specific configuration of social relations, institutions and culture that the idea of rights can be understood and realized.

Kymlicka's goal is to advance a new 'distinctively liberal approach to minority rights' that preserves the basic principles of individual freedom but that is not limited by the traditional liberal conceptualizations of citizenship that all rights must be 'difference-blind' and which refuse to allow for any form of group rights (Kymlicka, 1995a, p. 7). He notes that modern societies are increasingly 'multicultural' but adds that the ways in which this is formulated are exceedingly vague and ambiguous, primarily because the concept has not been grounded in an analysis of 'how the historical incorporation of minority groups shapes their collective institutions, identities, and aspirations' (Kymlicka, 1995a, p. 11). In order to overcome this lack of specificity, Kymlicka proposes four types of difference: separate nations within an existing state; immigrant ethnic groups; refugees and exiles; and the special circumstances of African-Americans. The rights-claims of distinct cultural groups need to be understood and evaluated in terms of the different institutional articulations that define each of these categories. But it is the first two that are really the focus of concern.

In developing and examining the situation of diversity that arises from the multination position, the nation is understood as a 'historical community, more or less institutionally complete, occupying a given territory or homeland, sharing a distinct language and culture' (Kymlicka, 1995a, p. 11). The second source of cultural difference is immigration, a situation where groups seek affirmation of their ethnic identity but do not intend to establish a separate 'nation', and instead aim to 'modify the institutions and laws of the mainstream society to make them more accommodating of cultural differences' (Kymlicka, 1995a, p. 11). Kymlicka identifies these as 'two broad patterns of cultural diversity' and the specifics of the incorporation of these multinational and polyethnic groups require three forms of group-differentiated rights for these groups to acquire effective citizenship status: self-governmental rights, polyethnic rights and special representation rights. Far from rejecting the incorporation of the cultural distinctiveness of these groups as a basis for rights-claims, Kymlicka argues instead that the meaning of liberal freedoms can only be realized in the context of a cultural context of choice. Central to the concept of freedom that is the basis of the liberal tradition is the premise that individuals have the right to choose how to live their lives, to live according to their beliefs about what gives meaning and value to their existence. But determining the value and meaning of different options and choices depends on, indeed requires, the existence of a societal culture that provides the context without which these determinations cannot be made. It is 'a matter of understanding the meanings attached to it by our culture' (Kymlicka, 1995a, p. 83). Thus the cultural disjunction that characterizes the circumstances of the historical incorporation of multinational and immigrant groups require that they be given certain 'group-differentiated' rights (although different for each type) that incorporate and protect their cultural distinctiveness as the indispensable means that enable them effectively to pursue the freedom that is the foundation of the liberal form of citizenship.

Other scholars also argue for group-differentiated rights as the basis for citizenship claims. While Young's *Justice and the Politics of Difference* (1990) and Charles Taylor's 'The Politics of Recognition' (1994) differ from Kymlicka's as well as each other's substantive arguments, they essentially deal with the ways in which the politics of difference influence the boundaries of the public sphere. Nonetheless, these works are beset by similar problems. For while they acknowledge the institutional dimensions of the problematic they confront, their theorization of the structural changes that constitute the very context that they argue must be incorporated remains at a level of generality and abstraction that at best makes it difficult to determine the validity of these formulations and at worst distorts or obscures the very reality they seek to address. Thus, for example, Kymlicka acknowledges the vagueness of the ways in which multiculturalism has been used, and even alludes to the processes of 'globalization' as having a determinative effect on the issue.

> Globalization has made the myth of a culturally homogeneous state even more unrealistic, and has forced the majority within each state to be more open to pluralism and diversity. The nature of ethnic and national identities is changing in a world of free trade and global communications, but the challenge of multiculturalism is here to stay.
>
> (Kymlicka, 1995a, p. 9)

Yet nowhere in his book is there a systematic analysis of multiculturalism as a set of specific *institutional social practices* that are part of a broader process of social transformation. Even more problematic is the lack of specification of the processes of globalization that Kymlicka acknowledges is a crucial factor in producing the particular pattern of cultural differences that are now so much contested. And it is not simply that a more 'complete' analysis of these phenomena would fill out the argument, for an accurate understanding of globalization at the level of institutional specificity of the practices that constitute it would in fact alter the very way in which the issue of citizenship in a multicultural context must be conceptualized (Rocco, forthcoming a). What needs to be addressed then, is how to ground the analysis of the practices of rights-claims within specific institutional sites of multicultural societies, how to incorporate adequately the dimension of institutional specificity in the formulation of both the theory and practices of rights-claims, which constitutes the contested terrain of citizenship.

Beyond multiculturalism

The most effective approach to this needs to theorize these institutional sites, spaces or places, as *constitutive* of multicultural social relations rather than simply a contextual or additive dimension. One of the formulations of the constitutive role of the spatial dimension is reflected in attempts to theorize these spaces of difference as third space, hybridity, borders, the 'in-between' or margins. These constructs have emerged from efforts, often but not always under the rubric of post-colonialism, to rethink the disjunctions between Eurocentric and Third World constructions of cultural formations and configurations so as to capture the complexity of the conditions of articulation.

These attempt to theorize the complexity of these relations in terms that reject the privileging of the West and which delineate the nature of institutional locations of Third World peoples. While not arguing for the reductionist conflation of these terms and the complex theoretical frameworks within which they have been elaborated, and without assuming a sameness of content, it is nevertheless clear that these operate within a field of constructs that overlap considerably. This overlap is noted in a recent essay on boundaries.

> A jumble of cultural-political practices and forms of resistance have emerged that have variously been named hybrid, border or diasporic. The most creative and dynamic of these resistances are located on the borders of essentialism and conjuncturalism. They refuse the binarism of identity politics versus post-modernist fragmentation. ... We name this terrain of practice and theory, this zone of shifting and mobile resistances that refuse fixity yet practice their own arbitrary provisional closures, the third time-space.
>
> (Lavie and Swedenburg, 1996, p. 154)

In his most recent book, Soja reviews a group of affiliated positions that he designates 'third-space', and provides the following description, which, although advanced in the discussion of bell hooks, nevertheless captures the central thrust of his own conceptualization. He states that a hook 'attempts to move beyond the modernist binary oppositions of race, gender, and class into the multiplicity of *other* spaces that difference makes' (Soja, 1996, p. 96). In their study of popular culture in Latin America, Rowe and Schelling propose a useful definition of cultural hybridity as 'the ways in which forms become separated from existing practices and recombine with new forms in new practices' (Rowe and Schelling, 1991, p. 231). But this deceptively simple definition does not convey the complexity of both the processes involved and the modes of theorizing them. Works by theorists such as Bhabha, Spivak and Said have sought to delineate these in great detail and with great sophistication. These conceptualizations all reject binary theoretical constructions and the privileging of mono-causal factors, and insist instead on the notions of multiple subjectivities and voice, on complex modes of positioning.

However, these concepts and the frameworks they are nested in, are clearly not without difficulties. They have been the subject of wiBerkeley, CAranging critique from a variety of positions and the shortcomings of these formulations have been amply delineated. One line of critique is particularly relevant to the focus here. A position advanced by Hall, and by Frankenberg and Mani maintains that while the notions of the margins, borders, hybridity and third space seek to address fundamentally important phenomena, these relations are even more complex than many formulations maintain (Hall, 1996; Frankenberg and Mani, 1993). What is called for is careful attention to and delineation of problems that arise in applying these concepts to issues of, for example, periodization, historical appropriateness and correlation, and both historical and institutional contextualization. For those of us exploring these themes within the context of the USA, one of the most helpful efforts to delineate the difficulties in applying these notions is found in the critique of post-colonial theorizations advanced by Frankenberg and Mani. They point out that terms such as post-colonialism and affiliated ideas need to be situated within the specific and particular historical circumstances and experiences that are being addressed. And they specifically focus on the issue of the appropriateness of the concept of post-colonialism in comprehending the US situation. They provide a summary of the historical and political elements for which such an endeavour would have to account:

> White settler colony, multiracial society. Colonization of Native Americans, Africans imported as slaves, Mexicans incorporated by a border moving south, Asians imported and migrating to labor, white Europeans migrating to labor. US imperialist foreign policy brings new immigrants who are 'here because the US was/is there', among them Central Americans, Koreans, Filipinos, Vietnamese and Cambodians. The particular relation of past territorial domination and current racial composition that is discernible in Britain, and which lends a particular meaning to the term 'post-colonial', does not, we feel, obtain here. Other characterizations, other periodizations, seem necessary in naming for this place the shifts expressed by the term 'post-colonial' in the British and Indian cases.
> (Frankenberg and Mani, 1993, p. 293)

They suggest the use of the term 'post-Civil Rights' as a possible way to talk about the US case, but immediately indicate their reservations of its adequacy:

> Let us emphasize at the outset that we use the term 'post-Civil Rights' broadly, to refer to the impact of struggles by African Americans, American Indian, La Raza and Asian American communities that stretched from the mid 1950s to the 1970s. ... However, the name, 'post-Civil Rights', would only grasp one strand of our description of the US. The term would have to be conjugated with another, one that would name the experience of recent immigrants/refugees borne here on the trails of US imperialist adventures, groups whose stories are unfolding in a tense, complicated relation – at times compatible, at times contradictory – with post-Civil Rights USA.
> (Frankenberg and Mani, 1993, p. 293)

It is in these substantially different, particular (local) historical and institutional circumstances that one of the major difficulties is encountered in finding ways of characterizing and theorizing notions of borders, margins, third space and hybridity. There are two dimensions of this problematic, in particular, that need to be addressed and disentangled: the connection between the colonizing–decolonizing contexts and histories that are the root of much of the theorizing about these concepts; and the connection between the long-standing populations from formerly colonized countries and the most recent immigrants from the same countries, as well as others from distinct regions and with substantially different cultural contexts. Again, Frankenberg and Mani put the issue succinctly and clearly. In referring to recent immigrants to the USA, they state that

> Their travel to the US has been occasioned by a history related to, but distinct from, that of people of color already here. Their historical experiences stretch existing categories – 'Hispanic', 'Asian' – inflecting them with new meanings. Relations between recent immigrants/refugees and those already here, whether whites or people of color, are constituted through discourses that draw heavily on colonial and racist rhetoric both in form and content. … *Nothing but the most complex and historically specific conceptions of identity and subjectivity can sufficiently grasp the present situation and articulate a politics adequate to it.*
>
> (Frankenberg and Mani, 1993, p. 302, emphasis mine)

Multiplicities of identity and place

The question arises as to whether the notions of these spaces have been theorized in ways that can adequately account for the realities of the substantive experiences, particular networks, modes of engagement and relations of political configurations that revolve around substantive historical and institutional axes and moments. To repeat, *nothing but the most complex and historically specific conceptions of identity and subjectivity can sufficiently grasp the present situation and articulate a politics adequate to it.* My premise here is that while some of the formulations of citizenship in multicultural societies move in the right direction and articulate positions that are adequate at one level of theory, they are still incomplete in terms of elaborating and providing for the institutional grounding for these concepts. To borrow a phrase from an Argentine theorist, Walter Mignolo, they have not for the most part established a theoretical basis for elaborating the multiple institutional configurations and manifestations in terms of which 'colonial legacies [are] at work in the present'. As an empirical example, I confronted this dilemma in developing my analysis of the processes of transformation of Latino communities in Los Angeles, where one of the most difficult dimensions to explain is the dynamic between recent Latino immigrants and earlier generations of Latinos, who have a long history of engagement with US culture and systems of subordination and power. These are two different yet complexly related trajectories or axes of engagement, and these in turn provide conditions and opportunities for cultural and political strategies that have qualitatively distinct centres of gravity.

In addition to this aspect, we need to suspect that some of the accents, emphasis and limitations of theorizing third space have to do with another factor that is less often discussed. It is clear that the critical examination of both colonialism and decolonization is hardly a new focus of attention, particularly in decolonized Third World countries. But it appears that the reason that this concern has become a major preoccupation in the present historical moment of the Eurocentric academy has less to do with theory than with demographics. It is the enormous and rapid migration of Third World peoples into the heart of Euro-US cities that has burst the boundaries of canonical paradigms. The pervasiveness of radical cultural differences in the major Euro-US metropolitan centres has sounded a dissonant chord for some, brought welcome decentring for others, but it can hardly be ignored by anyone. The world has changed and sooner or later theory had to confront it. The grounding of this particular theoretical enterprise in this reality requires not only that the parameters of these spaces be delineated but, to paraphrase Michael Kearney's critique of ethnography, that the theorizing 'must situate the production and consumption of representations of' subaltern spaces 'within the relationships that join' the theoretical self to the subaltern 'other it presumes to represent' (Kearney, 1996, p. 3). There needs to be, in other words, an accounting as well of the ways in which the theorizing itself may function as what Jameson calls strategies of containment.

Both of these dimensions, expanding and deepening the boundaries of the conceptions of third space, and including the self-reflexive moment as part of that enterprise, can be advanced by specifying their specific institutional grounding. With regard to the former dimension, the necessity to move in this direction is reflected in the following:

> Third spaces, third texts, third scenarios are concepts articulated in the interdisciplinary field of Minority Discourse through usage of Cultural Studies methodologies. Thus the cultural materials currently analyzed by using the modalities of 'the third' are highly stylized domains of knowledge, framed as dramatic, literary, cinematic, artistic and musical texts. Bridging Ethnography, Cultural Studies, and Minority Discourse will be possible if we return to the primary daily realities from which such textual representations are derived. *We call for reconceptualization, from lived identities and physical places, not just from texts, of the multiplicities of identity and place.* As they are forced into constantly shifting configurations of partial overlap, their ragged edges cannot be smoothed out. Identity and place perpetually create both new outer borders, where the overlap has not occurred, and inner borders between the areas of overlap and vestigial spaces of non-overlap.
>
> (Lavie and Swedenburg, 1996, pp. 168–9)

The 'lived identities' and realities of these hybrid and third spaces, of the margins, the borders, of the spaces 'in-between', are not random, epiphenomenal or transient. They are *institutional spaces*, structures of cultural, economic and political practices, that simultaneously limit and enable the parameters, conditions, strategies and options for social and political action. And their quality as spaces of the hybrid, border or margin are directly linked to the variety of changes in the nature of the relationship between territory, space, identity and community that have resulted from the processes of globalization and transnationalization. This is not a simple, linear causal relationship, but a complex set of interdependent and multidimensional constellations of institutional practices.

The theorizations of third space, then, must be reconfigured to incorporate these institutional spaces as necessary, inherent and internal dimensions of the organic discursive and material complexes that constitute societal relations. It is only when we understand that all cultural statements and systems are constructed in this contradictory and ambivalent space of enunciation that we begin to understand why hierarchical claims to the inherent originality or 'purity' of cultures are untenable, even before we resort to empirical historical instances that demonstrate their hybridity (Bhabha, 1995, p. 208).

In other words, the articulation of theorization is not reducible to nor dependent in a mechanistic or reductive manner on empirical 'reality'. Rather, it is a constitutive element of that reality (constitutive and not causal, which would return us to the tradition of idealism), and as such it is not sufficient to situate third space within the 'transnational' or 'global' context. Instead, the modes of discourse and frames of representations of third space themselves need to be part of that same process of contextualization.

Thus, for example, Dirlik argues that

> with rare exceptions, post-colonial critics have been silent on the relation-ship of the idea of post-colonialism to its context in contemporary capital-ism; indeed, they have suppressed the necessity of considering such a possible relationship by repudiating a foundational role to capitalism in history.
>
> (Dirlik, 1994, p. 331)

Similarly, Benita Parry points out that post-colonial writers like Spivak and Bhabha share a 'programme marked by the exorbitation of discourse and a related incuriosity about the enabling socioeconomic and political institutions and other forms of social praxis' (Parry, 1995, p. 43).[7]

Now the characteristics of fragmentation and cultural disjunction, and the emergence of these third spaces that contest US-Eurocentric representations and dominance, are indeed constitutive of the social relations in large urban centres in the USA, Canada and Europe. The theoretical formulations reviewed above are useful precisely because they establish a discourse that enables the analysis of the complexity of the consequences of the transforma-tions in social patterns, now characterized by a series of elements that have either emerged or intensified within the last thirty years, referred to by a number of terms, including globalization, restructuring and transnationaliza-tion. The literature on these processes has demonstrated the centrality and importance of the pattern that has characterized the globalization and transnationalization of both capital and labour since the late 1960s (Cox, 1997; Featherstone et al., 1995; King, 1996; Knox and Taylor, 1995; Sassen, 1988; 1991).

The specific institutional grounding, then, for the field of forces, practices and theorizations that are the axes of these theoretical constructions of third space is the particular configuration of interrelated processes of the restructuring and transnationalization of global capitalism. To recognize the centrality and influence of these processes does not necessarily privilege them nor reduce the theorization of third space to mere ideological expressions. It is precisely to avoid this facile dismissal of the complex reality for which theorizations of third space account that a more structurally rooted elaboration of these relations is needed. For to ignore them, or to construct them in institutionally ungrounded ways, leads to an incomplete analysis at best, or the obfuscation of the reality of domination at worst.

Margins, borders and third spaces need to be framed and contextualized as components and expressions of how these processes of social transformation, of globalization and transnationalization, are being lived. Nederveen Pieterse observes that

> Hybrid formations constituted by the interpenetration of diverse logics manifest themselves in *hybrid sites* and spaces. ... Global cities and ethnic mélange neighborhoods within them (such as Jackson Heights in Queens, New York) are other hybrid spaces in the global landscape.
>
> (Nederveen Pieterse, 1995, p. 51)

The emergence of these new types of institutional spaces or sites challenges traditional ways of understanding and explaining culture, identity and community, primarily because they are expressions of a different relationship between space and place that characterizes the dynamics of transnationalism.[8] The degree, extent and pervasiveness of the changes in patterns of social relations, cultural configurations and forms that are part of the processes of transnationalization have disrupted long-established boundaries that assumed specific representations and constructions of those populations that were constructed when 'they' were 'there', and 'we' were 'here'. But the viability and adequacy of these constructions have been undermined now that 'they' are 'here' and challenged the notion of who the 'we' are. Hence, although the focus of analysis of these concepts of third space has been on those marginalized in different ways, in fact the emergence of transnationalism has impacted long-established populations as well. Thus the meaning of, and hence the stability and orientation provided by, established notions of 'here' and 'there', of 'we' and 'them', have been fundamentally problematized.[9]

Theorizing space and identity

Gupta and Ferguson have advanced a convincing critique of contemporary forms of cultural analysis that continue to assume an isomorphic relationship between nations, territory, space and identities:

> In a world of diaspora, transnational culture flows, and mass movements of populations, old-fashioned attempts to map the globe as a set of culture regions or homelands are bewildered by a dazzling array of post-colonial simulacra, doublings and redoublings, as India and Pakistan apparently reappear in post-colonial simulation in London, prerevolution Tehran rises from the ashes of Los Angeles, and a thousand similar cultural dreams are played out in urban and rural settings all across the globe.
>
> (Gupta and Ferguson, 1992, p. 10)

And while they appreciate the effort to describe this dislodging of identities from a fixed and stable territorial 'place' through the notion of deterritorialization, they opt instead to characterize this dimension as 'reterritorialization' to avoid the connotation that space and place are no longer significant dimensions of social formations. Space and place still matter, but in a different way.

Incorporating 'place' in the study of the processes, dimensions and manifestations of transnationalization and globalization, then, means that we must rethink the concept of what constitutes a nation, of what role territory plays, as well as the nature of the claims of sovereignty and citizenship, and how these are related to the processes of community and identity formation. And as the particular configuration of these change, so too must our conceptions of the complex ways that these dimensions are incorporated in the institutional structures of the state and of civil society. But in developing this reformulation, the central role of institutional specificity expressed in and through particular places must be incorporated. One way of addressing this project is found in the more recent work of the urban theorist Saskia Sassen, who, after concentrating on explaining the specific dynamics of globalization for several years, has joined the effort of a growing number of scholars who have focused on analysing the implications and consequences of these processes for both the discourse and institutional arrangements of citizenship (Sassen, 1996a; 1996b; Garcia, 1996; Holston and Appadurai, 1996).[10]

Let me very briefly outline that part of her argument most relevant to the issues being discussed here. One of the major objectives of Sassen's most recent work is to use the notion of situated space, or 'place' as she calls it, to ground the specific processes that constitute globalization. Sassen argues that as she develops it, the concept 'allows us to recover the concrete, localized processes through which globalization exists and to argue that much of the multiculturalism in large cities is as much a part of globalization as is international finance' (Sassen, 1996a, p. 206). By examining the actual, situated practices that constitute globalization, she demonstrates that the latter is defined by a very specific configuration or pattern of transnational relations and actors, but points out that it is primarily the role and activities of transnational capital that are focused on as constitutive of globalization in many analyses. This is understandable since the new forms of transnational legal regimes 'privilege the reconstitution of capital as an internationalized actor and the denationalized spaces necessary for its operation' (Sassen, 1996a, p. 217). However, these formulations obscure the fact that it is not only the configuration of capital that has changed, but that the spaces and places that serve as the necessary basis of their practices and activities have also been altered fundamentally because the nature of what binds people and places together in these spaces has changed, as have the corresponding forms of the claims made on the economic, social, political and cultural dimensions of these spaces.

As a result, these conceptualizations or theorizations of globalization have overvalorized the role of capital and undervalorized that of labour as a necessary and constitutive element. The phenomena of immigration and ethnicity that are in fact constitutive of globalization are construed and positioned theoretically by theorists such as Kymlicka, who uses these factors as major elements in his attempt to reformulate citizenship, in ways that limit the ability to perceive the reconstituted spaces that emerge from this process of globalization wherein different types of claims to citizenship are pressed by the cultural others that typically inhabit these spaces.

> What we still narrate in the language of immigration and ethnicity, I would argue, is actually a series of processes having to do with the globalization of economic activity, of cultural activity, of identity formation. Too often immigration and ethnicity are constituted as otherness. Understanding them as a set of processes whereby global elements are *localized*, international labor markets are constituted, and cultures from all over the world are de- and reterritorialized, puts them right there at the center along with the internationalization of capital as a fundamental aspect of globalization.
>
> (Sassen, 1996a, p. 218)

Hence, while the new claims of transnational capital on the state are represented as a major component of globalization, both the spaces and the claims being made within them by immigrants and other disempowered sectors, are either erased, ignored or construed in terms of a discourse that is anchored in figuration of social and economic relations long ago eclipsed by the forces of globalization. Instead, what must be acknowledged is that the spaces created by the complex and multidimensional processes of globalization have become strategic sites for the formation of transnational identities and communities, and for the corresponding emergence of new types of claims within these transformed spaces (Rocco, 1999).

Others have offered similar arguments, proposing that new and different types of citizenship claims are part of restructuring and globalization, and that these claims are difficult to conceptualize or reconcile with the assumptions of the liberalism that underlies efforts like Kymlicka's. For example, Holston and

Appadurai argue that the transnational processes constitutive of globalization have generated claims to 'new kinds of rights outside of the normative and institutional definitions of the state and its legal codes' (Holston and Appadurai, 1996, p. 197). And in her essay on 'Cities and Citizenship', Garcia reviews the debates on the 'rapid changes in the practice of citizenship' and argue that these require the development of new forms of conceptual and empirical analysis (Garcia, 1996, p. 7). From this perspective then, it is crucial that attempts to reformulate our conceptions of notions of citizenship incorporate the contending claims of all the actors that occupy different spaces in the new globalized city, a process of political contestation that is likely to change the boundaries and parameters of the discourse of sovereignty and citizenship.

The challenge that emerges from these analyses that either suggest or explicitly call for the reformulation of the parameters of citizenship, then, is to develop a theoretical framework that allow us to perceive and examine these types of new claims and their relationship to the processes of globalization, one that enables us to ground the social practices of these sectors and the processes that produce them within specific institutional sites, 'spaces' or 'places'. Such a framework can be formulated by drawing on some of the insights and arguments found in the various ways that the discourse on civil society configures the relationship between citizenship, the state and democracy.

Civil society and associational citizenship

The claim advanced here, then, is that existing conceptions of citizenship are limited in their ability to recognize as such, rights-claims that arise from within marginalized social, political and cultural locations, and that by taking seriously the notion of 'place', at least some of these limitations can be addressed.[11] Even work that is sympathetic to this effort remains at a level of abstraction that makes it difficult to clarify and assess the nature and significance of these claims. However, a question remains about how to incorporate place as a theoretical opening that facilitates inclusion of these new types of claims into the field of discourse on citizenship and rights. One approach that addresses this is suggested in the critiques and formulations of Somers and Sassen reviewed earlier, which argue that rights and citizenship claims arise from the associational practices and activities of communities.

Now since the nature and role of associational practices and activities that take 'place' outside the sphere of the mechanisms of the state is the primary focus of recent analysis and debate regarding civil society, we might find here an approach that expands the conceptions of rights-claims and citizenship in a way that allows them to account more adequately for changing realities of globalization and transnationalism.[12] This associational basis of civil society is reflected in Walzer's description of it as 'the space of uncoerced human association and also the set of relational networks – formed for the sake of family, faith, interest and ideology – that fill this space' (Walzer, 1992). But the reason behind the turn to civil society is the actual or potential role of this associational sphere in promoting more inclusive and responsive forms of democratic governance and citizenship.[13]

A particularly relevant conceptualization of this relationship is provided in a recent volume on social movements in Latin America (Alvarez et al., 1998). The authors adopt the discourses of civil society to advance a conception of citizenship and rights-claiming practices that expands the parameters of both democracy and the public sphere. This position is based on a series of case studies that document the central role of associational behaviours and practices based on relations of trust, reciprocity and mutual exchange in the development of new forms of rights-claims and modes of citizenship. The introductory essay states that these chapters

> call attention to the cultural practices and interpersonal networks of daily life that ... infuse new cultural meanings into political practices and collective action. These frameworks of meaning may include different modes of consciousness and practices of nature, neighborhood life, and identity.
> (Alvarez et al., 1998, p. 14)

These practices have come to articulate claims about rights *within* society, and not solely against the institutions of the state. Sites or 'places' normally construed as apolitical were transformed in these cases as re-articulated public spaces, where 'market stalls, local bars, and family courtyards' served as localities where both processes of political affirmation and contestation were enacted and resulted in rights-claiming practices (Rubin, 1998, p. 155). Similar conclusions are advanced in a recent volume that focuses on examining civil society in non-western societies, arguing that 'there is ... a need to shift the debates about civil society away from formal structures and organizations and towards an investigation of beliefs, values and everyday practices' (Hann, 1996, p. 14).

The central role of these types of associational behaviour in promoting democratic practices is also supported in the work on social capital. Putnam, for example, contends that 'networks of civic engagement' and norms of reciprocity are crucial to promoting the expansion of democratic participation and 'good' government (Putnam, 1993; 1995).

> Networks of civic engagement, like the neighborhood associations, choral societies, cooperatives, sports clubs, mass-based parties ... are an essential form of social capital: the denser such networks in a community, the more likely that its citizens will be able to cooperate for mutual benefit.
> (Putnam, 1993, p. 173)

Thus social capital, which Putnam defines as 'features of social organization, such as trust, norms, and networks' (Putnam, 1993, p. 167) that establish relations of reciprocity, is activated by social trust, which, according to Putnam, arises from 'two related sources – norms of reciprocity and networks of civic engagement' (Putnam, 1993, p. 171). Thus, as in the social movement literature referred to above, the fostering of democratic social relations and forms of government require a broad network of activities and practices that are rooted in 'the submerged networks of daily life' (Alvarez et al., 1998, p. 14). This of course argues for a much broader concept of the political than that found in much traditional political science and sociology, which is defined primarily in terms of the primacy of formal, institutional apparatus of governing. The implications for understanding the dynamic nature of the processes that define the boundaries of the 'political' are summarized by Roniger in his study of civil society and clientelism:

> the 'construction of reality' hinges on social interaction and exchange as a contextual, pragmatic phenomenon. It is at this level of interplay between the logic of modern constitutional democracy and the praxis and pragmatics of everyday life and social action that moral obligations and commitments are enmeshed and can be reformulated in recurrent patterns of action and exchange through a complex web of movements, communities, associations, and interpersonal relations.
>
> (Roniger, 1994, p. 8)

These approaches, then, suggest a way of expanding the theoretical and conceptual parameters of the notions of citizenship and rights-claims which enables a level of analytic and empirical specificity that can account for the new strategies of political inclusion and rights-claims rooted in the associational strategies and practices characterized by relations of trust, reciprocity and mutual exchange developed within the sites of civil society in response to the effects of globalization.[14] These associational networks function within very specific institutional sites or 'places' that mediate the relationship between the household and the institutions that control the primary resources of economic, political and cultural power. Referring to the political significance of the relationship between the state and civil society, Chandhoke argues that

> states invariably seek to control and limit the political practices of society by constructing the boundaries of the political. The state attempts in other words to constitute and contain the political discourse. However, politics as articulatory practices which mediate between the experiential and the expressive are not only about controls and the laying down of boundaries. They are about the transgressions of these boundaries and about the reconstitution of the political. The site at which these mediations and contestations take place; the site at which society enters into relationship with the state can be defined as civil society.
>
> (Chandhoke, 1995, p. 9)

While agreeable, this position requires the inclusion of the mediations not only with the state, but with the macro institutions of economic and cultural power as well. These sites of mediation are the 'places' of everyday life, where individuals and groups engage and encounter the norms, boundaries, customs and networks that define institutional relationships, where they experience the consequences and effects of economic and political policies. Schools, churches, the workplace, parks are all sites where not only the activity of everyday life is carried out but where the effects of the practices of power are experienced, where the boundaries set by the configurations of privilege, status and access are encountered as the limits of action. And these are sites where the impact of globalization take effect and where strategic community responses to these consequences are developed. But they are also the sites of association, where individuals and groups establish a wide variety of relatively stable networks of activities that not only sustain their survival, identity and sense of worth, but which have also served as the basis for the development of practices and activities that are concerned with the direction of community and collective life, with the constitution of a 'public sphere'.[15]

Incorporating this notion of 'place' allows for concretizing the categories of the civil society construct so that the nature, range and validity of rights-claims advanced within the marginalized lived spaces of civil societies that have undergone the transformations entailed by globalization can be addressed and assessed. My contention is that arguments that seek to address the issue of citizenship within multicultural societies remain limited and incomplete as long as the constructs of the marginalized 'others' they have adopted are relatively ungrounded. Claims to citizenship are not isolated phenomena, they always take place within a specific ensemble of relations that *enable* those claims. Forms of civic association that strengthen solidarity and trust in a community may not in themselves constitute citizenship claims, but they can be vital in leading to the activities that do. Hence those forms of association that support the development of strong identities enhance the degree of mutual trust and solidarity, and promote a stronger sense of participatory rights and responsibilities in traditionally non-political spheres, while not themselves constituting citizenship claims, can nevertheless provide the necessary conditions for these to emerge. The point is that the discourse on citizenship is likely to be inadequate without grounding rights or citizenship claims within the associational contexts that enable them.

Without incorporating this dimension, analysis of the normative parameters of citizenship will resonate only with the lives of those in communities that have already gained political visibility within the dominant cultural landscape, and cannot possibly perceive, much less address, the needs and experiences of those that lie outside that vision. The result, unfortunately and ironically, is that the partial and distorted image on which these analyses are based is likely to undermine the very notion of the just and democratic polity that these theories seek to promote.

Notes

1 For the difference and relationship between these two sets of phenomena, see Ribeiro (1998).

2 For detailed accounts and explanations of these transnational migrations, see Sassen (1988) and Castles and Miller (1993). And on the need to rethink the issues of citizenship in light of these and other types of changes, see the discussions in Kymlicka and Norman (1995), Beiner (1995) and Habermas (1995).

3 The institutional context of citizenship is, however, a main concern in the literature on the sociology of citizenship. See, for example, the work of Somers (1992; 1993), Roberts (1995 and 1996) and the articles published in issues of the journals *Public Culture* (8, 1996) and the *International Journal of Urban and Regional Research* (20, 1996), both of which were completely devoted to exploring the theme of 'citizenship and the city'.

4 See, for example, the essays by Somers (1993) and McClure (1992).

5 For a critical discussion of these traditions, see Axtmann (1996).

6 These challenges have of course not been based on the same premises or theoretical positions. There are considerable theoretical as well as political differences between, for example, those who stress an essentialist position and those who draw upon versions of post-modernism as a means of providing alternatives to the universalism of the more traditional discourse of identity.

7 One way of incorporating this dimension is found in the model of mediation that I developed to study the processes of Latino community transformation in Los Angeles. See Rocco (1996; 1997; forthcoming b).

8 For an analysis of the implications of the processes and consequences of transnationalism for rights and citizenship, see Rocco (1999b).

9 Here I am summarizing the way in which Gupta and Ferguson (1992) have characterized and delineated the issue.

10 The growing concern to understand and explain the implications of globalization and restructuring for the concepts and practices of citizenship is reflected in the fact that several scholarly journals have devoted entire issues recently to the issue. See the following: *Public Culture* (8, 1996); *International Journal of Urban and Regional Research* (20, 1996); *Environment and Planning* (A 26, 1994); *Theory and Society* (26, (4), August, 1997).

11 There is obviously a difference between rights-claims and citizenship. However, my analysis does assume that rights-claims are what are incorporated as the basis of citizenship. Of course not all rights-claims lead to citizenship status; in fact, the former are often the basis on which struggles about citizenship status are fought.

12 For discussions tracing the historical development of civil society, see Cohen and Arato (1992), Seligman (1992) and Chandhoke (1995). For a critical discussion of some of the central issues raised in these analyses, see Alexander (1997).

13 For example, see the discussions in Hann and Dunn (1996). For an excellent explicit discussion of the linkage between civil society and citizenship, see chap. 2, 'Citizenship and Civil Society: Liberalism, Republicanism, and Deliberative Politics' in Roland Axtmann's analysis of democracy and citizenship in the context of globalization (Axtmann, 1996). Because of limitations of space, I do not review the various issues that are contested in the extensive literature on civil society. Instead, I offer a brief grounding for the particular formulation that I have found most useful in the analysis of the new claims to citizenship

14 It is precisely these types of contestations of citizenship that are found in my studies of Latino immigrants. See Rocco (1996; 1997; 1999).

15 I recognize that this formulation of the concept of public sphere deviates fundamentally from the discussions informed by Habermas's original analysis, and that it is subject to a range of objections and criticisms. However, while I believe it can be adequately defended, again, the limitations on the length of this chapter lead

me to present it simply as an assertion in the hope that the remainder of the argument provides a general idea of the reasons for my adoption of it. See Habermas (1989) and the discussion by Cohen and Arato (1992), particularly pages 211–31 and 241–51.

Bibliography

Alexander, J.C. (1997) 'The Paradoxes of Civil Society', *International Sociology*, 12: 115–33.

Alvarez, S.E., Dagnino, E. and Escobar, A. (1998) 'Introduction: The Cultural and the Political in Latin American Social Movements', in S.E. Alvarez, E. Dagnino and A. Escobar (eds), *Cultures of Politics-Politics of Culture: Re-visioning Latin American Social Movements* (Boulder, CO: Westview Press).

Axtmann, R. (1996) *Liberal Democracy into the Twenty-First Century: Globalization, Integration and the Nation-State* (Manchester: Manchester University Press).

Beiner, R. (1995) 'Introduction: Why Citizenship Constitutes a Theoretical Problem in the Last Decade of the Twentieth Century', in R. Beiner (ed.), *Theorizing Citizenship* (Albany: State University of New York Press).

Bhabha, H.K. (1995) 'Cultural Diversity and Cultural Differences', in B. Ashcroft, G. Griffiths and H. Tiffin (eds), *The Post-Colonial Studies Reader* (New York: Routledge).

Castles, S. and Miller, M.J. (1993) *The Age of Migration: International Population Movements in the Modern World* (New York: The Guilford Press).

Chandhoke, N. (1995) *State and Civil Society: Explorations in Political Theory* (Thousand Oaks, CA: Sage Publications).

Cohen, J. and Arato, A. (1992) *Civil Society and Political Theory* (Cambridge, MA: MIT Press).

Cox, K.R. (ed.) (1997) *Spaces of Globalization: Reasserting the Power of the Local* (New York: The Guilford Press).

Dirlik, A. (1994) 'The Postcolonial Aura: Third World Criticism in the Age of Global Capitalism', *Critical Inquiry* 20 (Winter): 328–56.

Featherstone, M., Lash, S. and Robertson, R. (eds) (1995) *Global Modernities* (Thousand Oaks, CA: Sage Publications).

Frankenberg, R. and Mani, L. (1993) 'Crosscurrents, Crosstalk: Race, "Postcoloniality" and the Politics of Location', *Cultural Studies*, 7 (2): 292–310.

Garcia, S. (1996) 'Cities and Citizenship', *International Journal of Urban and Regional Research*, 20: 7–21.

Gupta, A. and Ferguson, J. (1992) 'Beyond "Culture": Space, Identity, and the Politics of Difference', *Cultural Anthropology*, 7 (1): 6–23.

Habermas, J. (1962 [1989]) *The Structural Transformation of the Public Sphere* (Cambridge, MA: MIT Press).

—— (1995) 'Citizenship and National Identity: Some Reflections on the Future of Europe', in R. Beiner, (ed.), *Theorizing Citizenship* (Albany: State University of New York Press).

Hall, S. (1996) 'When was "the Post-Colonial"? Thinking at the Limit', in I. Chambers and L. Curti (eds), *The Post-Colonial Question: Common Skies, Divided Horizons* (New York: Routledge).

Hann, C. (1996) 'Introduction: Political Society and Civil Anthropology', in C. Hann and E. Dunn (eds), *Civil Society: Challenging Western Models* (New York: Routledge).

Hann, C. and Dunn, E. (eds) (1996) *Civil Society: Challenging Western Models* (New York: Routledge).

Holston, J. and Appadurai, A. (1996) 'Cities and Citizenship', *Public Culture*, 8: 187–204.

Kearney, M. (1996) Reconceptualizing the Peasantry: Anthropology in Global Perspective (Boulder, CO: Westview Press).

King, A.D. (ed.) (1996) *Re-presenting the City: Ethnicity, Capital and Culture in the 21st Century Metropolis* (New York: New York University Press).

Knox, P.L. and Taylor, P.J. (eds) (1995) *World Cities in a World-System* (Cambridge: Cambridge University Press).

Kymlicka, W. (1995a) *Multicultural Citizenship: A Liberal Theory of Minority Rights* (Oxford: Clarendon Press).

—— (ed.) (1995b) *The Rights of Minority Cultures* (Oxford: Oxford University Press).

Kymlicka, W. and Norman, W. (1995) 'Return of the Citizen: A Survey of Recent Work on Citizenship Theory', in R. Beiner (ed.), *Theorizing Citizenship* (Albany: State University of New York Press).

Lavie, S. and Swedenburg, T. (1996) 'Between and Among the Boundaries of Culture: Bridging Text and Lived Experience in the Third Timespace', *Cultural Studies* 10 (1): 154–79.

McClure, K. (1992) 'On the Subject of Rights: Pluralism, Plurality and Political Identity', in C. Mouffe (ed.), *Dimensions of Radical Democracy: Pluralism, Citizenship, Community* (London: Verso Press).

Mignolo, W. (1997) 'The Allocation and Relocation of Identities: Colonialism, Nationalism, Transnationalism', unpublished draft presented at workshop on 'Hybrid Cultures and Transnational Identities', UCLA, March.

Nederveen Pieterse, J.P. (1995) 'Globalization as Hybridization', in M. Featherstone, S. Lash and R. Robertson (eds), *Global Modernities* (Thousand Oaks, CA: Sage Publications).

Parry, B. (1995) 'Problems in Current Theories of Colonial Discourse', in B. Ashcroft, G. Griffiths and H. Tiffin (eds), *The Post-Colonial Studies Reader* (New York: Routledge).

Putnam, R.D. (1993) *Making Democracy Work: Civic Traditions in Modern Italy* (Princeton, NJ: Princeton University Press).

—— (1995) 'Bowling Alone: America's Declining Social Capital', *Journal of Democracy*, 6 (1): 65–78.

Ribeiro, G.L. (1998) 'Cybercultural Politics: Political Activism at a Distance in a Transnational World', in S.E. Alvarez, E. Dagnino and A. Escobar (eds), *Cultures of Politics – Politics of Culture: Re-visioning Latin American Social Movements* (Boulder, CO: Westview Press).

Roberts, B.R. (1995) The Making of Citizens: Cities of Peasants Revisited (London: Arnold).

—— (1996) 'The Social Context of Citizenship in Latin America', *International Journal of Urban and Regional Research*, 20: 38–65.

Rocco, R. (1996) 'Latino Los Angeles: Reframing Boundaries/Borders', in E. Soja and A.J. Scott (eds), *The City: Los Angeles and Urban Theory at the End of the Twentieth Century* (Berkeley, CA: University of California Press).

—— (1997) 'Citizenship, Culture and Community: Restructuring in Southeast Los Angeles', in W.V. Flores and R. Benmayor (eds), *Latino Cultural Citizenship: Claiming Identity, Space, and Rights* (Boston: Beacon Press).

—— (1999) 'The Formation of Latino Citizenship in Southeast Los Angeles', *Citizenship Studies*, 3.

—— (forthcoming a) 'Reframing Postmodernist Construction of Difference: Subaltern Spaces, Power and Citizenship', *Latin American Perspectives*.

—— (forthcoming b) 'Citizenship, Civil Society, and the Latino City: Claiming Subaltern Spaces, Reframing the Public Sphere', *Latin American Perspectives*.

Roniger, L. (1994) 'The Comparative Study of Clientelism and the Changing Nature of Civil Society in the Contemporary World', in L. Roniger and A. Günes-Ayata (eds), *Democracy, Clientelism, and Civil Society* (Boulder, CO: Lynne Rienner Publishers).

Rowe, W. and Schelling, V. (1991) Memory and Modernity: Popular Culture in Latin America (London: Verso).

Rubin, J. (1998) 'The Cultural Politics of Ethnicity, Race and Gender', in S.E. Alvarez, E. Dagnino and A. Escobar (eds), *Cultures of Politics – Politics of Culture: Re-visioning Latin American Social Movements* (Boulder, CO: Westview Press).

Sassen, S. (1988) The Mobility of Labor and Capital: A Study in International Investment and Labor Flow (New York: Cambridge University Press).

—— (1991) *The Global City: New York: London: Tokyo* (Princeton, NJ: Princeton University Press).

—— (1996a) 'Whose City Is It? Globalization and the Formation of New Claims', *Public Culture*, 8: 205–23.

—— (1996b) *Losing Control?: Sovereignty in an Age of Globalization* (New York: Columbia University Press).

Seligman, A.B. (1992) *The Idea of Civil Society* (Princeton, NJ: Princeton University Press).

Soja, E.W. (1996) *Thirdspace* (Oxford: Blackwell).

Somers, M.R. (1992) 'Narrativity, Narrative Identity, and Social Action: Rethinking English Working Class Formation', *Social Science History*, 16: 591–630.

—— (1993) 'Citizenship and the Place of the Public Sphere: Law, Community, and Political Culture in the Transition to Democracy', *American Sociological Review*, 58 (October): 587–620.

Taylor, C. (1994) 'The Politics of Recognition', in A. Gutmann (ed.), *Multiculturalism: Examining the Politics of Recognition* (Princeton, NJ, Princeton University Press).

Walzer, M. (1992) 'The Civil Society Argument', in C. Mouffe (ed.), *Dimensions of Radical Democracy: Pluralism, Citizenship, Community* (London: Verso Press).

Young, I.M. (1990) *Justice and the Politics of Difference* (Princeton, NJ: Princeton University Press).

Part IV
Globalism, politics, city

13 Urban citizenship

Robert A. Beauregard and Anna Bounds

Societies require a variety of integrative devices. From without, the allure (or the aggression) of other societies, whether real or imagined, threatens. From within, smaller-scale affiliations such as families and over-arching affiliations such as ethnic groups erode the strength of societal commitments. The integrative devices might be coercive, remunerative or simply functional, but they cannot be effective in the absence of moral ties. Integration is more effective when people identify with and feel a moral obligation to society.

Citizenship is one of these morally based, integrative devices (Alexander, 1992; Habermas, 1996); it has both political and cultural meaning. Though its roots are in the Greek city-states of the fourth century BC, its full emergence paralleled the rise of the nation-state during the eighteenth and nineteenth centuries (Anderson, 1983; Hobsbawm, 1996, pp. 82–97). National citizenship was its initial form.

Today, the nation-state is under assault by globalization from without and identity-based social movements from within (Castells, 1997). In response, political theorists have mounted a search for new forms of citizenship. Committed to globalization, one group has set its sights on a citizenship that transcends national boundaries and nation-state restrictions. Another group has targeted a sub-national citizenship. Convinced of the need for strong, place-based affiliations at a scale below the nation and influenced by the 'rights revolution' of the last quarter century (Schudson, 1998, pp. 245–73), it calls for an urban citizenship.

The purpose of this chapter is to elaborate a normative model of citizenship that takes its meaning from the urban public realm. The public realm is 'the city's quintessential social territory' (Lofland, 1998, p. 9). It is where people of diverse backgrounds engage each other on a daily basis in a variety of activities and associations. There, the rights and responsibilities of citizenship are exercised, civic sentiments are formed and identities are realized. Consequently, we propose a normative and bounded (Miller, 1999, p. 69) model of citizenship that establishes a 'thick' relationship (Bosniak, 1998; Hutchings, 1999, p. 28; Isin, 1999a) between the users of cities and the public realm of cities. We propose an urban citizenship.[1]

Citizenships

The most common citizenship is national citizenship. One is a citizen of, say, Canada or South Africa; that is, of a nation-state that commands a political territory. This ties citizenship to a sovereign political entity and to a socially and spatially bounded political community.

Although nation-states and their citizens were often created in coercive ways, national citizenship has endured. Reinforced externally by economic competition, wars and ideological confrontations (for example, the Cold War between Russia and America) and internally by identification documents, taxation and the teaching of history among other mechanisms, national citizenship remained a strong affiliation for most people in most countries through to the 1970s.

Rights and responsibilities are the key to nation-state citizenship and neither has remained static over the last two centuries. In western democracies, initial civil rights (for example, liberty of the person) were successively augmented by political rights (for example, enfranchisement) and social rights (for example, guaranteed healthcare) (Marshall, 1964; Hirschman, 1991). These new rights came with new obligations; the provision of social rights required more extensive taxation, for example. This elaboration of a basic citizenship did not occur in all nations or include all who resided there. Neither did it come about without political struggle. Nevertheless, the extension of citizenship rights strengthened the functional and moral ties between the nation and its citizens, and in this way strengthened the nation-state.

As we enter the twenty-first century, the nation-state is no longer as dominant as it once was. Two forces have brought this about: globalization and resurgent cultural diversity. With the increasing power of transnational corporations, spread of telecommunication links and heightened international migration, the importance of nation-states has waned (Linklater, 1998). Trade barriers are less defensible, emigration and immigration less controllable, and nation-state influence over the behaviour of transnational corporations has diminished. Even though nation-states have become stronger in other ways (Sassen, 1996) and nationalism still functions as a powerful force supporting them, many nation-states are less able to command the sole political allegiance of their citizens (Smith, 1999).

Simultaneously, nation-state dominance has been eroded internally. In the last half of the twentieth century, ethnic and racialized populations and affinity groups based on religion, gender, sexuality and historical trauma (among other bases of affiliation) became more politically prominent. The women's movement, environmental activism, ethnic rebellions, and struggles for racial identity have been central, and independence movements on the part of colonized peoples have contributed to the weakening of existing nation-states, even as they increase their numbers.

In response to these circumstances, and thus to the need for new integrative mechanisms, theorists and activists have begun to consider alternative forms of citizenship. The quest is bifurcated along the universalism/particularism divide.

One group of theorists (Beiner, 1995; Linklater, 1998) focuses on commonalities. Another gives prime emphasis to difference; that is, to a citizenship that will enable an heterogeneous public to thrive – differentiated citizenship in Iris Young's (1995; 1999) terms. The former rejects radical pluralism and the localism of civil society; the latter rejects cultural conformity. They share a concern with the formation and quality of political communities.

One of the most prominent of these alternative citizenships is cosmopolitan citizenship (Hutchings and Dannreuther, 1999; Linklater, 1998). Cosmopolitan citizenship is motivated by a concern for vulnerable groups and oppressed communities, respect for the profound multiplicity of the world, and the recognition that national citizenship places obligations to fellow citizens above obligations to humanity. The last is particularly important. Proponents claim that national citizenship weakens popular and political inclination to intervene outside the nation and thereby precludes a global distributive justice (Beitz, 1979, pp. 143–53). Cosmopolitan citizenship is designed to counteract the parochialism of national citizenship with a transcendent set of obligations. From this perspective, sovereignty resides in the whole human race, not just in the nation-state (Linklater, 1998, p. 27).

Linklater's (1998) version of cosmopolitan citizenship draws from Jürgen Habermas; its premise is that one can expect people to be reasonable and empathic, as well as honest and forthright, when interacting with each other. His cosmopolitan citizenship is dialogic, requiring communicative communities that have the power to 'refuse and re-negotiate offers' and to contest unjust social structures (Linklater, 1998, p. 28). The goal is to replace power and coercion, defining characteristics of nation-states, with dialogue and consent. The primary function is 'to institutionalise the normative commitment to "limitless communication" through participation in diverse global communities of discourse which reflect the heterogeneous quality of international society' (Linklater, 1998, p. 36).

A variation on this approach is transnational citizenship (Smith, 1999).[2] Unlike cosmopolitan citizenship, which is dismissive of national ties, transnational citizenship recognizes that the nation-state has been transformed but not seriously weakened, and that people will continue to claim national affiliation. In addition, the numbers of migrants who circulate between the country of origin and destination, and the numbers of elites who live and work in multiple global cities are expanding. These groups have commitments to more than one country. A need thus exists for a citizenship that will give them rights in all the countries with which they identify and where they have familial and group obligations. In its rudimentary version, transnational citizenship bundles together national citizenships. It requires each nation-state to recognize multiple citizen affiliations.

The strength of cosmopolitan and transnational citizenships is in the rethinking of our relationship to the nation-state. In an era of transnational corporations, fluid financial markets, weak trade barriers and robust migration flows, common people have multiple allegiances and countries are more dependent on each other. Citizenship tied to the nation neither adequately recognizes these non-national or cross-national allegiances, nor has the institutional underpinnings to respond to environmental and humanitarian crises that require intervention across national boundaries.

These citizenships, however, suffer from an over-reliance on the goodwill of individuals and nation-states (Miller, 1999). They assume transnational interests and moral bonds; that we are all part of humanity is often the premise, but it is a premise whose idealism greatly exceeds its substance. Relatedly, too little attention is paid to the ways in which such citizenships threaten nation-states. Some nations might well welcome dual citizenship, but cosmopolitan citizenship is meant to attenuate national commitments.

In addition, the inherent individualism of the citizen relationship is retained. Although some citizenship rights (for example, the immigration of family members) have extension beyond the single person, individuals – not groups – become citizens. Neither cosmopolitan nor transnational citizenship responds adequately to the group-based claims that emerge out of cultural pluralism.

This is not surprising. Citizenship has its roots in liberal political theory and capitalism, for which liberalism was justification and ideology (Beiner, 1995, pp. 1–2; Hutchings, 1999). Individualism is central to it. In general, citizenship is a weak social category for dealing with the group-based nature of social life. This is reflected in the universalism that is a strength of citizenship status (Young, 1995). It is manifested in the bourgeois public sphere that fails to recognize the embodied way in which people – as women or immigrants – act as citizens (Fraser, 1990; Isin, 1997). When combined with a nation-state stripped to its service functions, citizens are turned into clients. Virtue is displaced by interests and citizenship is depoliticized (Bender, 1996).

Transnational citizenship does hint at a more collective formulation. Group migration and transnational relationships are central; immigration, at least in America, has always had a strong group dimension – national quotas have been common. Still, cosmopolitan citizenship remains deeply individualistic, particularly in its dialogic conceptualization (Linklater, 1998). Neither cosmopolitan nor transnational citizenship breaks cleanly from the essential universalism and individualism of citizenship based in the nation-state.

An interesting response to individualism and to the quest for a sub-national citizenship is Engin Isin's (1997; 1999a; 1999b) proposal for a citizenship anchored in professionalism. His formulation has two premises: first, that citizenship has always required class and group struggle and, second, that 'the city emerged not as a place of loyalty but as a space where new professions [were] organized' (1999b, p. 278). Accordingly, an urban citizenship has to identify a group that is central to struggles for rights and central to the city. As Durkheim anticipated at the end of the nineteenth century, Isin argues, with post-modernization and globalization professionals have become that group. Professionals embody the city and do so via their control over the cultural capital that enables collective problems to be addressed. Consequently, all new rights negotiated within the political space of the city are necessarily mediated by professions. However, the professional-citizen is loyal not to the city but to the professional associations that are organized across boundaries.

This line of reasoning has its origins in the historical claim that citizenship began in the city, a reference to the early Roman and Greek city-states (for example, Athens) and the sixteenth-century European city-states (for example, Amsterdam and Venice). To this is added a more contemporary motivation: the supposed ascendance of city-regions as the primary economic units in the global economy. When coupled with the lessened identification of peoples with nations and the devolution of state policy to the local level, an urban citizenship begins to make sense.

Thomas Bender (1999) has pointed to one version of urban citizenship. Looking back to the late nineteenth century in America, when the public debate over the fate of cities was quite robust, Bender (a historian) discovered a number of intellectuals (such as Charles Beard and Frederick C. Howe) who defended the city as a locale of political engagement. At a time of rapid industrialization and urbanization, with the attendant social and environmental problems, local governments were under siege. These intellectuals argued for an urban citizenship. The city was 'closer' than the nation to the issues that people faced in their daily lives. People identified more with it than they did with national or state governments. Hence, the city could be a significant locus of citizen activity.

For an urban citizenship to be realized, citizenship status had to be ex-panded beyond those who owned property and paid taxes, and the city government had to be given 'home rule'; that is, more powers and greater autonomy from other levels of government. At the same time, the city government would have to resist being turned into a public works corporation dominated by the delivery of services and run by experts. It had to remain a political body.

Eventually, voting rights were extended, but 'home rule' was not widely granted. In addition, the federalism that emerged in the twentieth century weakened the city relative to the nation and the state. City governments professionalized around service delivery. Although politics did not disappear, public debate regarding civic life was reduced to the jockeying of government claimants for attention. An urban citizenship was not realized.

James Holston's (1999) urban citizenship moves away from the conflict between city and the nation and examines the influence of civil society on the development of citizenship. Of central concern is the gap between formal citizenship status and substantive citizen rights. When this gap becomes intolerable – that is, when state-building displaces social welfare and dominant elites constrict the lives of the masses – people search for insurgent spaces where they can manage their daily existence and their history. City residents use their knowledge of and access to the city to evade surveillance and control. In doing so, they create a new urban citizen.

The public realm

Our focus on an urban citizenship is not a move to pre-empt other forms of citizenship. In complex and dynamic societies, multiple forms of integration, and thus multiple forms of citizenship, are necessary to maintain cohesion and stability. At the same time, these multiple affiliations can also challenge cohesion and stability. The point is to recognize that people's moral ties are multi-stranded, with no one fully displacing the others.[3]

The form of urban citizenship we propose is tied to the public realm of the city; that is to the spaces where social life takes place. In these spaces, people gather to interact, to observe others unlike themselves, and to shop, gossip, talk and play. Two types of spaces comprise the public realm: public and parochial. Public spaces (such as sidewalks, greenmarkets and plazas) are where people unknown to each other (strangers) congregate. Parochial spaces (for example, neighbourhood playgrounds and church halls) are where people who are acquaintances and neighbours (that is, who are part of the same social networks) come together.[4] In the public realm, everyday life is enacted (De Certeau, 1984).

This distinction is not just between strangers and acquaintances. It also has a political component. In public spaces, individuals and groups publicize their interests and identities to city-wide and even national audiences. They hold rallies, give speeches and parade. Union workers stage symbolic protests or street vendors march down city streets to protest onerous city regulations. In parochial spaces, they craft their interests and identities. Here, for example, urban citizens meet in community centres to discuss the issues that concern them. People have more in common than they do in public spaces and this enables more substantive deliberations.

The public realm is central to urban citizenship for two reasons. First, most people in the city pass through or linger in these spaces on a weekly or even daily basis. These are places where many of the tasks of daily life are performed. People enter them to shop, worship and work; they linger to observe and to talk. If citizenship is to be forged, it will only be done here.

Second, it is within the public realm, particularly in parochial spaces, that people debate shared concerns (Sennett, 1977). These are places where a democratic society is rooted and nurtured. They are places where differences are resolved, or not, through deliberation and collective actions (Bohman, 1996; Fraser, 1990; Young, 1996). One cannot separate democracy from the public realm where democracy happens (Bender, 1983).

Nonetheless, the possibility of non-democratic activities in the public realm cannot be ignored. Over the centuries, public and parochial spaces have served as places where anti-democratic regimes solidify their control. Using political rallies, parades and symbolic displays (such as large posters of state officials), they assert their power. Public spaces can also be places of violence, whether by states and their surrogates or by groups opposing the regime and meeting armed resistance. One cannot assume that the public realm, because it brings 'the people' together, is inherently democratic.

An urban citizenship does not have to be grounded in the public realm. The local government could serve as the base, although we reject it. This would put too much emphasis on an entity that is dominated by its service–delivery function. Citizens are turned into voters or clients of government programmes and the cultural richness of public life is marginalized.[5]

Although not the anchor to our urban citizenship, the local government still plays a role, albeit a peripheral one. The public realm cannot function or remain open and inclusive in the absence of a regulatory and service-providing body that maintains (not by itself) the public and parochial spaces of the city. Without a strong (and democratic) state, civil society suffers and urban citizenship is at risk (Fainstein, 1997; Young, 1994).

A citizenship of the public realm is thereby distinct from a state-based citizenship but not independent of the state. One might say that this urban citizenship is situated in civil society, except that civil society is often confined to private, civil and political associations (Young, 1997). The public realm, however, contains the whole range of social collectivities, from households to affinity groups; it is an expanded civil society. It offers a fluid arena of social relations, one where deviance and conformity, resistance and acquiescence, innovation and routinization co-exist.

Our goal is to develop the social nature of citizenship, deflate its identification solely with political community, and resist its inherent state-centredness. We emphasize the moral rights and responsibilities that people have as participants in the social activities of public and parochial spaces (Hutchings, 1999, pp. 2–11).[6]

Rights and responsibilities

Five clusters of rights and responsibilities strike us as central to an urban citizenship. They can be arrayed around the themes of safety, tolerance, political engagement, recognition and freedom. Each is specific to the public realm. Each is also a practice, requiring an active citizen (Hutchings, 1999, p. 6).

A citizenship anchored in the public realm has to begin with personal and group safety. People have a right to expect that they will not be harmed in public, whether that harm comes from demented individuals, marauding gangs, police action or vigilante groups. If people do not feel safe, then the public realm will atrophy. Too dangerous to linger, citizenship is diminished.

When public spaces become unsafe, elites often react defensively. They withdraw to fortified enclaves – gated communities, for example, and 'secure' office buildings – that give them protection but that also make public spaces more dangerous (Caldeira, 1996). By turning away physically and psychologically, public spaces are devalued, investment is discouraged, and fewer people venture into them.

Safety is not only a right but a responsibility shared by both the state and citizens. The local government is obligated to use its police power to maintain public order. Streets and sidewalks, public parks and government plazas must be protected from deterioration, encroachment by commercial activities, uncivil behaviour and excessive state presence. Important in this regard are the physical and design qualities of public and parochial spaces that can encourage or discourage lingering and conversation.

More importantly, the responsibility for safety must be internalized as a social norm. Citizens can exercise this responsibility through their physical presence. The potential for violence and criminal behaviour is diminished when public spaces are vibrant with people performing their daily tasks. Withdrawal into fortified enclaves and excessive privatization diminish this responsibility.

A second pair of rights and responsibilities focuses on tolerance. While safety refers to violent behaviour, tolerance addresses the kinds of non-violent behaviour that are permissable in public and parochial spaces (Kahn, 1987; Lofland, 1993). To be tolerant is to refrain from blocking activities and forms of expression with which one disagrees. Street preachers, for example, often express controversial positions, yet citizens can be expected to tolerate opposing viewpoints and even participate in debate. Tolerant people

> make room for men and women whose beliefs they don't adopt, whose practices they decline to imitate; they coexist with an otherness that, however much they approve of its presence in the world, is still something different from what they know, something alien and strange.
>
> (Walzer, 1997, p. 11)

Tolerance thus enables difference; it is a responsibility (and an expectation) of a multicultural democracy.

There are limits to tolerance. When actions and expressions are physically harmful to others, they should not be tolerated. When they are psychologically harmful (for example, hate speech), they should be criticized. When they violate generally accepted norms (for example, intrusive noise, lewd behaviour), they should be discouraged. Punitive actions might or might not be taken.

Citizens have a responsibility to engage in debates about tolerance's limits, be tolerant themselves and speak out against intolerance. Tolerance only becomes pervasive, however, when supported by political arrangements (Walzer, 1997). Here, once again, the government plays a role.

The state's responsibility is to support tolerance and enforce its limits. Support comes from educational policies, official persuasion, the sponsoring of public forums and the subvention of cultural activities. Police action and legal sanctions should be a final option. Enforcement must always be a second choice and must always be open to democratic direction. In general, the regulatory mechanisms (for example, social norms) of the public realm are preferable to state interventions.

A third component of urban citizenship concerns political behaviour (Bohman, 1996; Young, 1994). People have the right to organize and congregate in the public realm for political reasons. They also have a responsibility to be politically engaged. The right and the responsibility reinforce each other.

When political action is carried out by a small minority of activists and the bulk of citizens act politically only when they vote, democracy can become a tyranny of minorities. All urban citizens have to be politically engaged. This does not mean that all are obliged to join political organizations or take to the streets. Rather, it means that everyone has to establish a connection to the realm of politics. Everyone has to maintain an interest, even if it consists simply of staying informed and voicing one's opinions to others (Schudson, 1998, pp. 310–12).

The government can play an important, enabling role. It can show tolerance for political activity, remove barriers (for example, residency requirements, financial costs) to elected office, encourage voting, open up government to broad citizen participation, and publicize the importance of political engagement. Civic organizations can also contribute. Nurtured in these ways, wider involvement deepens democracy's legitimacy and reduces apathy.

Fourth, urban citizenship is not just about politics. It is also about recognition of, and moral responsibility to, others. One of the dominant forms of expression in contemporary societies is that of identity (Calhoun, 1995, pp. 193–230; Young, 1990). Under an urban citizenship, citizens have the right to express their identity and to expect that those expressions will be recognized (Young, 1999, p. 246). This 'difference' is what enriches the public realm. Suppression substitutes sterility and conformity for vibrancy and fluidity. It weakens democracy by confining political behaviour only to interests (Fraser, 1995).

What takes the right to recognition beyond simply an issue of tolerance is the moral responsibility attached to it. Because identity differences often stem from conditions or feelings of marginality and because marginality is frequently associated with unequal or unjust treatment, societal integration is threatened when identities are suppressed. The persistence of inequalities, injustices and disrespect have deleterious consequences for democratic interaction. Marginalized people, feeling that the political process is illegitimate, are likely to withdraw from the public realm or disrupt it. Recognition and inclusion are antidotes to this, as are collective actions (particularly through and by the government) that redistribute valued goods, resources and recognition (Appiah, 1997).

The responsibility attached to the right of recognition is the moral obligation to respect others and act, beyond one's group, to bring about more equality and justice. Moral commitments that arch over groups and places can energize just politics and support the diversity that makes cities such vibrant places. Without this, the right to recognition suffers.

Finally, urban citizenship is about freedom. In the public realm, citizens should expect to be free from the intrusion of both commercialism and political manipulation. Their presence makes public spaces interesting and their complete absence would be undesirable. Nonetheless, there must be parochial and public spaces in which advertising and shopping are subdued and political symbolism and state presence are minimized. This enables other types of activities and dialogues to occur; people come to these spaces for other reasons, reasons that they deem important.

Equally important is the fact that urban citizens have the responsibility to fill these spaces with 'other' activities. They might include grassroots political activities (those not orchestrated by the state), but should mainly consist of socializing and play, activities which nurture social relations. If citizens do not organize the public realm, capital or the state will.

Reflection

This version of urban citizenship is an ideal. It is a first attempt to craft a place-based citizenship that is relatively independent of the nation-state and local government.

Our formulation takes as one of its constituent elements the public realm of the city. It aims to capture what is unique about city life: the multitude of parochial and public places and the negotiation of the public realm by people unknown to each other. We rejected placing the local government in this position. It is too confining. Instead, we opted for an object of citizen orientation embedded in the myriad social groups and relationships of an expansive civil society.

The local government is incorporated as a supportive institution with its own rights and responsibilities regarding urban citizenship. The relationship of the citizen to the state is a mediated one; indirect rather than direct. It is the active and engaged citizen, however, who defines urban citizenship, not the state.

An urban citizenship encourages people to act collectively. All of its rights and responsibilities are relational and their exercise requires interaction with others. This is one benefit of privileging the public realm rather than local government. Safety, tolerance, recognition and moral obligations situate people in social relationships in which they have to acknowledge others. Urban citizenship thereby becomes less individualistic. Citizens are not turned into consumers or state clients and they are urged away from the passivity intrinsic to national citizenship.

This approach to urban citizenship is both political and cultural. Citizenship is an integrative mechanism that relies heavily on moral obligations. To highlight this, we grounded urban citizenship in the public realm where the behaviours and interactions of people are governed less by remunerative or legal compulsions than by common bonds and identities, voluntary associations and a sense of mutual belonging. Rights and responsibilities make no sense in the absence of moral ties.

These positive, even if contestable, qualities of urban citizenship co-exist with unresolved issues. First, the public realm does not have the cohesiveness and solidity of the nation-state or the local government. The latter are formal organizations with well-defined tasks and capacities; the former is not. Rights and duties can easily slip away, becoming the responsibility of everyone and no one. To prevent this, the local government has been introduced to guarantee and enforce them. That the local government might opt to occupy the void, thereby becoming a core element of urban citizenship, is a distinct (and undesirable) possibility.

In addition, the collective side of urban citizenship is only weakly realized. Within the world that we have imagined, people can act individually and live quite well by doing so. They can also withdraw into parochial groupings, thereby weakening democracy. Individualism lingers.

Nothing has yet been said regarding the criteria for urban citizenship status (Dahl, 1989, pp. 119–31). Broad enfranchisement – universalism – across class, gender and ethnicity is the premise, but when dealing with the contemporary city there is also the issue of whether only residents are eligible. Commuters, temporary visitors such as tourists, international businesspeople and global elites are hypothesized to be an increasing proportion of those who use the city (Martinotti, 1999).

Rights and responsibilities clearly lose all meaning if criteria are non-existent, vague or excessively flexible. Citizenship is a matter of inclusion and exclusion. This gives it value. Because the public realm is so open, people are so mobile, and government, corporate and associational spheres overlap each other and political boundaries (Frug, 1999, pp. 97–111) our citizenship criteria must include all those who use the city and benefit from it.[7]

Inclusion, as Young (1995) has convincingly pointed out, leaves two important issues unresolved. One is the tendency for group differences in capacities, histories and behavioural styles to produce privileges in the public realm. Individuals from some groups are advantaged and equal treatment only perpetuates those advantages. The second is the need for 'special rights' that recognize, rather than suppress, group differences. Neither of these issues has been addressed here.

Lastly, we have not considered how such a citizenship might be realized. The public realm is not an actor; it is incapable of creating the urban citizen. To allow local government to do so is fraught with the potential for an urban citizenship to be centred on the state. Still, it could be argued that the makings of an urban citizenship are already in place (Hall and Lindholm, 1999). Most of the rights and responsibilities are available in democratic countries in one form or another. What is lacking is their attachment to the public realm; that is the recognition of an 'urban' citizenship. This presents the problem differently: not as one of generating rights and responsibilities but one of articulating their interdependence.

Conclusion

In the search for new forms of citizenship, the city cannot be ignored. Even transnational migrants and global elites – rootless cosmopolites in Kahn's (1987, p. 12) phrase – live in and identify with specific places. For most people, these places, these cities, are the meaningful spaces of their existence. If we are to resist the disarticulating tendencies of contemporary societies, urban citizenship is a necessity.

As an integrative device, urban citizenship emphasizes the moral obligations that enable the public realm to nurture individuals, groups and democracy. The strengthening of social and spatial bonds stands in opposition to citizens as clients of the state or consumers and signals its grounding in a broadly conceived civil society.

Finally, urban citizenship is not meant to preclude other forms of citizenship but rather to exist in a world of multiple affiliations. In multicultural societies numerous integrative mechanisms are needed, and people are more than capable of negotiating a variety of relationships. That they will do so in relation to everyday life is the foundation on which our conception of an urban citizenship is built.

Notes

1   We use 'urban' in an expansive rather than exclusionary way. To wit, we do not confine urban citizenship solely to cities. Rather, 'urban' stands for communities of sufficient size and complexity to contain places where people congregate on a daily basis.

2   To be fair to Smith (1999) and others who write on transnationalism, we are extrapolating from their arguments to produce a concept of transnational citizenship.

3   Our understanding of the public realm, rights and responsibilities, state behaviour and citizenship comes from our experience in the USA. This is the point of reference for our argument.

4   We distinguish the public realm from political community, the usual focus of citizenship (Habermas, 1996). We would agree that political community is manifested in the public realm. The latter encompasses much more than the former.

5   Frug (1999, pp. 95–112) grounds his version of urban citizenship precisely in the service provision of local government.

6   Sentiments and identity have been set aside here. Our intent is, first, to establish urban citizenship as a social contract around rights and responsibilities.

7   Dagger (1997, pp. 154–72) argues that the size, cohesiveness and stability of political communities also mediate citizenship status.

Bibliography

Alexander, J.C. (1992) 'Citizen and Enemy as Symbolic Classification', in M. Lamont and M. Fournier (eds), *Cultivating Difference* (Chicago: University of Chicago Press).

Anderson, B. (1983) *Imagined Communities* (London: Verso).

Appiah, K.A. (1997) 'The Multiculturalist Misunderstanding', *The New York Review of Books* 44 (15): 30–36.

Beiner, R. (1995) 'Why Citizenship Constitutes a Theoretical Problem in the Last Decade of the Twentieth Century', in R. Beiner (ed.), *Theorizing Citizenship* (Albany: SUNY Press).

Beitz, C.R. (1979) *Political Theory and International Relations* (Princeton, NJ: Princeton University Press).

Bender, T. (1983) 'The End of the City?', *Democracy*, 3: 8–20.

—— (1996) 'Clients or Citizens?', *Critical Review*, 10 (1): 123–34.

—— (1999) 'Intellectuals, Cities, and Citizenship in the United States: The 1890s and 1990s', in J. Holston (ed.), *Cities and Citizenship* (Durham, NC: Duke University Press).

Bohman, J. (1996) *Public Deliberation* (Cambridge, MA: The MIT Press).

Bosniak, L. (1998) 'The Citizenship of Aliens', *Social Text*, 56: 29–35.

Caldeira, T.P.R. (1996) 'Fortified Enclaves: The New Urban Segregation', *Public Culture* 8: 303–28.

Calhoun, C. (1995) *Critical Social Theory* (Oxford: Blackwell).

Castells, M. (1997) *The Power of Identity* (Oxford: Blackwell).

Dagger, R. (1997) *Civic Virtues* (New York: Oxford University Press).

Dahl, R. (1989) *Democracy and Its Critics* (New Haven, CT: Yale University Press).

De Certeau, M. (1984) *The Practice of Everyday Life* (Berkeley, CA: University of California Press).

Fainstein, S.S. (1997) 'The Egalitarian City: The Restructuring of Amsterdam', *International Planning Studies*, 2 (3): 295–314.

Fraser, N. (1990) 'Rethinking the Public Sphere', *Social Text*, 8 (3)–9 (1): 56–80.

—— (1995) 'From Redistribution to Recognition? Dilemmas of Justice in a "Post-Socialist Age" ', *New Left Review*, 212: 68–93.

Frug, G. (1999) *City Making* (Princeton, NJ: Princeton University Press).

Habermas, J. (1996) 'Three Normative Models of Democracy', in S. Benhabib (ed.), *Democracy and Difference* (Princeton, NJ: Princeton University Press).

Hall, J.A. and C. Lindholm. (1999) *Is America Breaking Apart?* (Princeton, NJ: Princeton University Press).

Hirschman, A.O. (1991) *The Rhetoric of Reaction* (Cambridge, MA: Harvard University Press).

Hobsbawm, E. (1996) *The Age of Capital: 1848–1875* (New York: Vintage Books).

Holston, J. (1999) 'Spaces of Insurgent Citizenship', in J. Holston (ed.), *Cities and Citizenship* (Durham, NC: Duke University Press).

Hutchings, K. (1999) 'Political Theory and Cosmopolitan Culture', in K. Hutchings and R. Dannreuther (eds), *Cosmopolitan Citizenship* (London: Macmillan).

Hutchings, K. and Dannreuther, R. (eds) (1999) *Cosmopolitan Citizenship* (New York: St Martin's Press).

Isin, E. (1997) 'Who Is the New Citizen? Towards a Genealogy', *Citizenship Studies*, 1 (1): 115–31.

—— (1999a) 'Introduction: Cities and Citizenship in a Global Age', *Citizenship Studies*, 3 (2): 165–71.

—— (1999b) 'Citizenship, Class and, the Global City', *Citizenship Studies*, 3 (2): 267–83.

Kahn, B.M. (1987) *Cosmopolitan Culture* (New York: Atheneum).

Linklater, A. (1998) 'Cosmopolitan Citizenship', *Citizenship Studies*, 2 (1): 23–41.

Lofland, L. (1993) 'Urbanity, Tolerance and Public Space', in L. Deben, W. Heihnemei-jer and D. van der Vaart (eds), *Understanding Amsterdam* (Amsterdam: Het Spinhuis).

—— (1998) *The Public Realm* (New York: Aldine de Gruyter).

Marshall, T.H. (1964) 'Citizenship and Social Class', *Class, Citizenship, and Social Development* (Garden City, NY: Doubleday and Company).

Martinotti, G. (1999) 'A City for Whom? Transients and Public Life in the Second Generation Metropolis', in R.A. Beauregard and S. Body-Gendrot (eds), *The Urban Moment* (Thousand Oaks, CA: Sage Publications).

Miller, D. (1999) 'Bounded Citizenship', in K. Hutchings and R. Dannreuther (eds), *Cosmopolitan Citizenship* (London: Macmillan).

Sassen, S. (1996) 'Whose City Is It? Globalization and the Formation of New Claims', *Public Culture*, 8 (2): 205–23.

Schudson, M. (1998) *The Good Citizen* (New York: The Free Press).

Sennett, R. (1977) *The Fall of Public Man* (New York: Alfred A. Knopf).

Smith, M.P. (1999) 'Transnationalism and the City', in R.A. Beauregard and S. Body-Gendrot (eds), *The Urban Moment* (Thousand Oaks, CA: Sage Publications).

Walzer, M. (1997) *On Toleration* (New Haven: Yale University Press).

Young, I.M. (1990) *Justice and the Politics of Difference* (Princeton, NJ: Princeton University Press).

—— (1994) 'Civil Society and Social Change', *Theoria*, (October): 73–94.

—— (1995) 'Polity and Group Difference: A Critique of the Ideal of Universal Citizenship', in R. Beiner (ed.), *Theorizing Citizenship* (Albany, NY: SUNY Press).

—— (1996) 'Communication and the Other: Beyond Deliberative Democracy', in S. Benhabib (ed.), *Democracy and Difference* (Princeton, NJ: Princeton University Press).

—— (1997) 'State, Civil Society and Social Justice', in I. Shapiro and C. Hacker (eds), *Democracy's Value* (Cambridge: Cambridge University Press).

—— (1999) 'Residential Segregation and Differentiated Citizenship', *Citizenship Studies*, 3 (2): 237–52.

14 The city as a heroic public sphere

Judith A. Garber

Introduction

This chapter reconsiders the dominant post-modern approach to politics and space in the city, suggesting how this approach works against the substantive vision of the urban public sphere to which post-modernism aspires. It focuses on the ways in which the post-modern understanding of politics in cities – as a contest over definitions or meaning – goes hand-in-hand with the dramatic shifting of spatial reference points from the physical to the abstract and metaphorical. This dual shift has left a noticeable impression on how post-modernists and other critical theorists think about a range of urban matters.[1] Because the public sphere is widely regarded as the meeting point for politics and space in the city, the adoption of abstract politics and metaphorical space has especially transformed the context in which the urban public sphere can be conceptualized and theorized.

My argument is not that the post-modern approach to space and politics is wholly defective or useless from the perspective of encouraging an urban politics of difference. Rather, it is that the distinctively post-modern project of situating politics in the particularities of experience, embodiment and identity is crucial to any effort to validate difference in the urban public sphere. To this end, the reappropriation of space and politics for more figurative, subjective usage has rendered them vastly more sympathetic to the possibilities of difference than they have been in modernism's less imaginative moments. Introducing specificity and subjectivity to urban questions has not only opened up the ideas of politics and space to a diversity of visions, it has also undermined the inherited, stagnant understandings of key urban notions like community, locality and publicity.[2]

Notwithstanding these achievements, abstract space and politics have considerably more complicated and unpredictable implications than post-modern students of cities acknowledge. First, over-abstraction can have perverse results, in that it works against the validation of politics, and especially political *action*, that springs from people's specific positions. At the least, the kinds of political goals that are tied up with expressing difference in the city cannot be realized solely or even primarily by means of a 'politics of definition'; eventually, abstraction and specificity become frankly incompatible goals. Nor is it possible to appreciate the complex linkages between space and politics if they are removed from their material urban contexts, since many of the most important political referents in cities are located literally on the ground.

Second, post-modern formulations that work well for cultural critique are not infinitely extensible to the realm of urban politics because what goes on in the urban public sphere is distinct from the politics of culture. A politics of definition simply does not have much to say about central political matters such as what constitutes meaningful citizenship in the global city or how to democratize relations in the urban public sphere. Its capacity for conceptualizing or theorizing the public sphere is, in fact, quite limited. Ultimately, one of the most crucial political goals for the post-modern city – the sustenance of multiple, insurgent urban 'publics' (Fraser, 1993) – depends partly on articulating the connection between physical space and the public sphere of collective political action and interaction. By turning away from the desire drastically to abstract urban politics and space as a corrective to modernism, it may actually be possible to reconstruct their relationship in a way that is conducive to the primary post-modern political aims of recognizing relations of difference, and embracing and empowering particularity.

Abstract politics

In the essays introducing and concluding their edited volume, *Post-modern Cities and Spaces*, Sophie Watson and Katherine Gibson forcefully articulate a common post-modern perspective on urban politics. They write 'what interests us is how *heroic visions of modernist politics*, that of mass mobilization and emancipation of the oppressed, have eclipsed our own view of the many possibilities of a post-modern politics' (Gibson and Watson, 1995, p. 254, emphasis added). Modernist politics 'homogeniz[es] categories, fix[es] difference along rigid lines, fail[s] to recognize the interplays and complexities of powers, and disallow[s] a multiplicity of subject positions' (1995, p. 260). In contrast, 'post-modern politics … defines an end to simplistic notions of class alliances or urban social movements' (1995, p. 262).

Watson and Gibson do not claim to be speaking for a unitary post-modern position on what constitutes politics (and, indeed, they do not). They also express tolerance for those who remain 'wistful' (Watson and Gibson, 1995, p. 9) for the old (i.e. modernist) political vision of cities as, in effect, latently 'heroic'. Nonetheless, their statements encapsulate a fundamental element of post-modern thinking about cities, politics and the politics of cities. Not only does post-modern urban politics reject the primacy of fixed categories such as class, but it often also attempts to move beyond – or, perhaps more accurately, above – the mere practice of politics to another, much more encompassing realm. Increasingly, in post-modern scholarship, to say simply 'politics' commits one to a distinctive, non-obvious usage of the word. With respect to cities, urbanity and space, politics is most typically articulated as the politics of culture, the politics of ideas or the politics of representation. These main strands of politics are explicitly defined with reference to one another; hence, they end up being treated as pieces of one, big, post-modern urban politics, because culture, ideas and representation are themselves closely interrelated. To take one well-developed version of this approach, Gillian Rose conveys, approvingly, the contribution of 'current social and cultural theorizing' in terms of the following chain of relationships that it elucidates: 'The politics of knowledge is understood in terms of the politics of representation, and the politics of representation is interpreted in terms of a geopolitics of location' (1996, p. 57). Politics exists, in other words, as an insight or entrée into various other phenomena.

Some political theorists have talked about the widespread use of the 'politics of x' formulation, worrying that its high level of abstraction can dampen the possibilities for concerted political action around gender, sex or other oppressions (Fuss, quoted in Phelan, 1994, pp. 98–9). This same concern lies at the heart of my discomfort with much of the post-modern usage of 'politics'. However, according to the predominant post-modern understanding, the politics of cities is, quite strikingly, a politics of *definition* or *meaning*. The politics of meaning is meant to stand in high contrast to liberal, socialist or communitarian politics. Although these forms of politics are certainly informed by grand theories and abstract ideas – about justice, the common good, rights, authority, equality, citizenship, and so on – they are in the end concerned with providing a guide for tangible aims and conduct in the world. Moreover, these aims and conduct have significance in their own right and in ways that may be readily perceived, as in the question of whether a local government's assigning policing and surveillance powers to a private company is a good or a bad thing, and for what specifiable reasons.

Another sample of the post-modern understanding of urban politics – as a 'site for contestation of meaning around … images' (Ruddick, 1996, p. 141) – reveals a basic disparity between this form of politics and the others. What the actual substance of *this* politics would be, and why it would be significant, is elusive. It is difficult to envision how it could be given content over time, or provide either an instrumental or ethical guide to conduct in the city; it is even unclear how people would recognize this as politics. The politics of meaning may be expressed as action or material accomplishment: for Watson and Gibson, a crucial political endeavour in cities is 'to design and build post-modern spaces' (1995, p. 255), including physical places and structures. In actuality, however, it is unquestionably the representative, expressive or definitional force of these activities that renders them political for many post-modern urbanists. To count as political, 'designing and building' need not have any end other than whatever meta-statements they make in public space; they need not engage discussion or action in the public sphere.[3] Again, this post-modern understanding of politics consists, at base, of the contestation over and fluidity of cultural, social, aesthetic, psychological, sexual, linguistic and epistemological *meanings*.

The post-modern understanding of specifically urban matters is not solely a result of this desire to assert an actual or potential political role for the cultural, symbolic or ideational aspects of the city. It is, rather, a joint product of the overall move toward politics as a struggle over meanings or definitions, plus the abstraction of spatial referents from their physical aspects. Together, abstract politics and metaphorical space determine the nature and size of the role attributed to the urban public sphere within the overall schema of post-modern city politics.

Metaphorical space

Lying behind the post-modern reconception of politics-as-definition is, of course, an attentiveness to difference, contingency, movement and multiplicity as basic facts of social life, and also as the highest aspirations for it. Politics, definition and difference are connected in numerous ways. Difference is largely determined by who makes and applies definitions – in the USA and Canada, households with either zero or two adult males signify (within the dominant discourses) 'different' kinds of families; in most countries throughout the world, immigrants from elsewhere are often assigned the status of 'different' from citizens. Not surprisingly, defining is thus a politicized act with real political consequences, and difference is political precisely because it is a product of definitional moves taken from disparate positions of power. Further, if we believe that politics is (or should be) an open struggle over meanings, then it is through politics that multiple and competing meanings of difference and other matters might come to the fore.

Both the post-modern condition and the post-modern ideal are widely seen to be epitomized by cities, because cities, more than other geopolitical forms, foster variety, disorder, embodiment and strangeness. Indeed, as the quotes from Rose and Ruddick show, the politics of representation, culture and ideas are frequently packaged with the politics of space. Since space retains an undeniably strong and generalized association with cities, cities are vital to post-modern concepts of politics. This remains true despite concerted efforts in feminist and other critical theory to disrupt the perception of congruity between space and in particular, local places.[4]

The debate over space

To begin to appreciate the spatial elements of this post-modern understanding of urban politics, it is necessary only to conjure up the truly impressive array of space-related terms that have been abstracted from their physical (and urban or local) referents for the purpose of destabilizing their meanings and, hence, politicizing them. There is the now-ubiquitous use of 'space', as in 'spaces of resistance' or 'discursive space'. A look through recent critical work turns up these additional metaphors related to two-, three-, and four-dimensional space: geography, terrain, territory, landscape, topography, topology, plateau, (dis/re)place, (dis/hetero/u)topia,[5] site, situate, venue, boundary, border, frontier, horizon, (fore/back)ground, margin, interstices, wall, bridge, architecture, mobility, navigate, travel, tourist, nomad, diaspora, migrant, exile, reside, home(less), lost, (dis)orient, (dis)location, local, locale, position, intersection, standpoint, map, chart, plot, cartography and scale. Many of these words are employed in multiple, and sometimes playful, forms that educe subtle variations in the metaphorical possibilities of space.

The marked popularity of spatial metaphors at this time is not a coincidence; it is a critical mass. This extended family of metaphors helps support the wave of interest in matters spatial/'spatial', an interest that Margaret Farrar (1997) labels, metaphorically, 'the spatial turn' and 'going mobile'. It is undeniably the case, as Neil Smith and Cindi Katz observe, that 'spatial metaphors have become a predominant means by which social life is understood' (1993, p. 68). This now appears to be true for an overwhelming proportion of academics who have any truck at all with post-modern ideas. Janet Wolff has summed up the impetus behind the use of spatial metaphors:

> Theoretical developments in urban studies have questioned the sociological assumption that the starting point of the study of space is the existence of physical spatial structures which, though themselves the product of earlier social processes, confront social actors and affect (constrain, determine, allow, facilitate) their actions.
>
> (Wolff, 1995, p. 106)

Metaphors liberate space from 'physical spatial structures', of course; perhaps more importantly they also give actors leave to affect (reconceive, reform, enter/exit, empower/disempower) space at will.

Those who revel in (Rose, 1996), or at least accept (McDowell, 1996; Wolff, 1995), the vast possibilities of the metaphorical turn are equally likely to discuss it as those who are more cool to metaphors (Smith and Katz, 1993; Soja and Hooper, 1993; see also Soja, 1997). As a result, there is more and more debate in urban studies concerning the practice, meaning and consequences of employing spatial concepts in figurative ways. The debate has yielded three fundamental observations in support of the omnipresence of spatial metaphors in urban studies. First, no space is static, essential, sealed or asocial. Second, there is some temptation to ascribe to both physical and non-physical space characteristics that reproduce and 'perform' race, sexuality, class, gender, age, citizenship and other relations of dominance. Third, metaphorical space is no less 'real' than physical space (and, relatedly, the distinction between metaphorical and physical space is always unclear). The first and second points have been more or less conceded by *au courant* metaphor-sceptics; the last point remains subject to the epistemological gulf separating post-modernism from modernism, despite creative efforts to step completely outside of such dualisms

(Keith, 1997, p. 139; Soja, 1997, pp. 194–7). To the extent that these observations make sense – and to the extent that they are defining characteristics of the post-modern city – they must at least inform efforts to conceive of an urban politics that embraces difference. Efforts at transformative, radical or oppositional urban politics no longer make sense without actively considering how space – in theory and in practice – holds consequences for the distribution of exclusions and inclusions across various spheres of urban life. In sum, it must be acknowledged that space is *sometimes* best understood as a process of being imbued with relations of authority and power and that space is not ontologically static (Massey, 1994; McDowell, 1996).

There is no need to outline here theories of urban space. It is important, however, to emphasize that urban space is more than the idea of it, and that some of the politically germane characteristics of the myriad forms of space are indeed physical.[6] The urge to extrapolate urban space farther and farther from its physical referents ignores much of what makes it politically salient, if politics is more than the politics of something else.

Representing the politics of representation of urban politics

In an article entitled 'Establishing Ground: Representing Gender and Race in a Mixed Housing Development', Myrna Breitbart and Ellen-J. Pader (1995; see also Pader and Breitbart, 1993) recount and interpret an instance of urban political action around physical space. This political engagement concerned the private redevelopment in the 1980s of a Boston public housing project (Columbia Point), which was in receivership, into a new, mixed-income development (Harbor Point). Breitbart and Pader's article focuses on the group of Columbia Point tenants, mostly African-American and Latina females, who were largely responsible for instigating, designing, directing and implementing the redevelopment (1995, p. 6). The women, who were elected by fellow tenants, had previously organized to address conditions within the housing project (1995, p. 13). Their insistence on participating in the redevelopment was, moreover, an outgrowth of their recognition that their housing was sitting on very valuable waterfront real estate in a city that is high up on the global urban hierarchy (1995, p. 14). They were not, in sum, wholly naïve in the ways of traditional politics. Accordingly, through negotiations with city agencies and the private developer, the women participated in establishing the agreement to turn Columbia Point into Harbor Point, in choosing an architect and lawyer, in setting up technical development guidelines, in guaranteeing that no existing tenants would be displaced, and in selecting new tenants. As members of the Harbor Point Task Force, former Columbia Point residents and market-rate tenants manage the new housing.

Breitbart and Pader's primary aim is to resurrect the residents' accomplishments from the misleading media coverage of Columbia Point's redevelopment. To this end, they point out numerous instances in which, in covering the redevelopment process, the Boston media primarily ignored, trivialized or misrepresented the involvement of the tenants; glorified the mixed-income housing concept; and pathologized public housing and its residents. A section of the article is devoted to analysing how the coverage of the Columbia Point redevelopment fitted into pervasive media images of African-Americans, as embodied by Rodney King, Anita Hill and generic 'welfare queens' (Breitbart and Pader, 1995, pp. 11–12; Pader and Breitbart, 1993, pp. 36–7). The Columbia Point residents were well aware at the time of this negative coverage of public housing and of scepticism about mixed-income, ethnically diverse housing, and some thought that they were being 'set up by the media to fail' (Pader and Breitbart, 1993, p. 39).

Breitbart and Pader focus on 'the tension between what the women were accomplishing and what the media were willing and able to see' (1995, p. 14). This mismatch is striking, and it is indeed uncomfortably reminiscent of the controlling political discourse in America. Ironically, though, this tension is also reflected to a certain degree in Breitbart and Pader's own discussion, insofar as they insert their own priorities about what was significant and compelling about the situation (abstract politics) for what *seemed* to be the residents' own priorities (collective political action towards concrete ends). As related by Breitbart and Pader, the women's accomplishments are impressive, especially given the extreme power imbalance between the residents and the city and developers. However, the tangible accomplishments end up taking a backseat to the theme of the article, which is representation and images. In their analysis of media images, for example, the authors speculate that the women sought fewer subsidized (compared with market-rate) units in Harbor Point because 'they implicitly recognized the negative impacts that gendered and racialized stereotypes of public housing had had on their living conditions and self-esteem' (1995, p. 15). Perhaps this is true, but Breitbart and Pader present no evidence that the residents chose to manipulate the media as a political strategy in furtherance of their housing goals, or that they attempted to control how they were being publicly portrayed as a goal in and of itself. In other words, there is no evidence that the women contemplated engaging in a politics of representation or definition in this instance.[7]

One might gather that the residents came together to act because they hoped to assert some control over the physical spaces – over the actual real estate – where they lived, to accomplish something in the political arena created by the housing conversion project, and to exercise the same sorts of powers and privileges of citizenship that other groups rely on when they act politically in the city. They certainly looked like people who were acting from some combination of *material* conditions, which were intertwined with race, gender, class, motherhood and geography.[8] This assessment of the political goals of this group of women does not require the mythologizing of them, or all poor women of colour; nor does it require us to deny them a keen appreciation of how they are portrayed in popular and political culture. It does make the modest assumption that they expected that something noticeable would happen as a result of their efforts, that their material conditions would improve, that they would be taken seriously as political actors, and that they could achieve, from engaging in collective action in the public sphere, the kinds of results that they could not get from participating in either electoral politics or a symbolic 'politics of'.

From the perspective of metaphorical space and, especially, of abstract politics, however, this interpretation presents a problem. The problem stems from the fact that the political acts of the women powerfully intimate the 'heroic' political forms that Watson and Gibson reject as merely modernist. At the same time, the women were clearly acting from a context of locality and particularity, which is what many feminists and post-modernists so strongly value. It could also be said that the women of Columbia Point were 'occupying political space' and 'charting their own images'. But this is surely the least satisfying way of summing up the story of an organization of poor women of colour who managed to divert some – *any* – of the benefits of economically valuable property to people who are excluded from virtually all benefits of urban space. There is, in short, something wrong with this picture.

Political theory and the city

What is askew in the preceding picture of urban politics has a lot to do with the difficulty of working out the appropriate relationship between the forms of political activity and the ends of politics. Numerous questions about this relationship arise: Is there a genuine problem in wanting, as a theoretical and practical project, to marry modernist political forms with post-modern political visions? Why does the desire to theorize, conceptualize and analyse urban politics at the level of meaning and representation work against the impetus towards specificity and locality? How integral is space to the public sphere? What version of the urban public sphere cultivates the substantive political vision of post-modernism as well as the political tools of modernism?

Some tentative answers to these questions can be found in Peter Howell's (1993) consideration of public space, the public sphere and locality. Howell has taken to task geography, and by extension most of the social sciences, for being carried away by social theory while yet being inattentive to political theory. Normative political theories of the city and locality have hardly been a common concern during most of this century in any field of study, including political science and urban studies. But as Howell argues, serious theorizing about public space and the public sphere demands engagement with normative political theory. The imperatives of political theory lie in the realization that it entertains a distinctive set of concerns, that it has a language that is uniquely suited to the discussion of these concerns, and that it admits the continued existence of politics as a distinct human endeavour and area of inquiry.

Howell insists, persuasively, on the distinction between social theory and political theory. His articulation of the distinction places into sharp focus why social and cultural theorists tend to understand politics so abstractly. The social theory that interests Howell primarily is positive and *modern* – in other words, he is talking about postwar sociology. He criticizes its 'lack of a convincing political and normative theory', as well as its 'unremitting opposition to the idea that an autonomous and viable sphere of political action could survive in modern times' (1993, p. 307). Beyond the observation that post-modernism 'has brought the *politics of theory* to the fore' (1993, p. 306, emphasis in original), Howell has not much directly to say about how critical social theories deal (or do not deal) with politics or political theory. It is enlightening, however, to realize that Howell's characterization of mid twentieth-century social scientific efforts to make sense of the world also applies perfectly to post-modern and other late-century forms of critical social theory, including a significant part of feminist, queer and cultural studies.[9] Both modern sociology and critical social theory gravitate inexorably towards an understanding of politics as simply another wing of social relations. It is undeniable that critical theories are usually motivated by self-conscious and transparent normative visions; however, those visions are less reliably trained on recognizably political questions, that is questions about matters that have integrity apart from the social and cultural sphere (1993, p. 306). Paradoxically, then, under the 'politics of x' approach heavily favoured by social theorists, everything is *generally* political but nothing is *specifically* political.

Howell is quite right when he concedes that it is 'difficult indeed ... to disentangle the social and the political substantively' (1993, p. 305). Although this very large task is beyond the scope of this chapter, there are feminist political theorists, such as Anne Phillips (1993), who make compelling claims about recognizing the boundaries between the political, social, cultural and economic without trying to seal hermetically any of those categories (compare Benhabib, 1992, pp. 90–5). With respect to the city, there are identifiably political matters bearing directly on publicity that are not well served by relentlessly abstracting politics into the realm of the social or cultural. A list of these matters would be headed by justice, equality, collective action, community, representation, participation and citizenship. Their persistent relevance to post-modern urbanity can be traced back to the fact that they speak most closely to what is political in and of itself and, probably more importantly, to what is generally recognizable as political. Citizenship, rights and the rest of the list remain ripe for the picking by normative *political* theorists who will take them seriously in the urban or local context, as very few recent writers have done. This approach would be especially valuable to the extent that it contributes to normative theories of the urban public sphere, which is the political crux of cities but which is vastly under-theorized and largely ignored. (Conversely, sustained normative consideration of the urban public sphere would also advance wider-ranging political theories of citizenship and the like.)

Drawing on Hannah Arendt, whom he counterposes to Jürgen Habermas, Howell (1993, pp. 313–18) argues for the integral relationship between geographical, local, public space and the public sphere. Arendt's conception of public space has been contested – Seyla Benhabib (1992, p. 92), for example, points out that her 'topographical figures of speech' do not suggest that the public sphere necessarily inhabits physical space. However, Howell's discussion of Habermas – the premier contemporary theorist of the public sphere – does remind us of the strong tendency in modern political theory towards a public sphere that is primarily discursive, procedural and ideal, and public space that is only metaphorical.[10] Feminist and other critical theorists have effectively attacked the ancient public sphere for being overly confined (to the participation of male citizens) and the modern public sphere for being overly universalized (to male standards of citizenship), but the broadening and contextualizing of the public sphere to account for people, actions and issues that have been relegated to the private sphere are oddly aspatial.[11] The normative linkages between the public sphere and public space, and certainly urban public space, remain to be explored.

Thus, within the dominant academic discourse about cities, and especially for those who agree at base that modernism is exhausted theoretically or historically, there is no obvious starting point for normatively theorizing the urban public sphere. It is impossible to carry on a creative normative conversation about publicity and other political matters because they are either *conceptually* submerged or simply incoherent. Since the urban public sphere is seen as simultaneously spatial and political, it suffers the most from the dual shift to abstract politics and metaphorical space, and it all but fades into the conceptual wallpaper of post-modernism. Questions about conceptual issues must therefore precede questions about the (possible) role of the urban public sphere in advancing citizenship, equality, identity difference or any other normative political ideal.

Conceptualizing the urban public sphere

Making sense of the urban public sphere proves to be more easily said than done. In the city, the public sphere has a highly complex relationship with public space, and thus it is always a slippery concept. The politics-space shift instigated by critical theorists has further complicated the task of conceptual clarification. Among the limitations posed by the shift is that its overarching 'politics of space' formulation provides little impetus to think about the public sphere as having conceptual (or practical) integrity apart from the vast field where politics and space, very generously defined, interplay. Because abstract politics and metaphorical space are assumed to cover so many of the relationships of power that are played out in the city, and because they are viewed as supplying a vital antidote to merely modernist understandings of urban politics, the public sphere holds no special interest as a distinctly political slice of urban life.

Public spheres/public spaces

This chapter has emphasized that an urban politics flowing from particularity often arises from material conditions and physical spaces (both public and private), and thus abstract politics and metaphorical space may work at cross-purposes to the goal of promoting the interpretive and normative roles of particularity. Metaphorical space ('the landscape of struggle') has no necessary relationship to the political core of the public sphere; it is contingent on what the struggle is about. By the same token, what abstract politics ('the politics of scale') says about the public sphere depends on how this politics is carried out. A related observation is that the public sphere is not identical to or co-terminous with physical space. They may coincide physically, as in the buffer/protest zone surrounding an abortion clinic or in neighbourhoods where queer political history is communicated on streetside markers (Hertz et al., 1997), and they may coincide virtually physically, as over a municipal Freenet. Quite commonly, however, the public sphere and space have a diffuse and contestable relationship that is not captured well by either liberal or post-modern expectations. A debate between candidates to represent a district in city council and guerilla environmental theatre staged at a public park can be presented equally as the intersection of space and politics, but exactly how they fulfil the definition of the urban public sphere would require some explanation. The point here is not to try to judge the substantive, democratic quality of the urban public sphere in any of these examples. Evidence of the unpredictability of the space-politics relationship simply reiterates the need for a more basic outline of what the urban public sphere really is.

Four public spheres

To conceptualize the public sphere means understanding it as the reflection of intentional, recognizable political engagements and, hence, as a matter of political agency as well as political space. Given the numerous possible combinations of the parameters of the urban public sphere, it is probably more helpful to talk about urban public *spheres*. Sketching out four general relationships between urban politics and space captures the principal variations of the urban public sphere as a political place, but it also shows how these public spheres differ in part according to how people approach space politically.

In the first public sphere, people act *from* space because their identities, experiences and interests are materially intertwined with space. Either these attributes predict how people will (be allowed to) occupy and use space, or the space that they occupy helps to form their attributes, or both. World-wide, urban history is the history of some groups being relegated to inconvenient, dangerous, unhealthy, barren, ugly, hostile or impermanent urban space because of who they are, while other groups claim the rest of the space. Space is always, then, a material effect of specificity or relations of difference. Thus it is not surprising how often people proceed politically from these material conditions to seek alternative distributions of space or power. Whether in Los Angeles or Bombay (Masselos, 1995), slum-based riots are public spheres in which people on all sides are acting from space.

The second public sphere is one in which people act *on* space by working to 'own' it, to shape its physical or symbolic character, or to control the scope of conflict over its ownership and character. The notions of 'queer space' and 'queerscapes' (Ingram, et al., 1997) suggest this version of the public sphere. They include the possibility that lesbians and gay men will act intentionally (through political, economic, social or sexual practices) to mark a physical space with an overt group or community identity. Attempts to render spaces fundamentally public or private – an ongoing preoccupation in post-modern North American cities – turn space into a political object and also help determine what is open for political discussion in the first place. Evan McKenzie's (1994) study of home-owner associations in America demonstrates how their gaining the political and legal authority to be defined as private has consequences for the vitality of the public sphere in the local spaces governed by the associations and in the surrounding municipalities.

Third, people act *in* space, in the sense that physical space supplies a temporary container for the abstract concept of the public sphere. This is the relationship that Don Mitchell is referring to in his work on local state suppression of speech and protest, when he connects citizenship rights to free use of 'the material, physical public spaces of the city' (1996b, p. 129). As he argues,

> the fight to claim the streets, parks, court house, and other public spaces of the city is precisely the fight to claim ... rights as members of the polity, as citizens who have both the duty and the right to reshape social, economic, and political life after an image perhaps quite different from ... laissez-faire liberalism.
>
> (Mitchell, 1996a, p. 172)

In terms of providing platforms for politics – whether proclamation, display, debate, protest or violence – there is little at the level of the nation-state that is truly analogous to the spaces that Mitchell lists.

In the fourth urban public sphere, people *make* space, providing a link between metaphorical space and politics. Here, public sphere activity is the creation of opportunities and incentives for the expansion or multiplication of the public sphere itself. This public sphere is also characterized by the development of political efficacy, or the encouragement of people to see themselves as having the capacity to act as citizens, even in the face of prevailing attempts to make citizenship exclusionary and monolithic. What the urban public sphere looks like here is suggested by Caroline Andrew's (1995) work on policies in several Canadian cities to stem violence against women. Andrew's study shows how the women's organizations and city officials who initiated the policies and instigated the recognition of violence and safety as policy issues succeeded in making a political 'space' for those concerns. Once in use, new political opportunities take on greater significance because they may fundamentally transform the public sphere, making room for other participants who are acting from multiple positions of particularity.[12]

Concreteness, particularity and materiality

Drawing on the depictions of the four urban public spheres, it is possible to fend off the likeliest results of dramatically abstracting space and politics: the guarantee that politics remains definitional, more or less contentless, and consequently above particularity; and the repudiation of collective political action as hopelessly modernist, raced, sexed, gendered and otherwise unsalvageable. Under the first outcome, politics is denied its integrity as an endeavour that is not just a cipher for something else. Under the second outcome, the urban public sphere loses importance because the potential for politics to transform and transgress is denied. I disagree with the idea that a concretely political urban public sphere merits either of these dire assessments and, finally, with the idea that a 'heroic' urban public sphere is inimical to the substantive political vision of the city to which post-modernism aspires. 'Modernist' political forms are not only *not* irrelevant or harmful to the values of particularity and materiality, but in the urban context, modernist politics and these values can actually be drawn closely together.

Within my sketches of the four public spheres, citizen rights, freedoms and opportunities for political participation feature prominently. A central feature of these dimensions of citizenship is their intensely non-abstract, non-symbolic character; that is they are not simply contests over meanings or representations. Even such abstractions as the right to speak or to be left alone in the public places of the city manifest themselves as actual activity (assembling, loitering, kissing), or as dialogue that people could enter into and continue through activities such as speaking, listening, reading, writing or watching.

There is nothing in the public sphere composed of these actions and interactions that is inherently disruptive to a political vision of the city revolving around the recognition of specificity and relations of difference. Like the women of Columbia Point, citizens could be acting from any configuration of unhomogenized, unfixed and unsimplistic (see Gibson and Watson, 1995, pp. 260–2) positions of particularity. We should not expect to embrace or tolerate all of the positions of particularity that manifest themselves in concrete political forms such as protesting, but this is also true of abstract post-modern politics such as performance art.

It is also helpful to consider citizenship in the city as having material qualities in and of itself, and not just as reflecting people's material conditions. This is especially evident with regard to rights. Whereas rights are always framed, awarded and wielded within a dense field of discourse, relationships, stories, symbols and ideas – as absolutely any post-liberal theory of rights would explain (for example, Rose, 1994) – rights manifest themselves, in the world and in the city, as *things* or *tools*. Rights only make a difference because people use and invoke them (or because someone believes that they can). This does not assume that rights must be the liberal rights of the undifferentiated individual, for there are plenty of other models of rights to draw on for inspiration, or that rights are a sufficient tool of counter-hegemony; it does not even deny that rights lead a not-very-secret double life in service of both the powerful and the powerless. In the most important ways I am merely echoing Patricia Williams's powerful insistence that the tools that are rights, if fairly distributed to everyone, are prerequisite to rectifying the inequalities rooted in (racial and other forms of) difference (1991, pp. 3–14).

Finally, politics is unabstract if it can be identified by citizens as plausibly political in form. In the four public spheres sketched out above, politics is identifiable, including by those who are meant to benefit most from attention to difference in the city. What is recognizable as political depends, naturally, on who is being asked – voter turnout in North American cities is low because some persistent non-voters find municipal elections insufficiently political to make participating worthwhile, while some gay men believe that reopening bathhouses closed in the 1980s constitutes important political action.[13] Notwithstanding this caveat, it does seem fruitless to rest transformative politics on abstruse events, spectacles or structures of the sort that are peculiarly post-modern and urban. Concrete political forms such as group formation, collective action and debate have the advantage of being more open to recognition, participation and even critical response by diverse citizens. Since these forms do not limit or presuppose the content of politics – notably, they do not dictate the public-private split of either civic republicanism or liberalism – they can be seen as encouraging *more* politics and expanding the urban public sphere.

A heroic urban public sphere?

A useful ending point for a discussion of the urban public sphere is Gibson and Watson's reference to 'heroic' urban politics (1995, p. 254). Because they associate it with unitary tendencies in modernist political styles, Gibson and Watson worry that heroic politics inherently opposes the post-modern political vision of plurality, contingency and subtlety. A more elaborate, but related, critique of heroic politics has been made by Benhabib, who traces its roots to the classical Greek 'public realm … in which moral and political greatness, heroism and pre-eminence are revealed, displayed, shared with others' (1992, p. 93). This heroic politics, as revived by Arendt (for example, 1958, pp. 50–8, pp. 199–207), is deeply unsuitable to modernity (and by implication post-modernity), in Benhabib's view. Heroism is unsuitable because it only makes sense in a community of equals who have a shared understanding of what counts as great political actions. Heroism fails difference for Benhabib, as for Watson and Gibson, because it presumes the universality of citizens' status, interests and norms.

Rather than assuming that heroic politics must obliterate distinct identities, interests and experiences in a quest to fulfil rigid community or class aspirations, we can ask how an urban politics flowing from the markers and effects of difference could *not* be heroic. Even the urban politics of definition, which on one level purports to shift politics to the realm of the unassuming and quotidian, on another level sees politics as nothing less than a means of disrupting the power relations – cultural, social, sexual, racial, ethnic, economic, territorial and political – that shape (global) urbanity. Benhabib's reference to the 'struggle for justice' (1992, p. 94) sums up nicely the scope of the task facing groups that might participate in post-modern politics (a task that includes culling and cultivating some shared purposes from among all of the positions of difference). Is this not a call for a frankly heroic politics?

Perhaps a believable urban politics of particularity and materiality requires a vision of a heroic urban public sphere in which there are plural heroes, acting as members of more grounded versions of the kinds of multiple, competing 'publics' that Nancy Fraser has proposed (1993, pp. 13–19). Heroic politics would not then be confined to either centralized efforts to remake the world in a single image, as Gibson and Watson imagine, or displays of prowess intended for the consumption of a closed community, as Benhabib fears. It would instead characterize the larger political project of expanding urban public spheres, where people act from, on and in space, and where they make space. Conceived this way, the heroic urban public sphere is consistent with the substantive post-modern political vision of cities; however, the combination of abstract politics and metaphorical space is not enough to sustain a public sphere in which one of the most daunting goals is bringing particularity and difference to the fore.

Notes

1 The label 'post-modern' is infinitely problematic but cannot be ignored. The part of post-modernism I am interested in is work in which: (1) particularity (of identities and interests) serves as a theoretical framework, an analytical lens, a normative ideal or an instance of the contingency of meanings, and (2) there is a commitment to abstract conceptions of space or politics. 'Other critical theorists' refers to feminist, queer, race, and cultural theorists, who share with post-modernists some of these signs of a fundamental repudiation of modernism.

2 Annalise Acorn, Glenn Burger, Lesley Cormack, Susan Hamilton and Susan Smith suggested much of this paragraph and the next over tea and cookies at our writing group. I am most grateful for their insights and encouragement.

3 According to Watson and Gibson, 'one form of an urban post-modern politics' (1995, p. 255) is proposed by Benjamin Genocchio, who refers to 'multivalent public installation projects' that 'call into question the increasingly functionalist, repetitively replicated and electronically monitored spatial experience that constitutes post-industrial city life' (1995, p. 43).

4 It is with respect to space-place relationships that a resurgent (and insurgent) feminist 'locality studies' (for example, Massey, 1994) has most radically altered the common usage of the concept of urban politics.

5 These are Michel Foucault's (1986) metaphors; their popularity and significance are explored by Genocchio (1995).

6 I employ 'physical' to characterize non-metaphorical space, or space that exists apart from somebody's idea or representation of it. This descriptor is somewhat less obnoxious (and also more precise) than 'real' or 'geographical'. Still, I admit that

this solution would not satisfy those who believe that efforts to dualize space or fix it conceptually are inherently exercises of 'masculinist power' (Rose, 1996, p. 58).

7 A plausible alternative explanation is that the residents simply acted expediently, figuring that Harbor Point would enjoy greater support if it contained more market-rate units, but also acted in the interests of their 'constituents', winning a guarantee that 400 of the 1283 units would be subsidized, so that no existing tenants would be displaced.

8 Although Breitbart and Pader do not report directly or specifically on the aspirations of the resident *activists*, interviews with Columbia Point tenants who remained in Harbor Point suggest that their goals revolved around things like 'mak[ing] the community succeed' and 'basic security – of person and of mind' (Pader and Breitbart, 1993, p. 40).

9 Howell vaguely endorses feminist geographers for being more concerned with political theory than are the Marxist (male) geographers that he discusses, but he cites feminist political theorists rather than geographers (1993, p. 305).

10 I appreciate Engin Isin pointing this out to me.

11 The pieces in Calhoun's (1992) and Robbins's (1993) edited volumes are suggestive of this generally aspatial approach to the public sphere (but compare Ryan, 1992; 1997).

12 Metaphorical space of this type is obviously not uniquely urban, but it remains open to debate whether local politics provides a more conducive environment for this form of democratic expansion, and under what conditions.

13 Additional factors, including people's intentions, would come into play in answering the 'what is politics?' question.

Bibliography

Andrew, C. (1995) 'Getting Women's Issues on the Municipal Agenda: Violence Against Women', in J.A. Garber and R.S. Turner (eds), *Gender in Urban Research*, (Thousand Oaks, CA: Sage).

Arendt, H. (1958) *The Human Condition* (Chicago: University of Chicago Press).

Benhabib, S. (1992) 'Models of Public Space: Hannah Arendt, The Liberal Tradition and Jürgen Habermas', in S. Benhabib (ed.), *Situating the Self: Gender, Community and Post-modernism in Contemporary Ethics* (Cambridge: Polity Press).

Breitbart, M.M. and Pader, E-J. (1995) 'Establishing Ground: Representing Gender and Race in a Mixed Housing Development', *Gender, Place, and Culture*, 2 (1): 5–20.

Calhoun, C. (ed.) (1992) *Habermas and the Public Sphere* (Cambridge, MA: MIT Press).

Farrar, M.E. (1997) 'Going Mobile: Location and Mobility in Feminist Political Theory', paper presented at the Annual Meeting of the American Political Science Association, Washington, DC.

Foucault, M. (1986) 'Of Other Spaces', *Diacritics*, 16 (Spring): 22–7.

Fraser, N. (1993) 'Rethinking the Public Sphere: A Contribution to the Critique of Actually Existing Democracy', in B. Robbins (ed.), *The Phantom Public Sphere* (Minneapolis: University of Minnesota Press).

Genocchio, B. (1995) 'Discourse, Discontinuity, Difference: The Question of "Other" Spaces', in S. Watson and K. Gibson (eds), *Post-modern Cities and Spaces* (Oxford: Blackwell).

Gibson, K. and Watson, S. (1995) 'Post-modern Spaces, Cities and Politics: An Introduction', in S. Watson and K. Gibson (eds), *Post-modern Cities and Spaces* (Oxford: Blackwell).

Hertz, B-S., Eisenberg, E. and Knauer, L.M. (1997) 'Queer Spaces in New York City: Places of Struggle/Places of Strength', in G.B. Ingram, A-M. Bouthillette and Y. Retter (eds), *Queers in Space: Communities/Public Places/Sites of Resistance* (Seattle: Bay Press).

Howell, P. (1993) 'Public Space and the Public Sphere: Political Theory and the Historical Geography of Modernity', *Environment and Planning D: Society and Space*, 11 (June): 303–22.

Ingram, G.B., Bouthillette, A-M. and Retter, Y. (eds) (1997) *Queers in Space: Communities/Public Places/Sites of Resistance* (Seattle: Bay Press).

Keith, M. (1997) 'Street Sensibility? Negotiating the Political by Articulating the Spatial', in A. Merrifield and E. Swyngedouw (eds), *The Urbanization of Injustice* (New York: New York University Press).

McDowell, L. (ed.) (1996) 'Spatializing Feminism: Geographic Perspectives', in N. Duncan (ed.) *BodySpace: Destabilizing Geographies of Gender and Sexuality* (London: Routledge).

McKenzie, E. (1994) *Privatopia: Homeowner Associations and the Rise of Residential Private Government* (New Haven: Yale University Press).

Masselos, J. (1995) 'Post-modern Bombay: Fractured Discourses', in S. Watson and K. Gibson (eds), *Post-modern Cities and Spaces* (Oxford: Blackwell).

Massey, D. (1994) *Space, Place, and Gender* (Minneapolis: University of Minnesota Press).

Mitchell, D. (1996a) 'Political Violence, Order, and the Legal Construction of Public Space: Power and the Public Forum Doctrine', *Urban Geography*, 17 (2): 152–78.

—— (1996b) 'Public Space and the City', *Urban Geography*, 17 (2): 127–31.

Pader, E-J., and Breitbart, M.M. (1993) 'Transforming Public Housing: Conflicting Visions for Harbor Point', *Places*, 8 (4): 34–41.

Phelan, S. (1994) *Getting Specific: Post-modern Lesbian Politics* (Minneapolis: University of Minnesota Press).

Phillips, A. (1993) *Democracy and Difference* (University Park: Pennsylvania State University Press).

Robbins, B. (ed.) (1993) *The Phantom Public Sphere* (Minneapolis: University of Minnesota Press).

Rose, C.M. (1994) *Property and Persuasion: Essays on the History, Theory, and Rhetoric of Ownership* (Boulder, CO: Westview Press).

Rose, G. (1996) 'As if the Mirror Had Bled: Masculine Dwelling, Masculinist Theory and Feminist Masquerade', in N. Duncan (ed.), *BodySpace: Destabilizing Geographies of Gender and Sexuality* (London: Routledge).

Ruddick, S. (1996) 'Constructing Difference in Public Spaces: Race, Class, and Gender as Interlocking Systems', *Urban Geography*, 17 (2): 132–51.

Ryan, M.P. (1992) 'Gender and Public Access: Women's Politics in Nineteenth-Century America', in C. Calhoun (ed.), *Habermas and the Public Sphere* (Cambridge, MA: MIT Press).

—— (1997) *Civic Wars: Democracy and Public Life in the American City During the Nineteenth Century* (Berkeley: University of California Press).

Smith, N. and Katz, C. (1993) 'Grounding Metaphor: Towards a Spatialized Politics', in M. Keith and S. Pile (eds), *Place and the Politics of Identity* (London: Routledge), 67–83.

Soja, E. (1997) 'Margin/Alia: Social Justice and the New Cultural Politics', in A. Merrifield and E. Swyngedouw (eds), *The Urbanization of Injustice* (New York: New York University Press), 180–99.

Soja, E. and Hooper, B. (1993) 'The Spaces that Difference Makes: Some Notes on the Geographical Margins of the New Cultural Politics', in M. Keith and S. Pile (eds), *Place and the Politics of Identity* (London: Routledge), 183–205.

Watson, S. and Gibson, K. (1995) 'Post-modern Politics and Planning: A Postscript', in S. Watson and K. Gibson (eds), *Post-modern Cities and Spaces* (Oxford: Blackwell), 254–64.

Williams, P. (1991) *The Alchemy of Race and Rights* (Cambridge, MA: Harvard University Press).

Wolff, J. (1995) *Resident Alien: Feminist Cultural Criticism* (Cambridge: Polity Press).

15 Who governs the global city?

Evelyn S. Ruppert

> With unmistakable undertones, the rhetoric of freeing private-sector initiative
> and reclaiming the right to manage – in this case, the right to *manage the city* – is
> clearly central to both the self-image and the public representation of the new
> urban politics.
>
> (Cochrane et al., 1996, p. 1325)

The global city is increasingly emphasized as a site for the enactment of
citizenship for various social groups that have been marginalized and disempowered by the processes of globalization. Sassen (1996; 1999) now speaks
about the global city as a new site for making claims. Fincher and Jacobs (1998)
see the global city as a site of enacting a politics of difference. Sandercock
(1998) sees the global city as a place for advancing multiculturalism. Iris
Marion Young (1993) heralds the city as a place of being together with
strangers. Borja and Castells (1997) urge that the global city is of strategic
importance for socio-cultural integration and political representation. While
these arguments are significant in highlighting the emerging modes through
which the global city is being politicized, the global city has also become
remarkably apolitical in its administration and management during the last
twenty years. Under various neo-liberal regimes of central government, local
government structures and institutions in the global city have been radically
transformed from democratic and representative into increasingly professionalized, marketized, entrepreneurial and managerial forms. Making claims in the
global city by marginalized social groups increasingly comes up against a
complex machinery of special-purpose bodies, non-elected agencies, boards and
commissions and a bewildering array of privatized, marketized and professionalized procedures.

Herein lies the paradox of the global city. While some declare the dawn of a
new age of the city-state, the traditional powers and authorities of city
governments have been significantly curtailed. The ostensibly new economic
significance of global cities has not translated into greater political power as
state practices and strategies for regulating and administering local governments
have increased. Analyses of state–local relations in Australia and New Zealand
(Jacobs, 1992), Britain (Cochrane et al., 1996; Stewart, 1994), Canada

(Andrew and Goldsmith, 1998; Siegel, 1997) and the USA (Eisinger, 1998) have revealed a relative decline in the powers and authorities of city governments. Even the need for democratically elected governments at the local level has been questioned in light of the greater central control of local finance and the inability of local governments to deal with the impacts of global economic change (*The Economist*, 1997). What has changed is the mode of state control, which could be described as a change from government to management, or a shift from liberal technologies to neo-liberal technologies of government. As opposed to less government, states have supported and advocated neo-liberal approaches which represent a shift in the techniques, focus and priorities of government, as well as a rationality of government that is less associated with the *institutions* of government and more with a *field of governing practices* (Isin, 1998). This shift has profound consequences for any group that wishes to enact citizenship and make claims in the city.

This chapter focuses on state practices that have weakened local government institutions in the global city: state control of the local property tax base, reductions in state transfers to municipalities, state-enforced municipal restructuring, and the fragmentation of local service delivery to numerous non-elected agencies. These state practices have given rise to local government practices which have increased the influence of the private sector in the management of the city: entrepreneurial strategies focused on competitive economic development leading to a greater reliance on private sector funding and cooperation, and market strategies focused on the privatization of municipal services and the adoption of private sector service delivery and management practices. It is argued that these practices represent a shift away from the government of the city by the welfarist public sector to the management of the city by the entrepreneurial private sector.

With a specific emphasis on Toronto, and drawing some comparisons with cities in Britain, the chapter examines these different state and local government practices. Since comparisons are being made between different governing structures, the term 'state' is used to refer to that level of government that has constitutional authority for local government. For example, in the Canadian federal system, local governments are under provincial jurisdiction. While the discussion is generally focused on state–local relations, the examples highlight the implications for global cities such as Toronto where a new economic significance is not being translated into greater political power or local authority to govern.

Governing the local

A conservative provincial government politically aligned with Thatcherism was elected in Ontario in 1995. Under the leadership of Premier Mike Harris this government implemented fundamental reforms to local government finance, responsibilities and structures; reforms which the government claimed would increase municipal autonomy. While many of the reforms were vociferously opposed, the government implemented its agenda with only a few changes. However, assessments of the reforms have brought into question the claims regarding local democracy and suggest that state control of local government has increased (Andrew and Goldsmith, 1998; Isin, 1998; Siegel, 1997).

Yet this hardly comes as a surprise to students of Canadian municipal government. While its two founding principles – service delivery and democracy – are often asserted as the main roles of local government as 'organs of local autonomy' (Higgins, 1977; Siegel, 1997; Tindal and Tindal, 1995), its service delivery role has been the major focus of provincial legislation and municipal restructuring initiatives. For example, local government reforms have typically placed an emphasis on municipal structures and the delineation of optimal boundaries for efficient service delivery (Sancton, 1994) rather than democratic goals and principles. Furthermore, both roles have been significantly constrained by provincial legislatures, as represented in a general pattern of gradually increasing provincial supervision and control over local governments (Tindal and Tindal, 1995).

Indeed, provincial legislatures have long asserted a natural and inalienable right over municipal governments (Isin, 1992). The Constitution Act of 1982 enshrines this concept of municipal governments as 'creatures' of the provincial governments that incorporated them. This has meant that municipal corporations in Canada have two essential features: (1) that they are created at the pleasure of the legislature and do not require the consent of the people of the affected locality, the act of incorporation not being a contract between the legislature and the local inhabitants, and (2) that the authority conferred on municipal corporations is not local in nature but derives from the provincial government (Isin, 1995).

In Ontario, it was the extent of this provincial control over both the incorporation and authority of local government that was exemplified in a number of municipal reforms introduced in 1997. Following patterns of government restructuring occurring elsewhere (the USA, Britain, New Zealand, Australia) and already under way in Ontario and Canada, the provincial government adopted a multi-pronged reform agenda that included fiscal, legislative and structural changes to the local government system. While these reforms were quite complex and numerous, the following discussion focuses on the reform of state–local finances and the amalgamation of the six constituent municipalities in the former Metropolitan Toronto into one Toronto 'megacity'.

Financial reforms centred on (contested) arguments of efficiency and cost savings, ignoring issues of political and democratic representation in decision-making. A process called 'disentanglement' was implemented, ostensibly to establish a clearer division of provincial–municipal financial responsibilities and increased municipal decision-making autonomy. However, the reforms ultimately represented a departure from these principles through the provincial take-over and control of almost $9 billion Canadian dollars of the local property tax base as well as an equally complicated arrangement of provincial and municipal responsibilities in Ontario (Ruppert, 1997).

This outcome reflected the underlying objectives of the provincial govern-ment, which had less to do with strengthening local government and more with reducing the provincial deficit by controlling the costs of local services and reducing social expenditures, particularly on education and welfare programmes (Isin, 1998). For example, the provincial government took complete control over the spending and redistribution of local education property taxes (which were formerly collected and allocated by locally elected school boards), thereby removing local control over locally raised revenues. In the case of the City of Toronto, this amounted to 37 per cent ($1.5 billion CAD) of locally collected property taxes for education being centrally controlled and administered (based on the 1998 City of Toronto budget). The provincial government now sets the rate of the property tax which is collected by municipalities and then handed over to the province to redistribute. In the case of welfare services, the province increased municipal funding responsibility for provincially mandated welfare payments, resulting in a further 7 per cent or $300 million CAD of locally collected property taxes being provincially controlled. In addition, policing services, which are fully funded by municipalities but governed by police service boards and regulated by the provincial government, account for another 6 per cent or $234 million CAD. Finally, the elimination of provincial transfers in the form of unconditional grants (for use at the discretion of municipalities), and of provincial funding for hard services such as roads and transit, resulted in significant costs being downloaded to municipalities without additional powers or own-source revenues to pay for the higher infrastructure costs demanded of large urban centres such as Toronto.

The provincial government also asserted its constitutional power over municipal government through the unilateral creation of the Toronto megacity. Against great local opposition and criticism, and without supporting studies and analysis exemplified in white papers that typically precede such decisions, the provincial government eliminated the largest municipality in the province, Toronto, and implemented a new structure, all with astonishingly limited public consultation and due process. This was achieved relatively swiftly and easily despite a long history of municipal structural reform founded on elaborate government commissions, tribunals, studies and debates. The new structure significantly reduced the number of local politicians and local structures for citizen participation and deliberation. Through its control of the legislation and legislature, and the appointment of professionals to oversee implementation, the provincial government was able to shape the new city of Toronto structure in a manner that reflected its fiscal and service delivery goals at the expense of democratic objectives.

In sum, the changes in state–local finance and the restructuring of Toronto have constrained the capacity of the city of Toronto as decisions on local services and finances are increasingly centralized in and managed by the provincial government. This severely limits and undermines the municipality's capacity to respond to citizen demands and local needs that do not meet provincial criteria and standards. Yet, the government defended these reforms because it claimed that they would make the city more competitive in the global economy. This obviously speaks to the paradox mentioned above. A neo-liberal interpretation of global competitiveness obviously required the weakening of local democracy and citizenship and the strengthening of central control. The building blocks of this interpretation and the specific practices and technologies that it gave rise to need further discussion, which the following sections provide by focusing on fragmentation, entrepreneurialism and marketization of local government.

Fragmented local governance

Many analyses of state–local relations argue that there is a change under way from government to governance, implying a shift in the distribution of local power away from municipalities to other bodies (Andrew and Goldsmith, 1998; Imrie and Thomas, 1995; Malpass, 1994). 'Governance' is now being used to denote the range of service delivery mechanisms at the local level, and expresses the shift from provision by local and central government structures to a number of fragmented agencies within the public, business, voluntary and private spheres (Malpass, 1994).

This proliferation of special purpose bodies has led to a decline in support for local government as a multipurpose service producing and providing structure, and to the fragmentation of services amongst a plethora of providers (Andrew and Goldsmith, 1998). However, this is not a new phenomenon, but the expansion of a long tradition of establishing independent bodies to carry out local service delivery responsibilities. Most authorities on Canadian local government devote considerable attention to the role of appointed 'special purpose bodies' and to the problems associated with the fragmentation of local governance (Higgins, 1977; Tindal and Tindal, 1995; Graham et al., 1998). Again, arising from the focus on the service delivery as opposed to the democratic role of local government, special purpose bodies in the past were often created to insulate decision-making from 'politics' (Graham et al., 1998). More recently, they have been created to deal with a fragmented municipal structure which can stand in the way of delimiting optimal service boundaries for achieving economies of scale or containing inter-jurisdictional spillovers.

For example, an inventory of special purpose bodies in the Greater Toronto Area (GTA) identified 400 agencies, boards and commissions (Stevenson, 1995). While many of them are controlled and funded by local municipalities, over 100 were identified as inter-municipal and inter-regional agencies funded and controlled by the provincial government. And despite the criticisms of these bodies, the most recent review of local government structure in the GTA continued to hail their benefits and even proposed new bodies to deliver municipal services, since 'different services have different optimal geographic and population thresholds' (Greater Toronto Area Task Force, 1996, p. 185). The report went further to recommend that services be delivered by specially appointed boards or contracted out to private agencies, arguing that this would promote competition and innovation.

The multiplication of local bodies, however, has also been a product of retrenchment of the welfare state. Beginning in the mid-1970s, the regime of neo-liberalism, with its agenda of fiscal constraints, led to the abandonment of services which were picked up by numerous non-profit and community agencies which sought funding from alternative sources. For example, in Ontario, public housing programmes were replaced by a variety of municipal, charitable and cooperative agencies for which federal and provincial governments only provided token support (Magnusson, 1994). This increased the significance of the voluntary sector and community agencies in the delivery of social service programmes (Graham et al., 1998). Provincial funding eventually became one of the major sources of funding for these local agencies. In healthcare, for example, approximately 1,200 community agencies across Ontario provide visiting health professionals, homemakers and community supports funded in large part from provincial grants. Through these funding arrangements the provincial government is able to assert control over programme standards and delivery to the extent that in some instances agencies have become little more than delivery arms of the state.

Indeed, the focus on municipal governments as delivery agents, and the fiscal and legislative control over their activities have made much of what they do easily transferable to non-profit agencies governed by local boards. Consequently, during discussions of alternative models for delivering local services, municipal governments are often compared to special purpose bodies as simply one of many delivery options. For example, since the early 1990s the provincial government has been considering the transfer of responsibilities for delivering welfare services from municipal governments to provincially appointed boards. Programme delivery is already strictly administered, regulated, monitored, audited and evaluated by the provincial government, thereby making the transfer to a special purpose body relatively straightforward. While municipalities still deliver welfare, local employment training boards and long-term care access centres have already been established to assume these previously municipal government responsibilities.

In Britain, increasingly tight, centrally imposed controls over local government spending, and pressures to move away from direct service provision by local authorities have also led to a proliferation of locally based institutions outside electoral control, and a more fragmented provision of services (Cochrane, 1998; Imrie and Thomas, 1995; Jacobs, 1992; Malpass, 1994). Cochrane cites, for example, the establishment of Training and Enterprise Councils, health authorities, the expansion of the voluntary sector in housing, and the assumption of some responsibilities by the private sector. Similarly, Stewart notes the pattern towards a centralization of urban policy through the establishment of a number of initiatives which bypass the local political processes of planning, control and accountability, and fragment urban policy amongst a number of new organizations (Stewart, 1994).

This has also been manifest in requirements that local authorities partner with the private and voluntary sectors in order to receive state support (Malpass, 1994), thereby opening up a political space for businesses which can now sit directly on local governing bodies (Cochrane et al., 1996). Many funding programmes in Britain are based on a competitive bidding process between cities in which bids must come from partnerships involving business, local authorities and non-statutory organizations.

This kind of 'corporatist localism' seeks to involve a number of local interests in decision-making. Typically, an arms-length process is established for the development of local policies from which the majority of local elected politicians are distanced (Stewart, 1994). But, as a consequence, the institution of local government and hence the institutional means of citizenship have been weakened. The right to manage the city has therefore shifted to non-elected, locally unaccountable bodies which are mandated to focus on the cost-efficient delivery of services, not on democratic principles of representation, transparency, participation and accountability, and is well insulated from 'politics.'

Entrepreneurial local governance

Globalization and economic competition have demanded that global cities redefine their roles in a global context and emphasize entrepreneurial or proactive strategies in order to be competitive and market their cities (Borja and Castells, 1997; Hall and Hubbard, 1998). Similarly, as cities have lost both provincial transfers and control over a significant portion of their finances, they have in turn become more dependent on economic development for revenues. Attracting investment and economic development have therefore become prominent foci of municipal government activity.

This is particularly manifest in strategies for urban renewal that focus on marketing cities. 'Place marketing', 'urban growth coalitions' and 'urban regimes' have become emblematic of a shift from a municipal welfarist (bureaucratic, managerial) politics to that of a dynamic and charismatic (entrepreneurial) business leadership, an emphasis on potential gains from urban entrepreneurialism rather than the effective delivery of welfare services (Cochrane et al., 1996; Magnusson, 1994; Harvey, 1989). While local governments have long been involved in marketing their localities for business investment, the contemporary period is marked by a new complexity of issues, such as the mobility of capital, removal of trade barriers, economic restructuring, new telecommunications technologies, labour market adjustments, etc. (Graham et al., 1998). Old activities are therefore being repackaged, a repackaging which is no doubt a response to greater competition for business (Magnusson, 1994).

In Canada, competitive localism and the importance of cities in economic development have become central to arguments for restructuring Toronto which focus on taxation, infrastructure, service delivery and political fragmentation in terms of their implications for economic competitiveness

(Greater Toronto Area Task Force, 1996). In particular, public–private economic development bodies, which operate at arms-length from government and which 'rely on strong business leadership to spearhead marketing efforts for their regions' have become the dominant economic development model in Canadian cities (Graham et al., 1998). Cities such as Vancouver, Montreal, Calgary, and Ottawa have economic development bodies that include a number of other policy and programme levers beyond marketing and promotion, including planning and development actions such as infrastructure investment, fast-tracking development, designating business parks and improvement areas, and investments in cultural and recreational facilities to enhance the quality of life (Graham et al., 1998).

The marketing of the city to business is also extended to the state. With the loss of provincial transfers, particularly for major infrastructure projects, cities must now compete and find other ways of leveraging financial support from the state. Indeed, a prominent method that cities use to leverage funding is that of bids to host the Olympic Games. For example, one of the key arguments put forward in Toronto's bid to host the 2008 Olympics is that this will lever both provincial and federal investment in major civic infrastructure projects – funding that otherwise would not be forthcoming. However, the bid is being planned and led by a private sector corporation (TO-Bid) which consists principally of business professionals in sport, communications, tourism, marketing, law, government, arts and culture, with nominal representation from municipal government. The executive committee of TO-Bid meets in private and since its inception repeated requests by citizens for copies of budgets and or financial statements have largely been ignored.

In Britain, the development of arts, cultural, recreational or sports mega-projects are illustrative of a kind of competitive localism in which localities engage in active marketing and presentation of their cities in order not only to attract private sector financing but also predominantly to win funds from government (Stewart, 1994). Manchester's failed bids for the Olympics in the 1980s and 1990s are illustrative of the same reliance of local governments on leveraging state finance. The process involved attracting significant funding from central government through a competitive bidding process (Cochrane et al., 1996). It was also illustrative of this shift to new partnership bodies which have marginalized local authorities and insulated decision-making from processes of public accountability and even from political debate (Cochrane et al., 1996). Another example was Britain's City Challenge programme, which involves competitive bidding amongst municipalities with place marketing as a key objective of funding allocations (Stewart, 1994).

Attracting investment from both the private sector and the state has there-fore not only led to entrepreneurial and competitive municipal practices but also to the establishment of unelected, arms-length public–private 'partnership' boards or private corporations. In both cases, the private sector has gained new rights to manage the city and, as in the case of special purpose authorities, insulated decision-making from public input and scrutiny. Yet these bodies make major planning, distributive and resource allocation decisions which will have long-term impacts on the public domain of cities, decisions that are well insulated from public scrutiny and debate.

Marketized local governance

Municipal governments have also developed strategies to increase their revenues and decrease costs through a greater reliance on the private sector in terms of service delivery and management practices. The adoption of these strategies has been spurred on by a broader and pervasive shift in governing culture, in which the language and techniques of business management have become the answer for deficit-focused and cash-strapped governments.

The private sector has become increasingly important in the direct provision of services and the transfer of management practices to local government. Private sector firms have been delivering municipal services in Ontario for a long time, with contracting out being the most common form. Construction projects, water and sewage lines and treatment plants, professional services such as engineering, planning and legal advice, and waste management, tourism, recreation, transportation and administrative services are some of the major services which have been contracted out in Ontario (Greater Toronto Area Task Force, 1996). In the past, many of these services were delivered by local governments directly, but fiscal pressures resulting from reductions in provincial funding and perceived difficulties with raising property taxes have led to greater interest in increased private sector involvement.

Local government searches for costs savings have increasingly turned to contracting out as a solution. Greater reliance on funding services from user fees as opposed to general revenues has also made the step towards privatization easier. Once the full cost of a service (for example, water, waste) is covered by a fee, it is easier to resort to private sector delivery and collection.

The contract culture in municipal government has become instrumental in the adoption of new management practices. Various studies note that identifying cost savings through privatization requires the production of financial data for evaluating alternative delivery approaches. It is argued that in order to monitor and measure effectiveness and compare performance, defined outcomes and benchmarks need to be compiled (Greater Toronto Area Task Force, 1996). This requires collecting and analysing municipal service delivery data in order to provide benchmarks for comparison and the production of annual reports, requiring new accounting and measuring procedures and a data collection system that allows for auditing cost-effectiveness. These practices of enumeration, calculation, monitoring and evaluation are further examples of neo-liberal techniques of governance (Isin et al., 1998). The process of performance measurement has led to the adoption of private sector cost-saving programmes such as 'best practices'. This involves a process of competitive comparisons based on benchmarks or operating statistics that enable comparison of performance between organizations. For example, the new city of

Toronto's first budget exercise identified the introduction of 'best practices – the most efficient ways to provide services' as one means of finding savings to meet the deficit caused by provincial funding cuts (City of Toronto, 1998).

Thus the new fiscal self-reliance has led to local government officials speaking the language of modern public management: 'they believe in reinvention, innovation, privatization, competition, strategic planning, and productivity improvements' (Eisinger, 1998, p. 320). The language of restructuring and streamlining is pervasive in local government: becoming more entrepreneurial, developing public–private partnerships, 'steering' instead of 'rowing', measuring results and rewarding success, introducing a competitive atmosphere, efficiency and effectiveness, developing a stronger focus on the customer, and defining your core business, are all popular slogans in local government today (see Andrew and Goldsmith, 1998; Greater Toronto Area Task Force, 1996; Tindal and Tindal, 1995).

Local governments have looked increasingly to business for ideas. Several influential authors and studies have popularized this kind of convergence of public and private approaches, including David Osborne and Ted Gaebler (1992), who advocate radically different ways of 'doing business' in the public sector. They provide numerous examples of innovative and entrepreneurial practices – defined as practices that use resources in new ways to maximize productivity and effectiveness – as evidence that their principles are practical and can be successfully implemented.

The adoption of these practices has contributed to the 'marketization' of the public sector through processes of contracting out or compulsory competitive tendering or privatization (Andrew and Goldsmith, 1998). This contract culture has been accompanied by a 'consumerist' trend – the persistent search for increased effectiveness through a greater sensitivity to user needs, performance evaluations, and a changing relationship between the municipality and the individual.

In Britain this has been described as a kind of 'managerialist localism', represented in state programmes which direct local government bids to achieve strategic and operational objectives, identify measures of inputs and outputs, indicate milestones towards progress, and develop monitoring and evaluation techniques for assessing outcomes (Stewart, 1994). Local authorities are often required to open up to private competition services such as waste collection and street cleaning, as well as professional services which local authorities have traditionally provided in-house (Malpass, 1994).

Decisions to privatize the management of the city in these various forms are based largely on the recommendations of private sector consultants who have become prominent advisors to governments looking to 'reinvent' themselves in a global age. For example, reviews of local government often look to private sector consulting firms for advice on how to govern the global city, and are not surprisingly offered the answer: let the private sector manage the city (for example, Greater Toronto Area Task Force, 1996).

However, regardless of whether professionals work within the public or private sector, the same neo-liberal practices are employed that constitute a 'new public management' of governance at a distance through contracts, targets, performance measures or monitoring and audit, and where the emphasis is upon accountability, standards and measures of performance, contracts, competition and a budget discipline. Accounting and auditing have proven to be powerful technologies for acting at a distance upon the actions of others: 'whilst apparently devolving more decisional power to those actually involved in devising and delivering services in local sites it renders those activities governable in new ways' (Rose, 1999, p. 245).

This contract culture has shifted management of the city from the public sector to the private sector, both in terms of the privatization of local functions and the adoption of private sector management approaches. In both cases, these managerial approaches are represented as being 'apolitical' since they are focused on achieving objectives of efficiency and productivity and are based on accepted standards of enumeration, calculation, accounting and comparison. However, through both the direct provision of services and the transfer of management practices to local government the private sector has become more influential in the day-to-day decision-making and management of the global city. And through yet another mechanism, the institutional means of citizenship for influencing public policy-making have been undermined.

Who governs the global city?

The paradox of the global city – the coupling of a new age of citizenship with the curtailment of the powers and authorities of city governments – means that at a time when the importance of making claims in the city is ascending, the mechanisms of deliberative democracy are being dismantled, and local government is becoming a shell emptied of its content. This chapter has described how local decisions and control are being shifted elsewhere – to the state, other local authorities or the private sector. Given the decline in local government powers and authorities, the ability of local government to make public policy and serve as a site of local democracy is therefore being seriously undermined.

What are the prospects for the possibility of citizens governing their cities in the face of globalization, 'informationalization' and sprawling urban regions which are undermining the relevance and authority of local governing institutions? For Borja and Castells (1997), the answer lies in reinforcing local society and its political institutions, the site where the global and local come together: 'The strategic importance of the local as a managerial centre for the global in the new techno-economic system can be seen in three main fields: economic productivity and competitiveness, socio-cultural integration and political representation and management' (Borja and Castells, 1997, p. 3). However, at the same time they note that local governments are dependent on nation-states and have less power and resources to deal with global and economic change. For them the question then becomes how to strengthen local governing institutions and thereby bring together economic, participatory democracy and cultural integration. Yet, in the 1990s reviews of local government have repeatedly spoken of globalization and the imperative of reform to meet the challenges of a 'new era'. They typically focus on economic and fiscal considerations, while ignoring other significant challenges and changes under way in the global city. They undermine the 'other' global city, where various groups are claiming rights.

A new politics of difference, tolerance, recognition and affirmation is receiving considerable attention, and not simply as difference but as a located politics of difference sited in the city (Fincher and Jacobs, 1998). In the face of this change, the city and region are argued to be where citizenship can be located and where a shared notion of a common destiny as a coming together, a being together of strangers can be formulated (Young, 1993). Sandercock (1998) turns to cities and regions as the answer, as the locus of citizenship in the future which must nurture difference and diversity through a democratic cultural pluralism based on social justice, difference, citizenship, community and civic culture. If power is shifting from the nation-state to transnational institutions and from the nation-state to the city-state, then cities are the more important and relevant political-administrative units. And they take on this role in conjunction with their changing demographic and economic roles as 'receptors of global movements of peoples as well as economic transactions' (Sandercock, 1998, p. 182). For Borja and Castells, local governments are also the institutional agents for achieving this kind of social and cultural integration in territorial communities, and in this regard are better situated than nation-states: 'Without a system for social and cultural integration that respects differences while also establishing codes for communication between the various cultures, local tribalism will be the other side of the coin of global universalism' (Borja and Castells, 1997, p. 4). This link between local government and citizenship and the direct involvement of diverse groups in the making of public policy is recognized in a growing literature on cities and citizenship (Andrew and Goldsmith, 1998). The sense of citizenship as rights to the city highlights the potential of local governments to create a public space for debate and deliberation and the governance of diversity, as a means of increasing equity, accessibility and political participation. This sense of citizenship sees the local level as not merely a deliverer of services but also as a democratic government.

While liberal local government structures and practices were far from meeting the demands of democratic citizenship, this chapter has argued that neo-liberal mentalities towards the city shifted power to professional, procedural, performative and auditing techniques without democratic mechanisms of deliberation, accountability and responsibility. This suggests that the real question is not whether the global city is a 'primary locus of economic activity and power in today's global context' but how the right to govern the city is claimed, and how rights-claiming practices shifted away from the institutions of local government to a field of fragmented management practices. These questions are not about the rights *of* cities but rather of citizens to govern their cities. For while local government is diminishing and being fragmented amongst a plethora of local bodies and private sector organizations, the city is indeed being governed. To enact *any* kind of democratic citizenship in the global city requires working through these new governing practices and institutions.

Bibliography

Andrew, C. and Goldsmith, M. (1998) 'From Local Government to Local Governance-and Beyond?', *International Political Science Review*, 19 (2): 101–17.

Borja, J. and Castells, M. (1997) *Local and Global: Management of Cities in the Information Age* (London: United Nations Centre for Human Settlements (Habitat) and Earthscan Publications Limited).

City of Toronto (1998) 'City Budget' (Toronto: City of Toronto).

Cochrane, A. (1998) 'Globalization, Fragmentation and Local Welfare Citizenship', in J. Carter (ed.), *Post-modernity and the Fragmentation of Welfare* (New York: Routledge).

Cochrane, A., Peck, J. and Tickell, A. (1996) 'Manchester Plays Games: Exploring the Local Politics of Globalisation', *Urban Studies*, 33 (8): 1319–37.

The Economist (1997) 'The Music of the Metropolis' (2 August): 43–4.

Eisinger, P. (1998) 'City Politics in an Era of Federal Devolution', *Urban Affairs Review*, 33 (3): 308–25.

Fincher, R. and Jacobs, J.M. (eds) (1998) *Cities of Difference* (New York: Guilford).

Graham, K.A., Phillips, S.D. and Maslove, A.M. (1998) *Urban Governance in Canada: Representation, Resources, and Restructuring* (Toronto: Harcourt Brace and Company).

Greater Toronto Area Task Force (1996) 'Greater Toronto: Report of the GTA Task Force' (Toronto: Queen's Printer for Ontario).

Hall, T. and Hubbard, P. (eds) (1998) The Entrepreneurial City: Geographies of Politics, Regime and Representation (New York: John Wiley and Sons).

Harvey, D. (1989) 'From Managerialism to Entrepreneurialism: The Transformation of Urban Governance in Late Capitalism', *Geografiska Annaler B*, 71: 3–18.

Higgins, D. (1977) *Urban Canada: Its Government and Politics* (Toronto: Macmillan).

Imrie, R. and Thomas, H. (1995) 'Urban Policy Processes and the Politics of Urban Regeneration', *International Journal of Urban and Regional Research*, 19 (4): 479–94.

Isin, E.F. (1992) *Cities Without Citizens* (Montreal: Black Rose Books).

—— (1995) 'The Origins of Canadian Municipal Government', in J. Lightbody (ed.), *Canadian Metropolitics: Governing Our Cities* (Mississauga: Copp Clark).

—— (1998) 'Governing Toronto Without Government: Liberalism and Neoliberalism', *Studies in Political Economy*, 56 (Summer): 169–91.

Isin, E.F., Osborne, T. and Rose, N. (1998) *Governing Cities: Liberalism, Neoliberalism, Advanced Liberalism* (Toronto: Urban Studies Programme Working Paper no. 19, York University).

Jacobs, B.D. (1992) *Fractured Cities: Capitalism, Community and Empowerment in Britain and America* (New York: Routledge).

Magnusson, W. (1994) 'Metropolitan Change and Political Disruption', in F. Frisken (ed.), *The Changing Canadian Metropolis: A Public Policy Perspective* (Berkeley and Toronto: Institute of Governmental Studies Press, University of California, Berkeley, and the Canadian Urban Institute, Toronto).

Malpass, P. (1994) 'Policy Making and Local Governance: How Bristol Failed to Secure City Challenge Funding (Twice)', *Policy and Politics*, 22 (2).

Osborne, D. and Gaebler, T. (1992) *Reinventing Government: How the Entrepreneurial Spirit is Transforming the Public Sector* (New York: Penguin).

Rose, N. (1999) *Powers of Freedom: Reframing Political Thought* (Cambridge: Cambridge University Press).

Ruppert, E.S. (1997) 'The Provincial Property Tax', unpublished paper, Toronto.

Sancton, A. (1994) 'Governing Canada's City Regions: Adapting Form to Function' (Montreal: Institute for Research on Public Policy).

Sandercock, L. (1998) *Towards Cosmopolis: Planning for Multicultural Cities* (Toronto: John Wiley and Sons).

Sassen, S. (1996) 'Identity in the Global City: Economic and Cultural Encasements', in P. Yaeger (ed.), *The Geography of Identity* (Ann Arbor: University of Michigan Press), 481.

—— (1999) 'Whose City Is It? Globalization and the Formation of New Claims', in J. Holston (ed.), *Cities and Citizenship* (Durham, NC: Duke University Press), 177–94.

Siegel, D. (1997) 'Local Government in Ontario', in G. White (ed.), *The Government and Politics of Ontario* (Toronto: University of Toronto Press).

Stevenson, D. (1995) 'Inventory of Existing Governance Structures in the Greater Toronto Area' (Toronto: Canadian Urban Institute).

Stewart, M. (1994) 'Between Whitehall and Town Hall: The Realignment of Urban Regeneration Policy in England', *Policy and Politics*, 22 (2).

Tindal, C.R. and Tindal, S.N. (1995) *Local Government in Canada*, 4th edn (Toronto: McGraw-Hill Ryerson Limited).

Young, I.M. (1993) 'Together in Difference: Transforming the Logic of Group Political Conflict', in J. Squires (ed.), *Principled Positions: Postmodernism and the Rediscovery of Value* (London: Lawrence and Wishart).

16 Politicizing the global city

Warren Magnusson

> Although conceivably surpassed by Tierra del Fuego or Outer Mongolia, Tasmania's geographical location makes it just about the perfect place from which to assess the extent of globalization. If one can sit here at the spatial edge of human society, looking northward across the vast desert continent of Australia and southward towards emptiness and desolation, knowing that one is thousands of kilometres from the 'global cities' of Tokyo, Frankfurt, or LA, and still feel that one is part of the world, then globalization is an impressive process.
>
> (Waters, 1995, p. xi)

Like many, Malcolm Waters mistakes the rhetoric of the global city for reality. To pick particular locales like Tokyo, Frankfurt, and Los Angeles and award them stars for global influence is to engage in a mug's game. As Waters' own analysis reveals, the important thing about globalization is not that it creates centres of command and control – that is an old story – but that it delocalizes those centres and draws the most remote regions into a common way of life. Long ago, Louis Wirth (1938) described that way of life as 'urbanism'. Like many social scientists, however, Wirth wanted to de-politicize the phenomenon he was analysing. My purpose is precisely the opposite: to explore the means for *politicizing* the global city.

Nostalgia for sovereignty

This chapter argues that to comprehend the politics of such a global city, we need new categories, quite different from the ones we have inherited from the social sciences of the nineteenth and twentieth centuries. The conventional categories tend to displace, repress and conceal the political. As such, they inhibit any understanding of global citizenship. We need to begin again, with a different ontology of the political. As Foucault put it, 'We need to cut off the king's head: in political theory it has still to be done' (Rabinow, 1984, p. 63). At present, we are caught within a discourse of sovereignty that leads us on a merry chase for the centres of power, and deludes us into thinking that there are commanding heights to be seized and fortified. If not the castle, why not the king? If not the king, why not parliament? If not parliament, why not the nation? If not the nation, why not the economy? If not the economy, why not culture? If not culture, why not the global city? Surely, the centre of power is somewhere. Is that not the expectation that flows from sovereignty-thinking? And, if we break from this pattern of expectation – if we refuse the temptation to model the political universe in terms of highs and lows, centres and peripheries, interiors and exteriors – do we not also have to decentre the social sciences, cultural studies, and all the other disciplines that make politics into the great impossible?

In the popular imagination, politics is at once removed from humane and responsible activity. It is parasitic on the social, the economic and the cultural. It is inherently uncreative and usually a source of corruption. At best, it is an activity that generates much sound and fury, while ultimately signifying nothing. At worst, it is like a horrid disease that destroys everything it touches. These popular understandings are not at odds with the ones entrenched in the academy: on the contrary. In the categorical structure of the social sciences, there is little room for politics except as a source of disorder and unreason: something that must be confined to the margins if rational understanding and rational action are to occur. Politics taps into the deepest, darkest regions of the human soul, and as such it can never be entirely rational: that is what political scientists generally teach their students. Indeed, the whole discipline of political science is designed to replace naïve idealism in favour of a 'realism' that specifies attainable ideals and recommends an attitude of calculative rationality. (Hence, the popularity of so-called rational choice theory, an approach that aims to save politics by turning it into a form of economics.) From this perspective, politics is an unavoidable evil: an evil to be controlled by calculative rationality.

Of course, there are people who advance a different understanding. The legacy of the ancient Greeks, the Roman republicans, the Florentines and the early modern democrats is still with us. From this tradition we get a positive conception of politics (see Arendt, 1961; Crick, 1962; Connolly, 1987; Skinner, 1998; and Tully, 1999). Nevertheless, this is a minor current. In the dominant view, politics is something to be reduced to a minimum, if not by suppressing it directly, then by bringing it into line with economic calculation or cultural expression. Salesmanship, diplomacy and dispute resolution can thus be presented as the highest forms of political activity. It is difficult, if not impossible, to express a different conception of the political on a discursive terrain that has already been fixed by the dominant social sciences. Those who pursue a different tack are caught between nostalgia for the *polis* (or its surrogate, the modern state) and a nagging suspicion that the social sciences have already explained politics away (see Held, 1991; Vincent, 1997). The *polis*, the republic and the state are spatializations of sovereignty, spatializations that only work under specific conditions (as Aristotle himself must have known). Nostalgia for the *polis* is a powerful motivator (not least for the discussion that follows here), but it will lead us to repeat past mistakes if we do not see that sovereignty itself (and the spatial imaginary from which it derives) creates the idealized *polis* and the mundane 'political system' as conditions of possibility for one another (Agamben, 1998). The ideal is the justification for the real (Walker, 1993). To break out of this mode of thinking, we need to rethink our ontological assumptions.

In this context I think it is salutary that we are now presented with the global city: the city that has become the world, the world that has become the city. To comprehend such a phenomenon, we have to dispense with the seventeenth century spatial imaginary that has given us our state-centric conception of government, and that has thus told us what form our politics should take if it is to be at all rational. This old spatial imaginary still grounds most political philosophy including work by Rawls (1971; 1996), Habermas (1984–87; 1989), Taylor (1989), and their many interlocutors and commentators. Ironically, the same imaginary also grounds the social sciences that relegate political philosophy to the margins, giving it a status equivalent to the wishful thinking that Hegel condemned so long ago (Knox, 1952). To think seriously about our political possibilities is to think *through* this spatial imaginary, and discover other ways of conceptualizing space, time and identity. There is much in twentieth-century philosophy (and indeed in the natural and social sciences) that can aid us in this task (see, for instance, Foucault, 1980; Deleuze and Guattari, 1987; and Haraway, 1991). However, to focus on the global city is especially helpful, because it is a phenomenon that defies description within the old spatial imaginary.

Seeing ourselves politically

To politicize the global city is to make it into a domain in which we can act politically. The task is comparable to the one posed in the seventeenth and eighteenth centuries. In that era the modern state was formed. The early proponents of the modern state wanted to repress politics by making authority incontestable (see especially Bodin, 1576; and Hobbes, 1651). However, the republicans and democrats were able to claim the state as a domain for political action within a framework of sovereignty. The theory and practice of liberal democracy have come out of these early efforts (Macpherson, 1977). The challenge for us now is to come to terms with a different spatial order, one in which the state no longer has such a decisive place. Eighteenth-century political economy, nineteenth-century sociology, and their twentieth-century successors all gesture towards the need for decentring the state as a focus for attention. On the other hand, these social sciences leave the political behind (in the domain of the state) or project it into the realm of ethics (where it can be expressed in pious wishes or moral injunctions). To overcome these disabling practices, we must claim the global city as a political space. That cannot be done without challenging the tendency to represent the city or 'urbanism' as a natural phenomenon.

The naturalization of the city is an effect of *social* scientific thinking. It is worth remembering that the social sciences were developed in more or less explicit opposition to Aristotelian *political* science. The Aristotelian approach was bound up with the ideal of a *polis* or republic: a self-contained community in which people could be active citizens (Barker, 1962). Although this ideal was long preserved in the western tradition by thinkers such as Cicero, Machiavelli and Rousseau, it was challenged effectively by the new 'social' scientists of the late eighteenth and early nineteenth centuries, who showed in various ways that 'political' self-government was not enough for genuine self-determination. The implication was that people who seemed to have political independence would still be subject to economic and social forces beyond their control. Moreover, these same people would act within the framework of a culture that largely determined what they would do. Thus, from the perspective of the developing social sciences, merely political activity seemed epiphenomenal. Attention was directed at the 'other' of politics: civil society. The social might be understood in terms of economic relations, biological necessities, cultural norms or whatever. The point was that it could not be comprehended by politicians or statesmen, let alone by ordinary citizens. Social science – or its 'other', cultural understanding – always trumped merely political science. Indeed, the only kind of political science that deserved the name was one that could be understood as just another branch of the naturalizing social sciences.

Often forgotten now, in the rush to demonstrate the aristocratic, ethnocentric and patriarchal assumptions of the classical political thinkers, is that the Aristotelian and later republican conception of political science was action-oriented. That is, the premise of this way of knowing was that the people who were fit for it had the responsibility for governing. Such people were rulers and had to decide what to do. The 'science' of politics was to help them get oriented and then to make the appropriate decisions. Such a science had to encompass philosophy, sociology, psychology, geography, history and so on: it had to be comprehensive, because everything was at stake in the matters at issue and anything might be relevant to the decisions at hand. In this context, political science had to be the study to which all other sciences contributed. The premise, of course, was that the people who used such a master science could and should take responsibility for the human affairs in which they were engaged. If they disclaimed responsibility – if they said that what was happening was determined by fate, or by nature, or by the requirements of God – they would be refusing to act politically. There have been many ideologies – Christianity and liberalism among them – that have encouraged such political passivity. One of the meritorious features of the critical social sciences and critical social theory is that they have exposed the ideological moves involved in such encouragement and shown how the quiescence of some has entrenched the political power of others. On the other hand, there has been much less clarity about the fact that political responsibility, like adulthood, is ultimately thrust upon every one of us. Either we behave like children politically – which is what many social and cultural theorists seem to recommend – or we take responsibility for ourselves and the world around us. If we opt for the latter, a political science of some sort is essential.

Unfortunately, the only sort of political science we have is disabling, insofar as it is focused on the state and on the political field constituted by the state. 'Policy studies' are the nearest modern equivalent to Aristotelian political science. The state-centricity of such studies is apparent. To develop a sociology or an economics or a geography or a cultural analysis of politics is not the appropriate alternative, because a move of this sort is vitiated by the depoliticizing assumptions of the discipline invoked. The terms 'culture', 'geography', 'economy' and 'society' were developed in opposition to politics. They were meant to denote a reality that was not the effect of politics, but that instead arose more or less naturally out of ordinary human activities. Having thus imagined human life as it would be without politics, we cannot then return politics to its place – as politically engaged writers would like to do – without making nonsense of the ideas that have underpinned the depoliticized social sciences. We cannot throw out 'the state' as a focus of our political attention (as some people would no doubt like to do), without also discarding 'culture', 'economy', 'region', 'nation', 'society' and all the other entities that we have invented as alternatives to the *polis*. In the end, the political is unavoidable, but it is no accident that we have such difficulty writing or even thinking about it, since we work within an intellectual tradition that is determined to put politics to one side.

Ultimately, a sociology of politics can only offer a naturalized account, which leaves the action-questions – the political questions – to be decided later. Other disciplinary (and interdisciplinary) analyses have the same effect: specifically political analysis is subject to infinite deferral. Taking a stance, proclaiming an allegiance or offering an ironic comment is not the same as developing a political analysis. And yet, these are the interventions we pass off as political, in response to the naturalizing accounts that dominate academic understandings of human possibility. This is not good enough, especially in an age which is supposed to be one of deepening democracy. Whatever else democracy means, it entails a broadening of political responsibility, in the sense that people who were once conceived as the innocent subjects of government now appear as agents of their own destiny. As political agents they need 'to think what they are doing' (to borrow a phrase from Hannah Arendt) and thus to take responsibility for their own actions. If we have learned anything from two centuries of social science, it is that the most innocent-seeming, depoliticized activities – caring for our children, disposing of our household wastes, purchasing the things we need, arranging for our own security – can have widespread political effects. Thus, to be responsible political agents, we need to think about our lives as a whole, relate what we are doing to the actions of others and consider our individual and collective responsibilities. It is not easy to do any of this well and it will be doubly difficult if we continue to substitute cultural commentary, pious moralizing, and pseudo-scientific description for political analysis.

Globalization as urbanization of politics

The question of the global city brings these issues into view in a particularly helpful way. This is because the globalization of an urban way of life gives a discernible form to the politics of the world as a whole – a form which is analytically familiar in various respects. Although the existing disciplines obstruct the effort to come to terms with this form, we do have resources in urban analysis that could be tapped in an effort to work out a new political science.

The concept of the global city has been most fully developed within the allied disciplines of urban geography and urban sociology (Friedmann and Wolff, 1982; Knox and Taylor, 1995). Geography has long been the least respected of the social sciences, because of the spatial determinism that seems implicit in its concept of human affairs. Urban sociology has been a bastard study because most of what is important in modern societies is urban, and the focus on that feature seems to beg the question of analytical significance. In this context, the concept of the global city is of some importance to both disciplines, because it suggests that there is a spatial form of the urban that bursts the bounds of particular societies. By analysing the hierarchy of cities in a globalized urban system and giving particular attention to the peak command centres – especially London, New York and Tokyo (Sassen, 1991) – it seems possible to analyse patterns of development and forms of social power in new ways. This elevates the status of the spatial sciences. On the other hand, sociologists and historians who want to put the urban back in its place prefer the concept of 'globalization' – a looser formulation that enables them to look at cultural and economic relations, without relating them to patterns of urban development. Sociology has been somewhat embarrassed by its lack of global theory, which has put this discipline at a disadvantage in relation to political science and economics (Robertson, 1992; Waters, 1995). The latter disciplines have the state system and the market respectively to account for world order. Modernity – or, in more radical versions, capitalism – has been the closest analogue to a sociological concept of the global, but it is more useful for analysing the transition from then to now, than for specifying the dynamics of the present itself. This opens the way for a sort of revenge of the spatial sciences, in the form of a theory of the global city.

Unfortunately, existing analyses of the global city tend to focus our attention on centres of command and control, and encourage us to think of the global order as some sort of world system. Notions of hierarchy, centricity, and systematicity lead inexorably to the idea of sovereignty; that is, to the idea that there is a point from which the world can be (or is being) organized or 'governed'. That the point should be conceived as a city, rather than as a state or a king, is not much of an improvement, since the same spatial imaginary is being invoked. Elsewhere in the geographical literature that spatial imaginary has been under challenge (see especially Lefebvre, 1991; Massey, 1994; Soja, 1996; and Brenner, 1998). To bring a more complex understanding of space into the analysis of the global city is essential. It is particularly important to recognize that space and time are dimensions of one another, and hence that the distinction between geographical and historical analysis is ultimately untenable. The concept of the global city invites us to abandon a number of old distinctions: between the local ('the city') and the global; between the economic, the social, the cultural and the political; and between the static ('structures', 'systems', 'space') and the dynamic ('movements', 'time'). However, these distinctions are bound to reassert themselves (as has occurred within the global city literature, when analysts have attempted to rate cities in relation to one another) if we are not attentive to ontological assumptions.

Within the existing discipline of political science, the concept of the global city has relatively little purchase, because there is already a powerful theory of the global, in the form of the 'realist' account of international relations (Walker, 1993). This account is deeply invested in the traditional spatial imaginary. It suggests that states are ultimately the dominant actors in global affairs, by virtue of their monopoly over the means of extreme violence, their command over popular loyalties and their legal supremacy in relation to economic, cultural, religious, social and other political institutions. One might well suggest that the dominance of states is not what it appears to be (and indeed this is a major theme in contemporary commentary on international affairs: see, for instance, Ruggie, 1993; Sassen, 1996). On the other hand, if municipalities are the political organizations on which the global city (or global cities) must rely, it is not clear how they are to match the power of states. Municipalities are conventionally understood as miniature states, stripped of sovereign authority. How can such stripped-down, miniaturized states be effective, when the organizations on which they are modelled seem to have lost control? An increasingly popular idea is that there is an emergent 'civil society' that brings people from different countries together (see, for example, Lipschutz with Mayer, 1996). However, to conceptualize world politics on the model of civil society is simply to project a familiar form onto a different scale (compare Shaw, 1994, and Walker, 1994). Something similar happens in current speculations about 'global governance' (see, for instance, Held, 1995 and Linklater, 1998). To think differently about world politics is extraordinarily difficult, because we are so used to the idea that there is a centre from which 'government' occurs and to which 'politics' must relate.

There is an ever-growing literature that suggests that the state system is historically specific and, moreover, that its form can be understood as an effect of economic, social, cultural or military conditions (compare McNeill, 1986; Braudel, 1984; Giddens, 1985; Mann 1986; 1994; Rosenberg, 1994). This mode of analysis has long antecedents. We can find it in Weber and Marx, for instance. Whatever the other merits of this mode of analysis, it does tend to put 'the political' into a narrow and dangerous space. To explain existing institutions as an effect of social conditions, broadly construed (including relations of production, religious sentiments, available military technologies and so on) is to present the world as something that developed behind our backs. Like Christ's crucifiers, we knew not what we were doing. But, what place can politics have under those conditions? The Weberian/Marxian answer points, on the one hand, toward the social science that enables us to understand the natural order of things (and attune ourselves accordingly) and, on the other hand, to the possibility of a violent intervention that will give form to something persistent. There is thus a secret complicity between the naturalism of the social sciences and the violence that substitutes for politics. The realist theory of international relations tells us that the leaders of states are bound to the use of violence by the logic of the system. Neo-classical economics offers a comparable account of the ruthless logic of economic competition. Stories about cultural difference – such as the ones now told about the Balkans – have a similar logic. The implication always is that there is a natural order to which *there is no alternative*. Politics cannot change anything of fundamental importance, and violence is required to restrain violence. This way of thinking is implicit in a social scientific approach. In an earlier era, we might have identified that approach with Marxism and Fabianism, but now its main expressions are in neo-liberalism and compassionate conservatism (compare Gill, 1995).

The point of focusing on the urban is to move away from social scientific categories, in the hope of recovering a sense of the political. Used in the way I suggest, the urban is both a spatial and a temporal category – that is, it is both geographical and historical. In its original sense, it denotes a difference between the urban on one side and the rural or simply natural on the other. At any moment this can be mapped in two or three dimensions. On the other hand, the urban is a historical movement, which can be traced to its origins in the ancient civilizations and followed in its development into a global system which actually encompasses the rural and the natural. The predominance of urbanism as a way of life thus can be shown geographically and accounted for historically. It is important to emphasize that urbanism is not just *any* way of life, but is a particular form of it, in which people gradually free themselves from their immediate dependence on the natural environment and create for themselves environments of their own making. As we know well, the latter environments are not always pleasant and their making is constrained by the parameters of the natural world. Nonetheless, it is obvious that the world in which we live is increasingly something of our own creation and it is this feature, more than the presence of dense clumps of buildings, that makes urbanism as a way of life so different from what went before.

To think of the urban in this way is to bring us nearer to a political conception of it, for the emphasis is on the process whereby we make the world in which we live. There is an Aristotelian echo here, for what Aristotle noted in *The Politics* was the fact that the ultimate political questions – the 'constitutional' questions that interested him most – related to the problem of producing and maintaining the *polis* in the form most conducive to human aspirations. What was at stake for the founders of a *polis* was the creation of a new way of life that could be self-sustaining. Genuinely political issues always related to these problems of founding and sustenance. Significantly, the *polis* was conceived as a city, that is as an organization of urbanism as a way of life. As urbanism became self-conscious, it became political in the fullest sense. To organize a city politically was to make a declaration of independence from agrarian, pastoral or hunter-gatherer life; it was to say that people could create and maintain their own artificial environment, which would be more or less adequate to their own purposes. We may believe, as some ecologists and religious thinkers do, that such an aspiration is a sign of *hubris* and that people are liable to destroy themselves if they push urbanism to its logical conclusion. However, it is hard to deny the fact that urbanism has become global and that the rural and the natural are quickly being reduced to the status of urban parks.

The nineteenth- and twentieth-century social sciences encourage us to think of urbanism as an unintended consequence of things we do for other reasons. Urbanism thus becomes susceptible to naturalistic explanation. A politicized understanding of the urban leads us to refuse this evasion of responsibility. It is true that no one planned the world to be exactly as it is – any more than anyone planned Athens to be exactly as Aristotle found it. Nonetheless, the world in which we live is largely of our own making and we sustain it as such in our daily routines. To take responsibility for that world – as the Athenians took responsibility for Athens – is to take responsibility for urbanism as a way of life. This means attempting to understand the global city – urbanism as a way of life – as a political order that people have created and that they continue to sustain. To appreciate what it is, we have to give up the idea that political order necessarily conforms to the sovereignty principle. The latter idea encourages us to think that there can be no real political order if there is no sovereignty present. Since urbanism does not conform to the sovereignty principle, it appears to be apolitical. But to mistake this appearance for reality is to make a grave theoretical error. To the extent that sovereignty exists, it is always localized and its existence is always in the form of a political claim (Magnusson, 2000). That claim is never uncontested and thus paradoxically sovereignty is always limited. In the wider politics of the global city, sovereignty-claims appear beside other sorts of political claims – rights-claims, property-claims, knowledge-claims, identity-claims and so on – which are not necessarily less important. What is contested politically is actually quite open, for it is always possible for someone to identify a new problem with the existing way of life and to demand fundamental change. That is what 'new' social movements are always about.

If urbanism denotes the process whereby we come to create and sustain our own environment – a place in the natural world in which we can live in accordance with human purposes – then the politics of urbanism is the activity by which this creative and sustaining process is put into question. To the extent that we assume responsibility for what we are doing, we become engaged politically, and in its broadest sense this engagement is with the phenomenon of urbanism.

It is worth pausing to consider the 'ism' in urbanism. As noted above, the term 'urbanism as a way of life' comes from Wirth (1938). He contrasted urbanism with industrialism and capitalism and appealed for a sociological understanding of the phenomenon. However, he was a *social* scientist, looking for social not political reasons. This led him towards the naturalism for which he was ultimately criticized by neo-Marxists such as Manuel Castells (1977; see also Smith, 1979, pp. 1–48). Castells attempted to rethink urbanism as an effect of the class relations implicit in capitalism. This led him to the idea of 'urban social movements' as modes of resistance to capitalism. His thinking has evolved since, as has the critical analysis of urban political economy, an analysis that he and David Harvey (1982; 1996) did so much to inspire. In a way, Castells and others have been trying to radicalize and politicize Wirth's original analysis. In so doing, however, they have pushed Wirth's original insight into the background. To retrieve that insight, we have to link it not only to the ancient Greek conception of politics as an ongoing activity (Arendt, 1961), but also to the modern notion of a social movement as a challenge to the existing order (Tarrow, 1994).

In a sense, a social movement is the modern equivalent of a *polis*. If the *polis* offered to its ancient inhabitants a sense of identity and purpose and constituted their collective existence in a form that enabled them to act together to carry this identity and purpose forward, then the contemporary social movement does something rather similar. There is a crucial difference, however, and this is that a movement is not necessarily tied to a particular place. A movement moves, in every sense of that word (Magnusson, 1997). In this respect, it is akin to urbanism as a way of life. Particular cities, habitations, modes of transportation, forms of cultural expression and patterns of economic activity may be established as this way of life develops, but these fixtures are always temporary. Urbanism is characterized by movement, flux, restlessness. The global city is never finished, because new possibilities are always being discovered. Thus, the politics of urbanism is a politics of movement, akin in this respect to the politics of any other social movement. So, does it make sense to conceive of urbanism as a sort of social movement?

To affix an 'ism' to the 'urban', as Wirth did, is to suggest such a possibility. Then as now, an 'ism' could be conceived as an ideological construct which ordered people's political activity in a movement towards a particular goal. The goal of urbanism is not easy to specify, but if the analysis above is correct we can identify urbanism with the effort to make human life self-dependent – that is, to free human beings from the limitations of their natural existence. There are many aspects to this aspiration and it is subject to constant revision, but we can well see that urbanism in this sense is associated with a broad political agenda. The space of urbanism is the space of the global city, but not in the sense in which the geographers and sociologists have tended to use that term. The global city is not just a particular site like New York or Tokyo. Rather, it is urbanism as a 'way of life'. The argument here is that we must learn to think of this way of life as a way of organizing ourselves *politically*. From this perspective, urbanism appears as an over-arching social movement, which constitutes the political hyperspace within which other, more familiar social movements appear.

Every important social movement creates its own political space. It defines 'us and them', 'here and there', 'then and now'. It establishes an identity and a set of goals for the people involved and thus sets a direction for their activity. This direction is both spatial and temporal: we are here and want to be there, we were this and want to be that. The political space that the movement defines is the terrain in which it must act if it is to be successful. Its enemies appear in particular locations on that terrain, with particular powers at their disposal. Its friends and potential supporters are in other locations, with powers to be developed and deployed in accordance with the strategic objectives and tactical capacities of the movement. The space of action must be defined if decisions are to be made, but it is impossible to know that space – and in particular to appreciate how it might change – without understanding how it was produced historically. Thus, the political space available to a movement must be interpreted temporally if it is to serve as a space for action. In the end, what a movement shapes out of what it can discover is a space and time for its own activity: a where and when for its own efforts. Movements such as socialism, feminism and environmentalism – like liberalism, secular humanism and scientific rationalism before them – create worlds of their own in which the friends and enemies, pasts and futures, homes and aways, opportunities and threats are quite distinctive. It would be a mistake to suppose that each of these movements conforms to the same model.

Urbanism seems to be distinctive in that it is an architectonic movement, which occurs in a more complex political space. The urban is associated with contrary 'affects': on the one hand, the excitement of human achievement, human expression and human contact; on the other hand, dismay at the effects of human activity in relation both to individual and social life, and to the natural environment. Thus, the urban is rarely posed as an unambiguous ideal. It is rather the form that our way of life has taken in consequence of our efforts to make the world over in accordance with our purposes. To the extent that different purposes are expressed in different social movements, urbanism is the ensemble of these purposes and more generally of the activities that give effect to them. The really powerful social movements are the ones like capitalism and statism which we can trace to the beginnings of the modern era, and which have obviously reshaped the space and time for human activity in fundamental ways. Capitalism and statism – to which one might add the ideological ensemble of secular humanism, scientific rationalism and political liberalism – appear to have been the most vital movements *within* urbanism as a way of life and to have given contemporary urbanism its most significant characteristics. Most of the other social movements can be understood in terms of their reaction to these hegemonic movements.

Hyperspace of urbanism as a way of life

Elsewhere I have suggested that we might invoke the concept of 'hyperspace' to make sense of the relation between urbanism and other social movements (Magnusson, 1996). I take this term from contemporary physics (Kaku, 1994), in which the currently dominant theory is that space actually has ten, rather than four dimensions. According to this theory, the four-dimensional world in which we live day-to-day is in a sort of giant, expanding bubble on the surface of a six-dimensional space curled up in a tiny ball. The only evidence that the other six dimensions are there is that, without hypothesizing them, we cannot make sense of the relations between the four fundamental forces of the universe. It would be wrong to suppose that the physicists' concept of an n-dimensional hyperspace could be applied directly in an anlysis of our social existence – what would it mean? – but two important ideas can be derived from this physical theory. The first is that there can be separate spatial domains, in which what is outside remains largely unnoticeable. And the second is that there are features of the interior of any domain that are unintelligible except with reference to what is outside. We can apply these ideas to the analysis of social movements. On the one hand, every major social movement seems to form its own political space – positing an identity (workers, women, whatever), developing an appropriate history, situating itself geographically. As a result, no two movements share exactly the same political space and so none can simply read off its future or pull down its lessons from the experience of another. On the other hand, there are parameters for each movement that are given by the character of the exterior space. A movement cannot simply give its political space the character it wants: that depends on what is outside. If the analysis above is correct, the 'outside' can best be understood as the 'inside' of a 'global city' – the hyperspace of urbanism as a way of life.

Arguably, the concept of urbanism that I am advancing is a functional equivalent of older theories of modernity. After all, it was by means of the distinction between the ancient and the modern or, later, between the traditional and the modern, that western thinkers began to make sense of what distinguished post-Renaissance Europe from what went before and what was outside. The modern was actually a four-dimensional, spatio-temporal concept which was heated up for explanatory purposes at points and times of transition. For good or ill, the concept is now burdened with the assumptions of western imperialism, which are ethnocentric and presentist. Much of the recent fascination with the concept of the *post*-modern derives from the frustration of intellectuals who are attempting to think beyond the tradition of modernism that they have inherited. However, the concept of the post-modern simply confirms the spatio-temporal assumptions it was supposed to challenge ('We were modern then, but now we are post-modern'). If we are to break out of this frame, we need to think of our lives in a way that does not burden us again with the same history and geography. The concept of urbanism as a way of life is not to be identified simply with Europe and its effects since 1492. On the contrary, we can see that this way of life has taken a variety of forms and has developed over thousands of years in different parts of the world. What is unique about the present era is that the various urbanisms have been integrated with one another in the context of a developing global city.

It is not hard to see that some elements of the contemporary global city – long-distance trading routes and universal religions, for example – were already in place two thousand years ago (*Times Atlas*, 1993, pp. 70–3). However, the world was still strongly separated into distinct regions and some regions – the Americas, southern Africa, Australia, the Arctic – were largely isolated from the rest of the world. In any case, the predominance of urbanism in relation to other modes of life was far from complete. Only with the long outburst of European expansionism in the so-called modern era did the various regions of the world become firmly integrated with one another and urbanism become everywhere predominant. In fact, it is only in the last few decades that most countries in Africa, Asia and Latin America have become preponderantly urban. To the extent that this process is as yet incomplete, there is every indication that it will continue until it is complete. People do not like starving in the countryside and they will make what efforts they can to join in the urban prosperity of which they are now aware.

To say this is not to reinvoke a theory of historical inevitability. Rather, it is to call attention to the political choices that are shaping the world in which we live. We are accustomed to assign a political character to the decisions made by national governments, international agencies and great corporations. We have a little more trouble thinking of a peasant's decision to move into the city as political. But what else is such decision? It is by no means simply an economic move, since it is vested with social and cultural aspirations. Moreover, it involves an implicit repudiation of one sort of political community in favour of another. The sum of these innumerable political choices is of enormous consequence for the world as a whole. On the other hand, it is difficult, if not impossible, to call the people concerned to account for the choices they have made, because those choices seem to have been impelled by dire necessity. What we can see from a distance is that the global city is organized in a way that offers only bad choices to the majority of people and gives others enormous power to organize global life in accordance with their own desires. The global city may be decentred, but it is by no means democratic in its mode of political organization. Indeed, the claim that the world is becoming 'more' democratic seems to depend on an extraordinarily narrow conception of democracy, which depends on the illusion that states normally govern human affairs.

If we want to understand the political organization of the contemporary world, we are well advised to look at the cities in which we live. These places are but nodes in the global city, but in their local and regional organization they seem to replicate most features of the global order. Anyone who has studied urban government carefully will tell you that sovereignty is illusory in urban affairs. Of course, there are states that claim authority over cities and intervene regularly in urban affairs, but what becomes apparent on the ground is that states have a very limited capacity to order things as they would wish. In fact, state authority seems to dissipate at the local level, as it spreads through a bewildering array of agencies that overlap the familiar analytical boundaries. Consider a state-funded charitable agency, with a board of directors representative of local elites, a mandate to raise funds from the community, a core of volunteers and professional workers and a set of elaborate procedures for consulting client groups and affected members of the wider community. Is such an agency within the state or in civil society? Is it economic, social, political or cultural? Or is it all these things simultaneously? The ambiguity we encounter in this instance is typical: nothing on the ground where political decisions are being made in the local community seems to conform to the state-centric categories of the social sciences. Concrete analysis pushes us towards categorical invention.

One such invention is 'the metropolis'. The idea of the metropolis was adopted about a century ago to make sense of the fact that there was a difference between the city proper – that is, the municipality with the name concerned or the densely built-up core – and the surrounding suburbs. As the distinction between suburban and rural areas blurred, people began to talk about metropolitan regions to denote the wider area of urban influence. From the beginning it was noticed that, in densely populated areas, one metropolitan region overlapped another, so that rather arbitrary distinctions had to be made for analytical or administrative purposes. Gradually, it was recognized that wider urban systems were national and international and had been so for some time. Thus, the obvious fact about the metropolis is that it is both centripetal and centrifugal: it draws activity towards itself and spins it outward, so that every metropolis interacts with other metropolises in extremely complicated ways. The relations between one metropolis and another cannot be understood as if the two entities were self-contained and factors like national boundaries are of only relative significance in determining the pattern of interaction. Every metropolis is characterized by an internal dispersal of political authority – a dispersal which is in part geographic and in part functional, but in the end much more complex. This dispersal does not conform to neat distinctions between state and society, public and private, national and local.

A similar ambiguity is implicit in the older idea of the municipality. Municipalities date from the medieval era and hence from a time when sovereignty had yet to congeal as a principle of personal and political identity. A municipality is a sort of *polis*, but it is not autonomous. It has come to be regarded as an organ of the state and yet it is always also in civil society. Not surprisingly, it has the legal status of a corporation: an artificial person without sovereignty. Although analysts sometimes treat municipalities as if they were miniature states, such an analytic strategy never works, because municipalities are not self-contained. The municipality is a liminal space. As such, it may be paradigmatic. Modern (or post-modern) identities are increasingly porous, complicated and ambiguous. If the personal is the political and the political is the personal, then the municipality is emblematic of our condition. It is limited, but never self-contained: always beyond itself, but nevertheless quite particular. Significantly, the organizations we call states are coming to resemble municipalities in their relation to the global economy and to replicate the patterns of municipal politics on a global scale.

If so, some will wonder why global analysis ought not be proceed under the rubric of 'capitalism'. The so-called triumph of the liberal democracies is obviously a triumph of capitalism and if there is a world order it is evidently now a capitalist world order. The global economy we now have is not just any economy: it is the one that emerged within the womb of European feudalism and that was established on a world scale in the context of European imperialism. It might be argued that, once we strip Marxism of its dross, what we have – especially in Marx's own writings – is a brilliant historical-geographic analysis of the way the contemporary world order came to be (Harvey, 1982; 1996). Moreover, we have in Marxist theory an account of the organizational principles of capitalism – the core system of the world order – which helps us to understand (at least in retrospect) why and how the world evolves as it does. What better analysis of the collapse of the Soviet Union could there be than the one we could derive from Marx? Was the Soviet planning system not one that had developed the economy in Russia to the point where the integument of the existing system of production had to be broken? If we were to reinvigorate Marxist analysis by applying it ruthlessly to the utopian socialists of the twentieth century – among whom Lenin, Attlee and Blair might all be numbered – then it might be possible to produce a convincing account of our world that put the phenomenon of capitalism at its centre.

Capital is a masterpiece of political analysis, in that it exposes as political a set of relationships that had been labelled as natural (or at least as apolitical). What Marx does so brilliantly is to explain how capitalism works as a political system. All subsequent analysis has to begin where he left off. On the other hand, we must be conscious now that an analysis of capitalism as a political system tells us only some of the things we need to know to make sense of the global politics in which we are engaged. A political science that centres itself on the phenomenon of capitalism may be superior in some respects to a state-centric political science, but it replicates many of the unfortunate features of sovereignty thinking. It misleads us into thinking that our world has a central determinant principle, one that can be comprehended naturalistically and that will somehow give us our political precepts directly. These were the presumptions of the political economy to which Marx was responding and they are presumptions from which he himself never fully escaped.

To conceive of capitalism instead as one of an ensemble of modern social movements is to situate it in a more complex political space. This space is not uniquely defined by the logic of capital or by labour's response to it. What is incommensurable with that logic – be it religious understanding, ethnic hatreds, feminist aspirations, or eco-centric concerns – is neither simply external nor simply subordinate. To understand this is to recognize that capitalism, like statism, produces a show of sovereignty to which we must respond, but respond in a way that does not reproduce the show's illusions.

With respect to citizenship, the state is the show we encounter first. It constitutes the political in a particular way, by attributing natural sovereignty to the individual. As Hobbes feared, such natural sovereignty can lead only to the worst of all possible worlds. So, the artificial sovereignty of the state seems necessary to produce social order. However, the global order thus effected turns out to be a place of mutually exclusive artificial sovereignties: hence, it reproduces the problems of violence and disorder on a different scale. According to the received view, both citizenship proper and politics proper are attributes of statehood (Linklater, 1990). States determine who may be citizens and constitute spaces within which citizenship can be practised. Citizenship thus defines a relation that absolves individuals of responsibility for what happens beyond the borders of their particular states. Political responsibility is state-centred and as such is distinguished from the personal responsibility that each person has for his or her own life. What cannot be assigned either to the personal or to the political is somehow beyond anyone's responsibility.

Conclusion

The depoliticizing social sciences enable us to analyse human affairs naturalistically and so to evade responsibilities that might otherwise come with citizenship. In deferring to such intellectual practices, we accept the shows of sovereignty as reality. To politicize the global city is to refuse these shows and to accept our responsibility for matters that we can never understand or control completely. Even more than a particular metropolis, the global city is decentred. It is not subject to a single, sovereign authority. There are multiple systems of power at work within it, some of which can be connected with capitalism, others with statism, still others with tribal nationalism, cultural imperialism, religious fundamentalism and so on. If there is a logic to the development of the global city, it can more easily be appreciated in terms of self-organizing systems or chaos theory than otherwise. However, to adopt such theories as a basis for analysis is to retreat once again into naturalism. A political analysis ought instead to return us constantly to the recognition that the city we have created is our own and that what happens in it is our own responsibility. The global city is both the venue and the product of our own struggles to become what we would like to be, and in the end there is no alternative but to take responsibility for what we have created.

Bibliography

Agamben, G. (1998) *Homo Sacer: Sovereign Power and Bare Life* (Stanford: Stanford University Press).

Arendt, H. (1961) *Between Past and Future* (New York: Viking Press).

Barker, E. (1962) *The Politics of Aristotle* (New York: Oxford University Press).

Bodin, J. (1576 [1992]) *On Sovereignty*, ed. J.H. Franklin (Cambridge: Cambridge University Press).

Braudel, F. (1984) *Civilization and Capitalism, 15th–18th Century*, 3 vols (London: Collins).

Brenner, N. (1998) 'Global Cities, Glocal States: Global City Formation and State Territorial Restructuring in Contemporary Europe', *Review of International Political Economy*, 5 (1): 1–37.

Castells, M. (1977) *The Urban Question* (London: Edward Arnold).

Connolly, W.E. (1987) *Politics and Ambiguity* (Madison: University of Wisconsin Press).

Crick, B.R. (1962) *In Defence of Politics* (Chicago: University of Chicago Press).

Deleuze, G. and Guattari, F. (1987) *A Thousand Plateaus* (Minneapolis: University of Minnesota Press).

Foucault, M. (1980) *Power/Knowledge*, ed. C. Gordon (New York: Random House).

Friedmann, J. and Wolff, G. (1982) 'World City Formation: An Agenda for Research and Action', *International Journal of Urban and Regional Research*, 6: 309–44.

Giddens, A. (1985) *The Nation-State and Violence* (Cambridge: Polity Press).

Gill, S. (1995) 'Globalisation, Market Civilisation and Disciplinary Neoliberalism', *Millennium*, 24 (3): 399–423.

Habermas, J. (1962 [1989]) *The Structural Transformation of the Public Sphere* (Cambridge, MA: MIT Press).

—— (1984–7) *The Theory of Communicative Rationality*, 2 vols (Boston: Beacon Press).

Haraway, D. (1991) *Simians, Cyborgs, and Women* (New York: Routledge).

Harvey, D. (1982) *The Limits to Capital* (Oxford: Basil Blackwell).

—— (1996) *Justice, Nature and the Geography of Difference* (Oxford: Basil Blackwell).

Held, D. (ed.) (1991) *Political Theory Today* (Oxford: Basil Blackwell).

—— (1995) *Democracy and the Global Order: From the Modern State to Cosmopolitan Government* (Stanford: Stanford University Press).

Hobbes, T. (1651 [1962]) *Leviathan*, ed. M. Oakeshott (New York: Collier Books).

Kaku, M. (1994) *Hyperspace: A Scientific Odyssey Through Parallel Universes, Time Warps and the Tenth Dimension* (New York: Oxford University Press).

Knox, P.L. and Taylor, P.J. (eds) (1995) *World Cities in a World-System* (Cambridge: Cambridge University Press).

Knox, T.M. (trans.) (1952) *Hegel's Philosophy of Right* (Oxford: Oxford University Press).

Lefebvre, H. (1991) *The Production of Space* (Oxford: Blackwell).

Linklater, A. (1990) *Men and Citizens in the Theory of International Relations*, 2nd edn. (London: Macmillan).

—— (1998) *The Transformation of Political Community: Ethical Foundations of the Post-Westphalian Era* (Cambridge: Polity Press).

Lipschutz, R.D. with Mayer, J. (1996) *Global Civil Society and Global Environmental Governance: The Politics of Nature from Place to Planet* (Albany, NY: State University of New York Press).

McNeill, W.H. (1986) *Polyethnicity and National Unity in World History* (Toronto: University of Toronto Press).

Macpherson, C.B. (1977) *The Life and Times of Liberal Democracy* (Oxford: Oxford University Press).

Magnusson, W. (1996) *The Search for Political Space: Globalization, Social Movements, and the Urban Political Experience* (Toronto: University of Toronto Press).

—— (1997) 'Globalization, Movements, and the Decentred State', in W.K. Carroll (ed.), *Organizing Dissent: Contemporary Social Movements in Theory and Practice*, 2nd edn (Toronto: Garamond Press).

—— (2000) 'Hyperspace: A Political Ontology of the Global City', in R.V. Ericson and N. Stehr (eds), *Governing Modern Societies* (Toronto: University of Toronto Press).

Mann, M. (1986, 1994) *The Sources of Social Power*, 2 vols (Cambridge: Cambridge University Press).

Massey, D. (1994) *Space, Place and Gender* (Cambridge: Polity Press).

Rabinow, P. (1984) *The Foucault Reader* (New York: Pantheon Books).

Rawls, J. (1971) *A Theory of Justice* (Cambridge, MA: Harvard University Press).

—— (1996) *Political Liberalism* (New York: Columbia University Press).

Robertson, R. (1992) *Globalization: Social Theory and Global Culture* (London: Sage).

Rosenberg, J. (1994) *The Empire of Civil Society: A Critique of the Realist Theory of International Relations* (London: Verso).

Ruggie, J.G. (1993) *Multilateralism Matters: The Theory and Praxis of an Institutional Form* (New York: Columbia University Press).

Sassen, S. (1991) *The Global City: New York, London, Tokyo* (Princeton, NJ: Princeton University Press).

—— (1996) *Losing Control? Sovereignty in an Age of Globalization* (New York: Columbia University Press).

Shaw, M. (1994) 'Civil Society and Global Politics: Beyond a Social Movements Approach', *Millennium*, 23 (3): 647–67.

Skinner, Q. (1998) *Liberty before Liberalism* (Cambridge: Cambridge University Press).

Smith, M.P. (1979) *The City and Social Theory* (New York: St Martin's Press).

Soja, E. (1996) *Thirdspace: Voyages to Los Angeles and Other Real-Imagined Places* (Oxford: Blackwell).

Tarrow, S. (1994) *Power in Movement: Social Movements, Collective Action and Politics* (Cambridge: Cambridge University Press).

Taylor, C. (1989) *Sources of the Self: The Making of Modern Identity* (Cambridge, MA: Harvard University Press).

Times Books (1993) *The Times Atlas of World History*, 4th edn (London: Times Books).

Tully, J. (1999) 'The Agonic Freedom of Citizens', *Economy and Society*, 28: 161–82.

Vincent A. (ed.) (1997) *Political Theory: Tradition and Diversity* (Cambridge: Cambridge University Press).

Walker, R.B.J. (1993) *Inside/Outside: International Relations as Political Theory* (Cambridge: Cambridge University Press).

—— (1994) 'Social Movements/World Politics', *Millennium*, 23 (3): 669–700.

Waters, M. (1995) *Globalization* (London: Routledge).

Wirth, L. (1938) 'Urbanism as a Way of Life', *American Journal of Sociology*, 44: 1–24.

Index